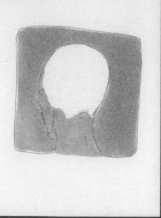

My editor, who had a perm, shaved his head. The following week a new editor was assigned to me: now I had two editors. The following week my new editor shaved his head. That same week I got a perm.

With the way things are going, I'm worried either Ichigo or I will end up with a shaved head due to some kind of accident.

–Tite Kubo

BLEACH is author Tite Kubo's second title. Kubo made his debut with *ZOMBIEPOWDER.*, a four-volume series for *WEEKLY SHONEN JUMP*. To date, *BLEACH* has been translated into numerous languages and has also inspired an animated TV series that began airing in the U.S. in 2006. Beginning its serialization in 2001, *BLEACH* is still a mainstay in the pages of *WEEKLY SHONEN JUMP*. In 2005, *BLEACH* was awarded the prestigious Shogakukan Manga Award in the *shonen* (boys) category.

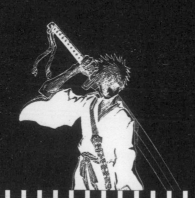

BLEACH
Vol. 42: SHOCK OF THE QUEEN
SHONEN JUMP Manga Edition

STORY AND ART BY
TITE KUBO

English Adaptation/Lance Caselman
Translation/Joe Yamazaki
Touch-up Art & Lettering/Mark McMurray
Design/Yukiko Whitley, Kam Li
Editor/Alexis Kirsch

Printed in the U.S.A.

Published by VIZ Media, LLC
P.O. Box 77010
San Francisco, CA 94107

10 9 8 7 6 5 4 3 2 1
First printing, July 2012

www.viz.com

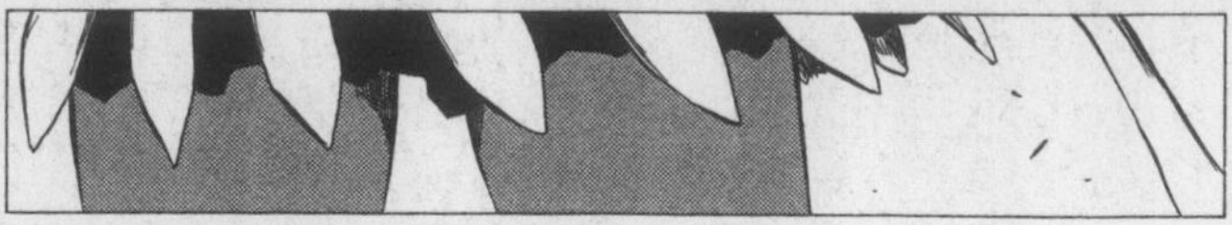

No world exists without sacrifice.
Do we not realize that we call
this hell where ash floats
upon a sea of blood, the world

BLEACH 42

SHOCK OF THE QUEEN

Shonen Jump Manga

STARS AND

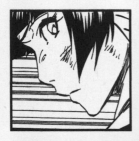

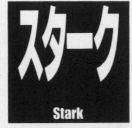

スターク

Stark

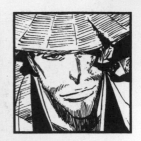

Soi Fon

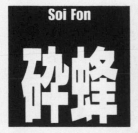

砕蜂

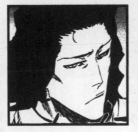

京樂春水

Shunsui Kyoraku

plot

When high school student Ichigo Kurosaki meets Soul Reaper Rukia Kuchiki his life is changed forever. Soon Ichigo is a soul-cleansing Soul Reaper too, and he finds himself having adventures, as well as problems, that he never would have imagined. Now Ichigo and his friends must stop renegade Soul Reaper Aizen and his army of Arrancars from destroying the Soul Society and wiping out Karakura as well.

Though Ichigo defeats Ulquiorra and saves Orihime, the battle between the Thirteen Court Guard Companies and the Espadas in Karakura rages on! Despite their wounds, the captains each challenge a high-ranking Espada! Now it's Kyoraku vs. Stark, Soi Fon vs. Barragan, and Hitsugaya vs. Halibel! Who will win, and who will perish in these deadly duels?!

BLEACH ALL

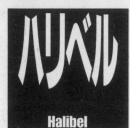

ハリベル
Halibel

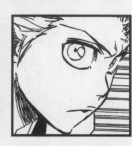

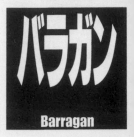

バラガン
Barragan

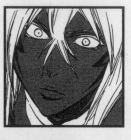

Toshiro Hitsugaya

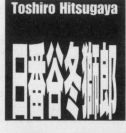

日番谷冬獅郎

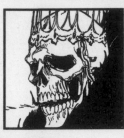

STORIES

BLEACH 42

SHOCK OF THE QUEEN

Contents

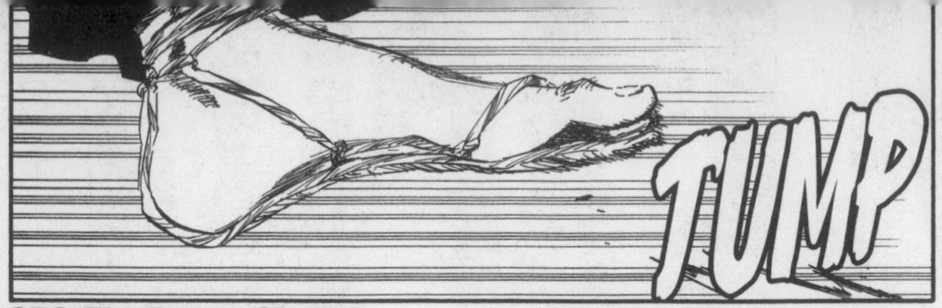
TUMP

359. The Frozen Obelisk

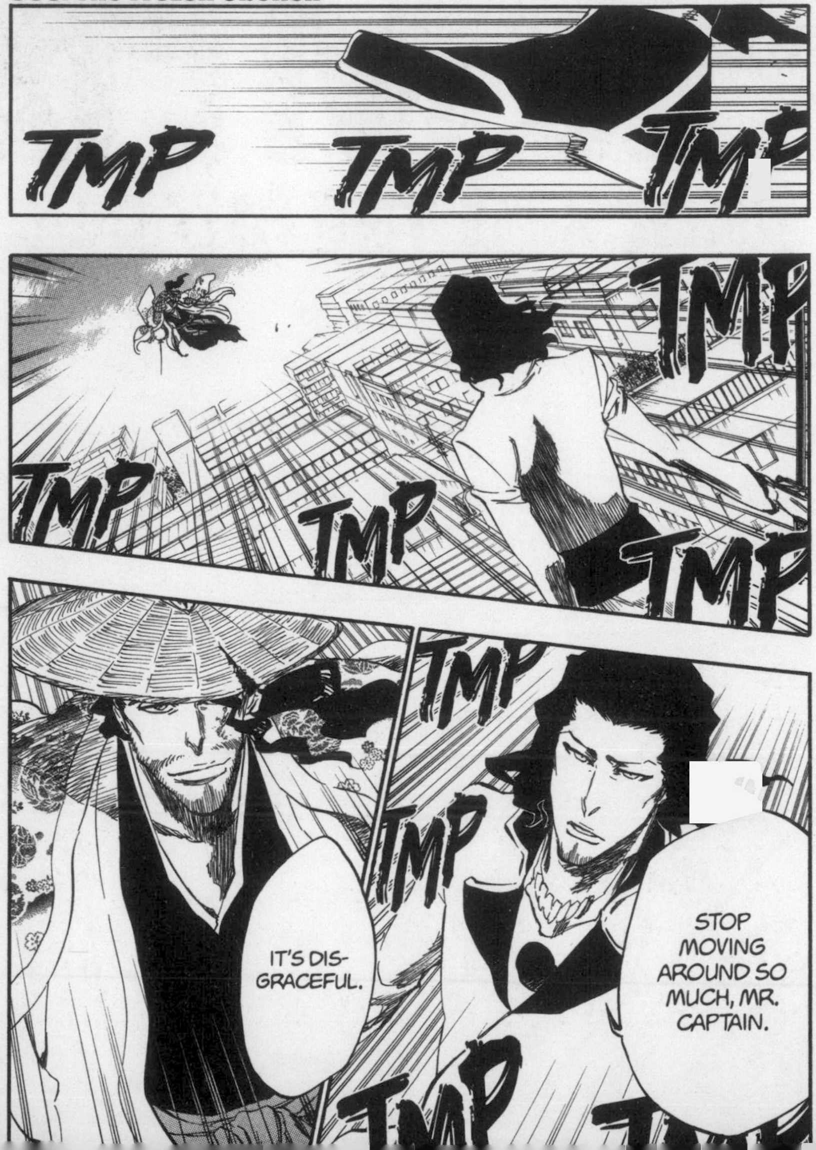
TMP
TMP
TMP
TMP
TMP
TMP
TMP
TMP
TMP
STOP MOVING AROUND SO MUCH, MR. CAPTAIN.
TMP
IT'S DISGRACEFUL.
TMP

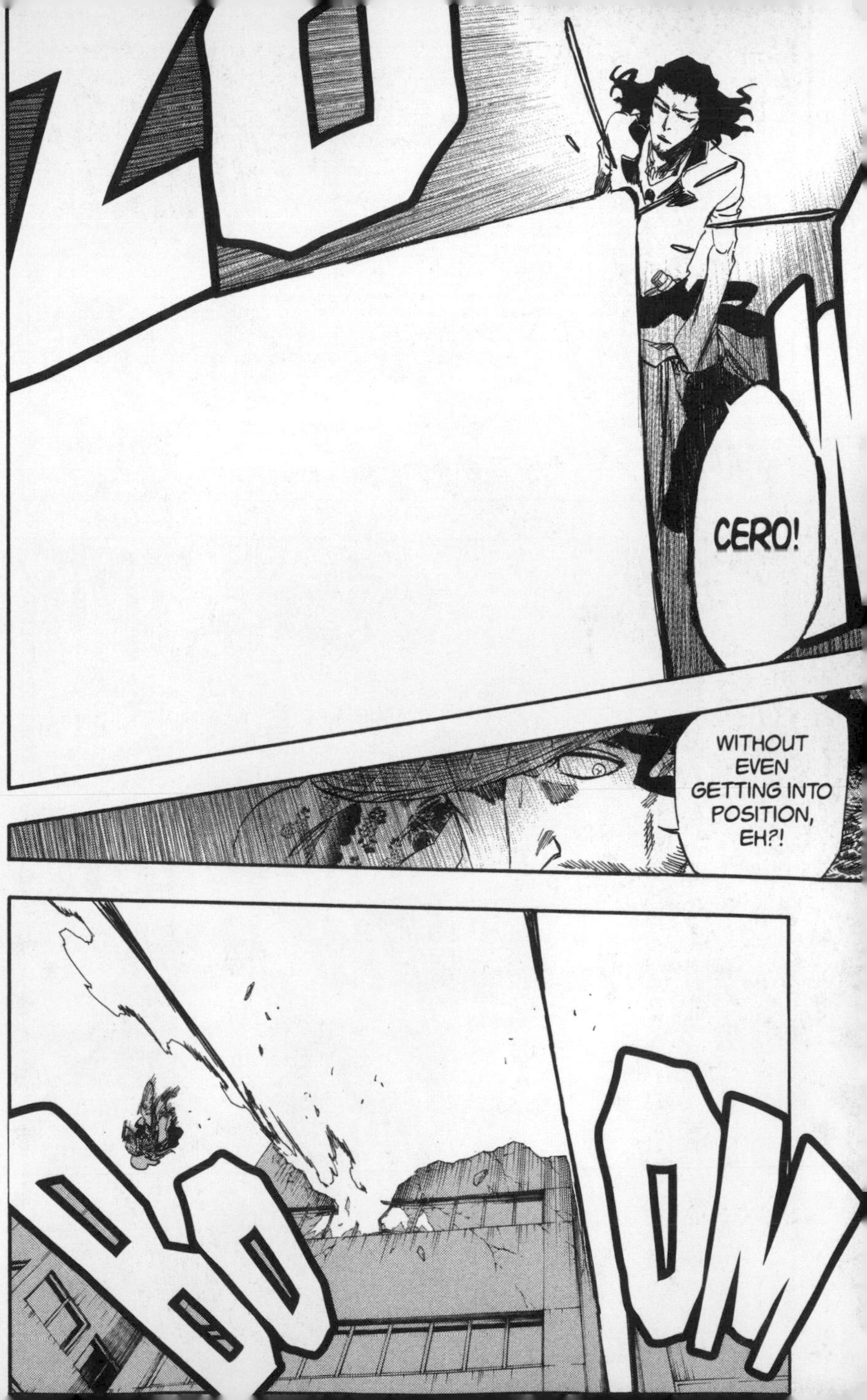
CERO!
WITHOUT EVEN GETTING INTO POSITION, EH?!
BOOM

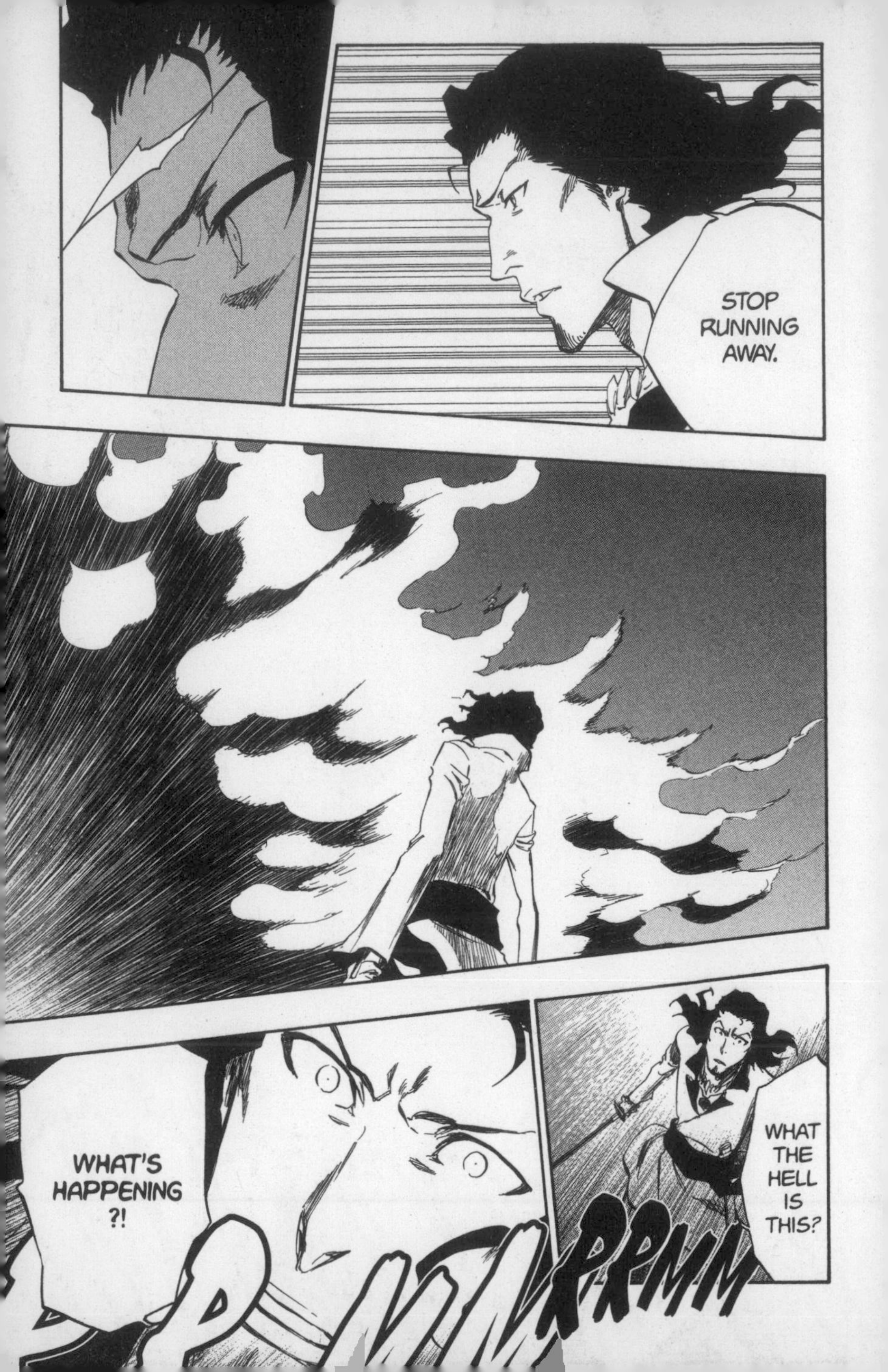
STOP RUNNING AWAY.
WHAT THE HELL IS THIS?
WHAT'S HAPPENING ?!

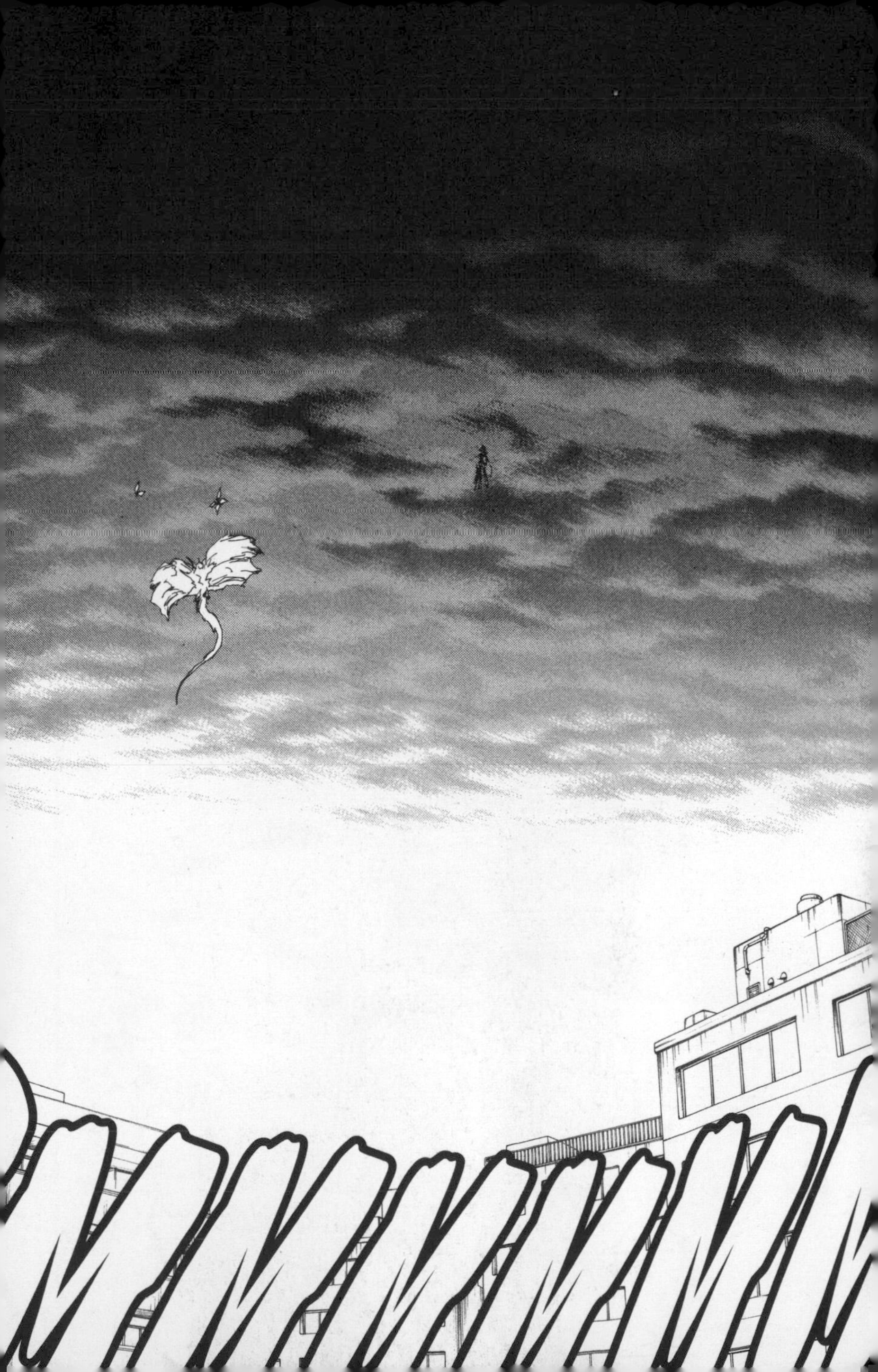

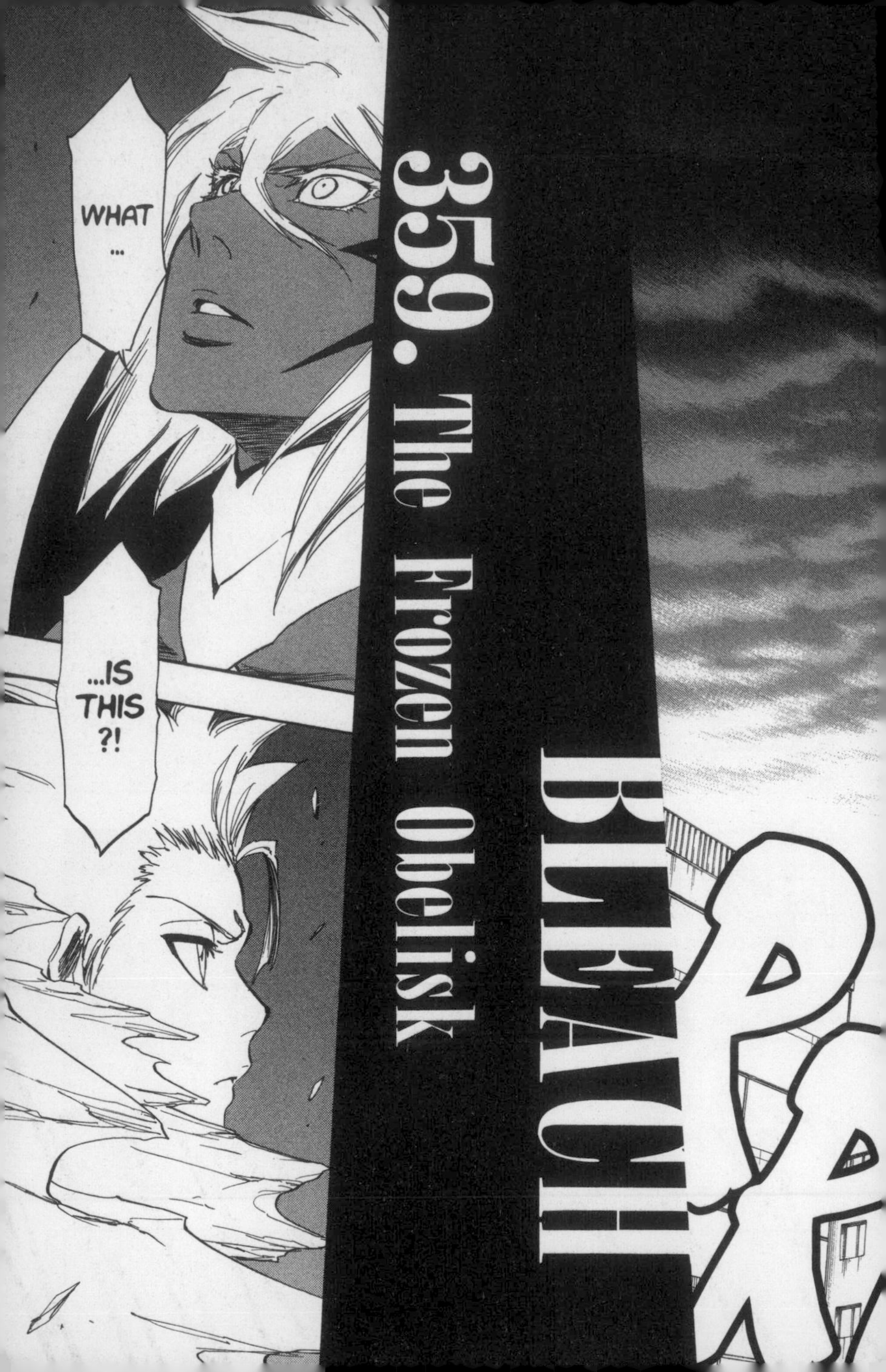
BLEACH
359. The Frozen Obelisk
WHAT ...
...IS THIS ?!

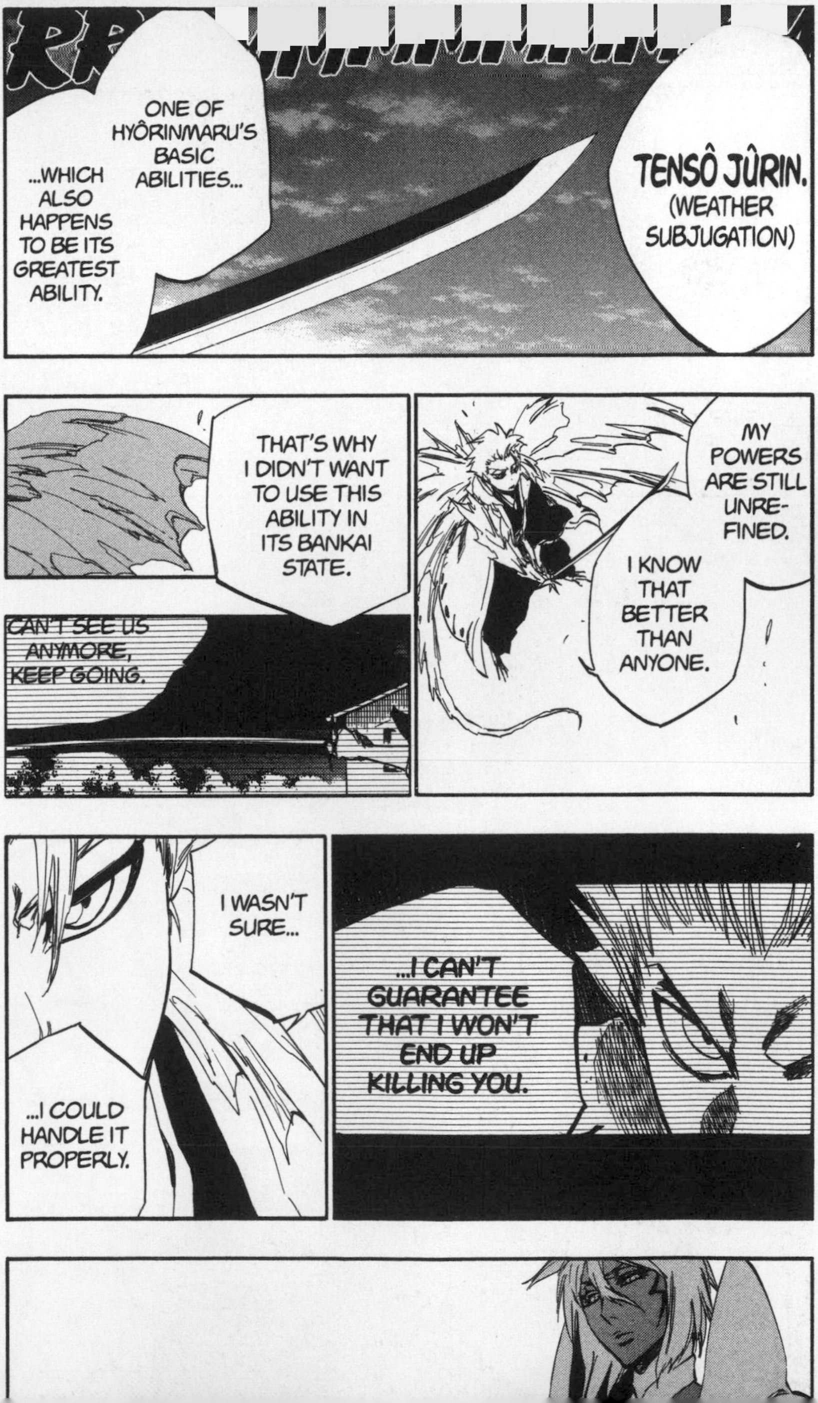
TENSÔ JÛRIN. (WEATHER SUBJUGATION)
ONE OF HYÔRINMARU'S BASIC ABILITIES...
...WHICH ALSO HAPPENS TO BE ITS GREATEST ABILITY.
MY POWERS ARE STILL UNRE-FINED.
I KNOW THAT BETTER THAN ANYONE.
THAT'S WHY I DIDN'T WANT TO USE THIS ABILITY IN ITS BANKAI STATE.
CAN'T SEE US ANYMORE, KEEP GOING.
...I CAN'T GUARANTEE THAT I WON'T END UP KILLING YOU.
I WASN'T SURE...
...I COULD HANDLE IT PROPERLY.

READ THIS WAY

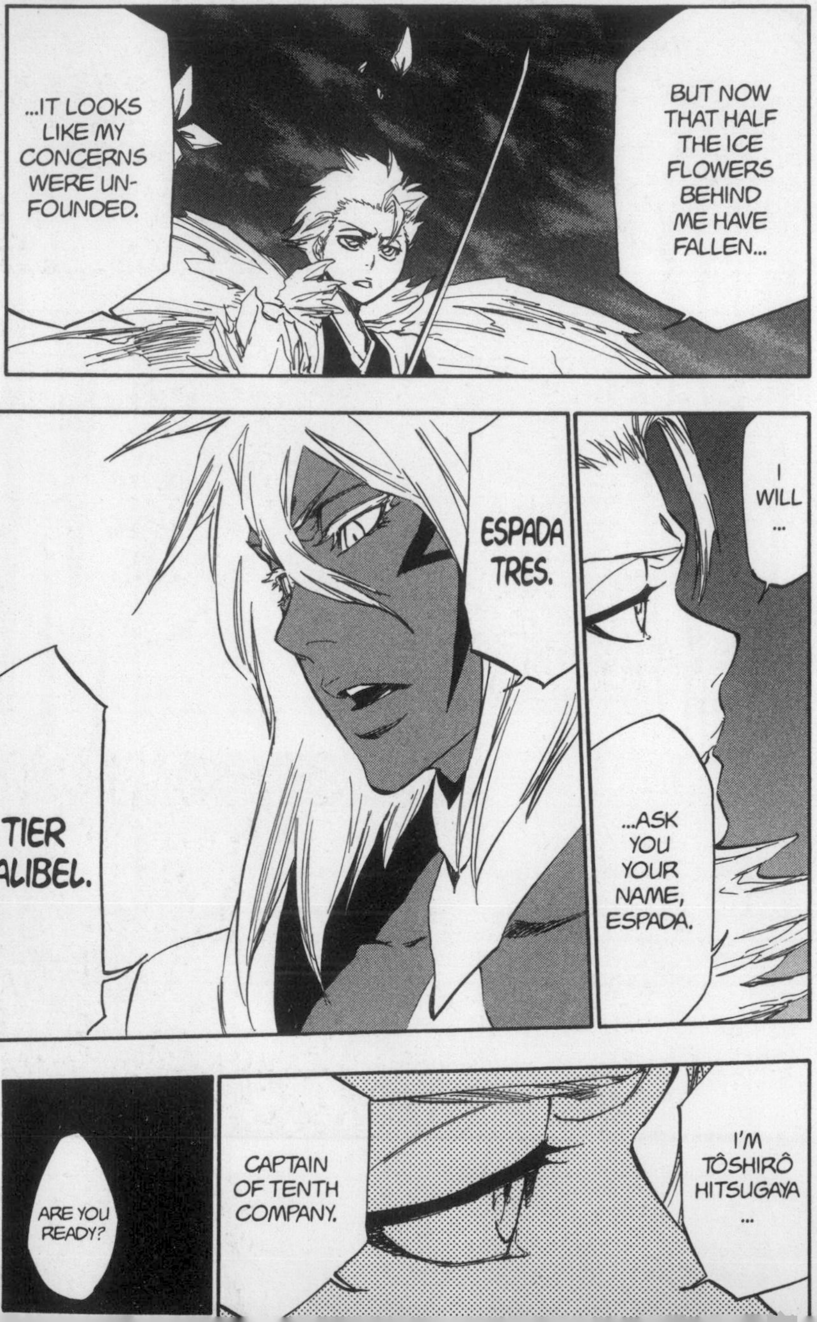
BUT NOW THAT HALF THE ICE FLOWERS BEHIND ME HAVE FALLEN...
...IT LOOKS LIKE MY CONCERNS WERE UN-FOUNDED.
I WILL ...
...ASK YOU YOUR NAME, ESPADA.
ESPADA TRES.
TIER HALIBEL.
I'M TÔSHIRÔ HITSUGAYA ...
CAPTAIN OF TENTH COMPANY.
ARE YOU READY?

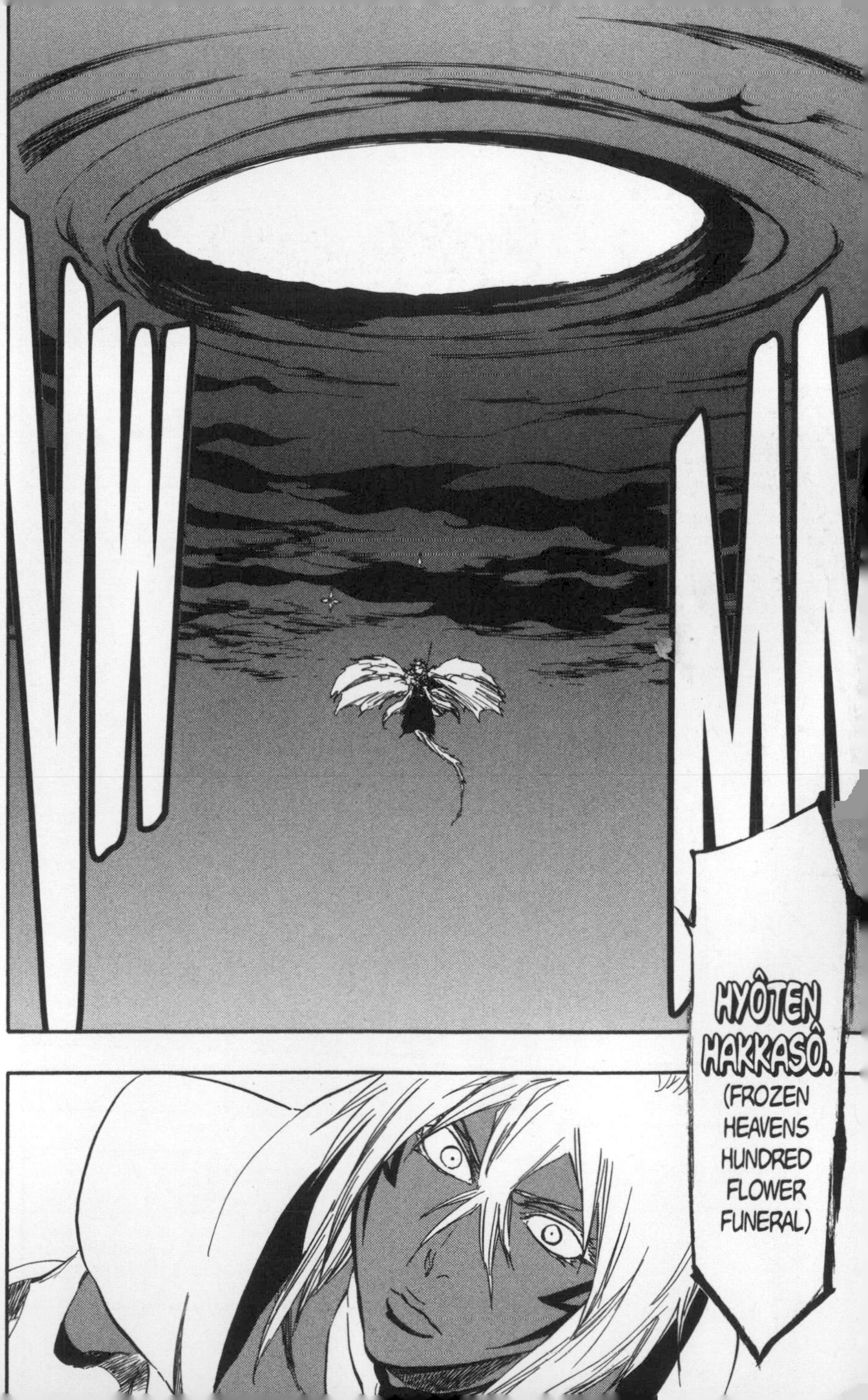
HYÔTEN HAKKASÔ.
(FROZEN HEAVENS HUNDRED FLOWER FUNERAL)

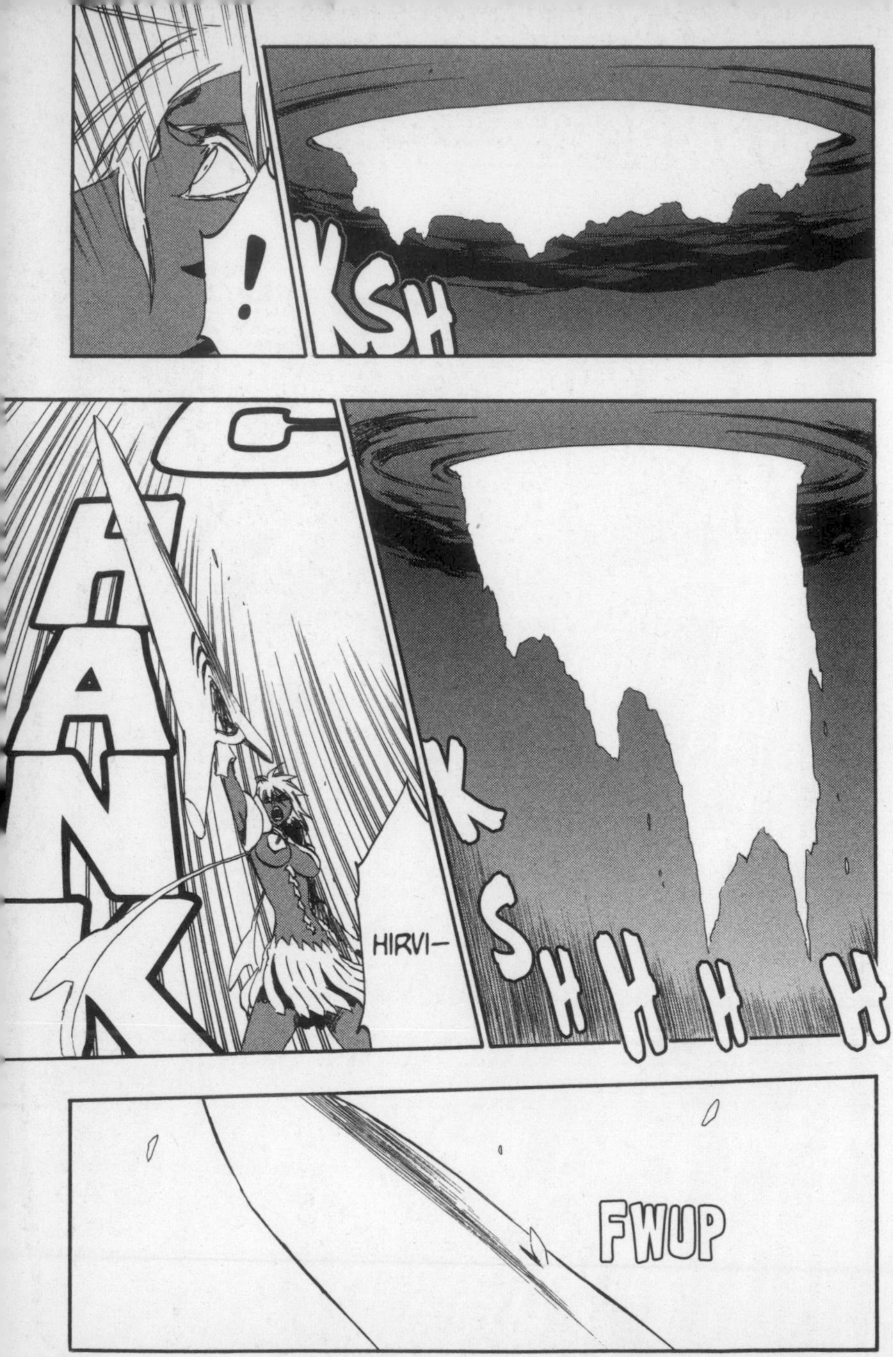
KSH
!
K
SHHHH
CHANK
HIRVI–
FWUP

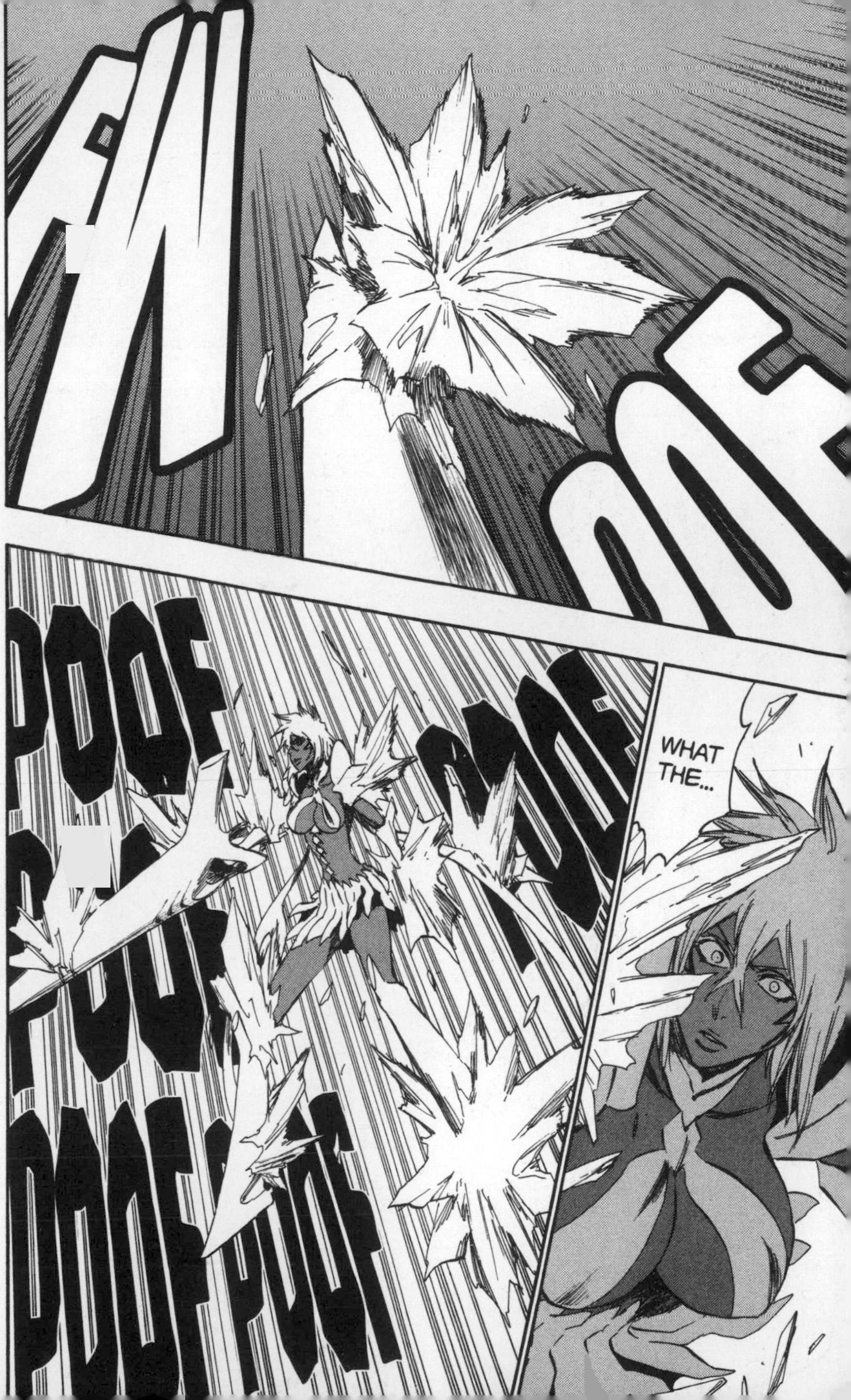
POOF
WHAT THE...
POOF
POOF
POOF
POOF
POOF

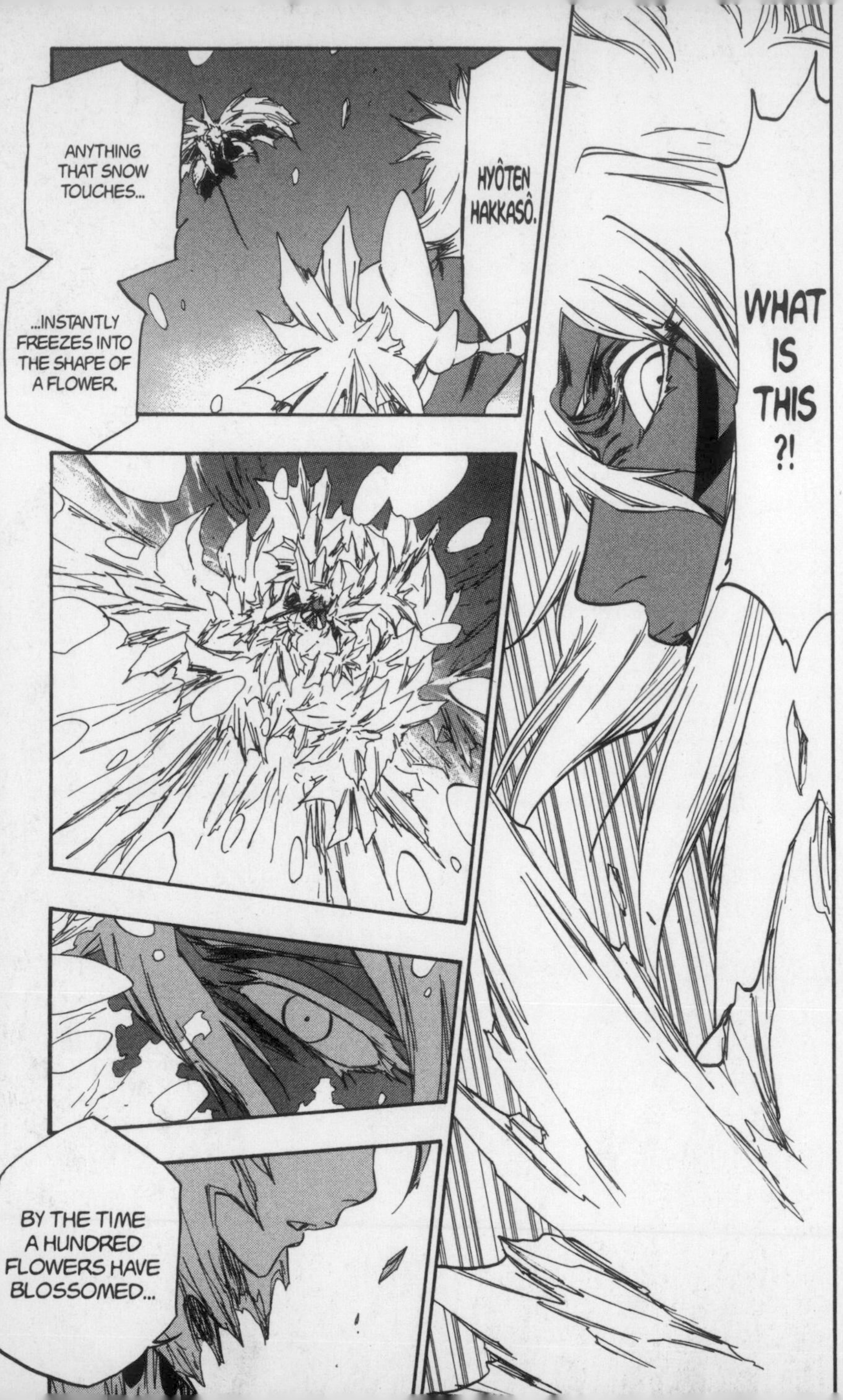
WHAT IS THIS ?!
HYÔTEN HAKKASÔ.
ANYTHING THAT SNOW TOUCHES...
...INSTANTLY FREEZES INTO THE SHAPE OF A FLOWER.
BY THE TIME A HUNDRED FLOWERS HAVE BLOSSOMED...

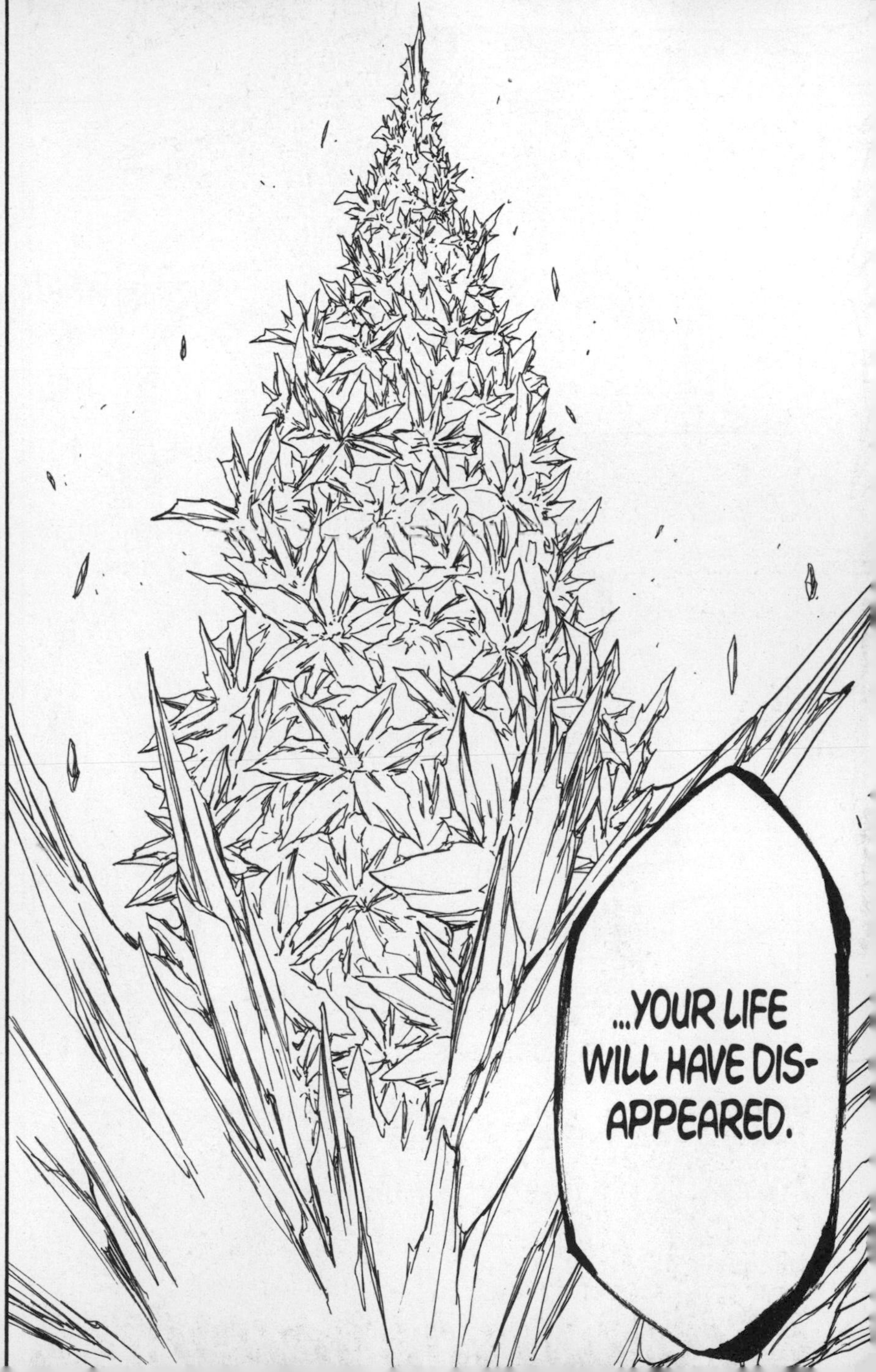
...YOUR LIFE WILL HAVE DIS-APPEARED.

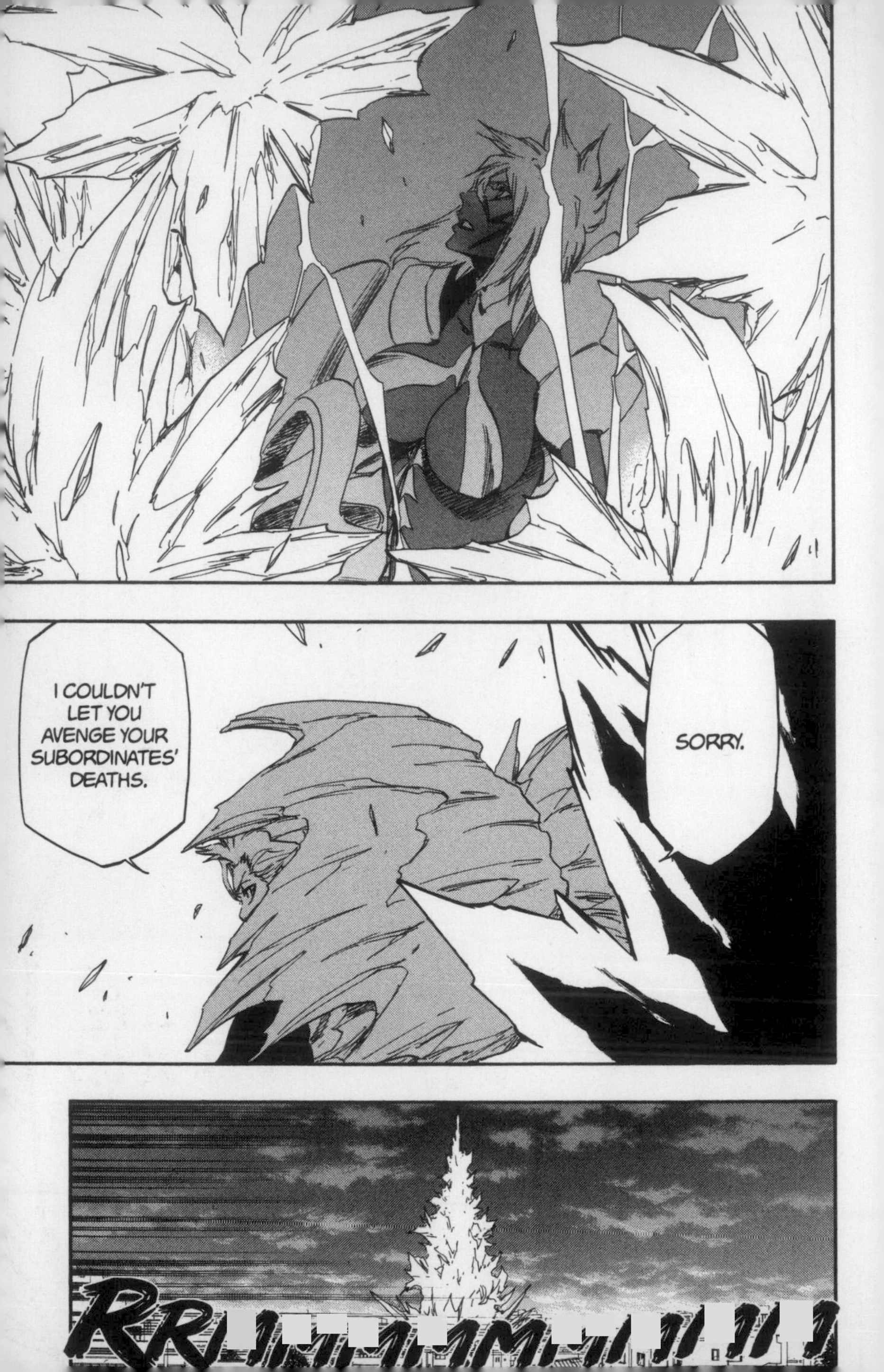
SORRY.
I COULDN'T LET YOU AVENGE YOUR SUBORDINATES' DEATHS.

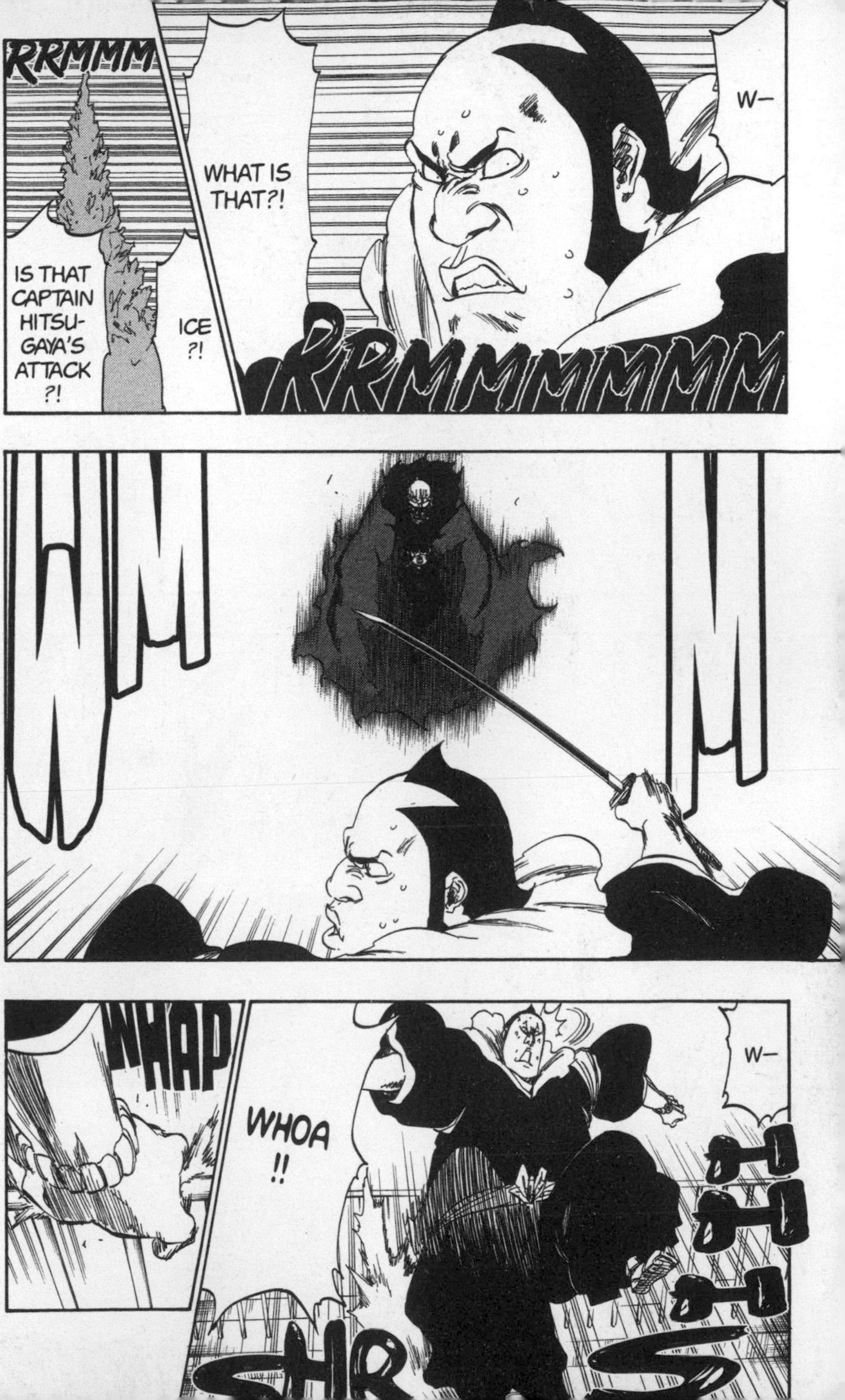
W–
WHAT IS THAT?!
ICE ?!
RRMMMMMMMM
RRMMM
IS THAT CAPTAIN HITSU-GAYA'S ATTACK ?!
M
WM
W–
WHOA !!
WHAP

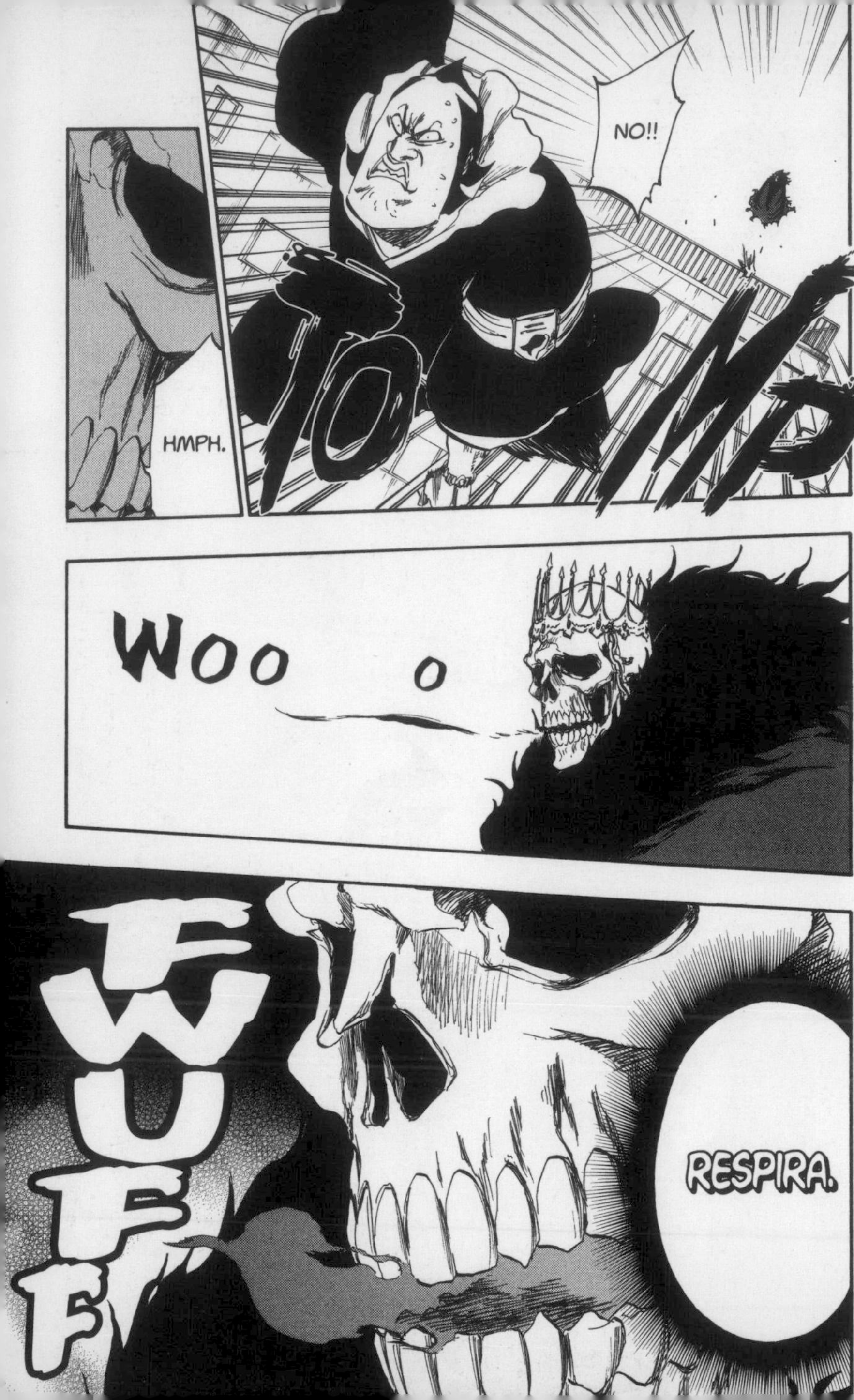
NO!!
HMPH.
WOO O
RESPIRA.
FWUFF

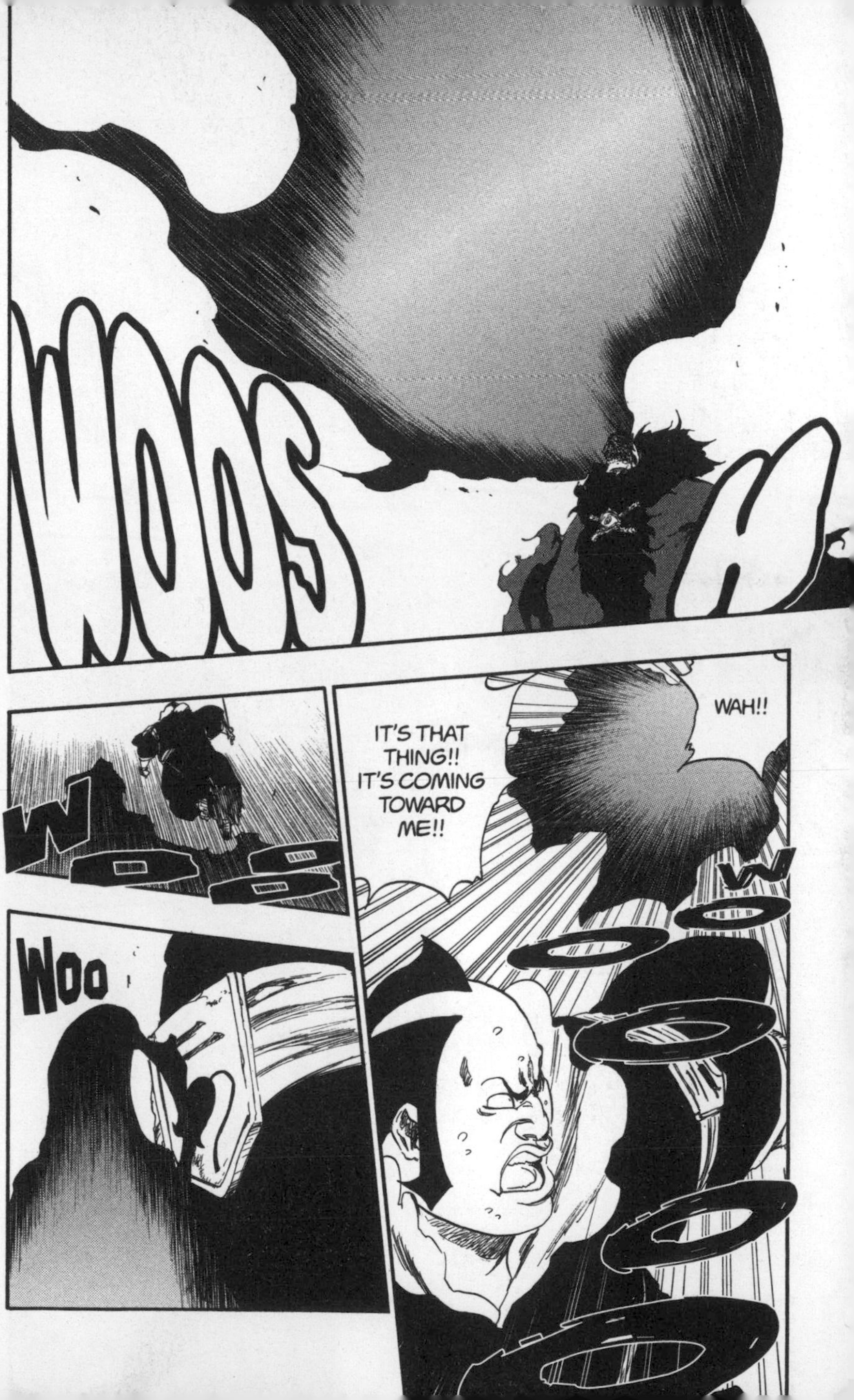
WHOOSH
WAH!!
IT'S THAT THING!! IT'S COMING TOWARD ME!!
WOOS
WOO

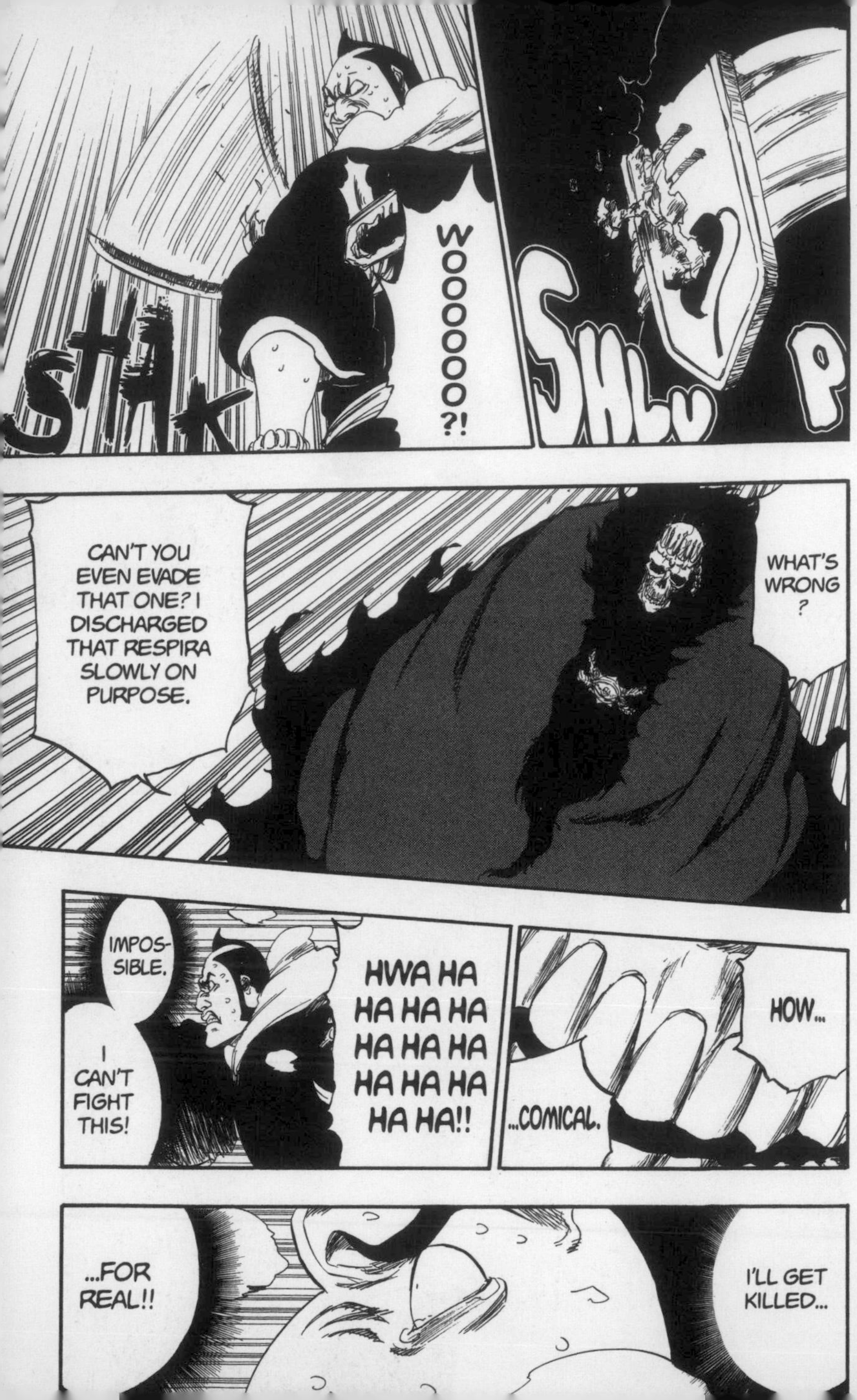
SHLUP
WOOOOOOO?!
SHAK
WHAT'S WRONG?
CAN'T YOU EVEN EVADE THAT ONE? I DISCHARGED THAT RESPIRA SLOWLY ON PURPOSE.
HOW...
...COMICAL.
HWA HA HA HA HA HA HA HA HA HA HA HA HA HA!!
IMPOSSIBLE.
I CAN'T FIGHT THIS!
I'LL GET KILLED...
...FOR REAL!!

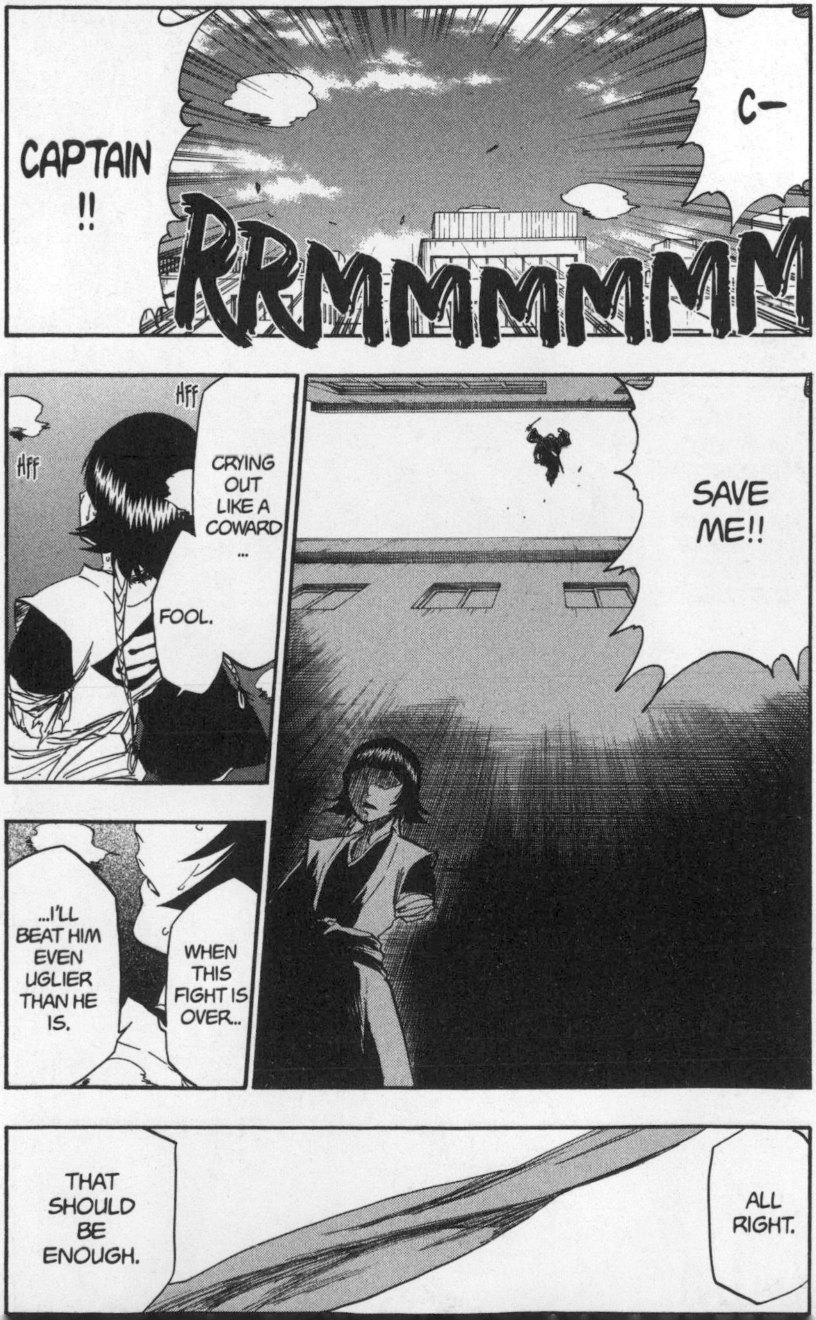
C—
CAPTAIN !!
RRMMMMMMM
SAVE ME!!
HFF
HFF
CRYING OUT LIKE A COWARD ...
FOOL.
WHEN THIS FIGHT IS OVER...
...I'LL BEAT HIM EVEN UGLIER THAN HE IS.
ALL RIGHT.
THAT SHOULD BE ENOUGH.

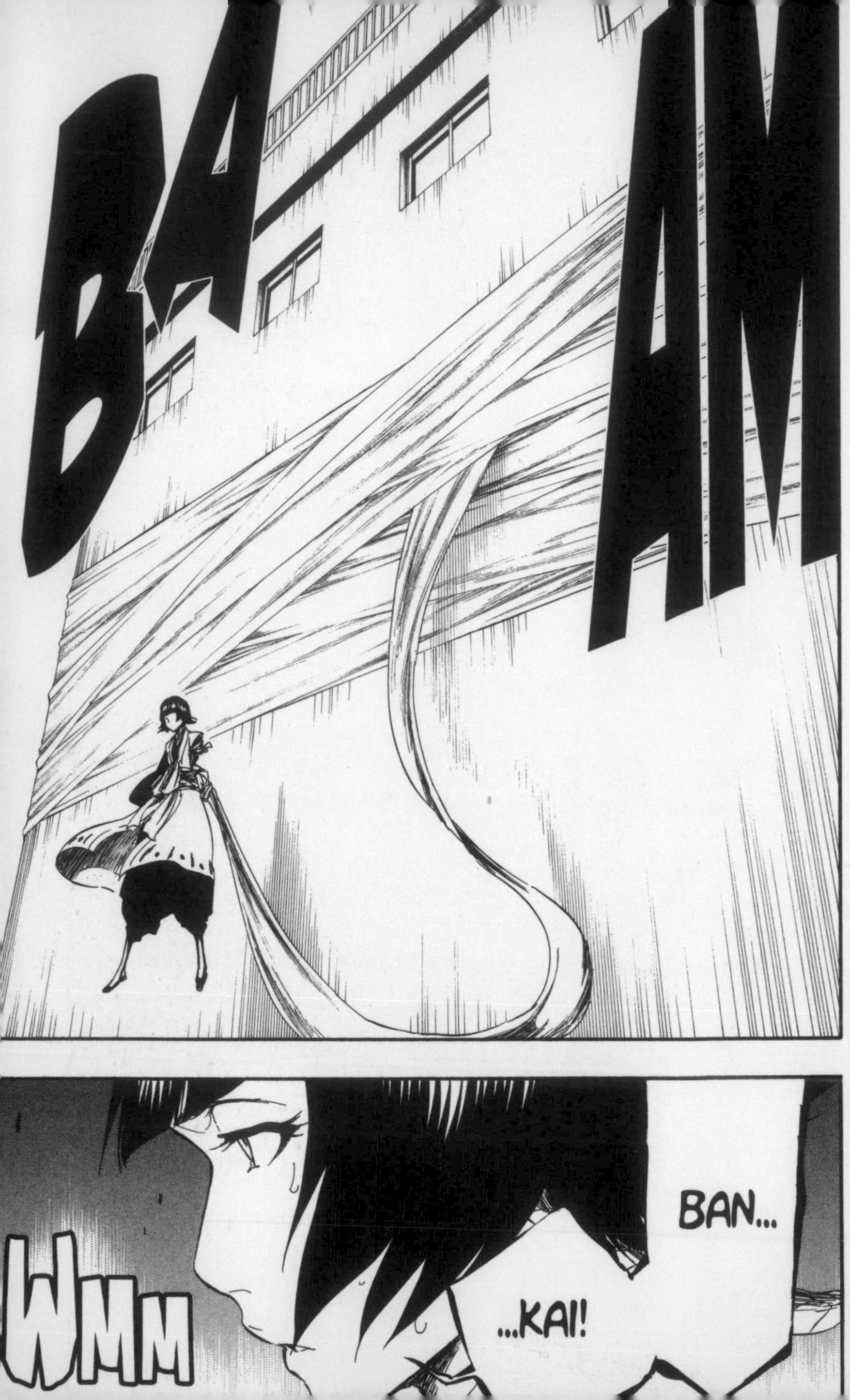
BA-AM
BAN...
...KAI!
WMM

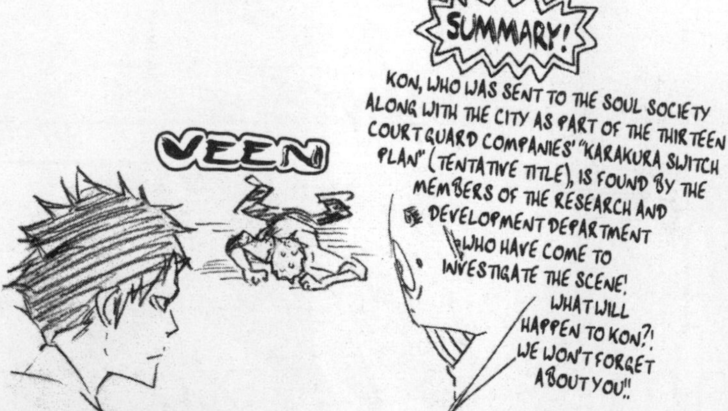
SUMMARY!
KON, WHO WAS SENT TO THE SOUL SOCIETY ALONG WITH THE CITY AS PART OF THE THIRTEEN COURT GUARD COMPANIES' "KARAKURA SWITCH PLAN" (TENTATIVE TITLE), IS FOUND BY THE MEMBERS OF THE RESEARCH AND DEVELOPMENT DEPARTMENT WHO HAVE COME TO INVESTIGATE THE SCENE! WHAT WILL HAPPEN TO KON?! WE WON'T FORGET ABOUT YOU!!
VEEN

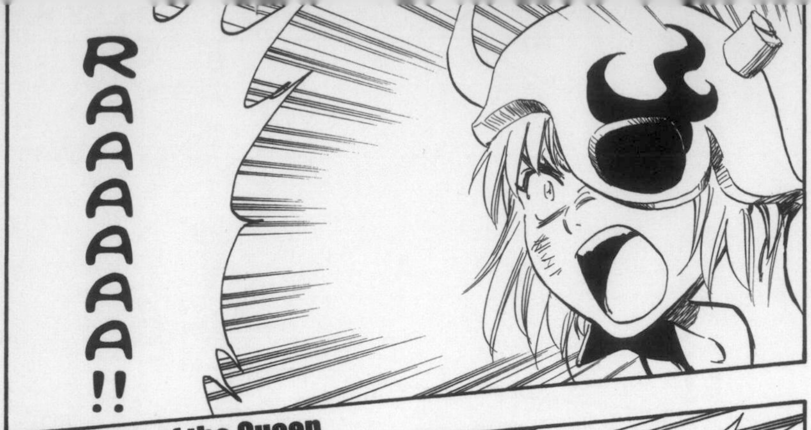
RAAAAAAA!!

360. Shock of the Queen

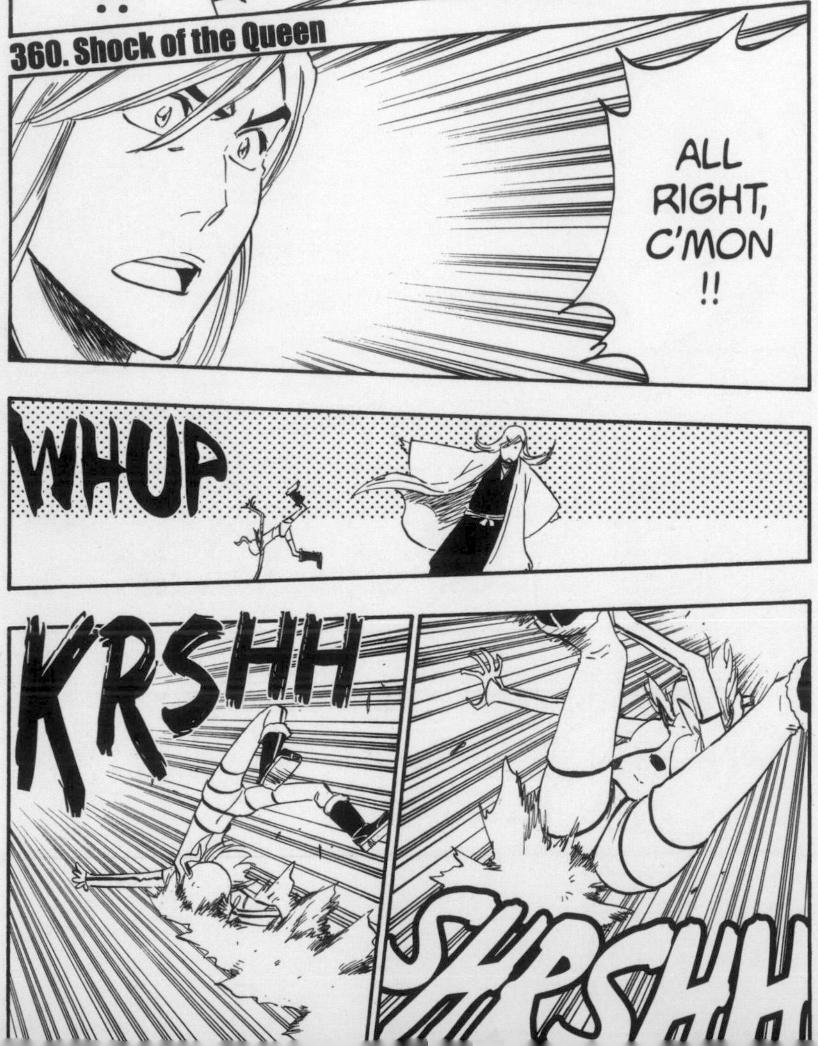
ALL RIGHT, C'MON!!
WHUP
KRSHH
SHPSHH

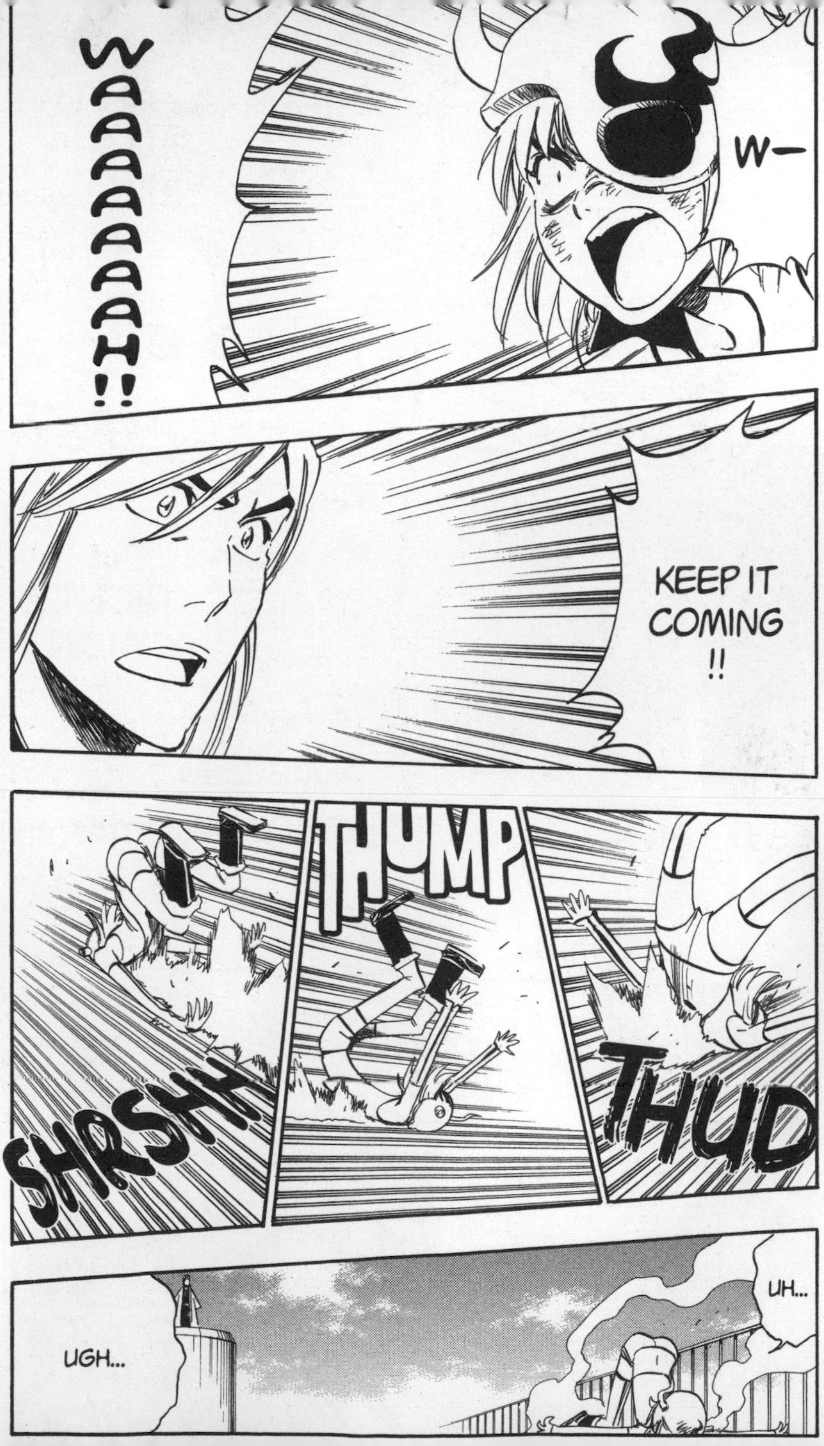
W—
WAAAAAAAH!!
KEEP IT COMING !!
THUD
THUMP
SHRSH
UH...
UGH...

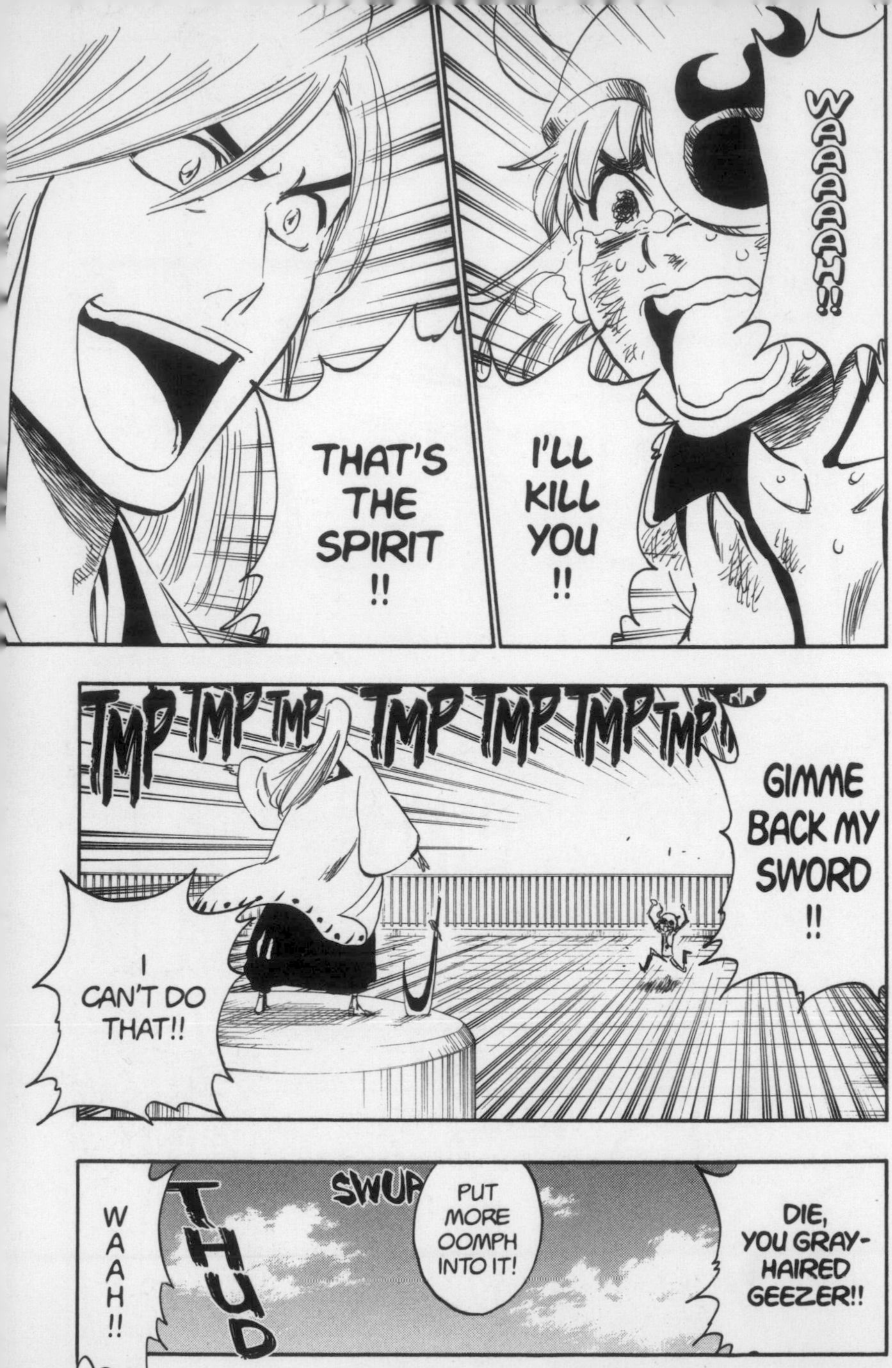
WAAAAAH!!
I'LL KILL YOU!!
THAT'S THE SPIRIT!!
TMP TMP TMP TMP TMP TMP TMP
GIMME BACK MY SWORD!!
I CAN'T DO THAT!!
DIE, YOU GRAY-HAIRED GEEZER!!
PUT MORE OOMPH INTO IT!
SWUP
THUD
WAAH!!

Bleach 360. Shock of the Queen

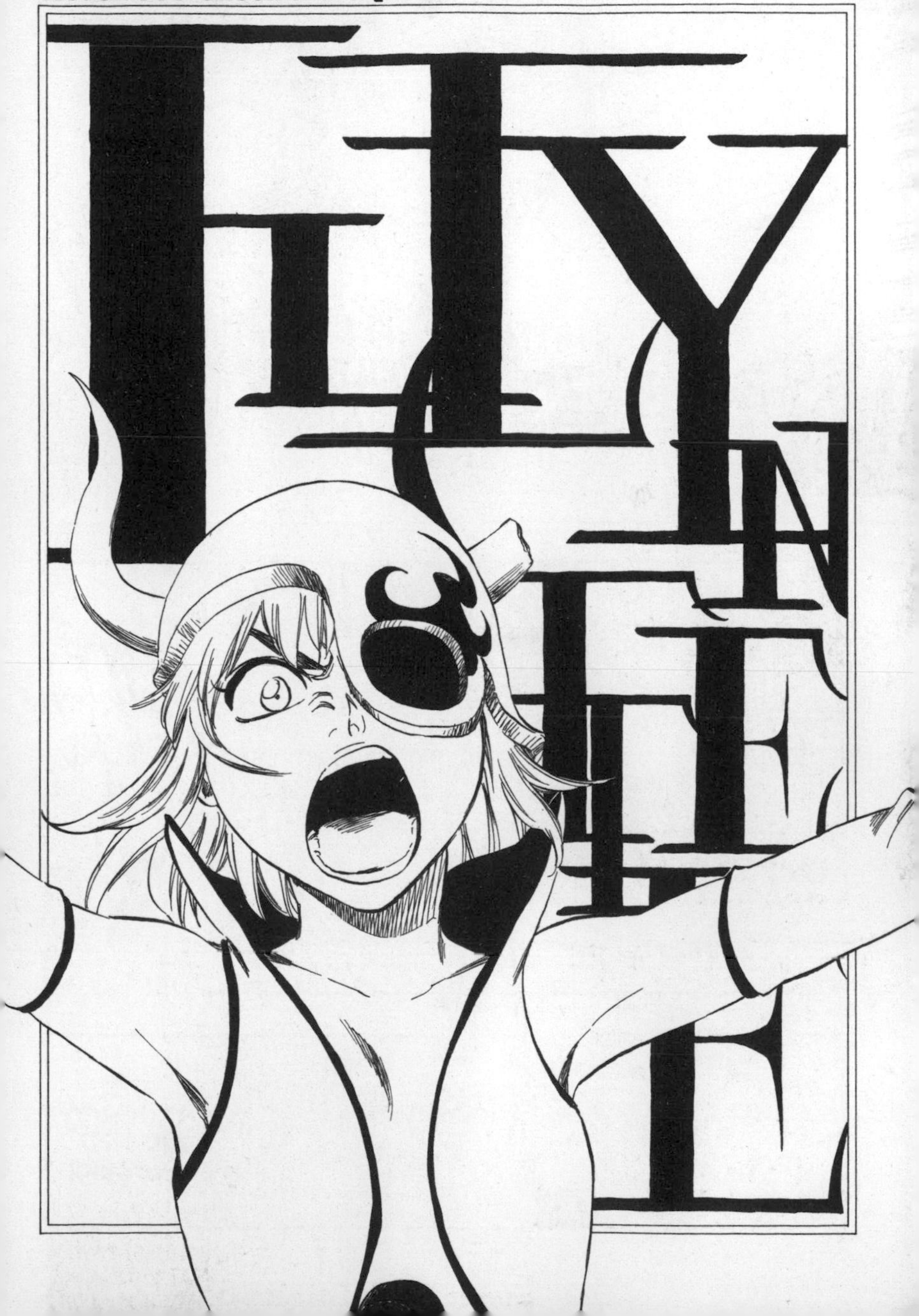

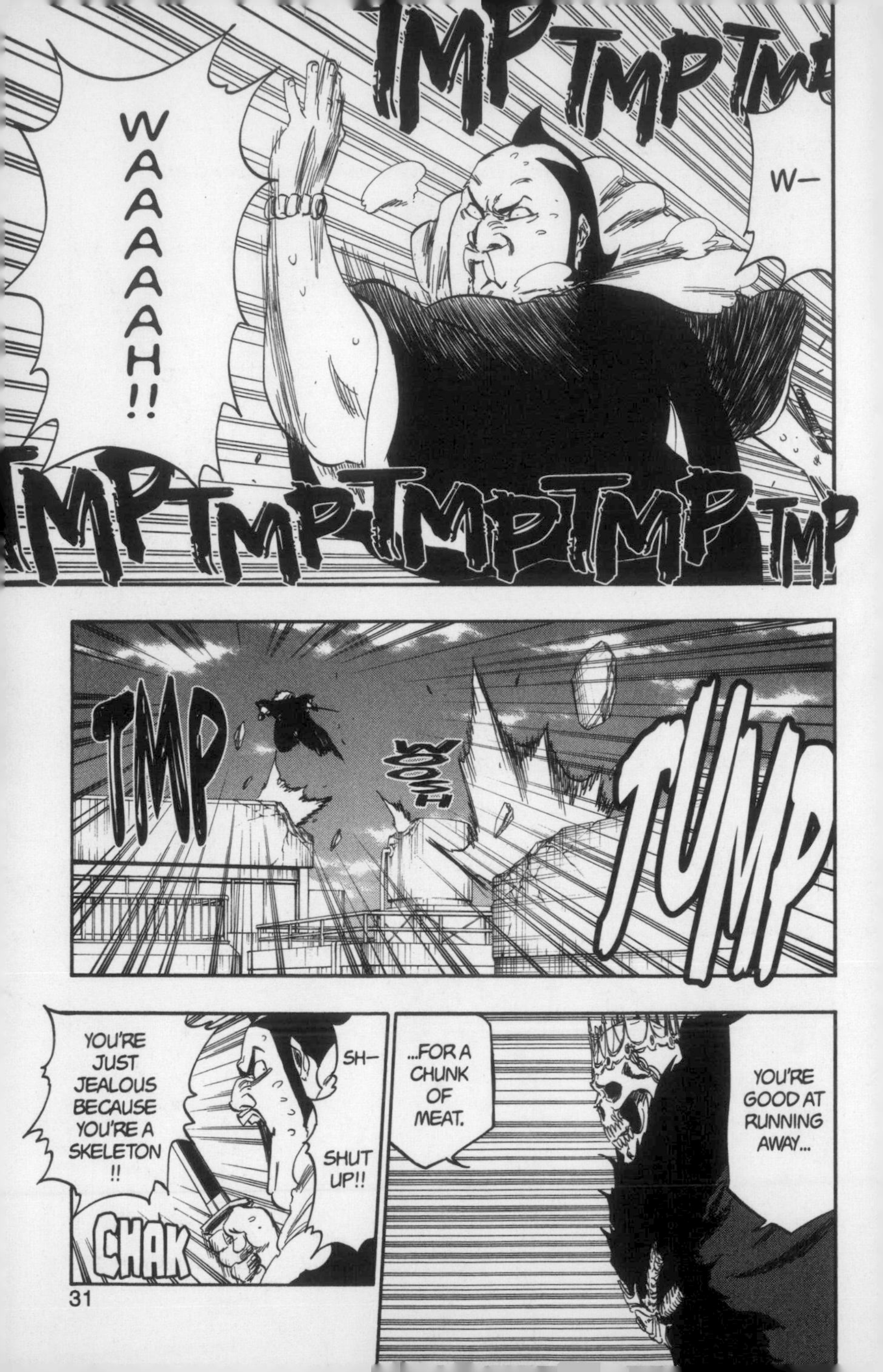
IMP TMP TM
W—
WAAAAAAH!!
MP TMP TMP TMP TMP
TUMP
WOOSH
TMP
YOU'RE GOOD AT RUNNING AWAY...
...FOR A CHUNK OF MEAT.
SH—
SHUT UP!!
YOU'RE JUST JEALOUS BECAUSE YOU'RE A SKELETON!!
CHAK

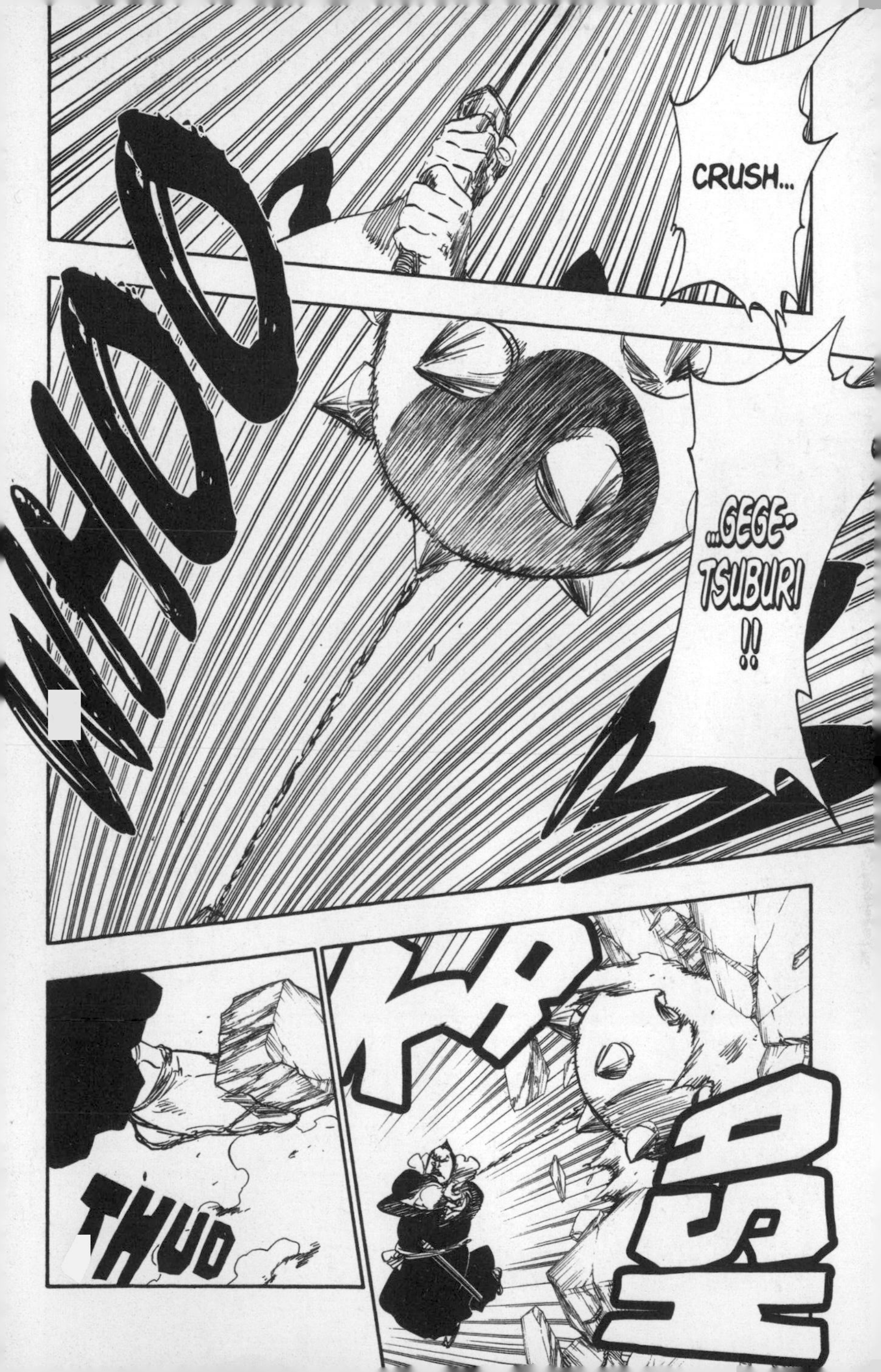
CRUSH...
...GEGE-TSUBURI!!
THUD

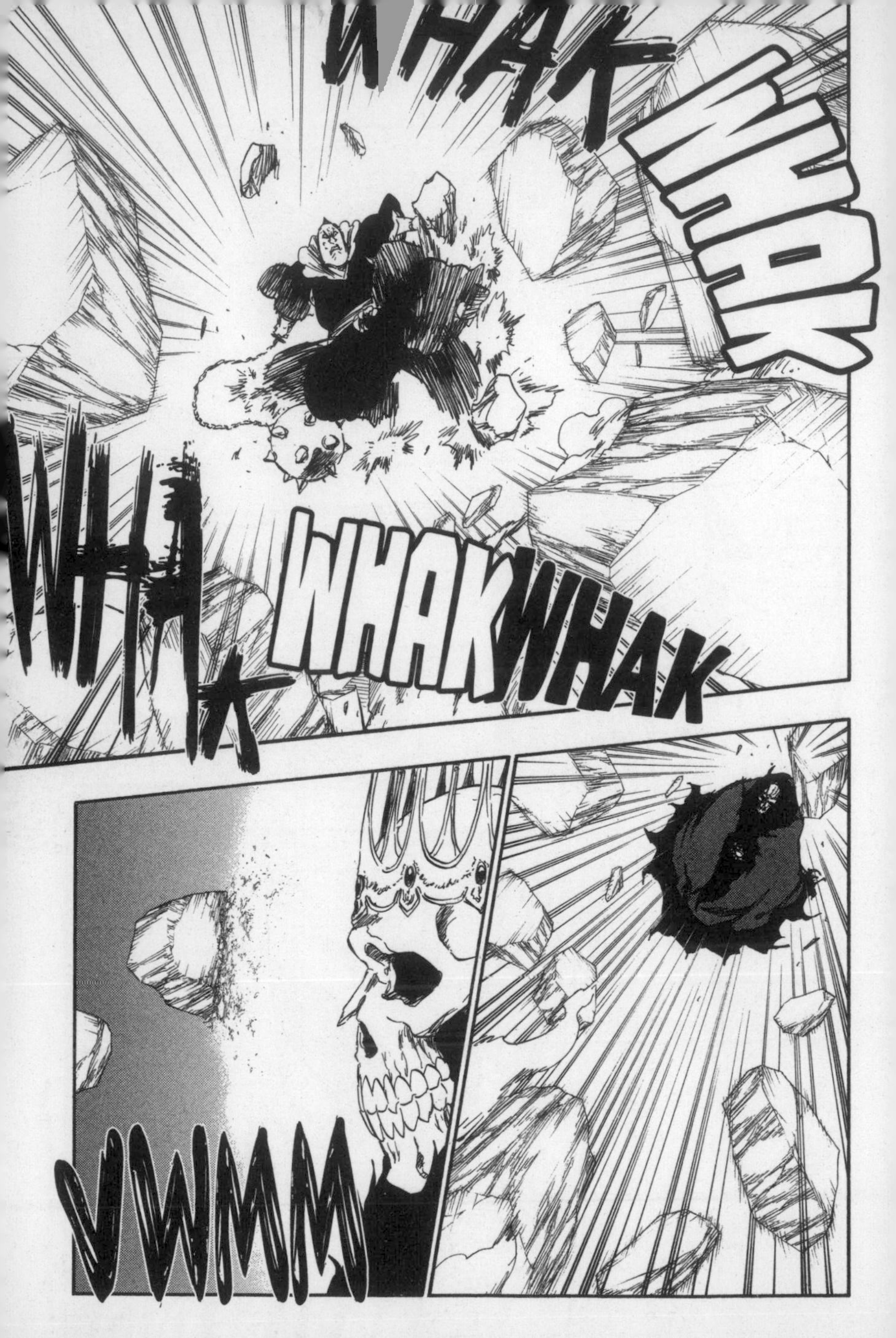
WHAK
WHAK
WHAK WHAK
WHAK
VWMMM

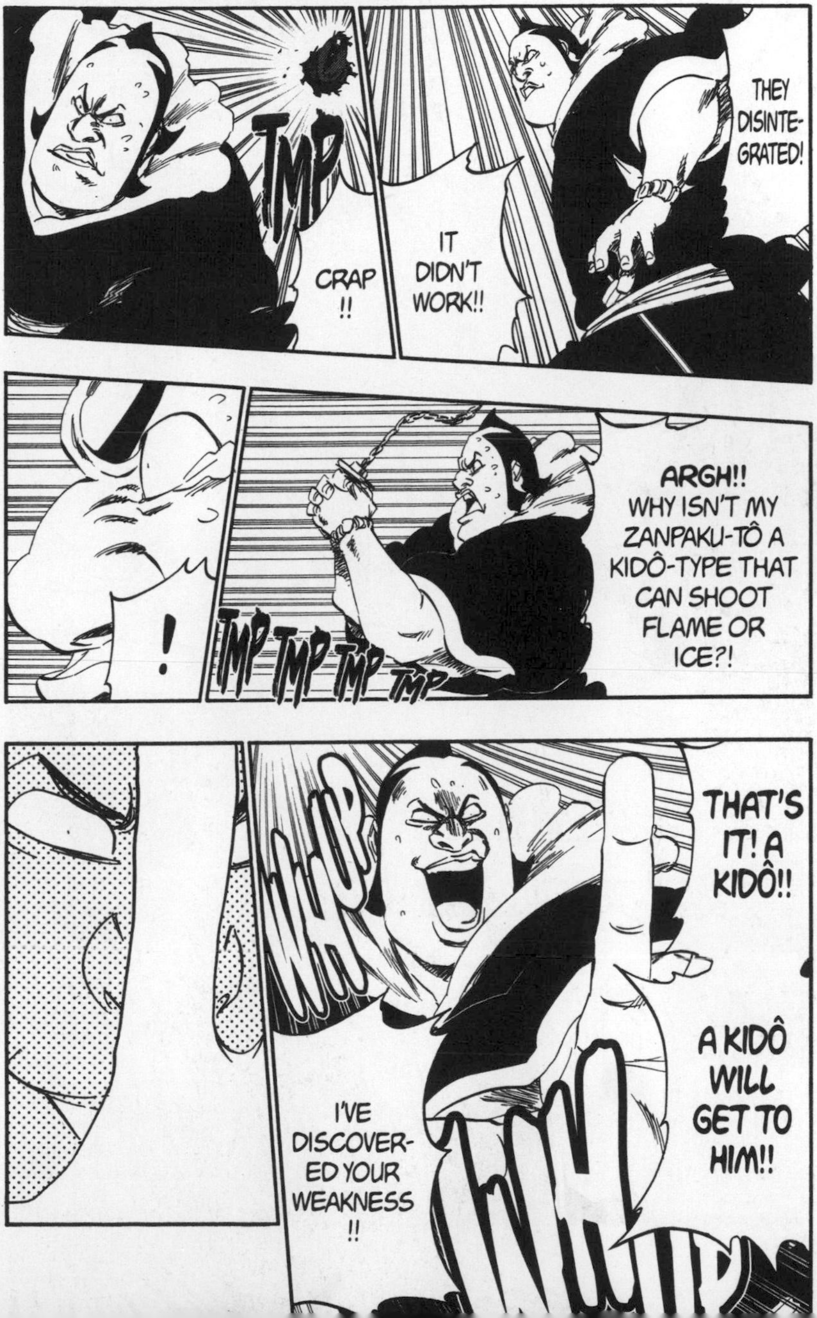
THEY DISINTE-GRATED!
IT DIDN'T WORK!!
TMP
CRAP!!
ARGH!! WHY ISN'T MY ZANPAKU-TÔ A KIDÔ-TYPE THAT CAN SHOOT FLAME OR ICE?!
TMP TMP TMP TMP
!
THAT'S IT! A KIDÔ!!
A KIDÔ WILL GET TO HIM!!
I'VE DISCOVER-ED YOUR WEAKNESS!!

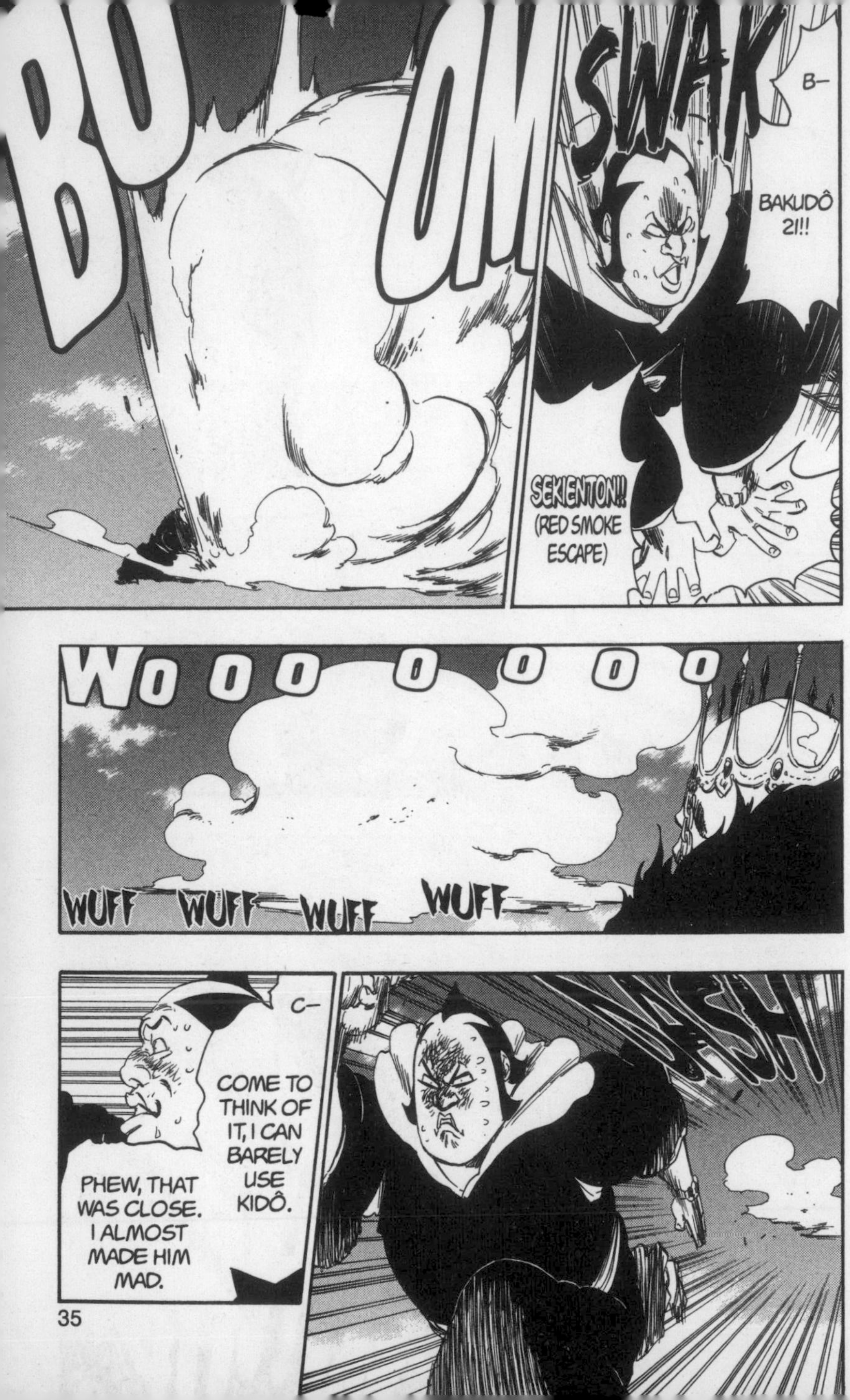
SWAK
B—
BAKUDÔ 21!!
SEKIENTON!! (RED SMOKE ESCAPE)
BOOM
WOOOOOOO
WUFF WUFF WUFF WUFF
C—
COME TO THINK OF IT, I CAN BARELY USE KIDÔ.
PHEW, THAT WAS CLOSE. I ALMOST MADE HIM MAD.

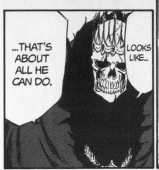

...THAT'S ABOUT ALL HE CAN DO. LOOKS LIKE...

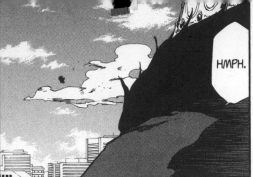

HMPH.

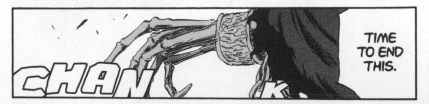

CHAN

TIME TO END THIS.

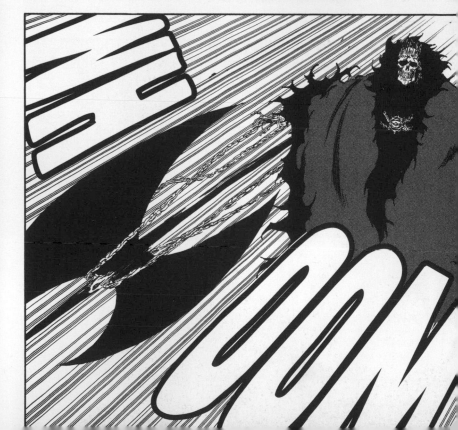

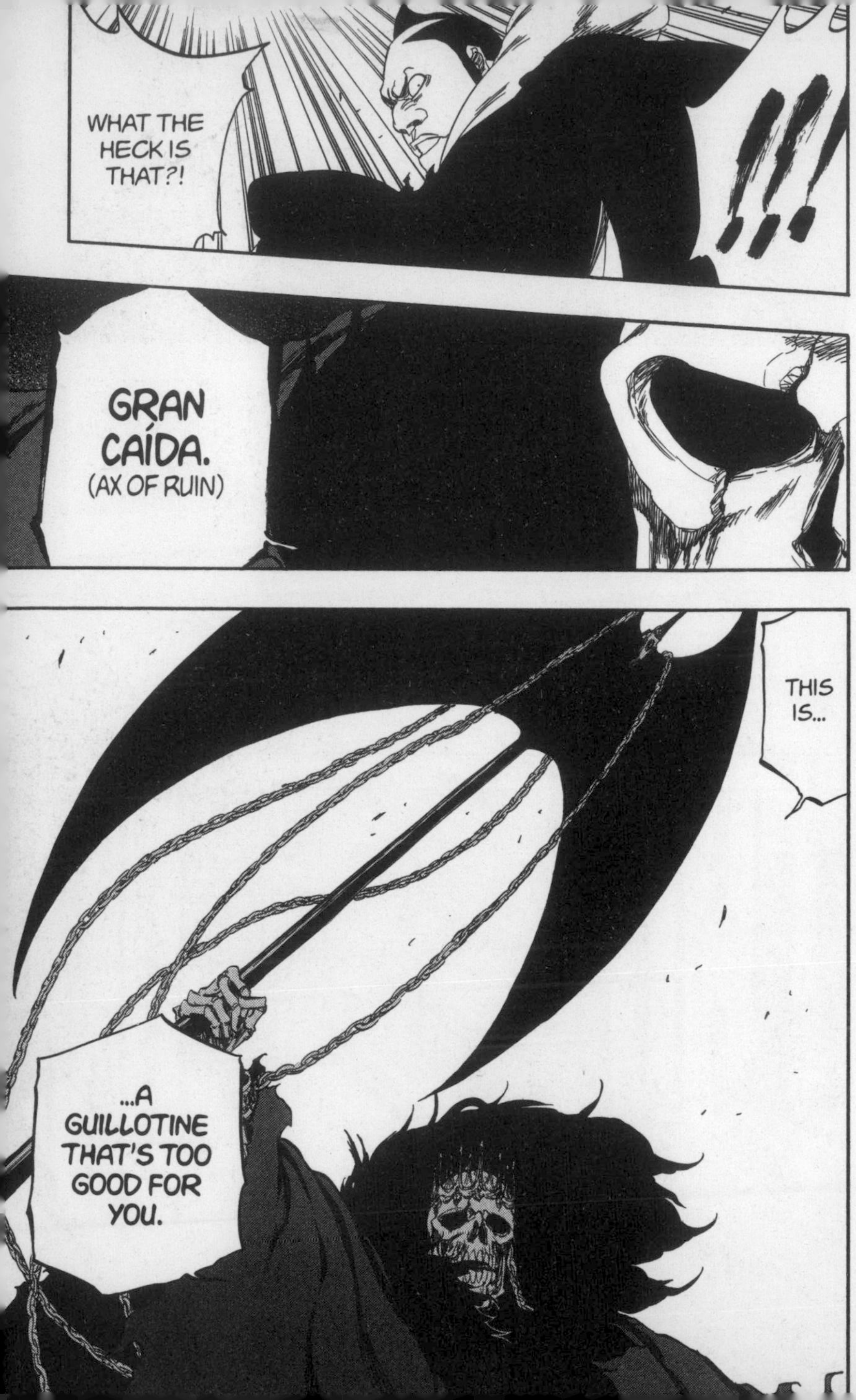
WHAT THE HECK IS THAT?!
GRAN CAÍDA. (AX OF RUIN)
THIS IS...
...A GUILLOTINE THAT'S TOO GOOD FOR YOU.

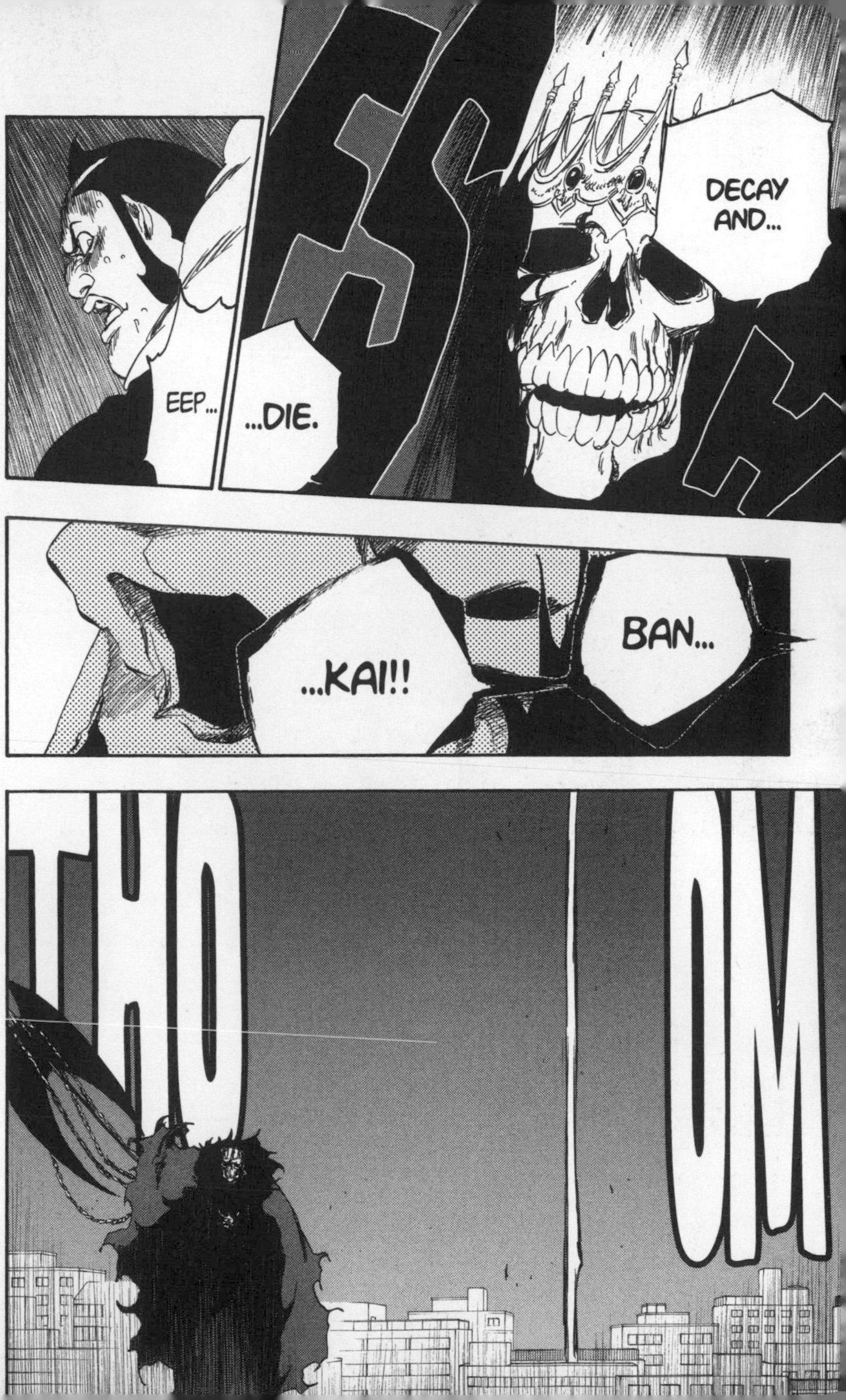
DECAY AND...
...DIE.
EEP...
BAN...
...KAI!!
THO
OM

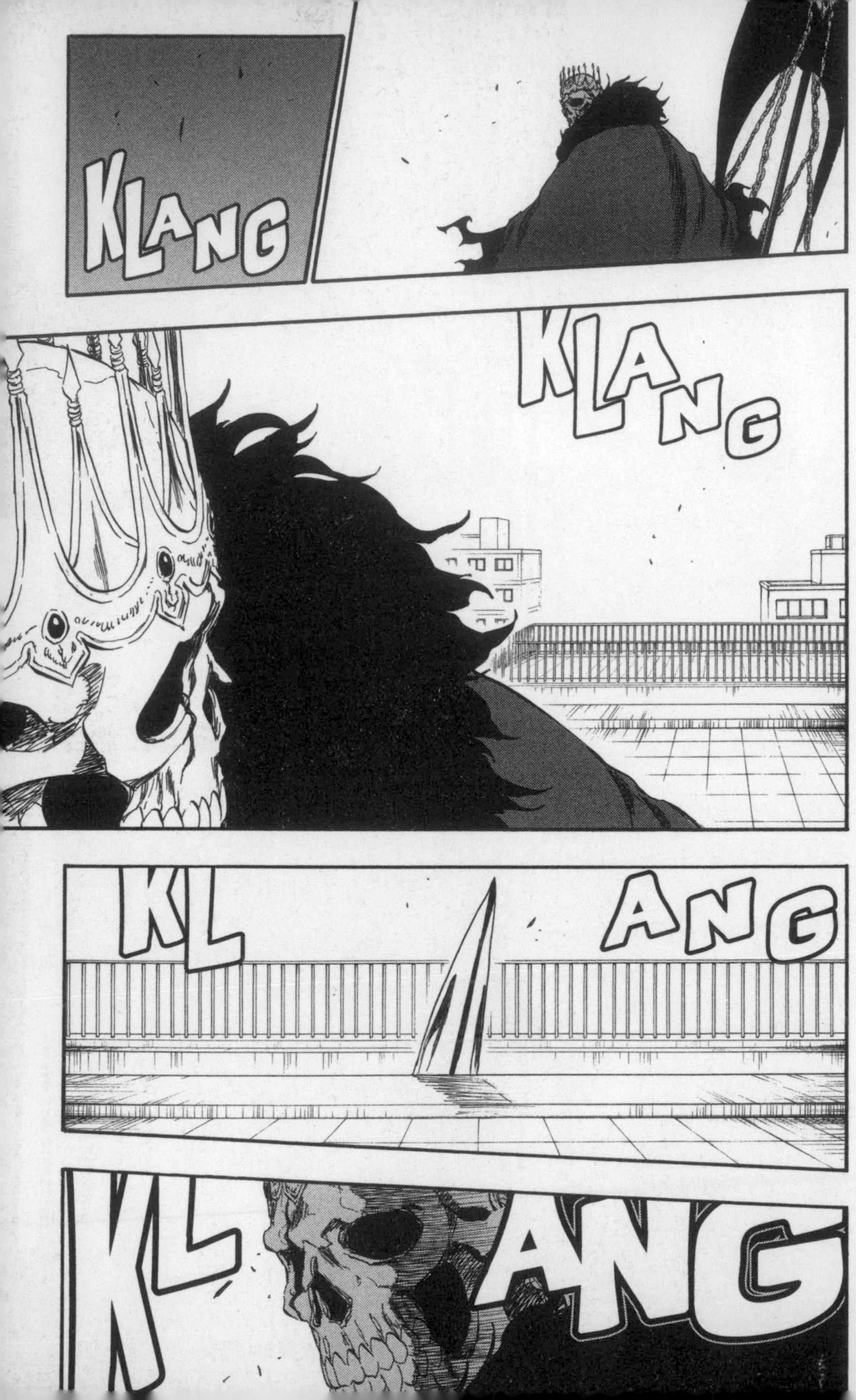
KLANG
KLANG
KL
ANG
KL
ANG

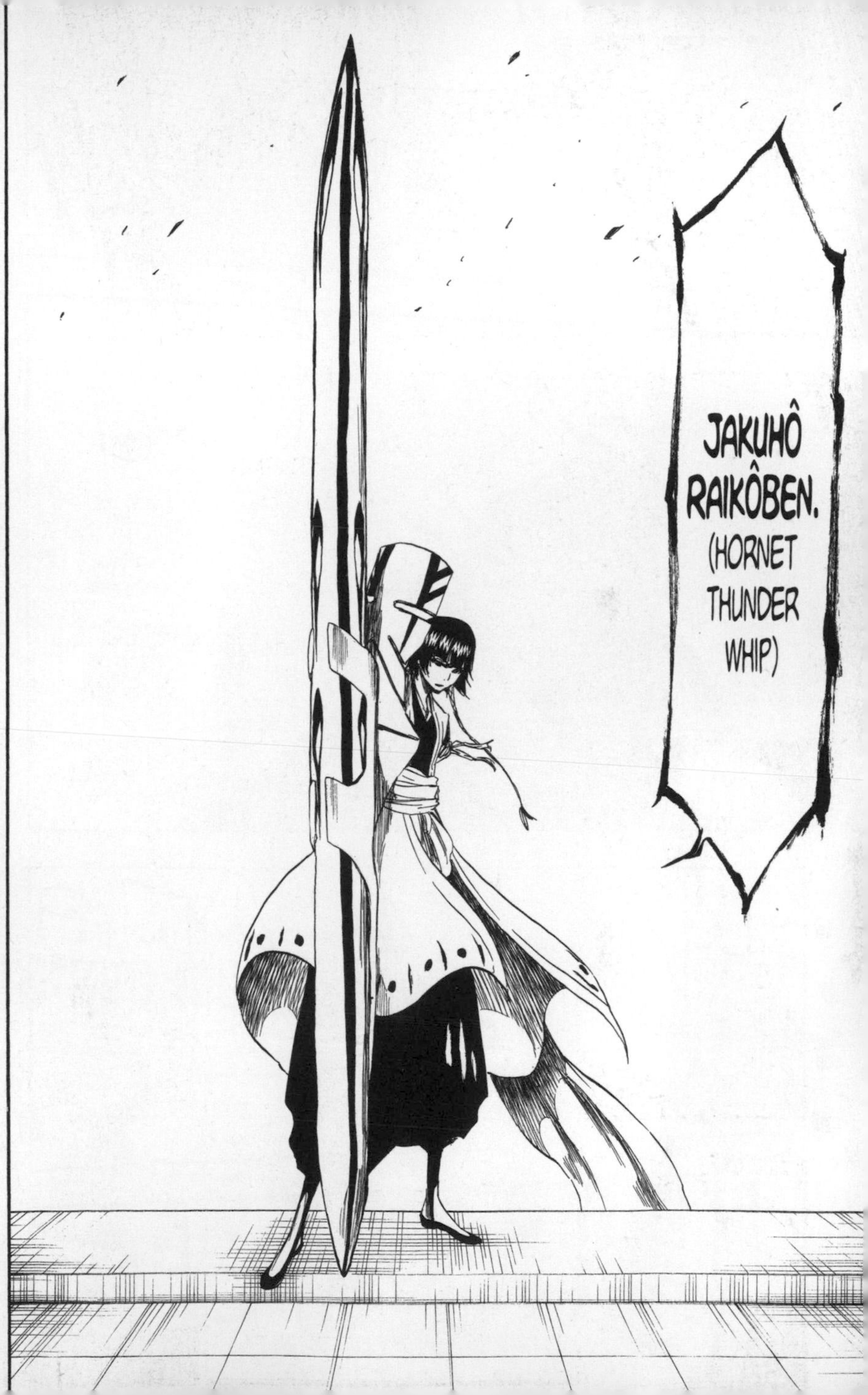
JAKUHÔ RAIKÔBEN. (HORNET THUNDER WHIP)

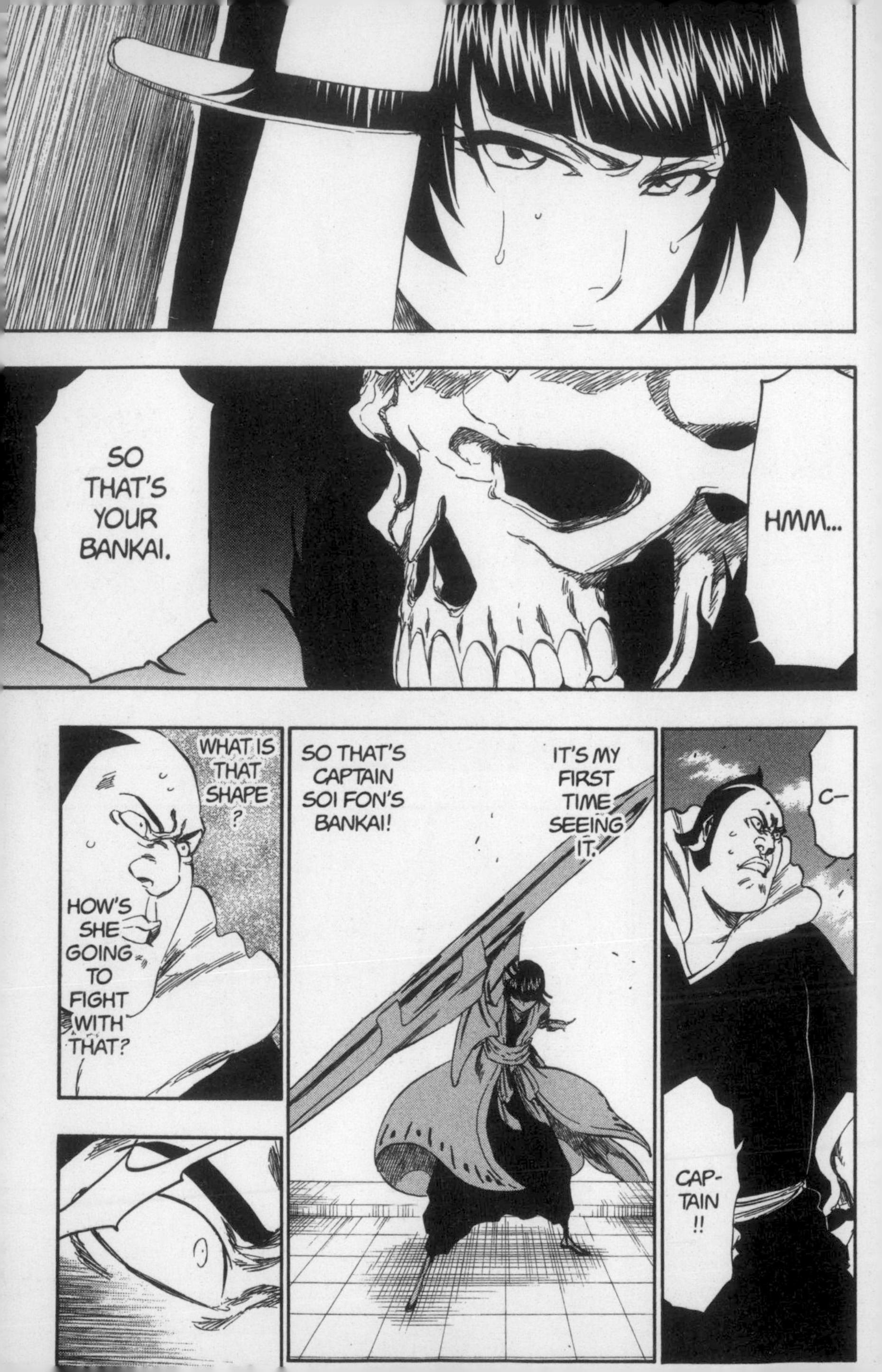
HMM...
SO THAT'S YOUR BANKAI.
C-
CAP-TAIN!!
IT'S MY FIRST TIME SEEING IT.
SO THAT'S CAPTAIN SOI FON'S BANKAI!
WHAT IS THAT SHAPE?
HOW'S SHE GOING TO FIGHT WITH THAT?

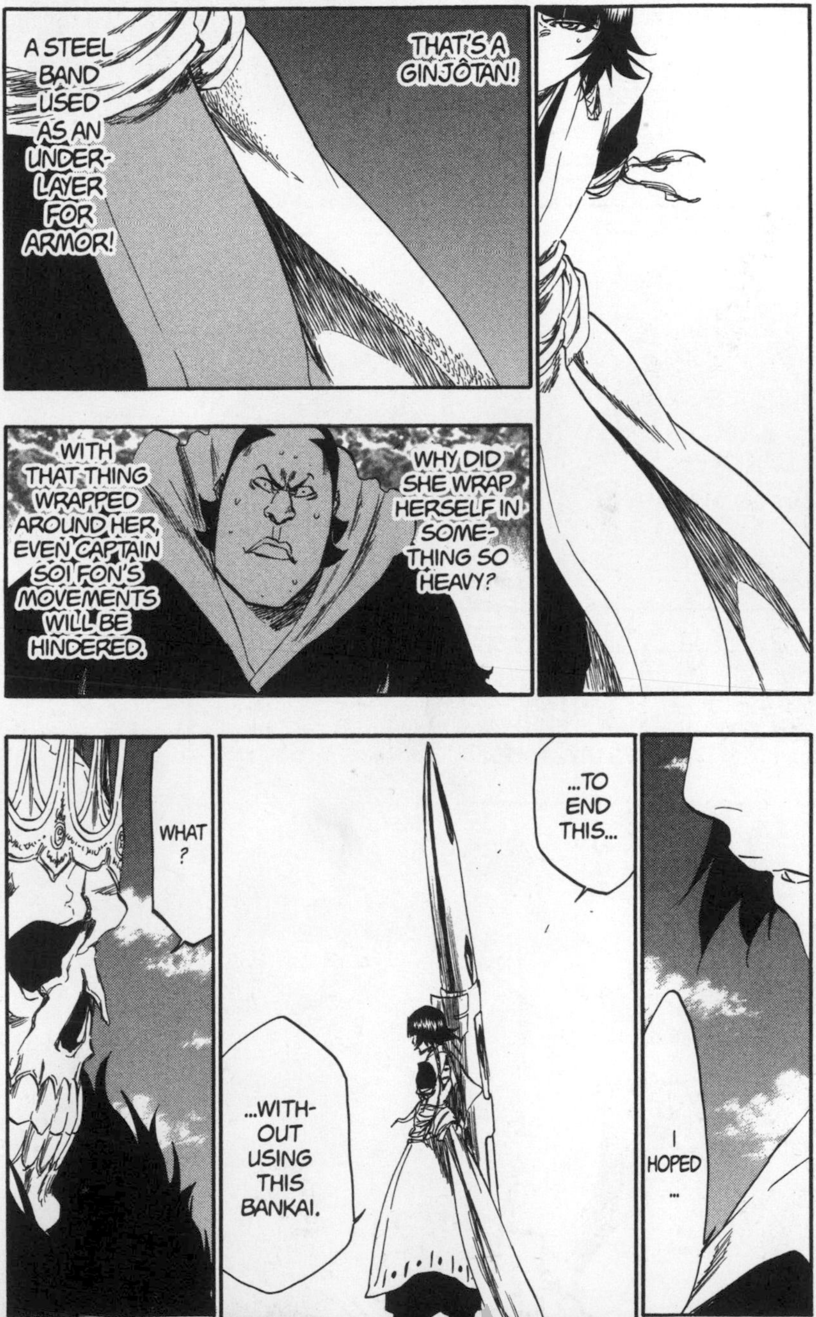
THAT'S A GINJÔTAN!
A STEEL BAND USED AS AN UNDER-LAYER FOR ARMOR!
WHY DID SHE WRAP HERSELF IN SOME-THING SO HEAVY?
WITH THAT THING WRAPPED AROUND HER, EVEN CAPTAIN SOI FON'S MOVEMENTS WILL BE HINDERED.
I HOPED ...
...TO END THIS...
...WITH-OUT USING THIS BANKAI.
WHAT ?

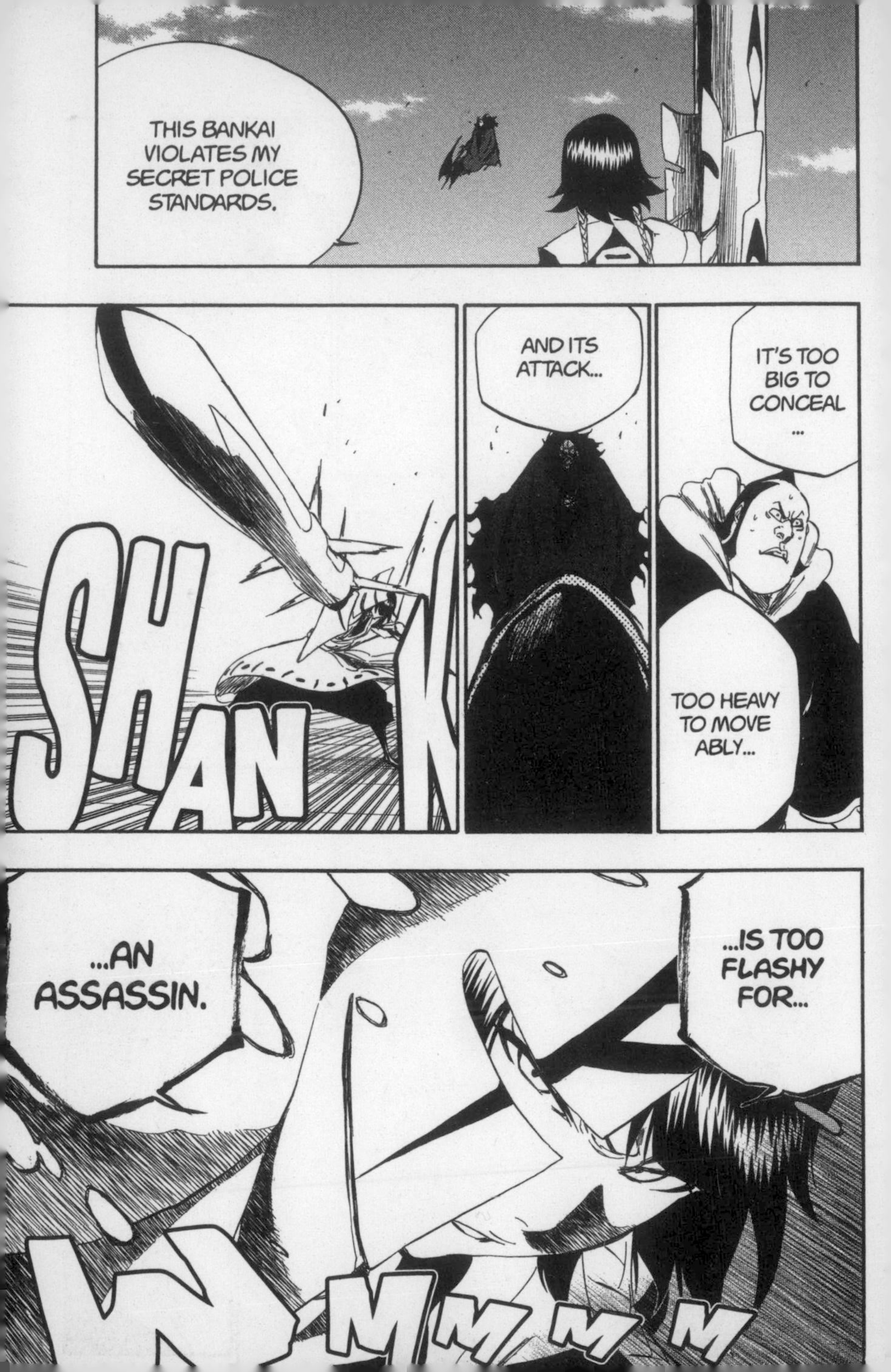
THIS BANKAI VIOLATES MY SECRET POLICE STANDARDS.
IT'S TOO BIG TO CONCEAL ...
TOO HEAVY TO MOVE ABLY...
AND ITS ATTACK...
SHANK
...IS TOO FLASHY FOR...
...AN ASSASSIN.
MMMMM

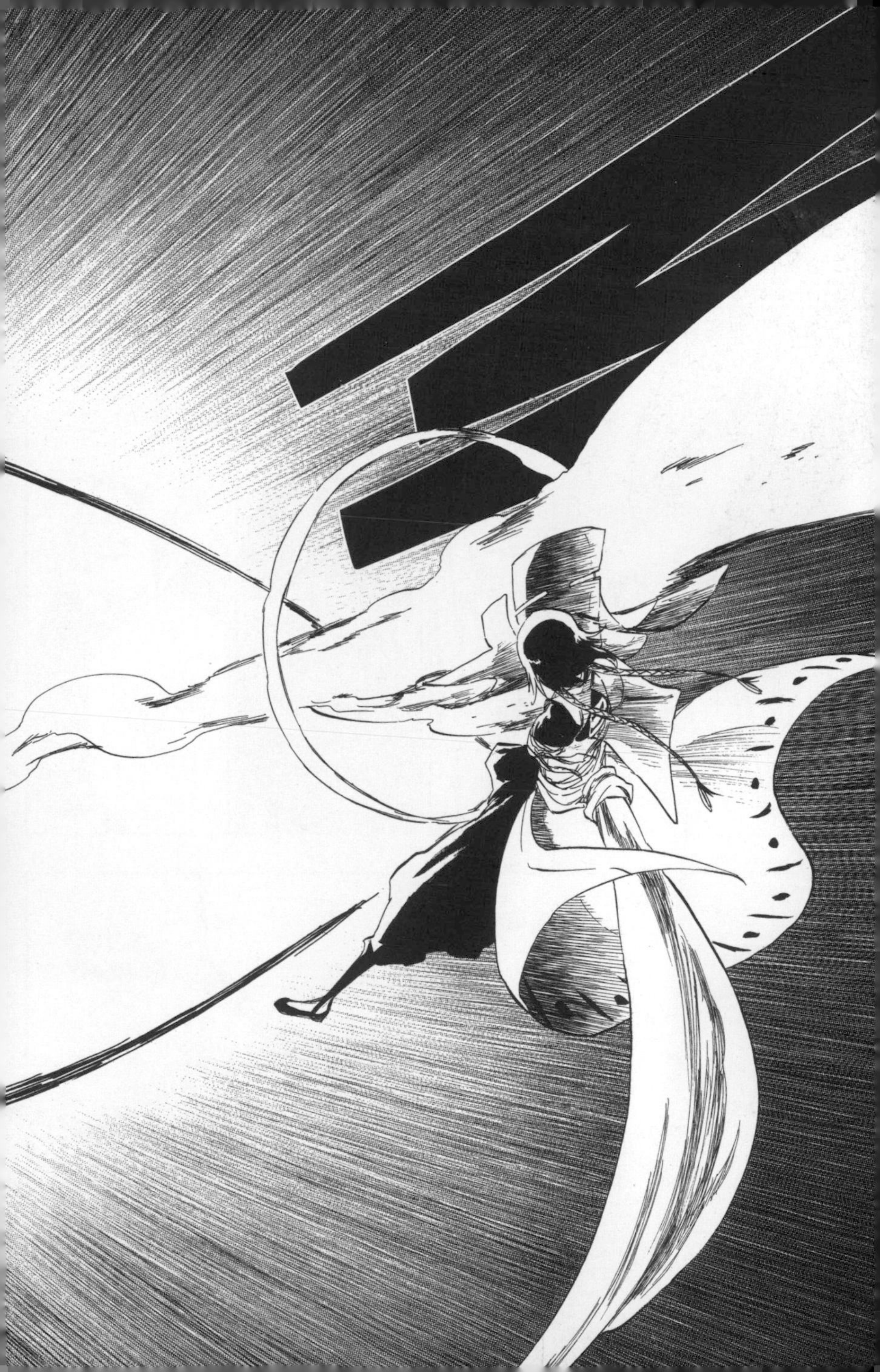

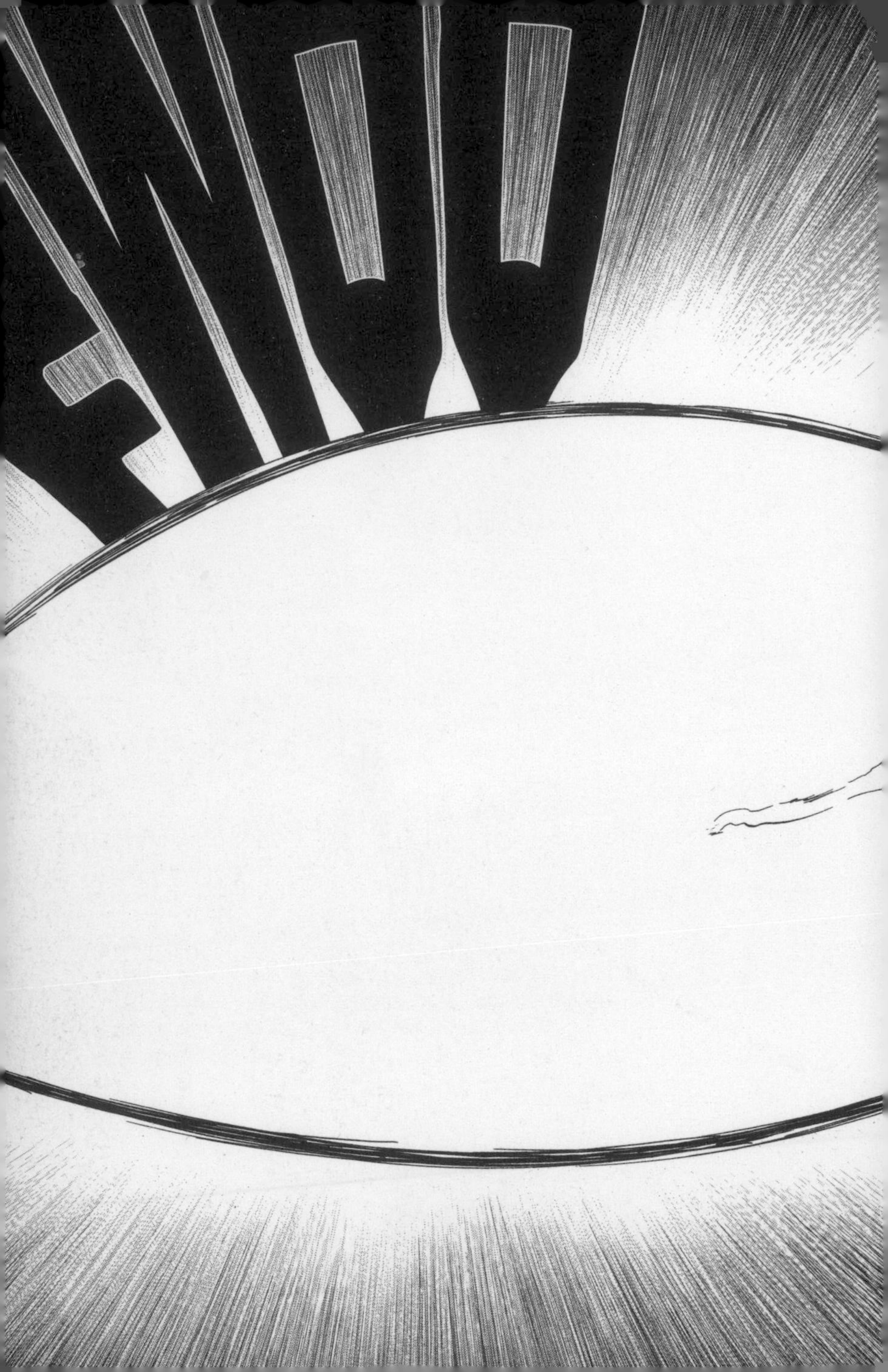

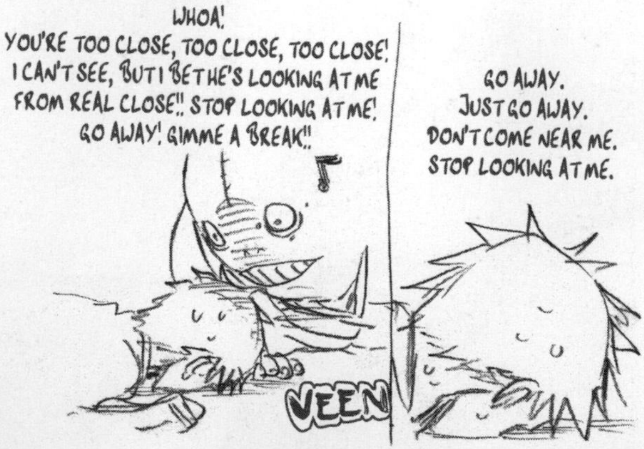
GO AWAY. JUST GO AWAY. DON'T COME NEAR ME. STOP LOOKING AT ME.
WHOA! YOU'RE TOO CLOSE, TOO CLOSE, TOO CLOSE! I CAN'T SEE, BUT I BET HE'S LOOKING AT ME FROM REAL CLOSE!! STOP LOOKING AT ME! GO AWAY! GIMME A BREAK!!
VEEN

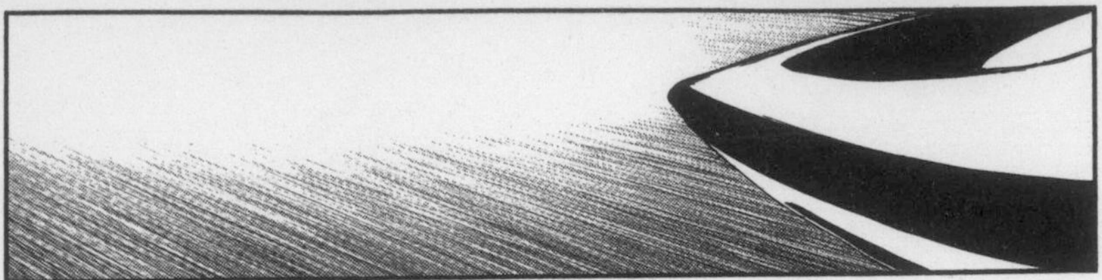

361. I Hate Loneliness, But It Loves Me

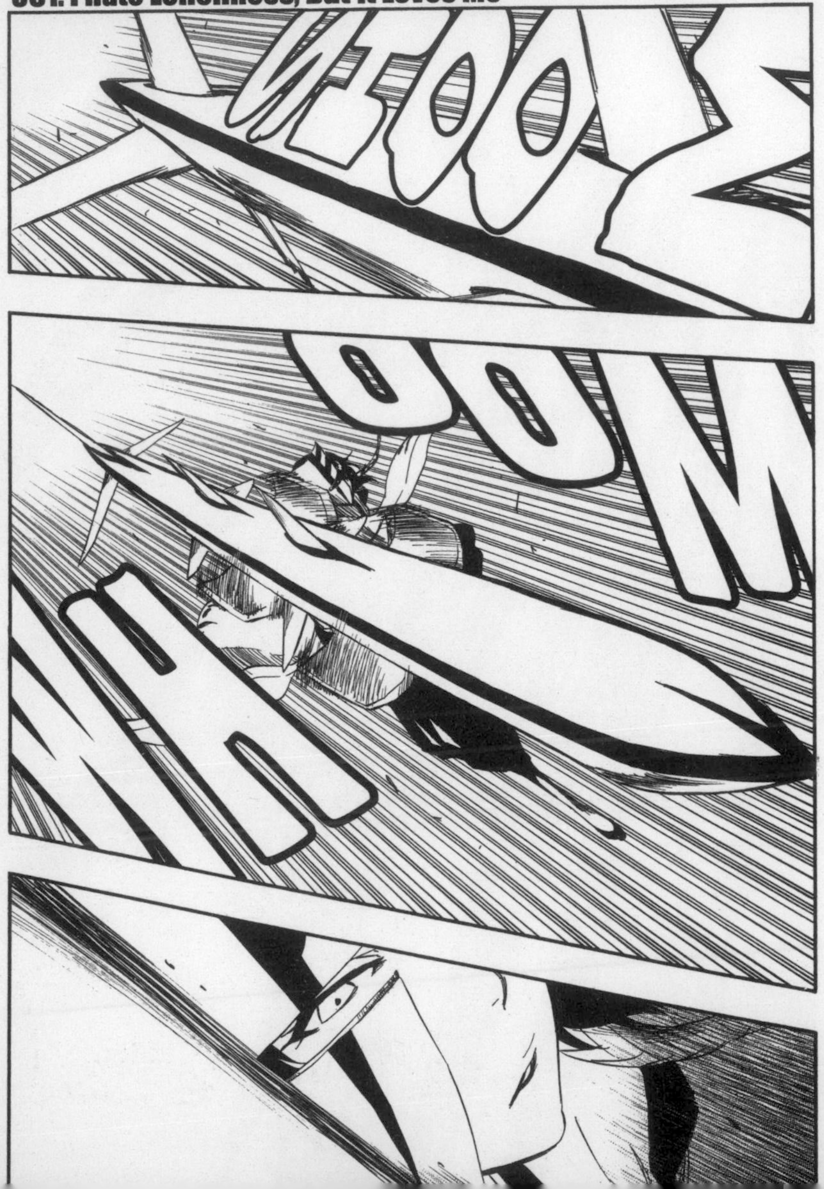

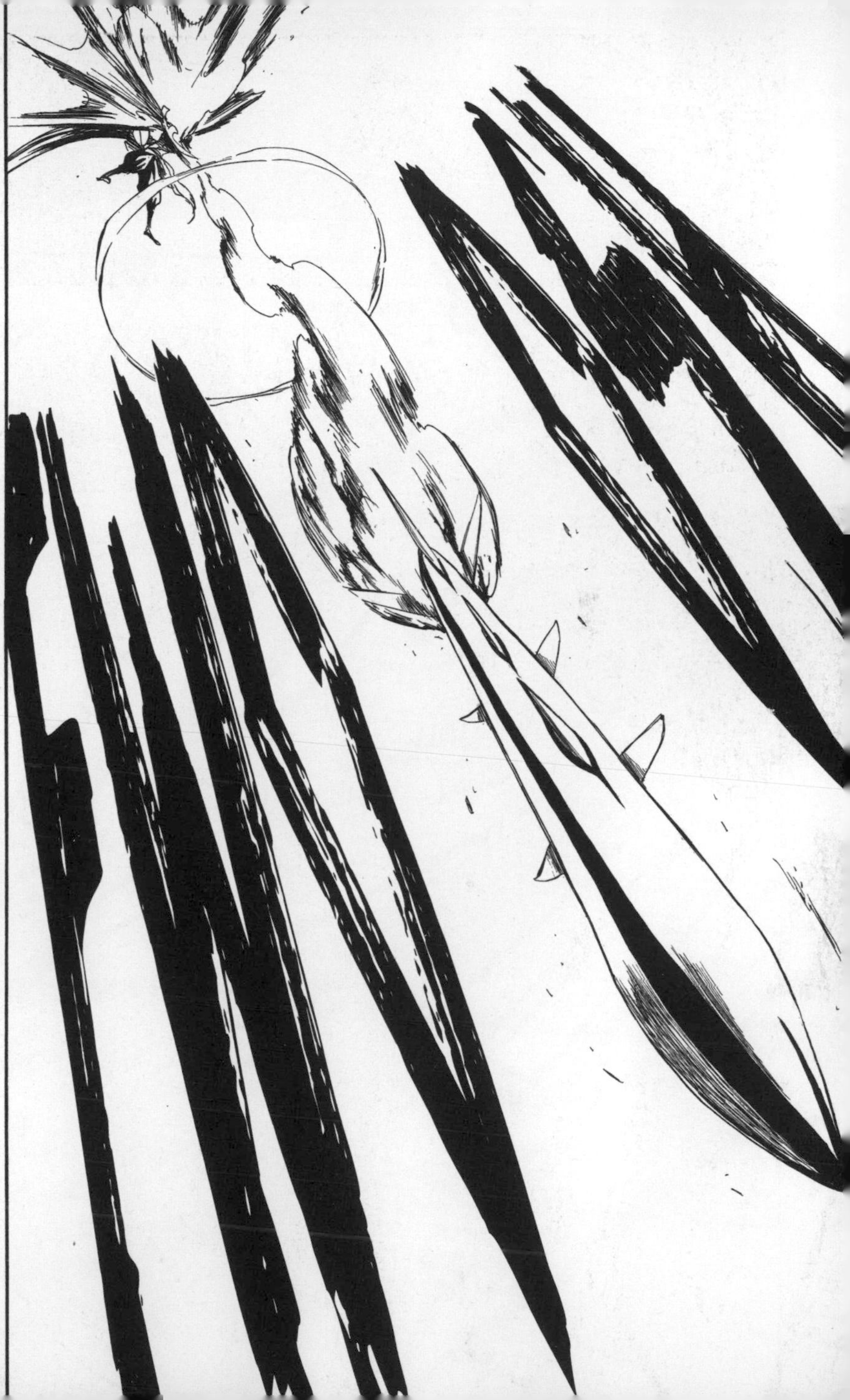

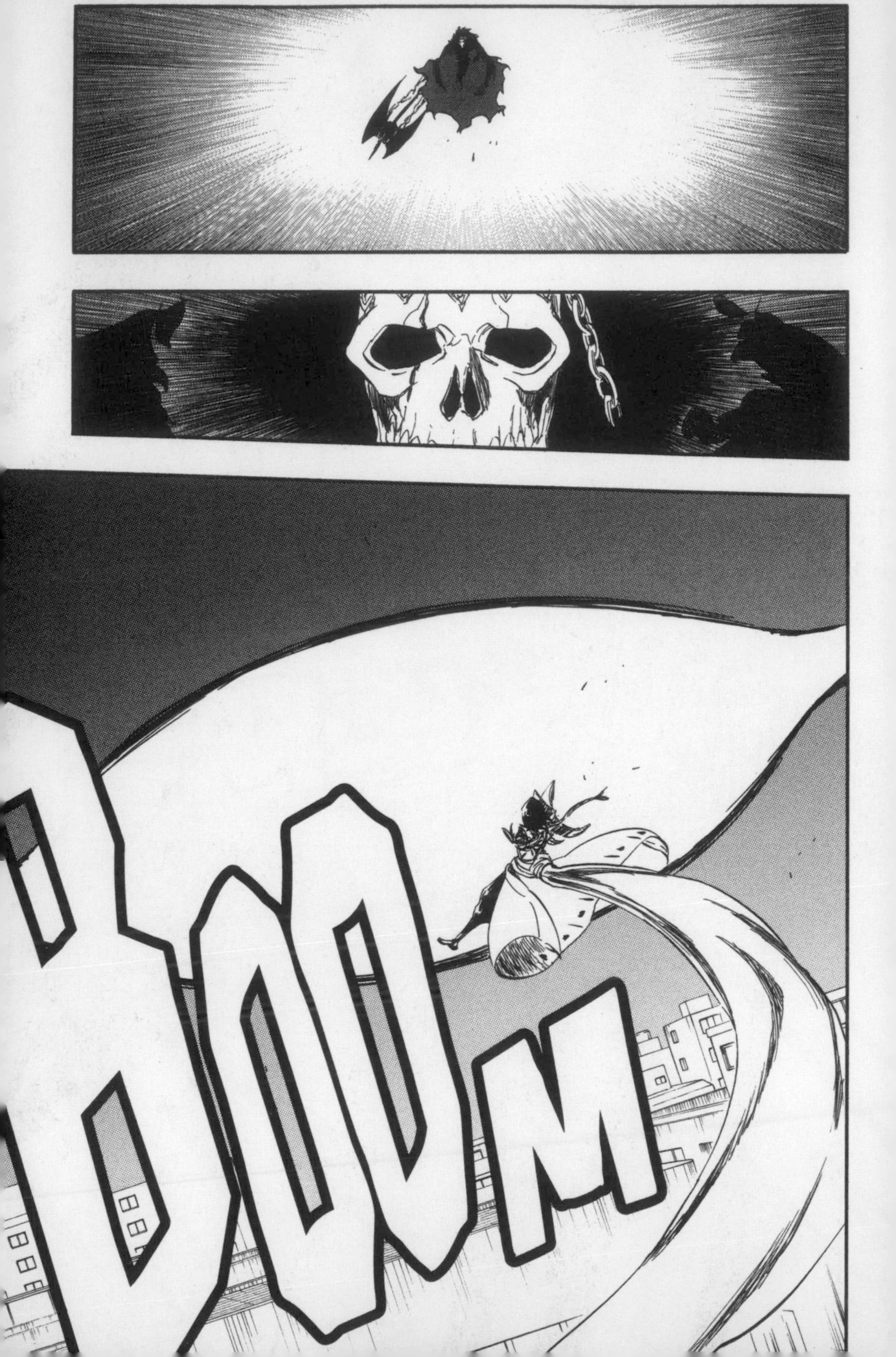
BOOM

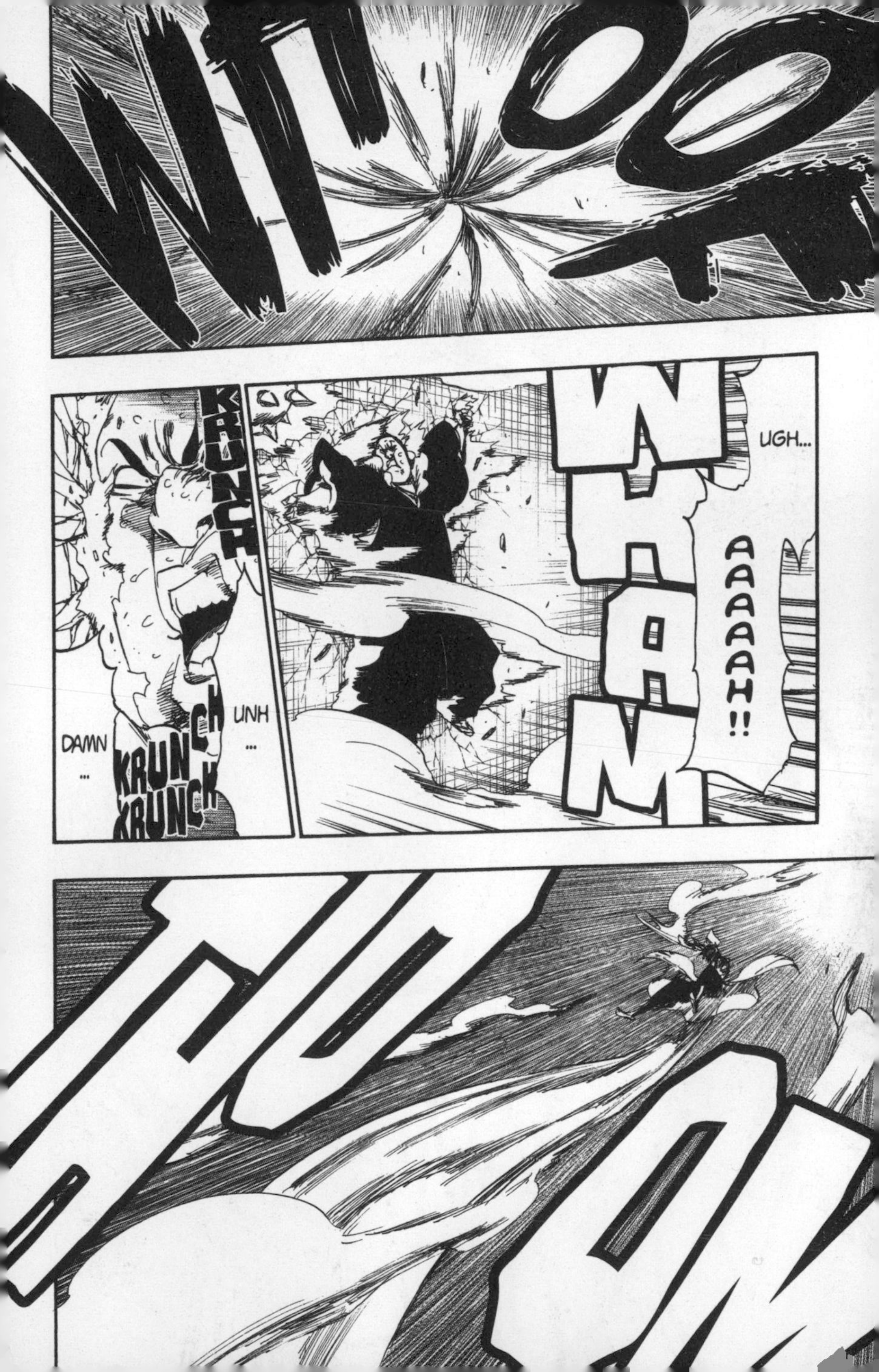
WHAM
UGH...
AAAAAH!!
KRUNCH
UNH...
KRUNCH
KRUNCH
DAMN...

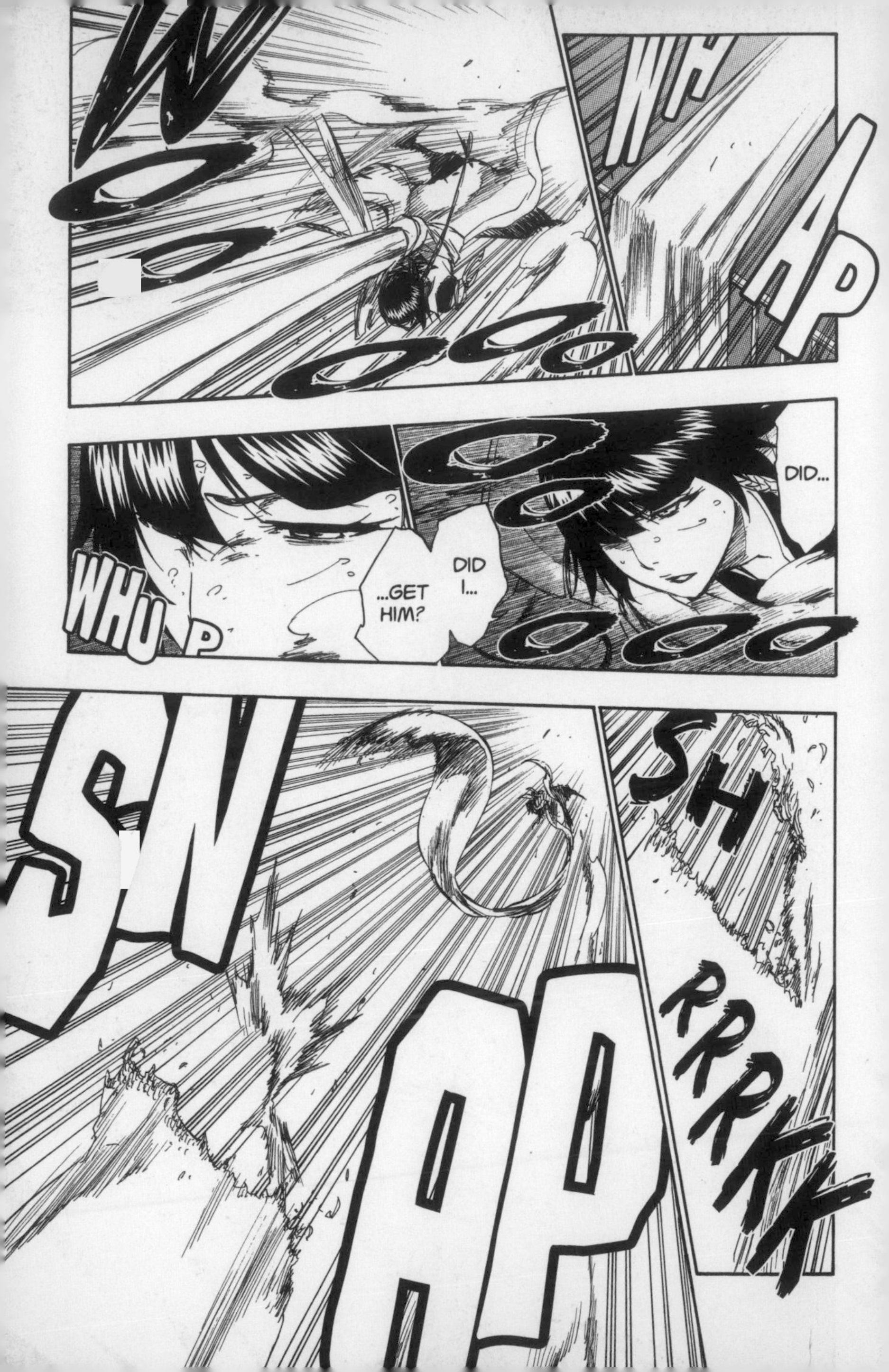
WHAP
DID...
DID I...
...GET HIM?
WHUP
SHRRRRKK
SNAP

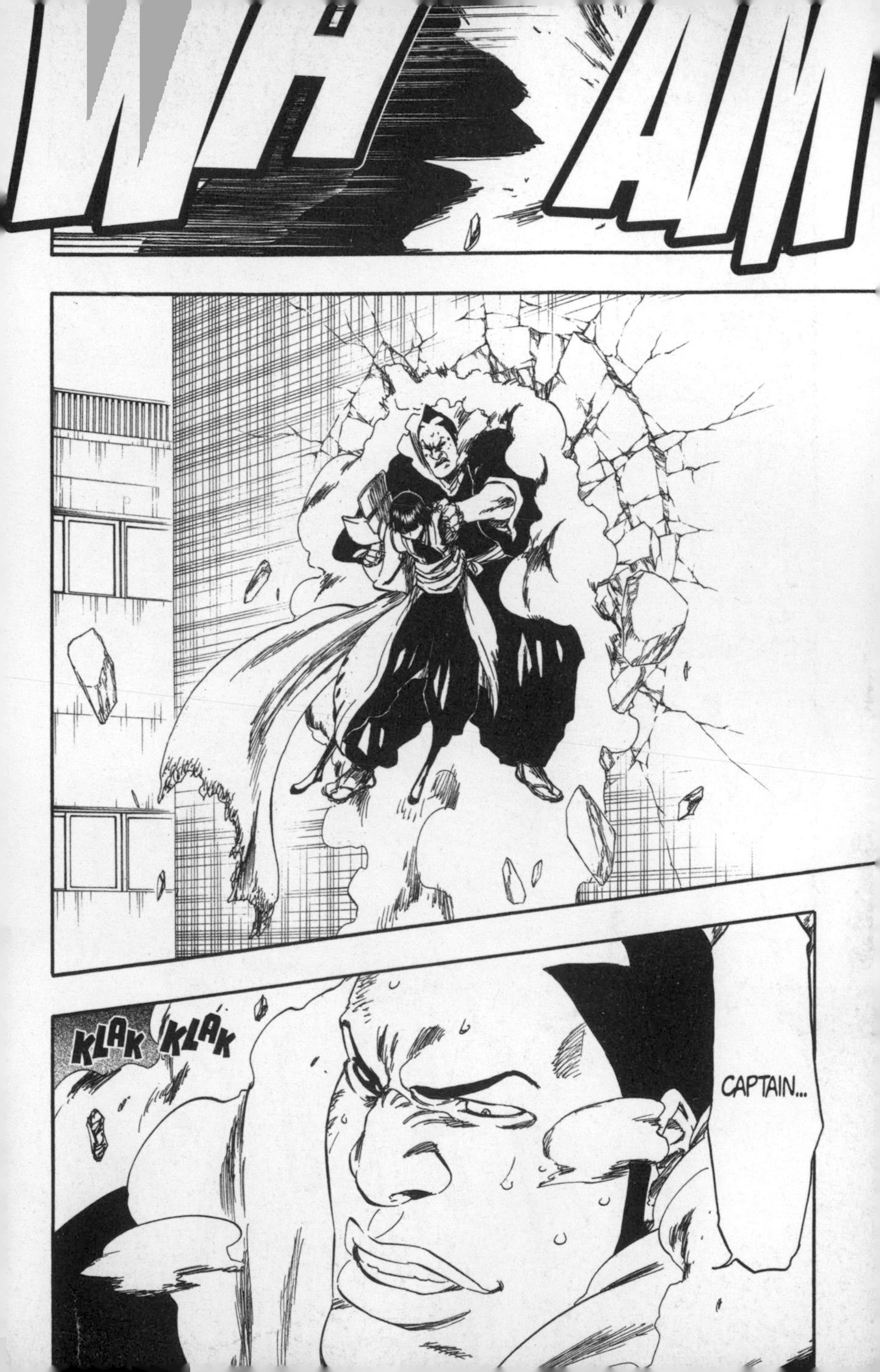
WHAM
CAPTAIN...
KLAK KLAK

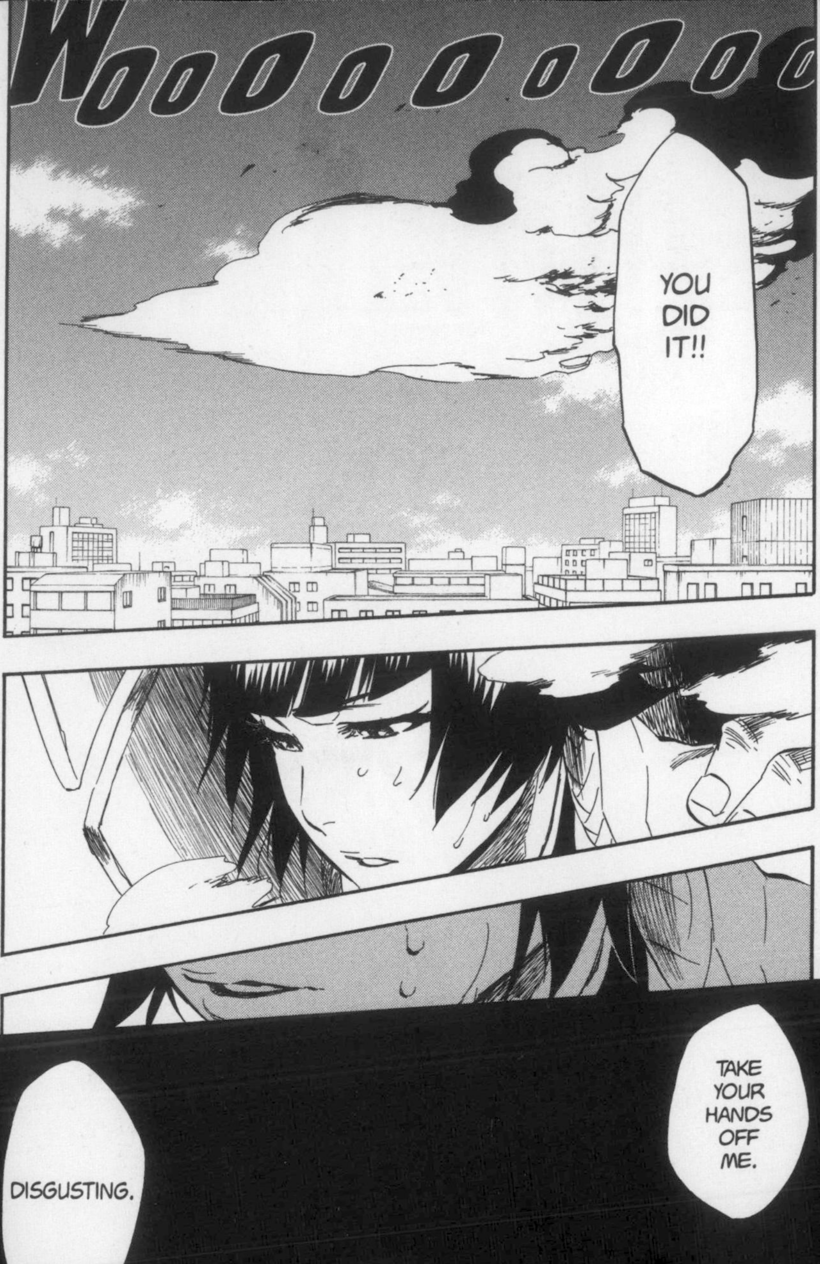
WOOOOOOOOO
YOU DID IT!!
TAKE YOUR HANDS OFF ME.
DISGUSTING.

361. I Hate Loneliness, But It Loves Me

BLEACH

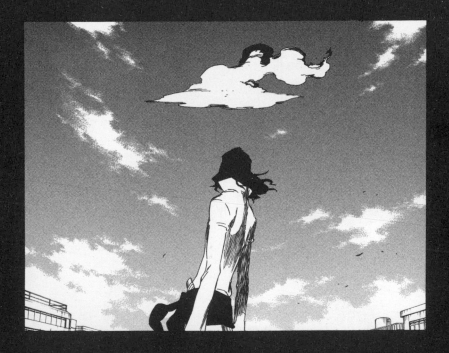

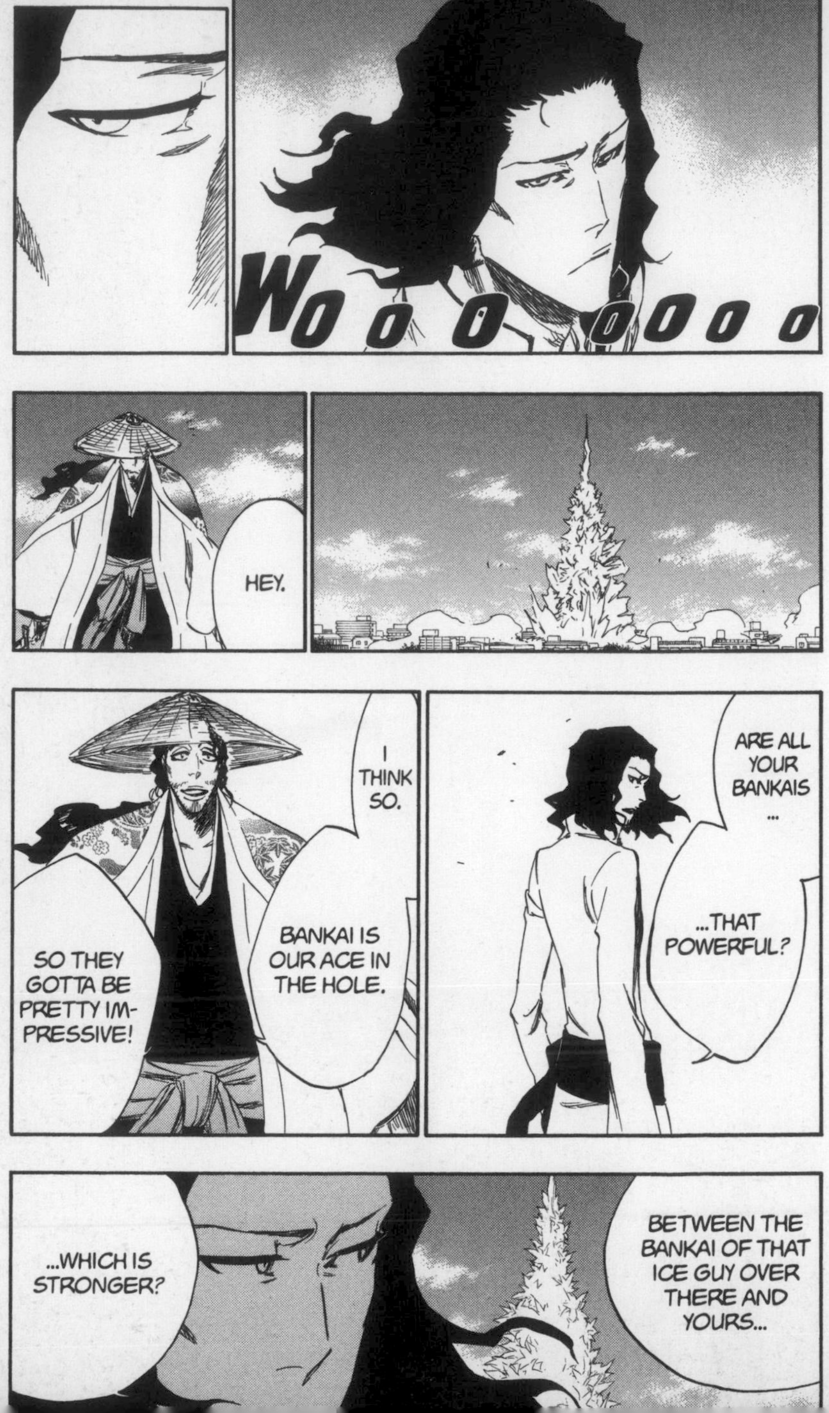
WOOOOOOO
HEY.
ARE ALL YOUR BANKAIS ...
...THAT POWERFUL?
I THINK SO.
BANKAI IS OUR ACE IN THE HOLE.
SO THEY GOTTA BE PRETTY IMPRESSIVE!
BETWEEN THE BANKAI OF THAT ICE GUY OVER THERE AND YOURS...
...WHICH IS STRONGER?

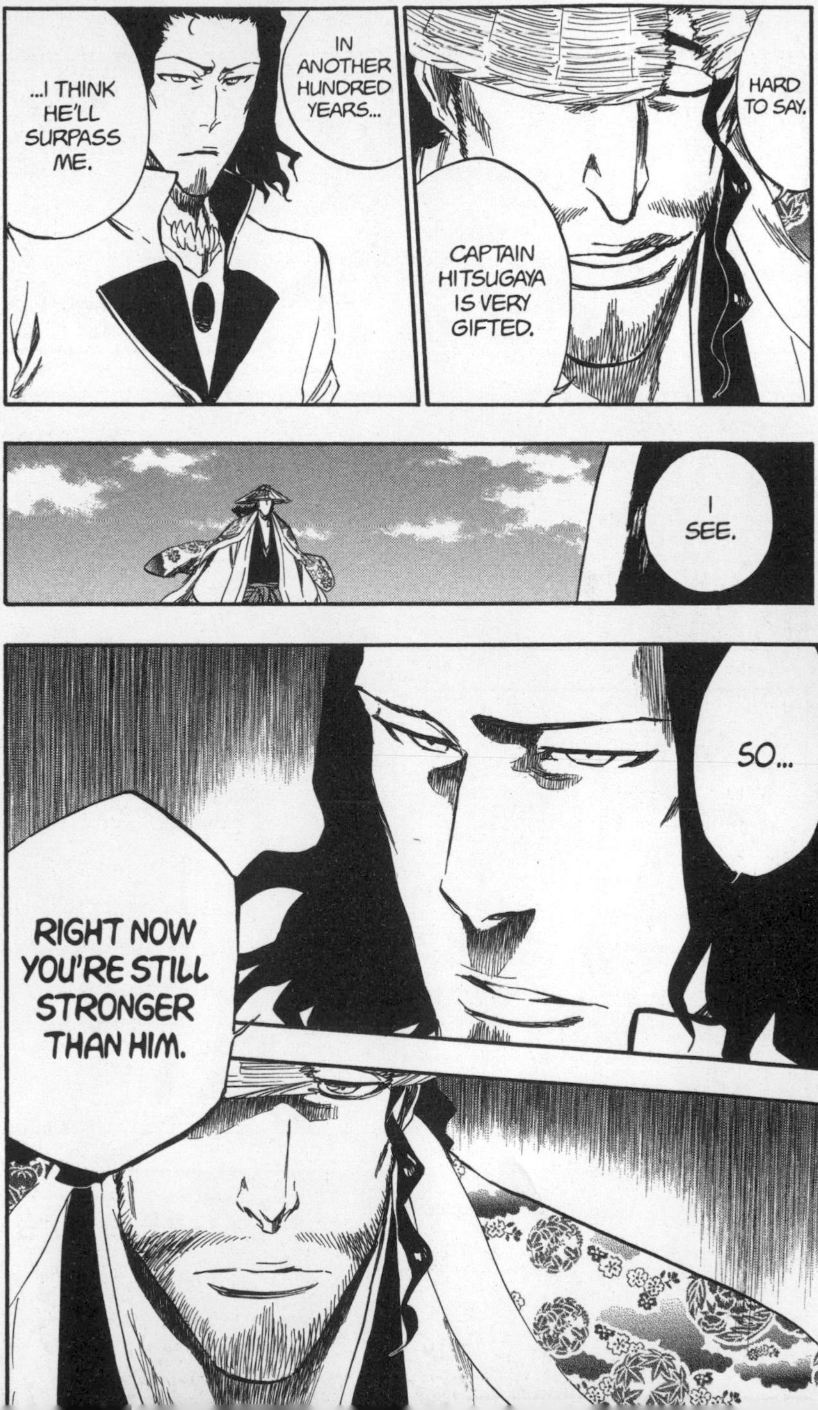
HARD TO SAY.
CAPTAIN HITSUGAYA IS VERY GIFTED.
IN ANOTHER HUNDRED YEARS...
...I THINK HE'LL SURPASS ME.
I SEE.
SO...
RIGHT NOW YOU'RE STILL STRONGER THAN HIM.

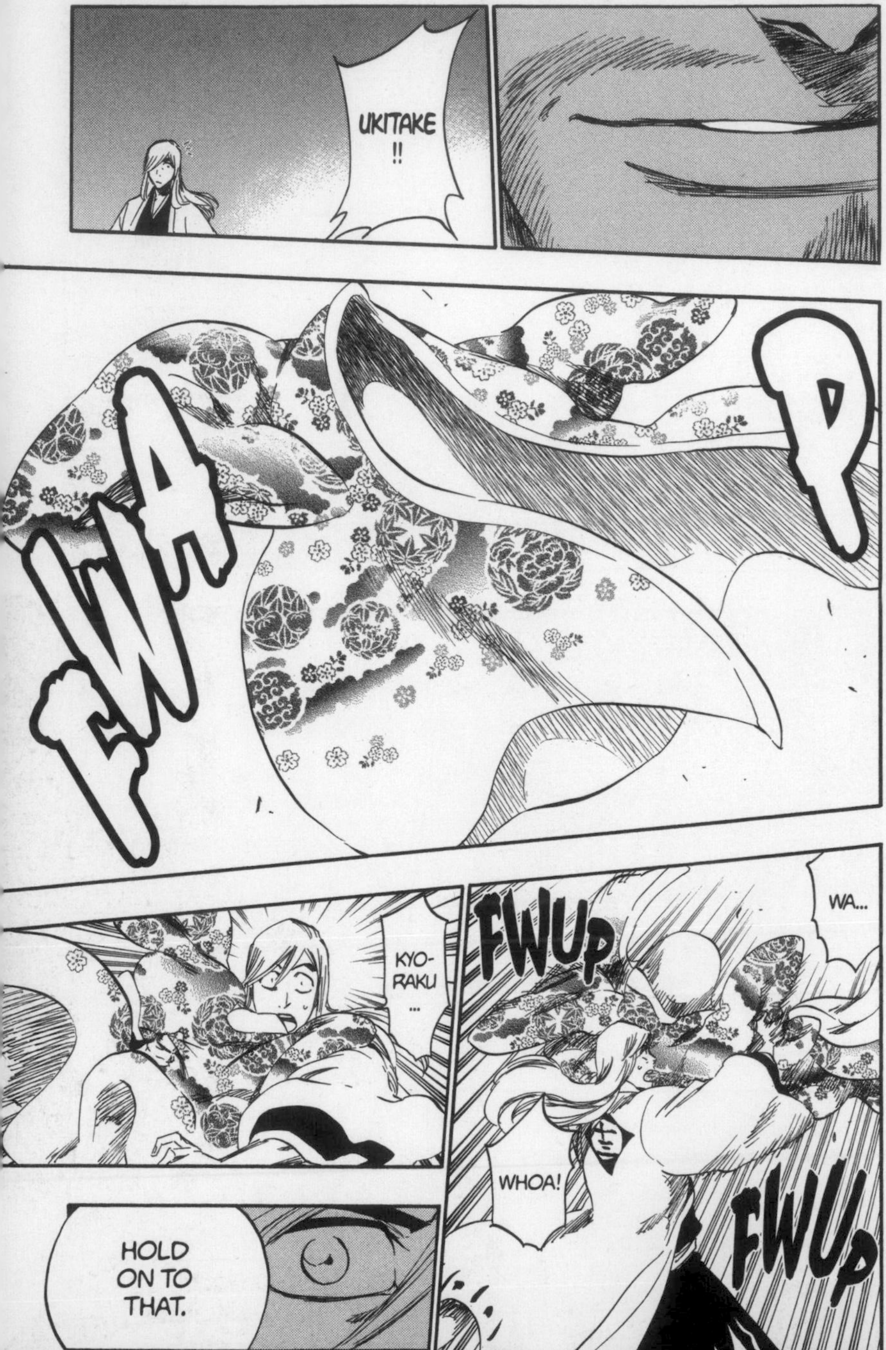
UKITAKE !!
FWAP
WA...
FWUP
WHOA!
FWUP
KYO-RAKU...
HOLD ON TO THAT.

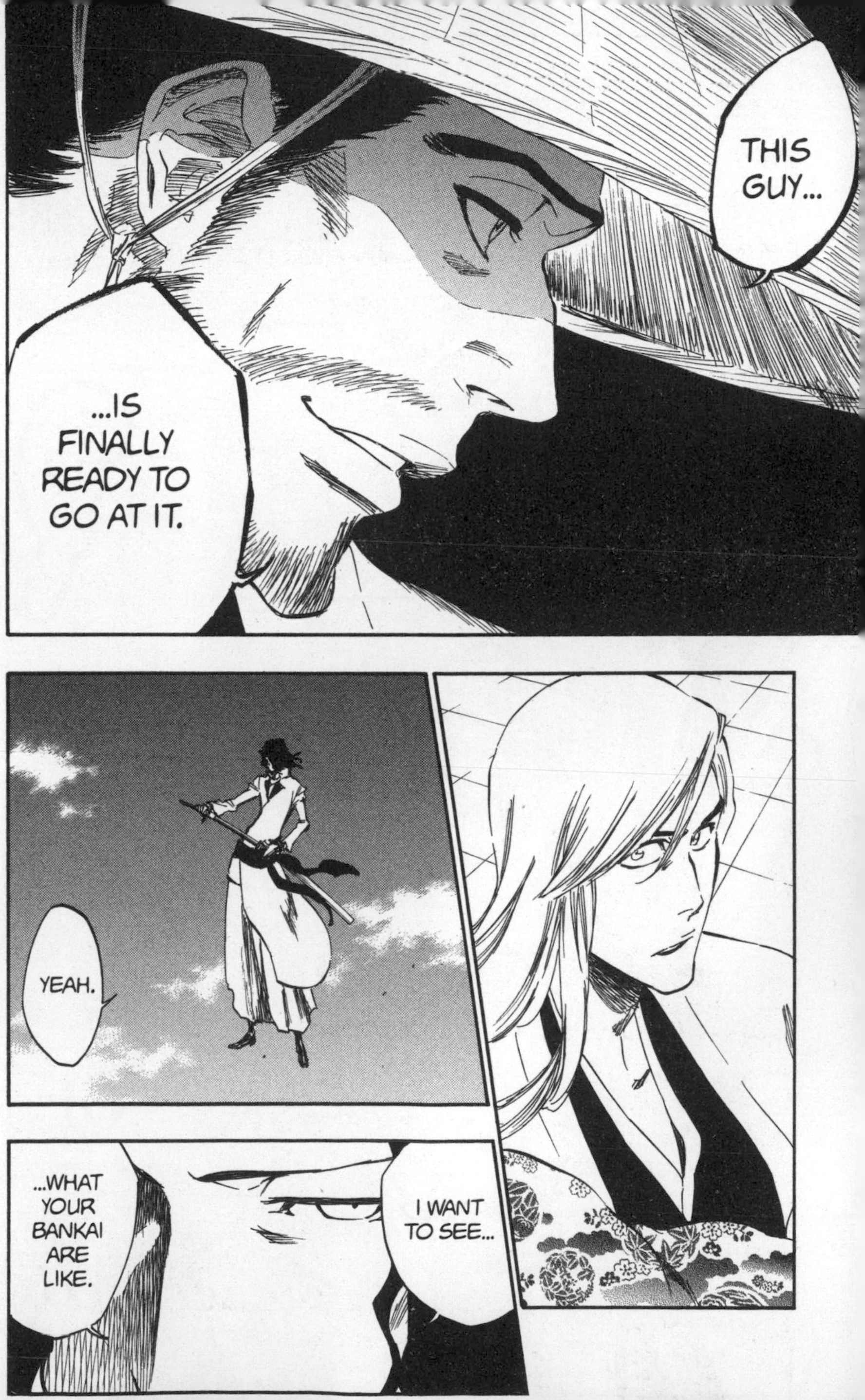
THIS GUY...
...IS FINALLY READY TO GO AT IT.
YEAH.
I WANT TO SEE...
...WHAT YOUR BANKAI ARE LIKE.

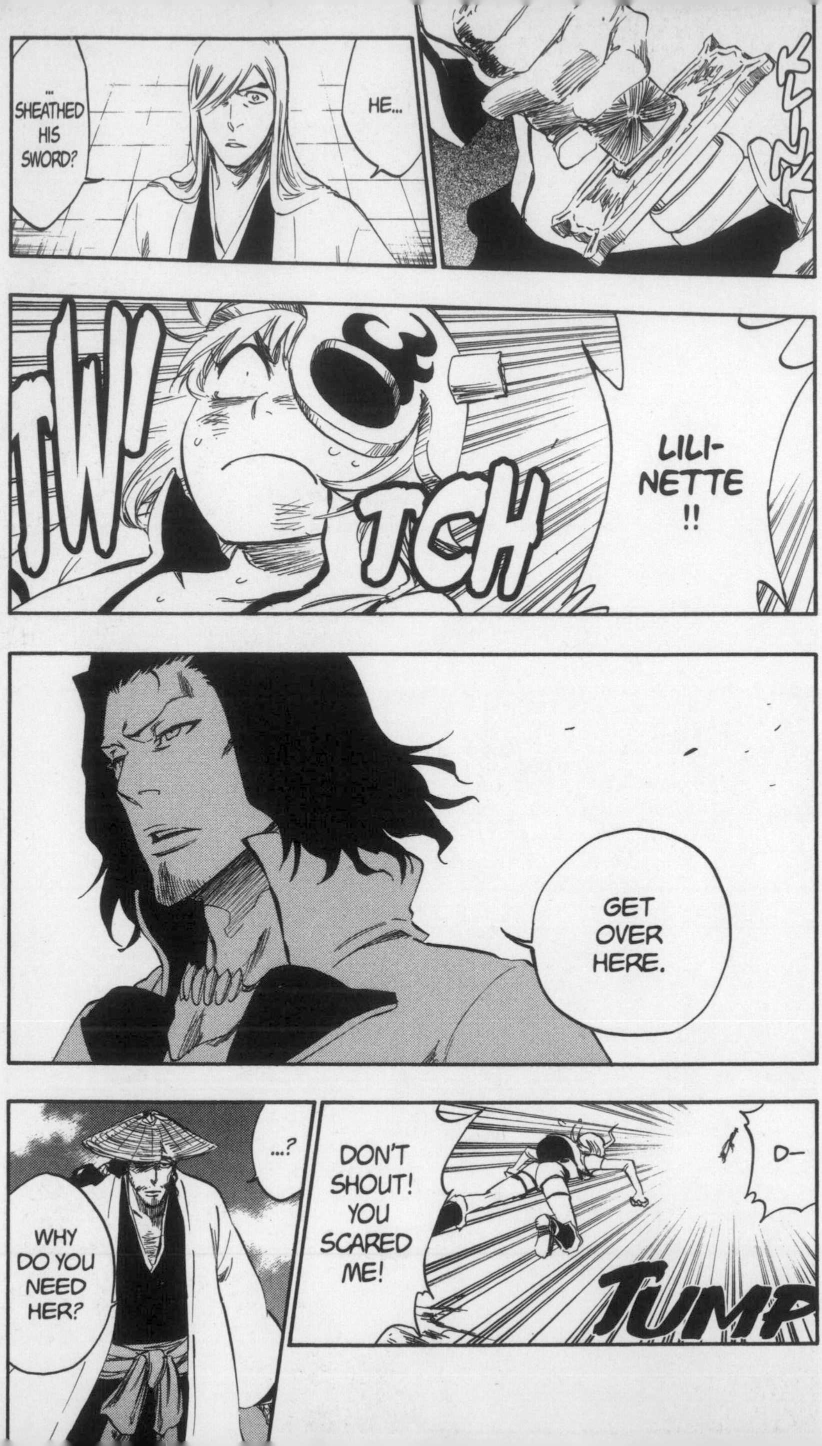
HE...
...SHEATHED HIS SWORD?
LILI-NETTE !!
TWI
TCH
GET OVER HERE.
D—
JUMP
DON'T SHOUT! YOU SCARED ME!
...?
WHY DO YOU NEED HER?

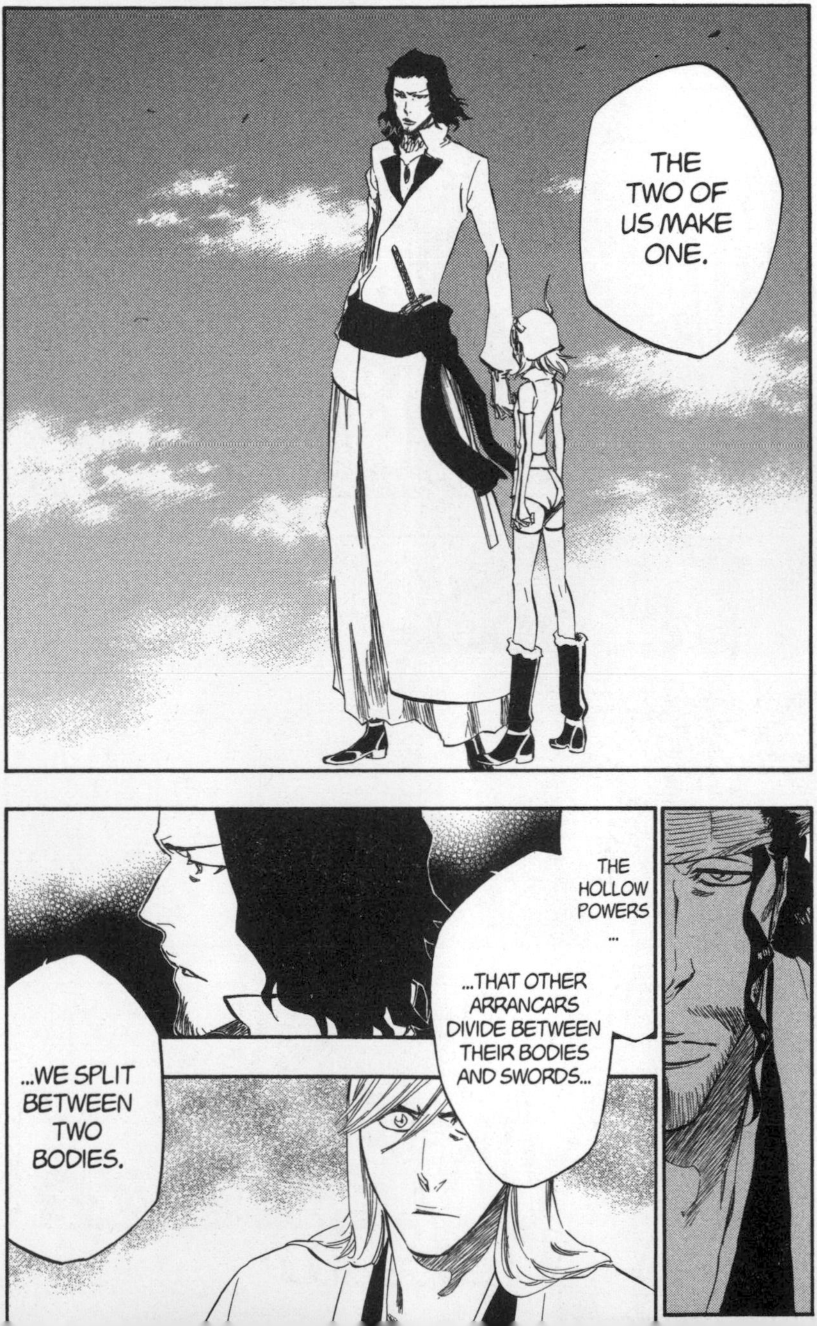
THE TWO OF US MAKE ONE.
THE HOLLOW POWERS ...
...THAT OTHER ARRANCARS DIVIDE BETWEEN THEIR BODIES AND SWORDS...
...WE SPLIT BETWEEN TWO BODIES.

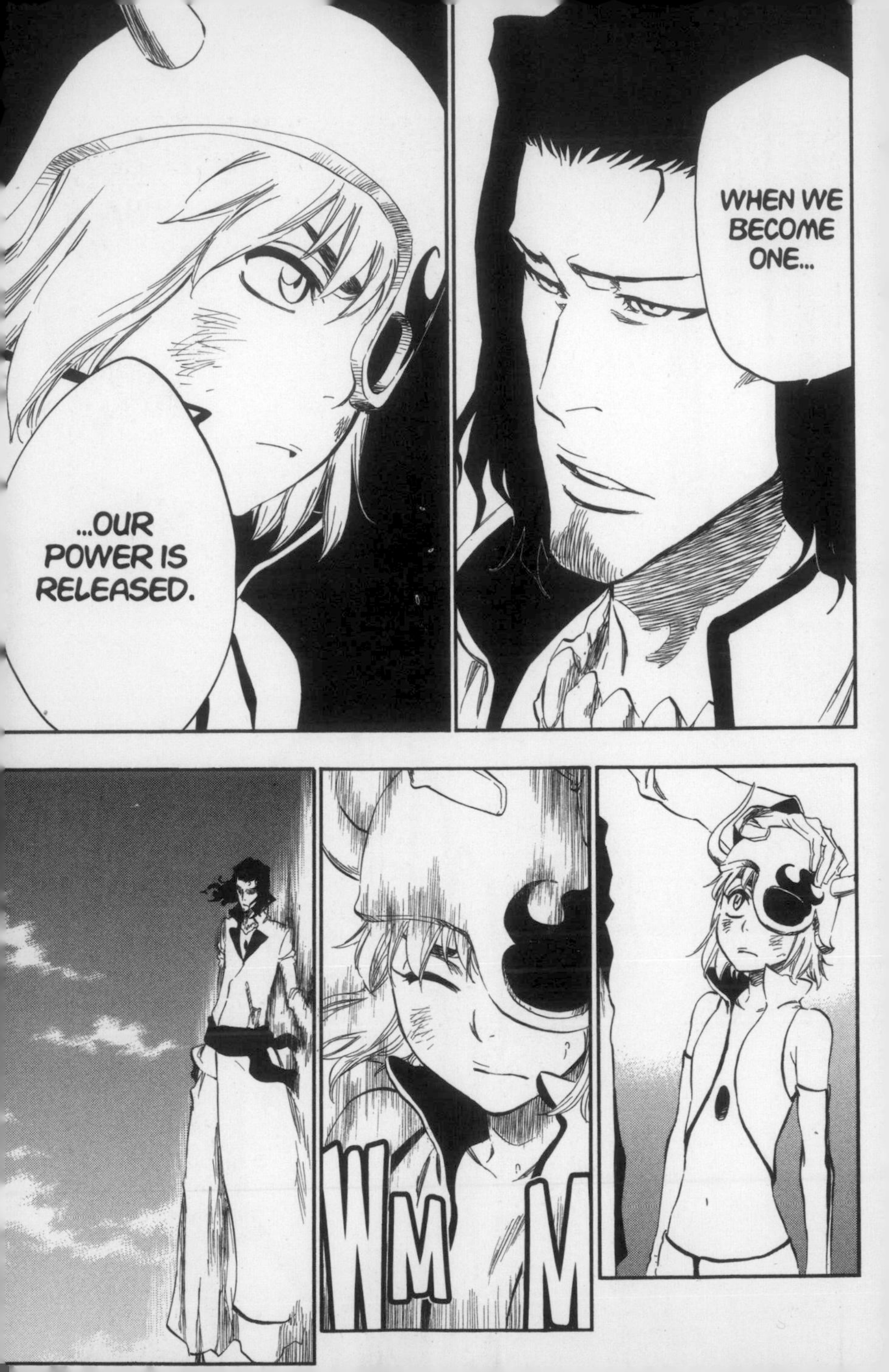
WHEN WE BECOME ONE...
...OUR POWER IS RELEASED.
WMMM

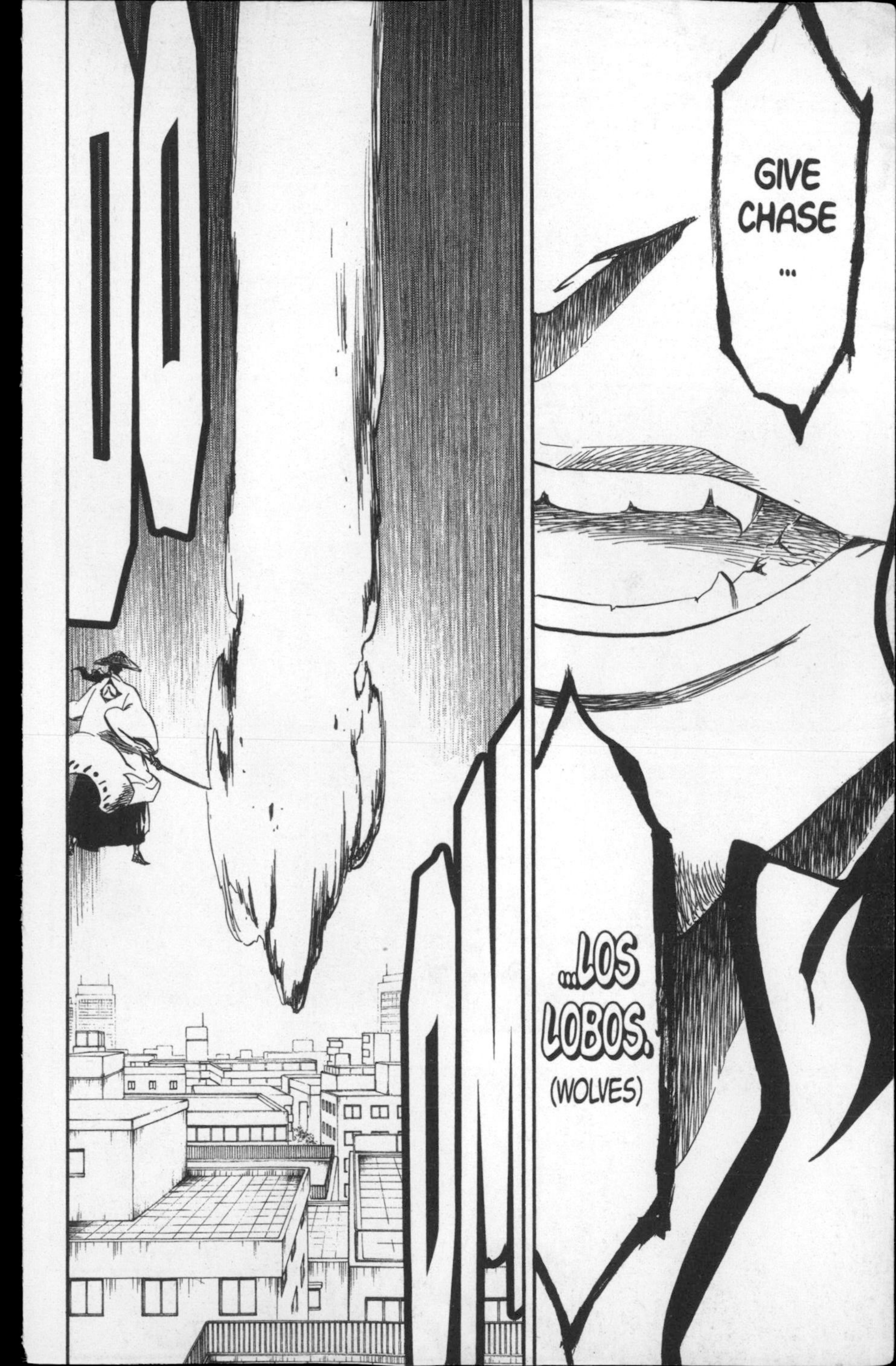
GIVE CHASE ...
...LOS LOBOS.
(WOLVES)

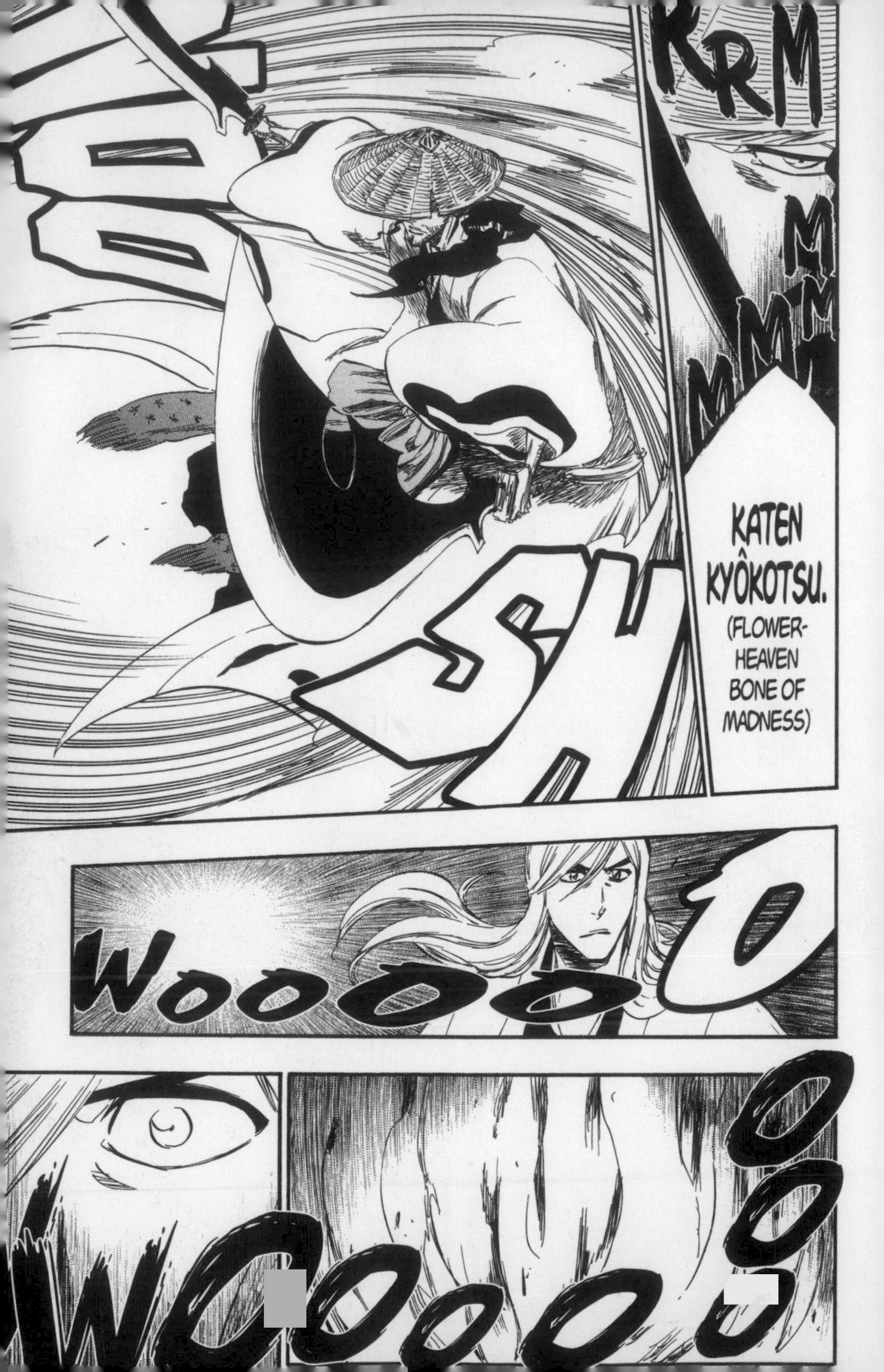
KRMMMMMM
KATEN KYÔKOTSU.
(FLOWER-HEAVEN BONE OF MADNESS)
WOOOOO
WOOOOOOOO

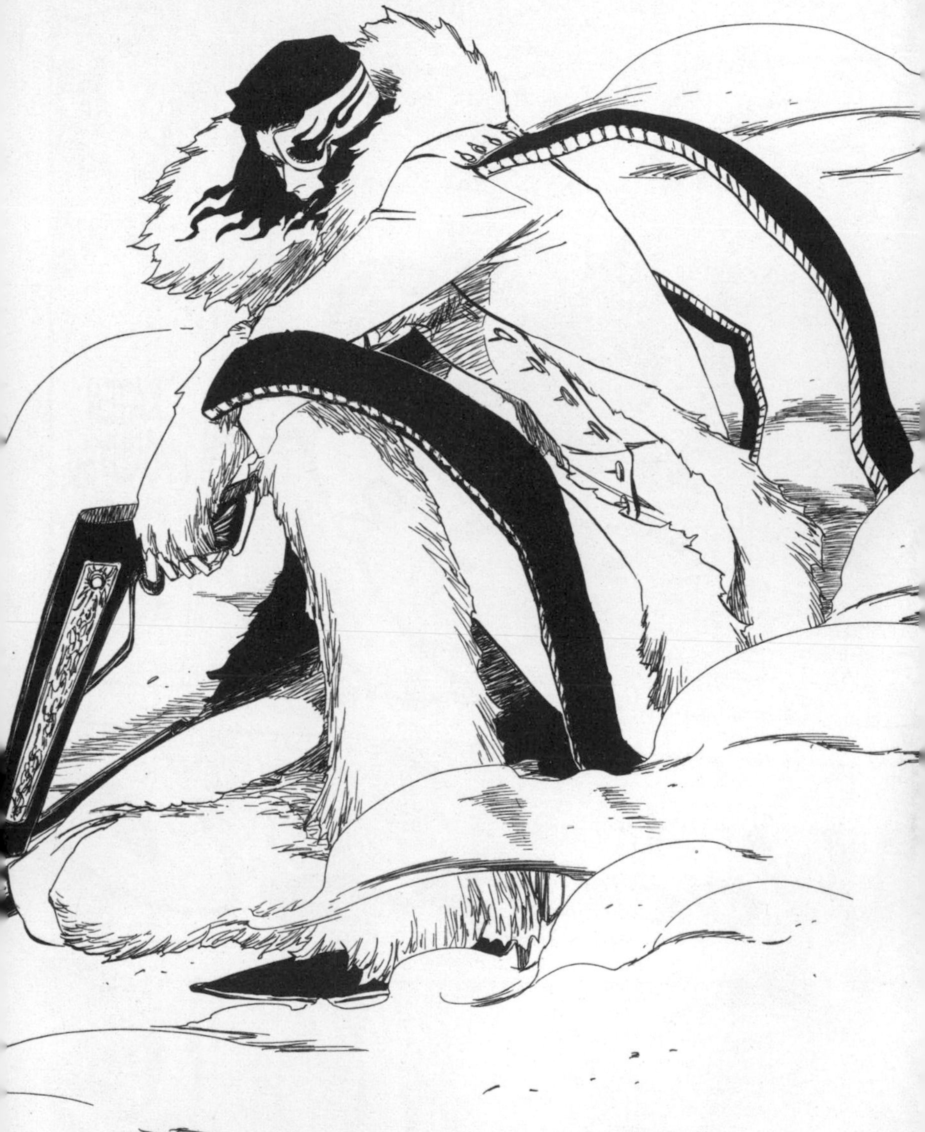

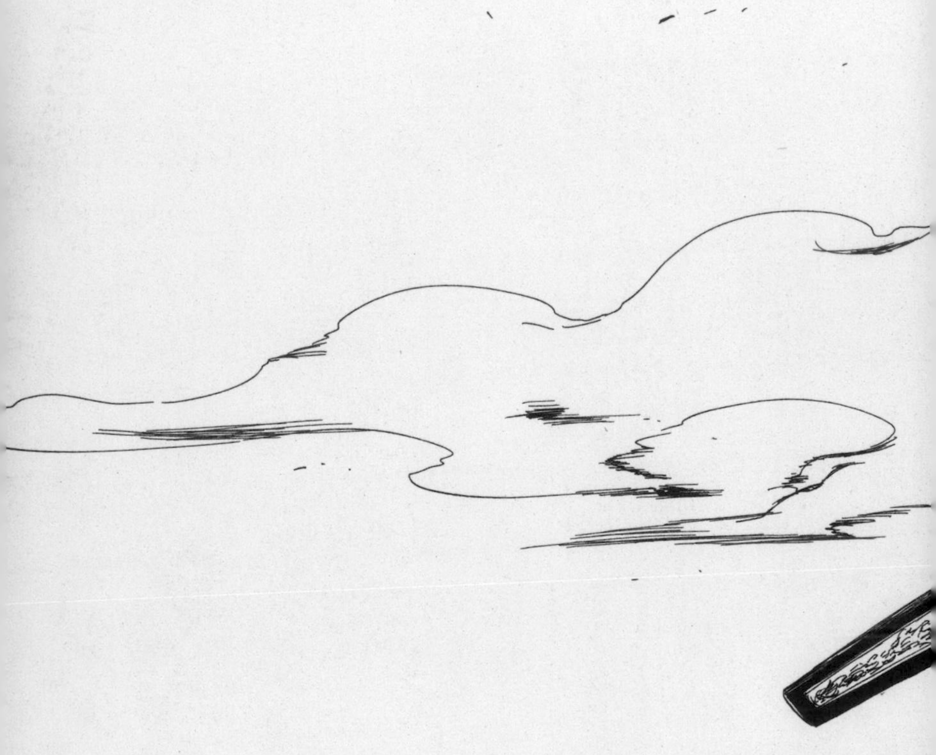

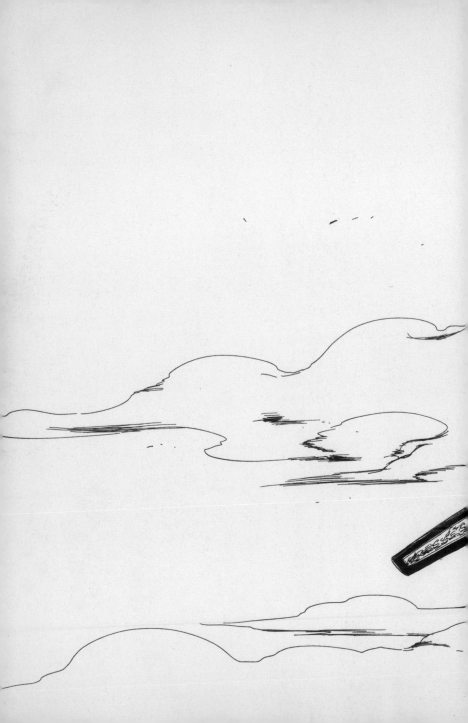

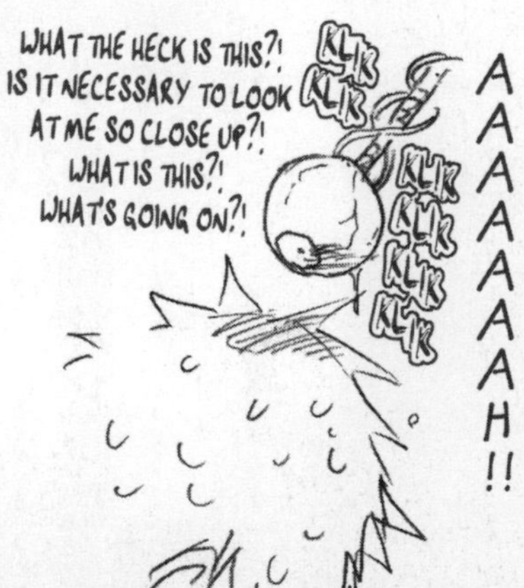
AAAAAAAH!!
KLIK KLIK
KLIK KLIK KLIK KLIK
WHAT THE HECK IS THIS?! IS IT NECESSARY TO LOOK AT ME SO CLOSE UP?! WHAT IS THIS?! WHAT'S GOING ON?!

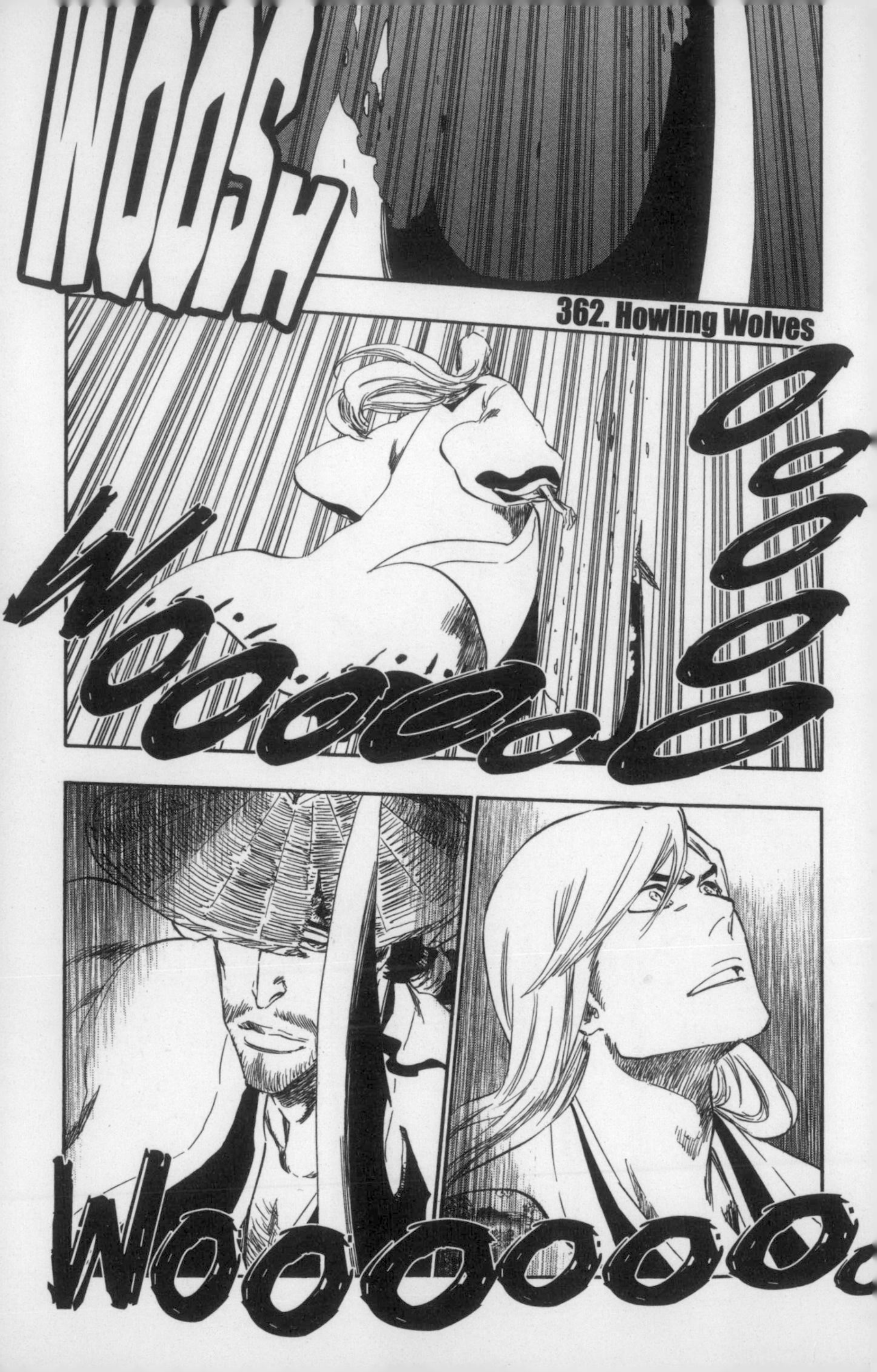

WOOSH
362. Howling Wolves
WOOOOOOOOOOO
WOOOOOOOOO

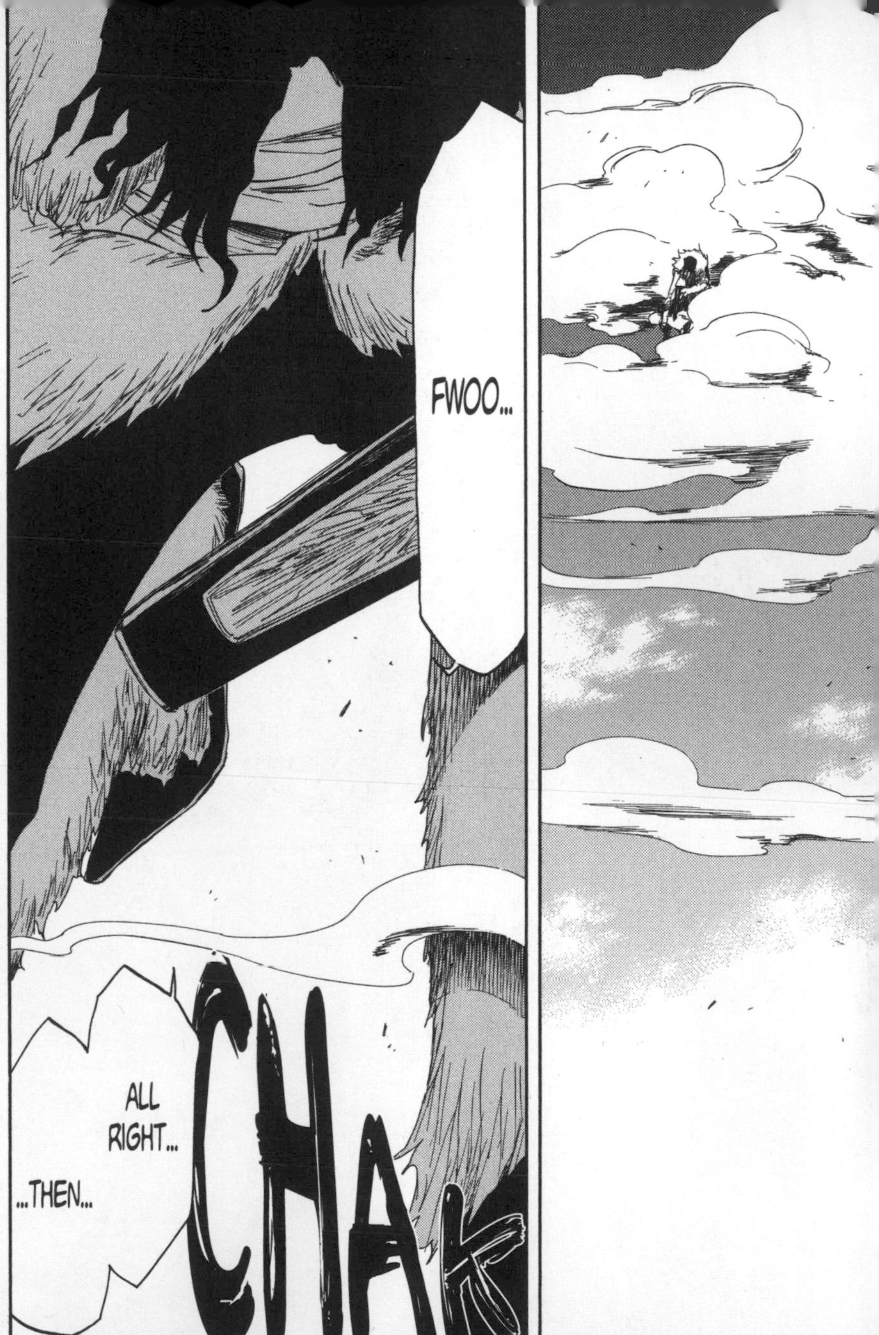
FWOO...
ALL RIGHT...
...THEN...
CHAK

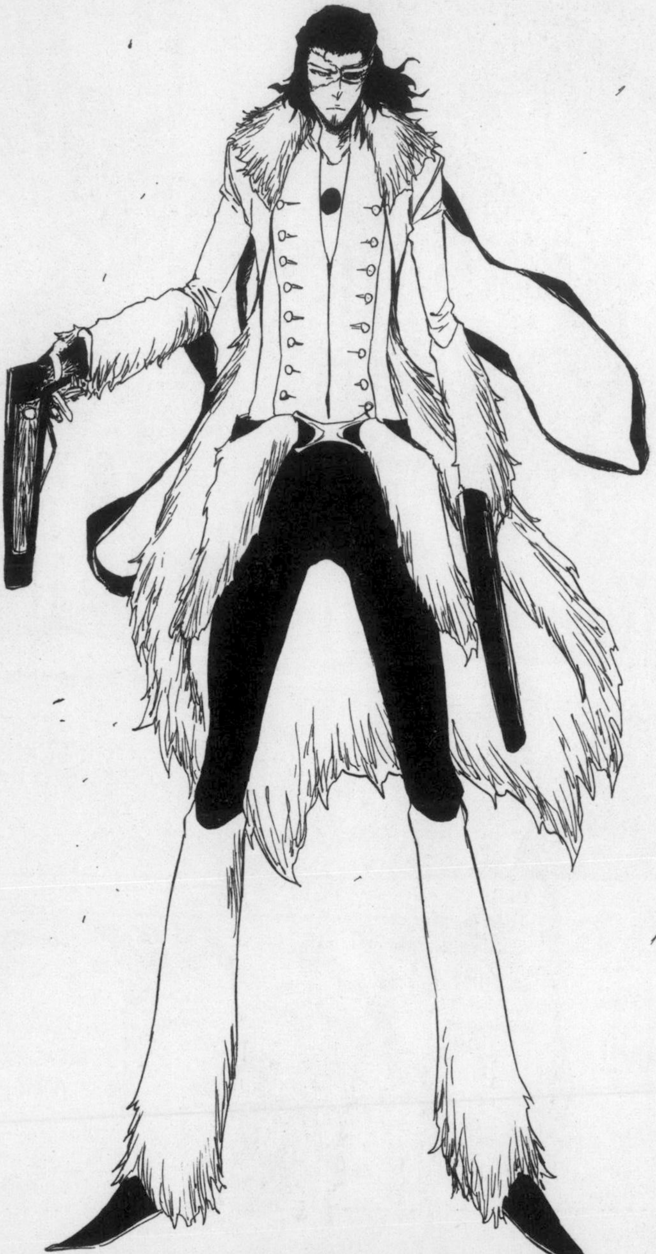

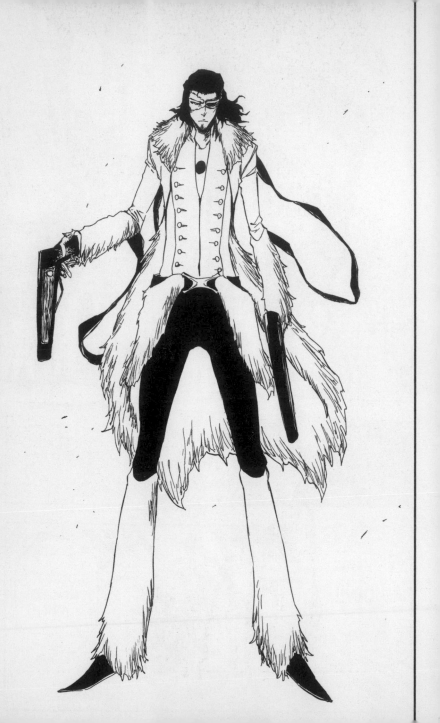

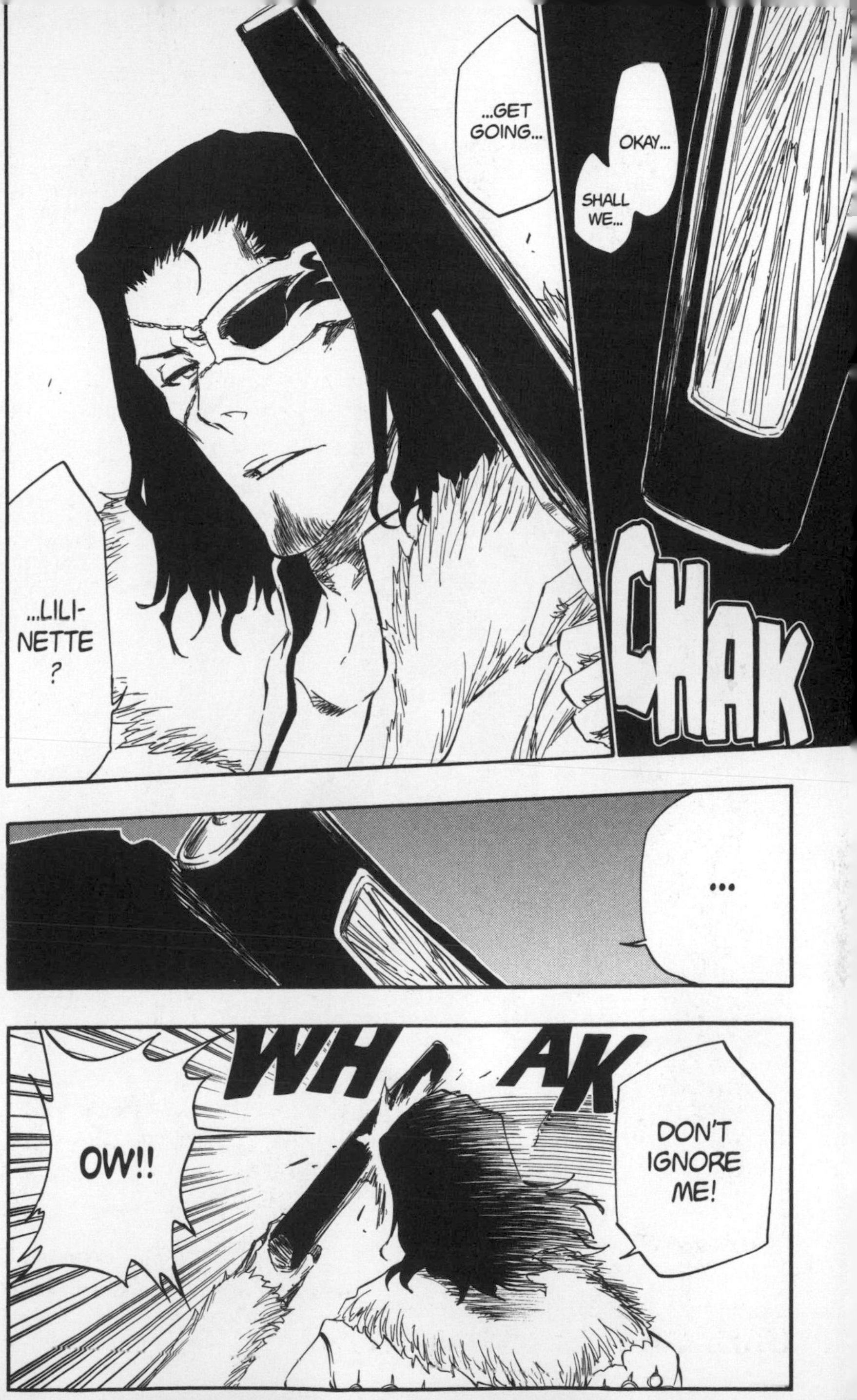
OKAY... SHALL WE...
...GET GOING...
CHAK
...LILI-NETTE ?
...
WH AK
DON'T IGNORE ME!
OW!!

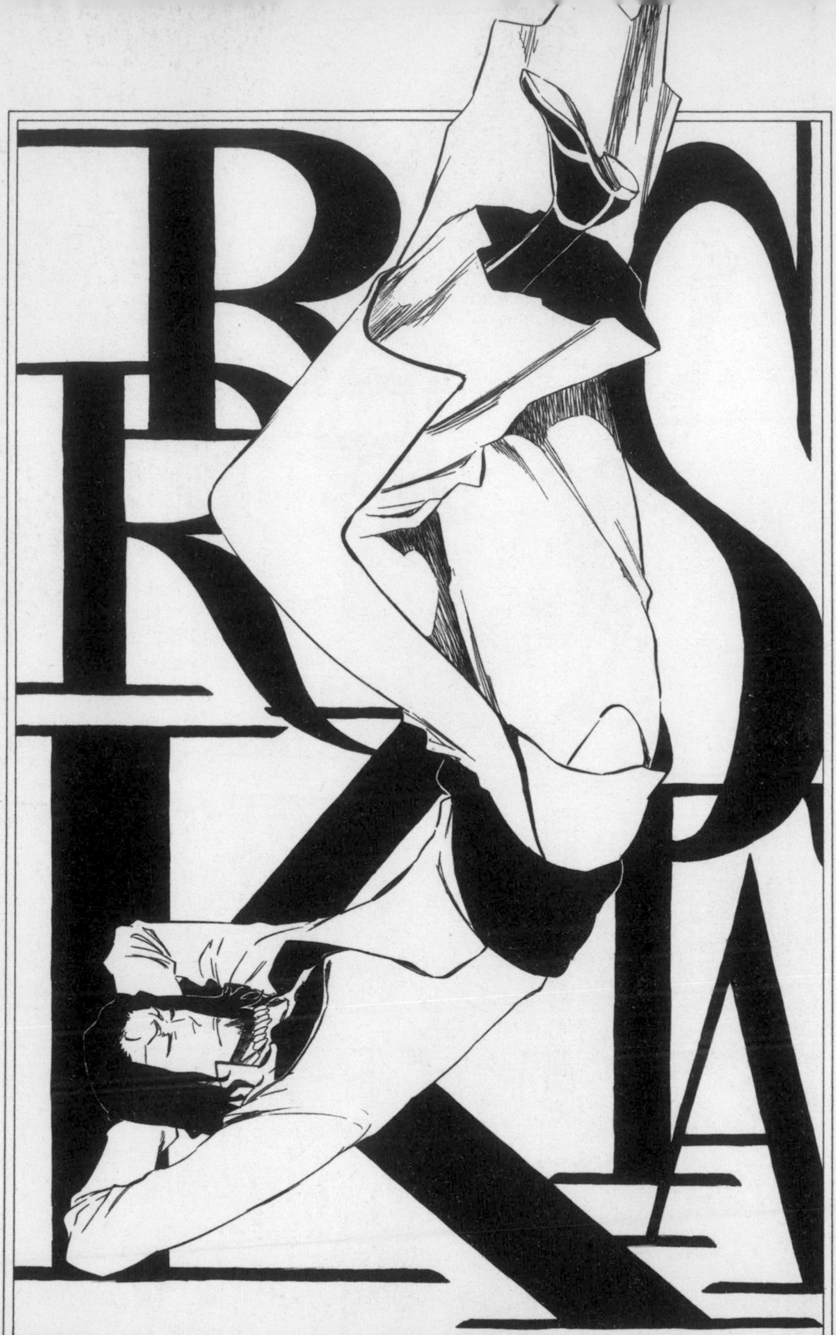

BLEACH 362. Howling Wolves

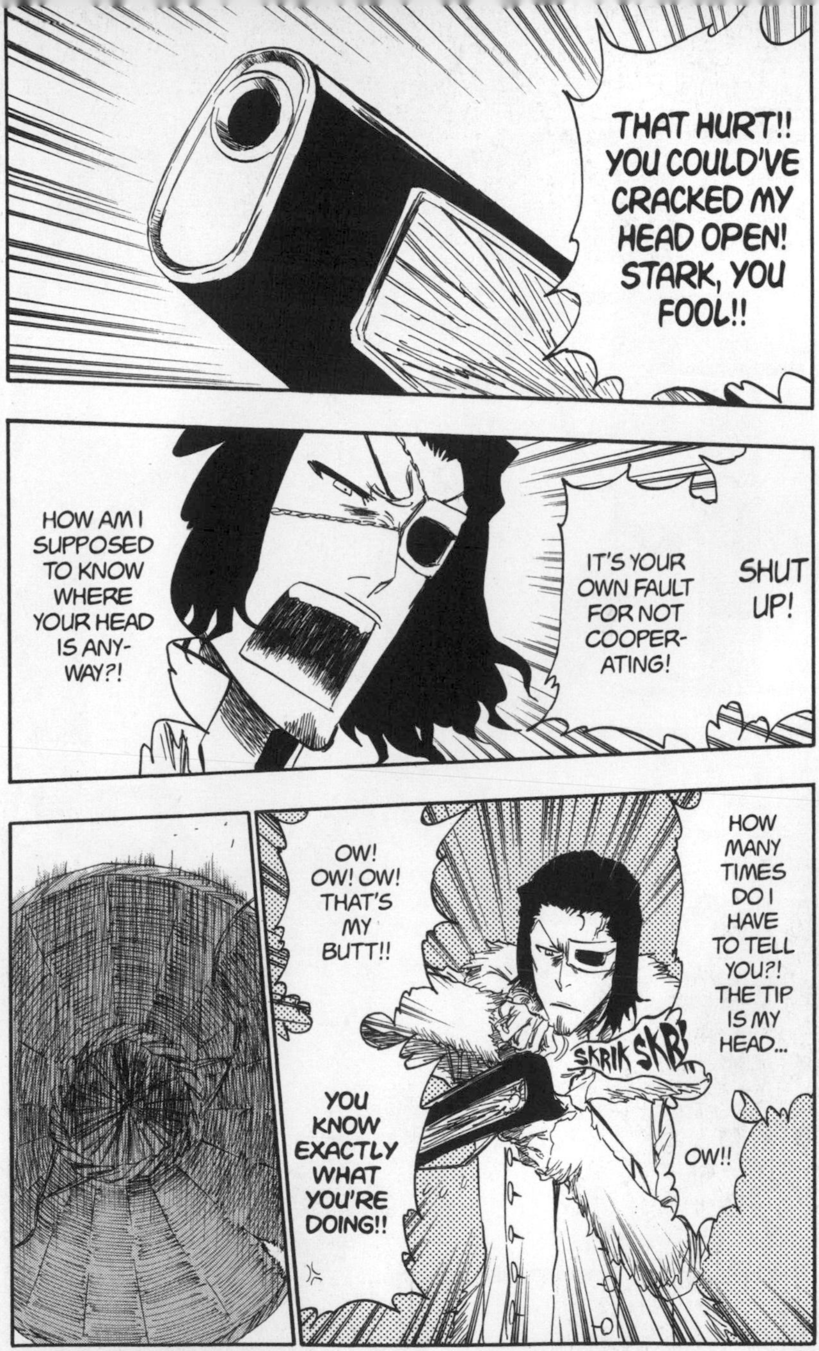
THAT HURT!! YOU COULD'VE CRACKED MY HEAD OPEN! STARK, YOU FOOL!!
SHUT UP!
IT'S YOUR OWN FAULT FOR NOT COOPER-ATING!
HOW AM I SUPPOSED TO KNOW WHERE YOUR HEAD IS ANY-WAY?!
HOW MANY TIMES DO I HAVE TO TELL YOU?! THE TIP IS MY HEAD...
SKRIK SKR
OW!!
OW! OW! OW! THAT'S MY BUTT!!
YOU KNOW EXACTLY WHAT YOU'RE DOING!!

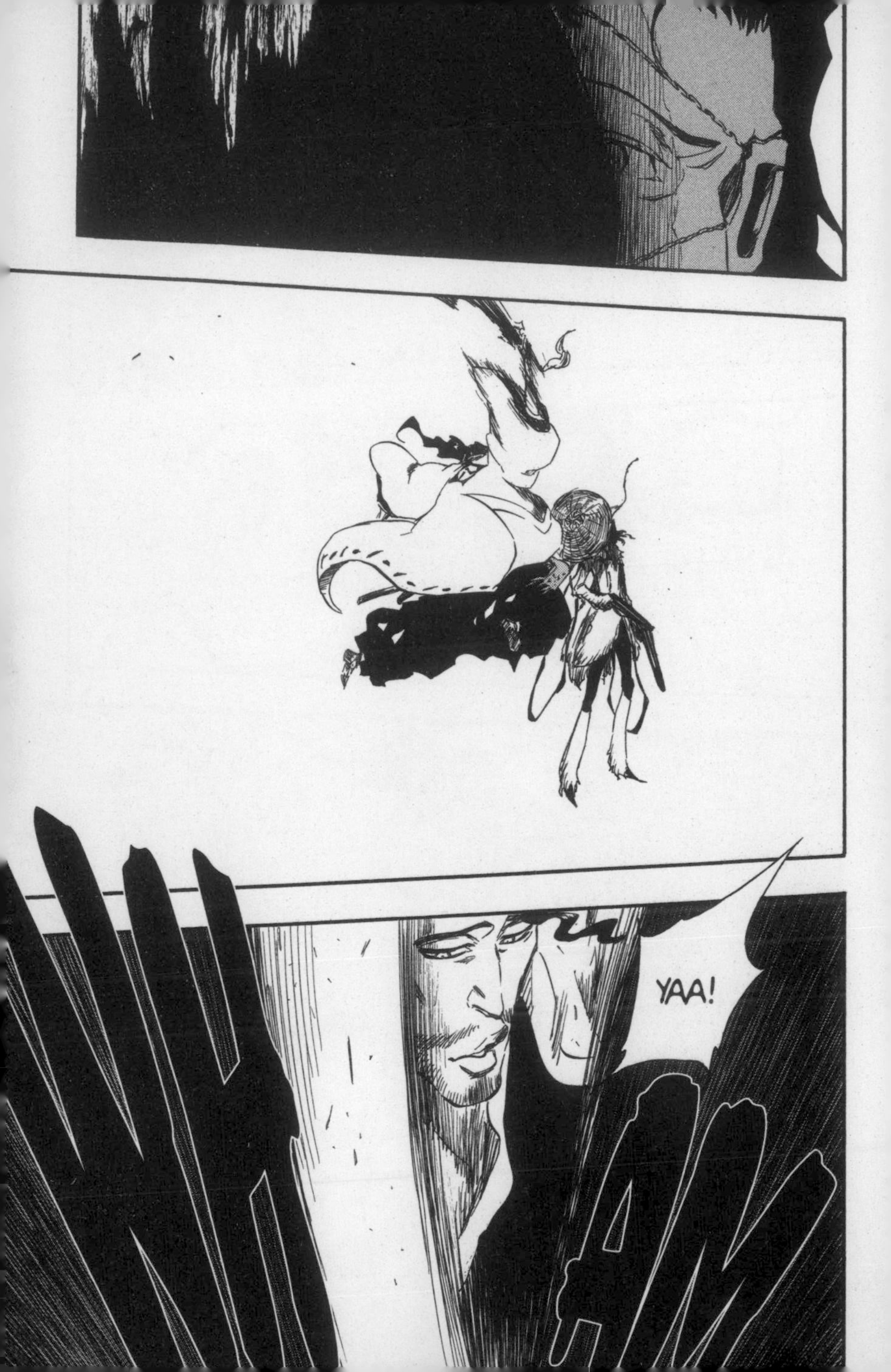
YAA!
WHAM

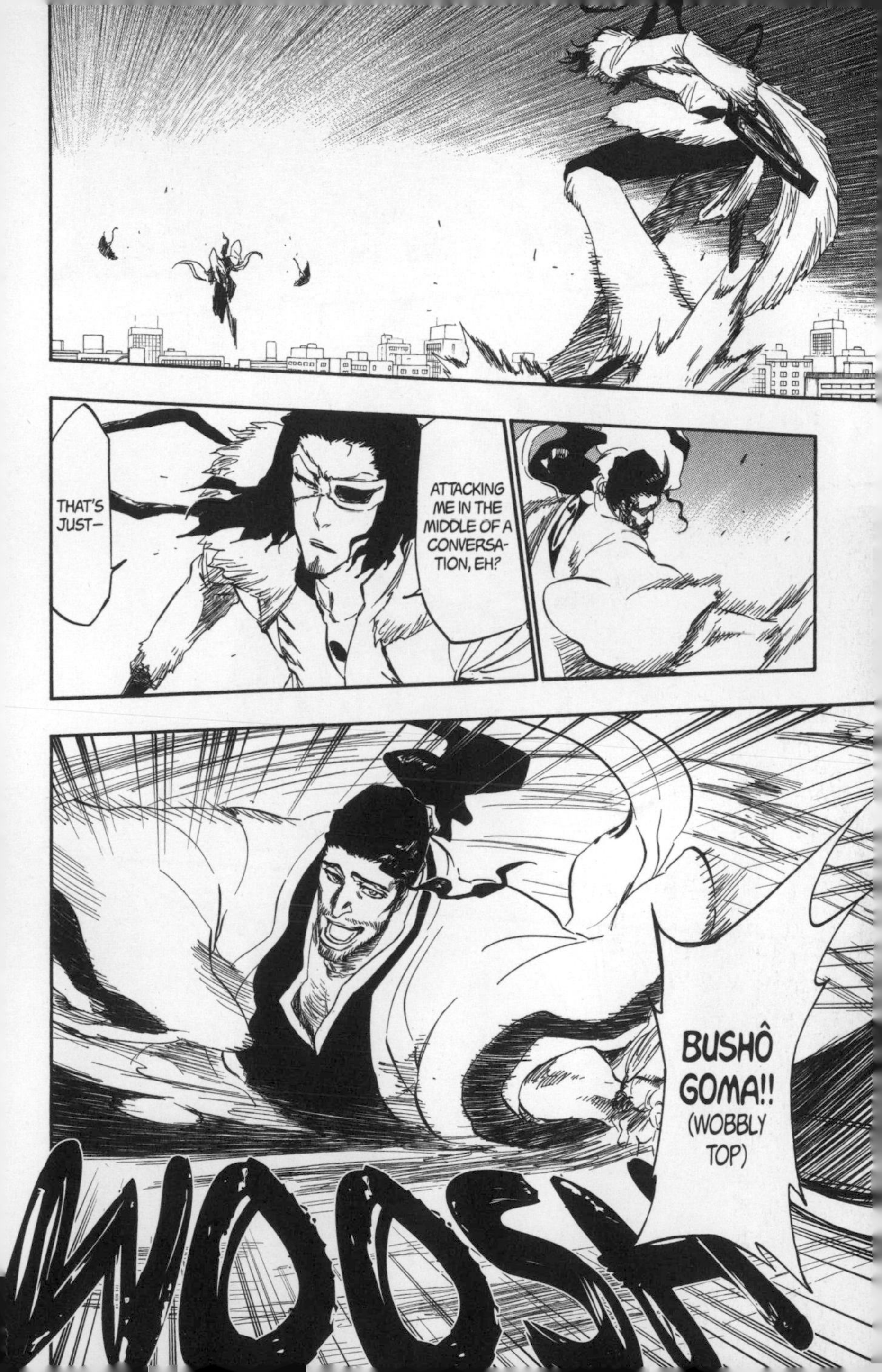
ATTACKING ME IN THE MIDDLE OF A CONVERSATION, EH?
THAT'S JUST—
BUSHÔ GOMA!! (WOBBLY TOP)
WOOSH

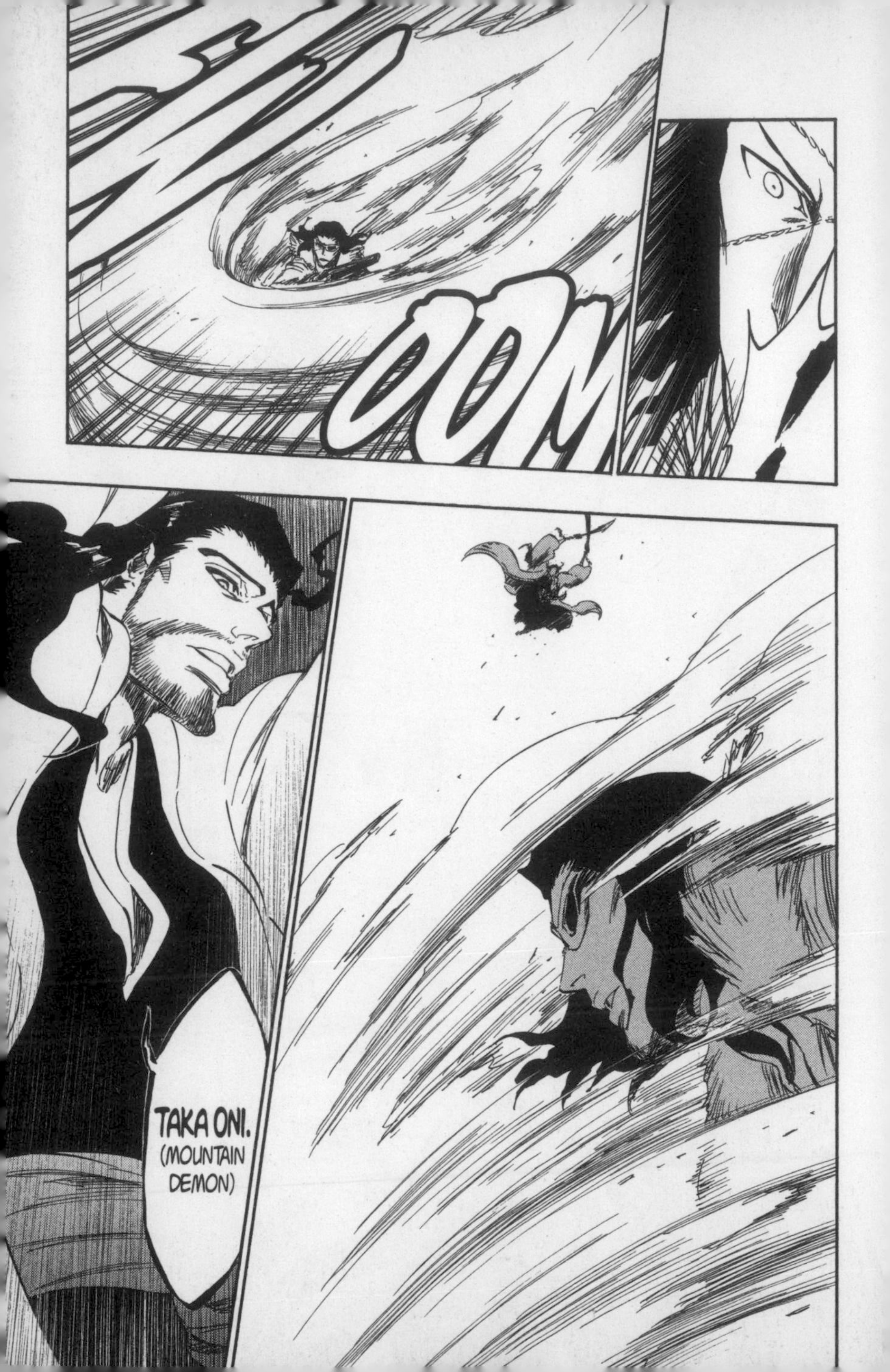
OOM
TAKA ONI.
(MOUNTAIN DEMON)

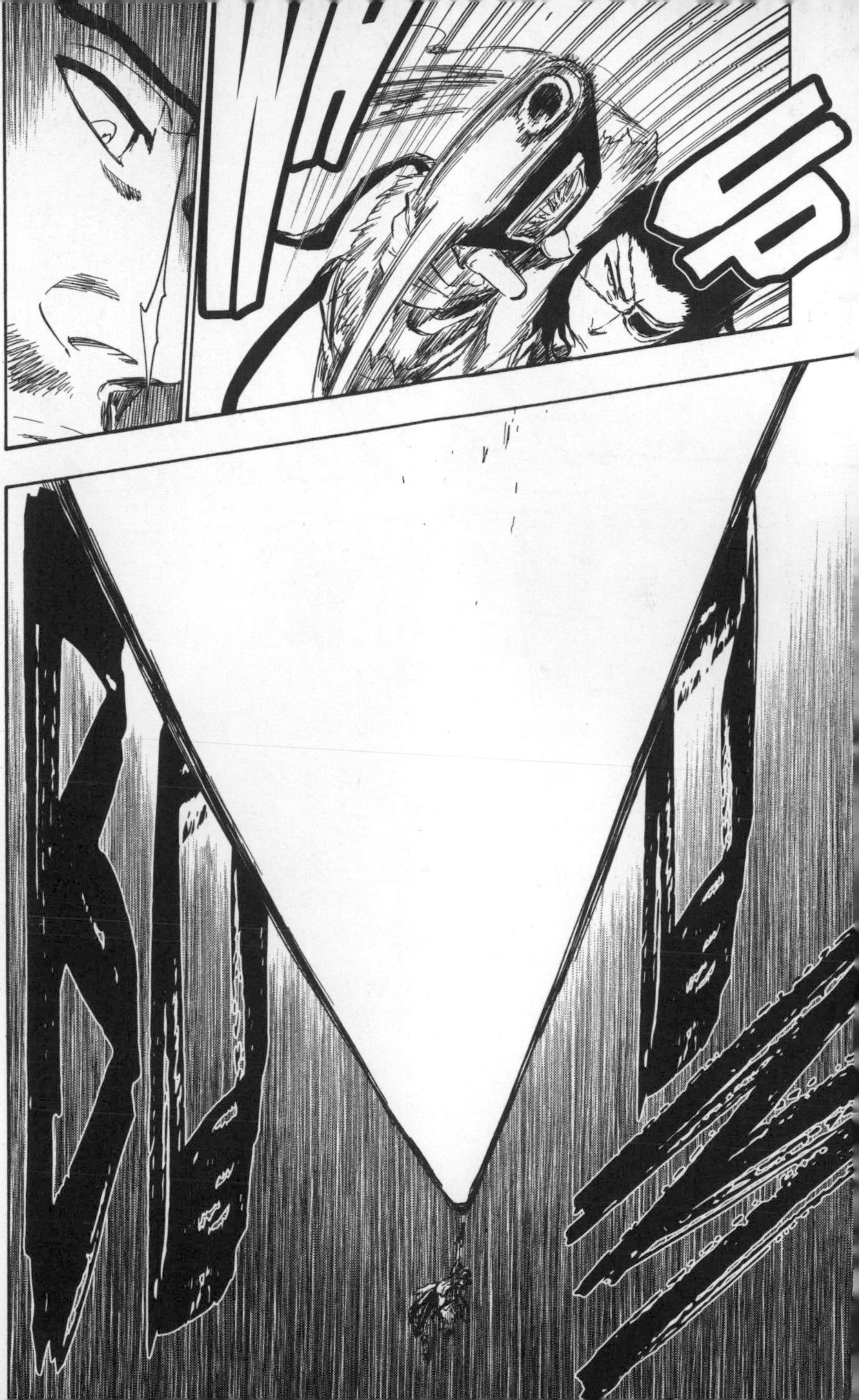

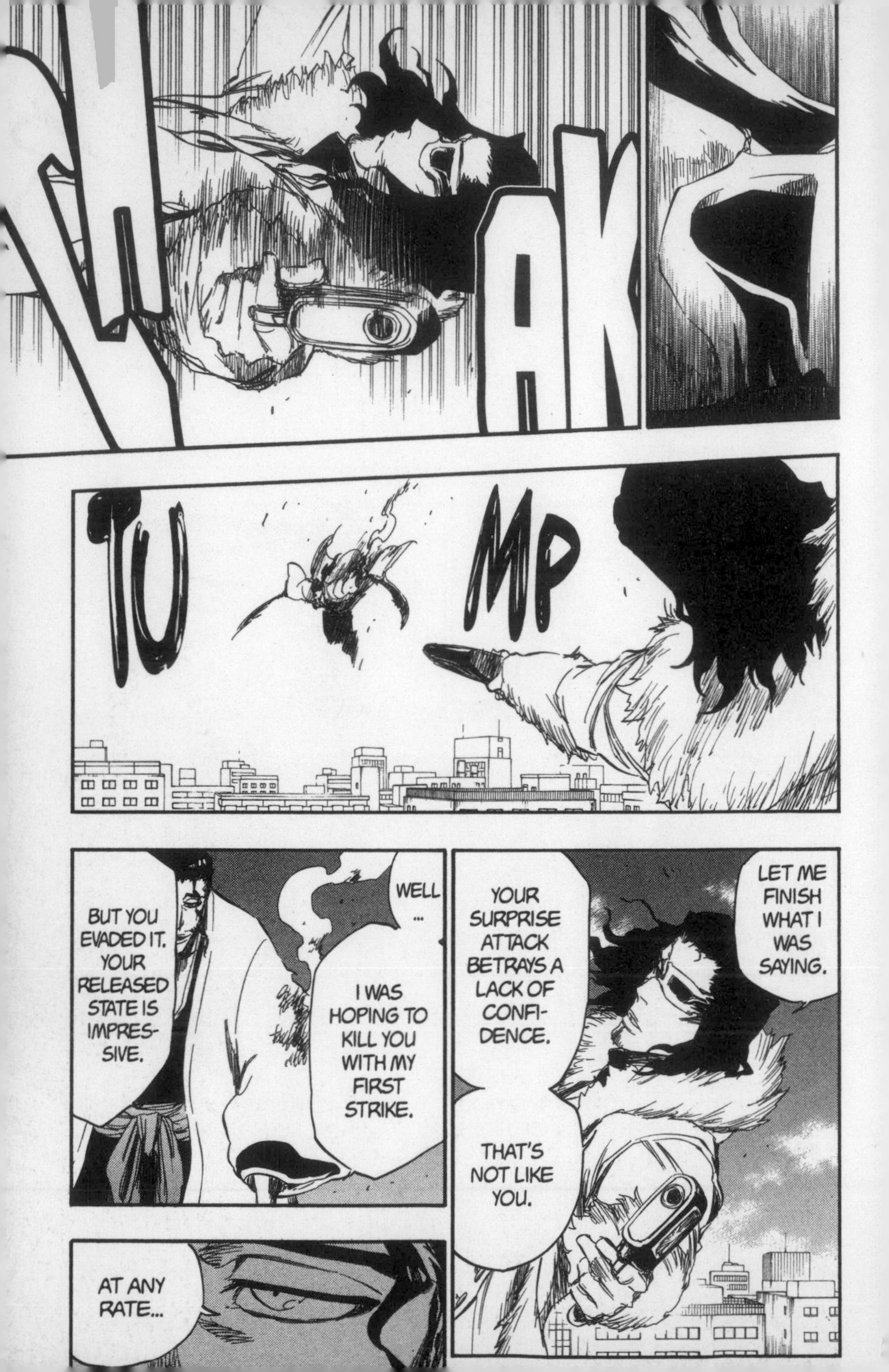
TU MP
LET ME FINISH WHAT I WAS SAYING.
YOUR SURPRISE ATTACK BETRAYS A LACK OF CONFIDENCE.
THAT'S NOT LIKE YOU.
WELL...
I WAS HOPING TO KILL YOU WITH MY FIRST STRIKE.
BUT YOU EVADED IT. YOUR RELEASED STATE IS IMPRESSIVE.
AT ANY RATE...

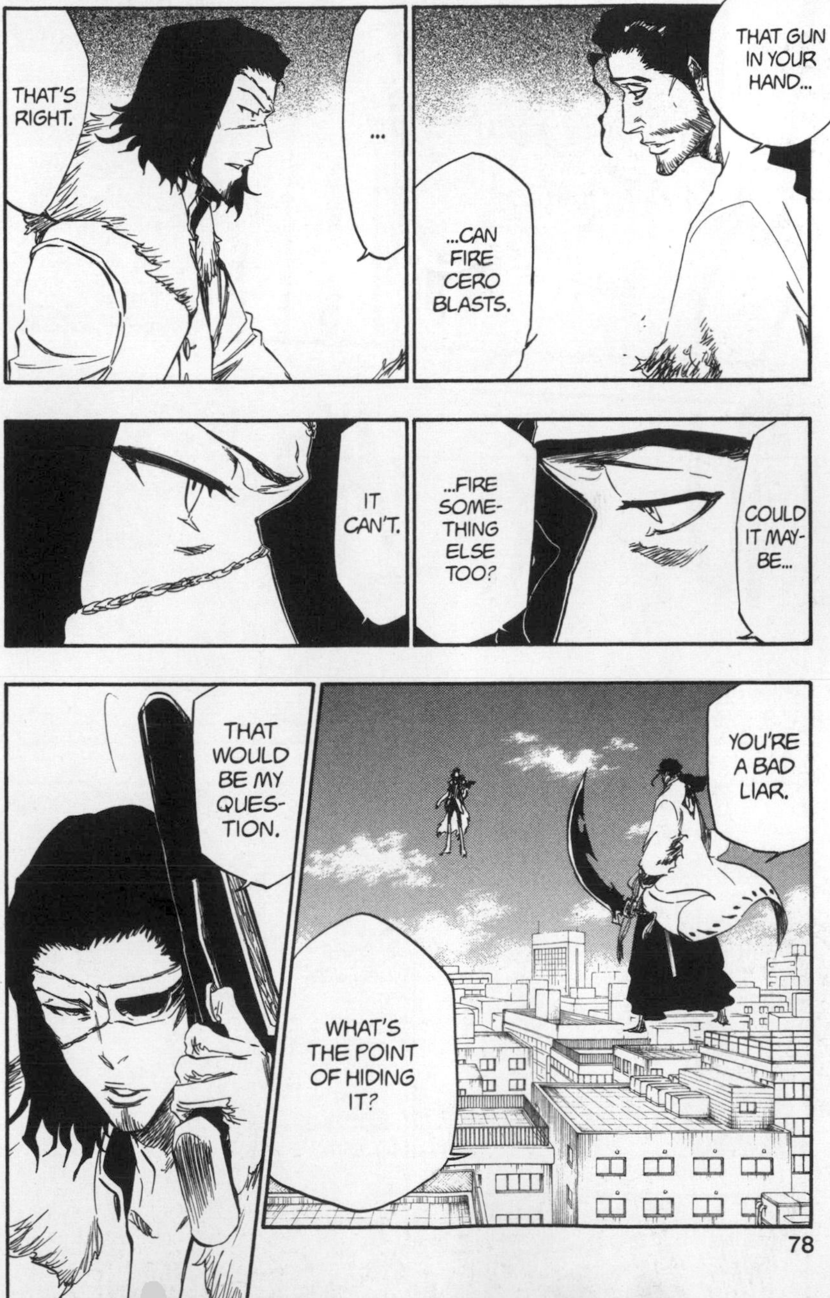
THAT GUN IN YOUR HAND...
...CAN FIRE CERO BLASTS.
...
THAT'S RIGHT.
COULD IT MAYBE...
...FIRE SOMETHING ELSE TOO?
IT CAN'T.
YOU'RE A BAD LIAR.
WHAT'S THE POINT OF HIDING IT?
THAT WOULD BE MY QUESTION.

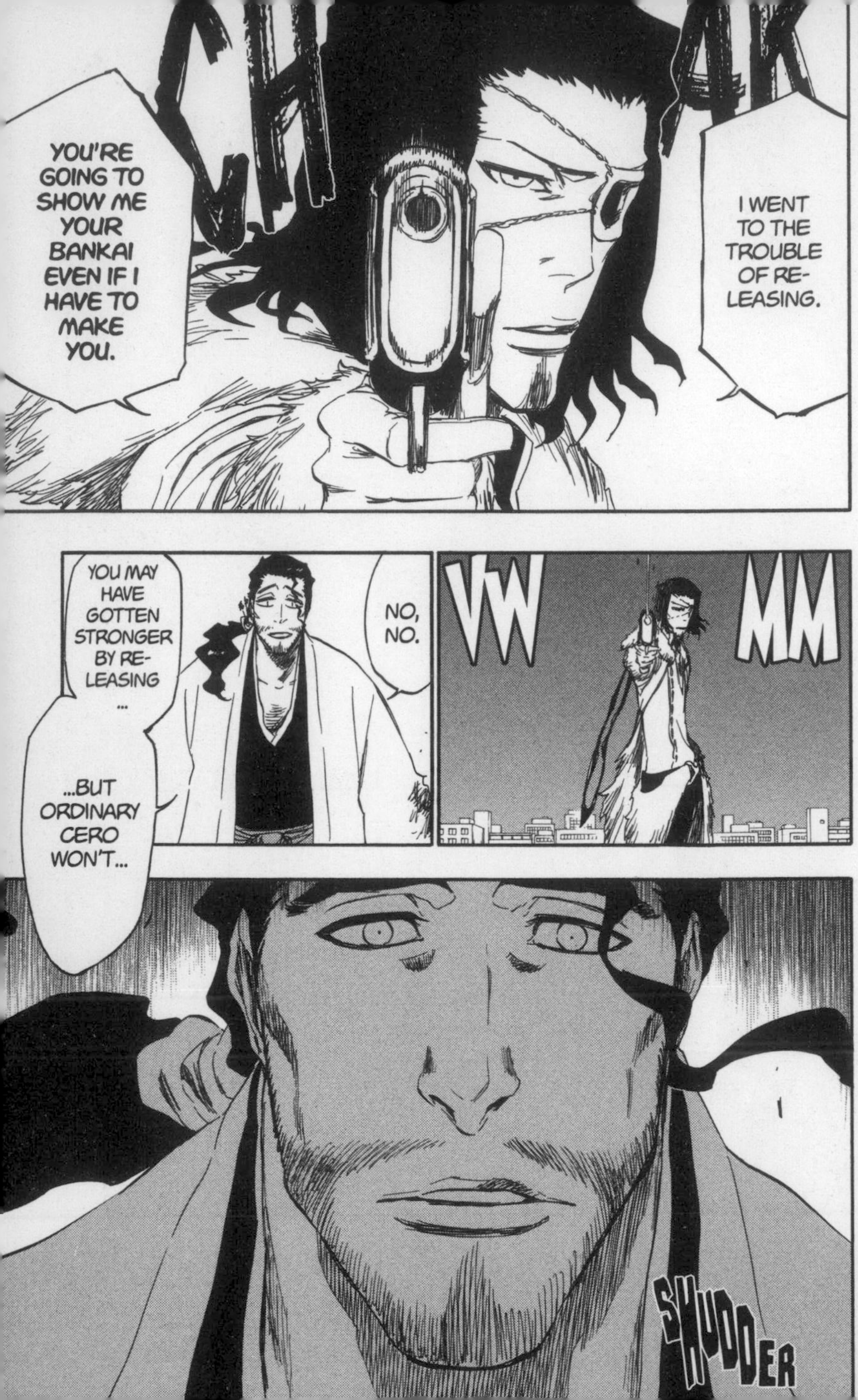
CHAK
I WENT TO THE TROUBLE OF RE-LEASING.
YOU'RE GOING TO SHOW ME YOUR BANKAI EVEN IF I HAVE TO MAKE YOU.
VWMM
NO, NO.
YOU MAY HAVE GOTTEN STRONGER BY RE-LEASING...
...BUT ORDINARY CERO WON'T...
SHUDDER

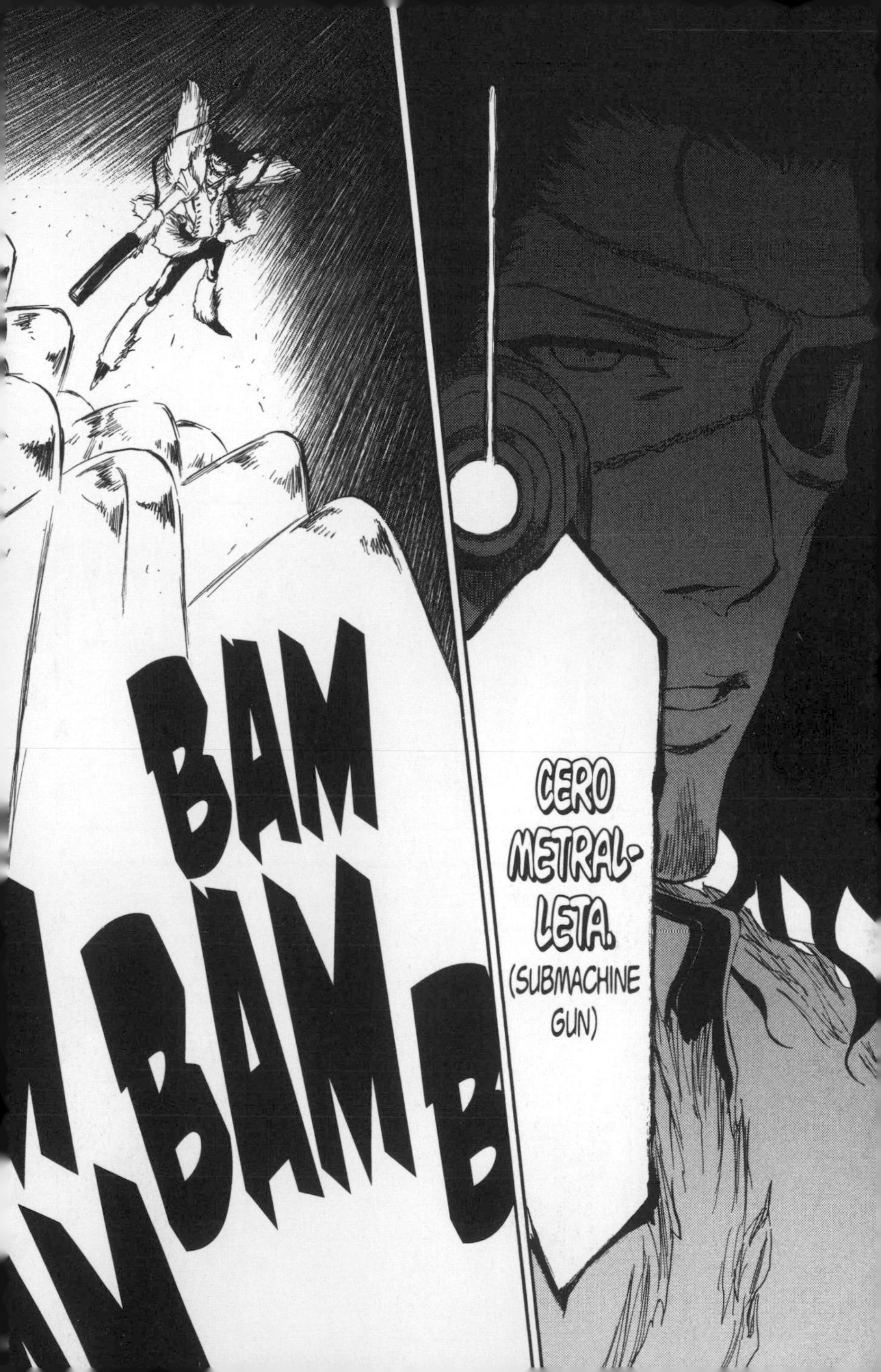
CERO METRAL-LETA.
(SUBMACHINE GUN)
BAM
BAM B

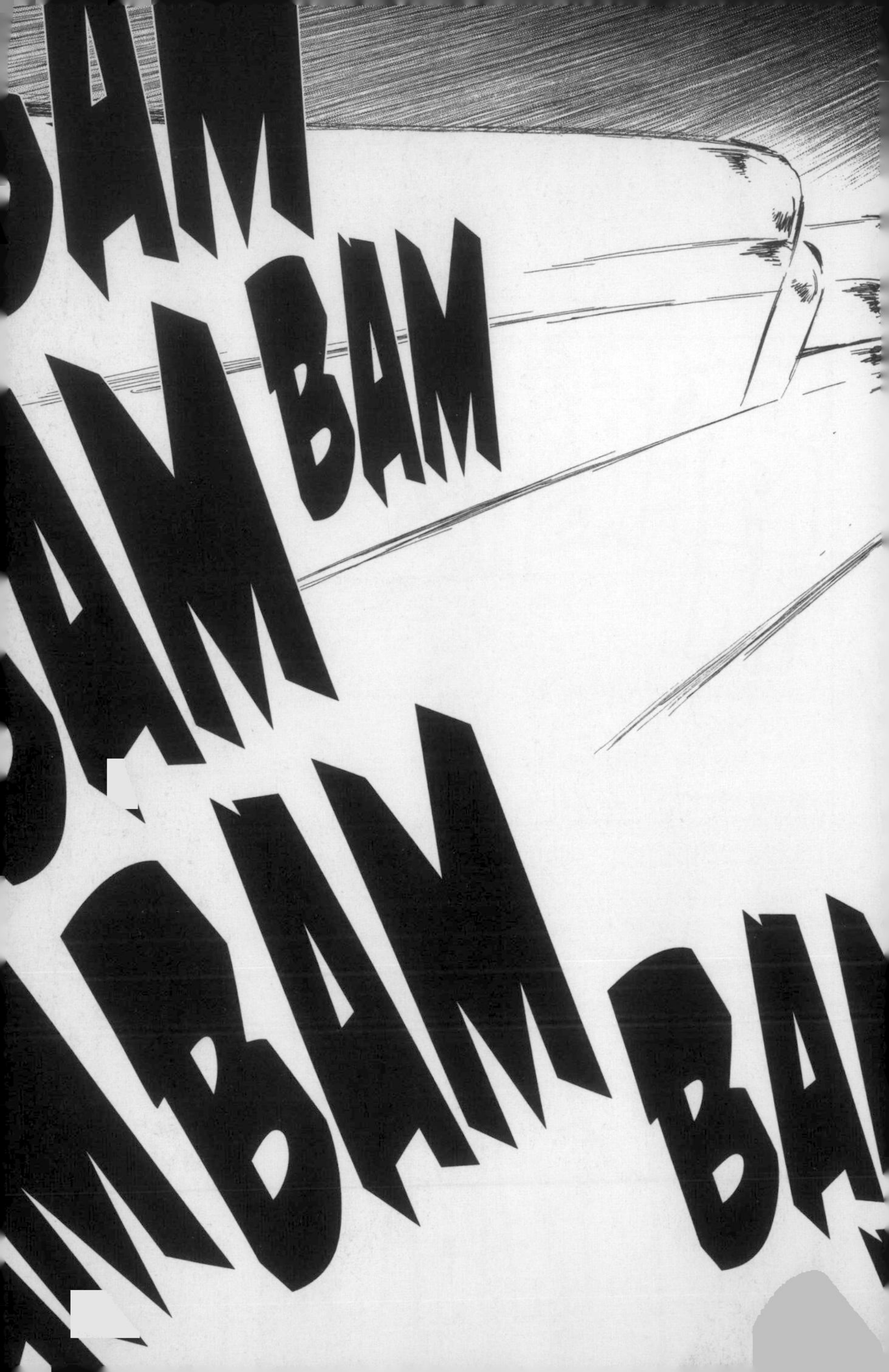
BAM
BAM

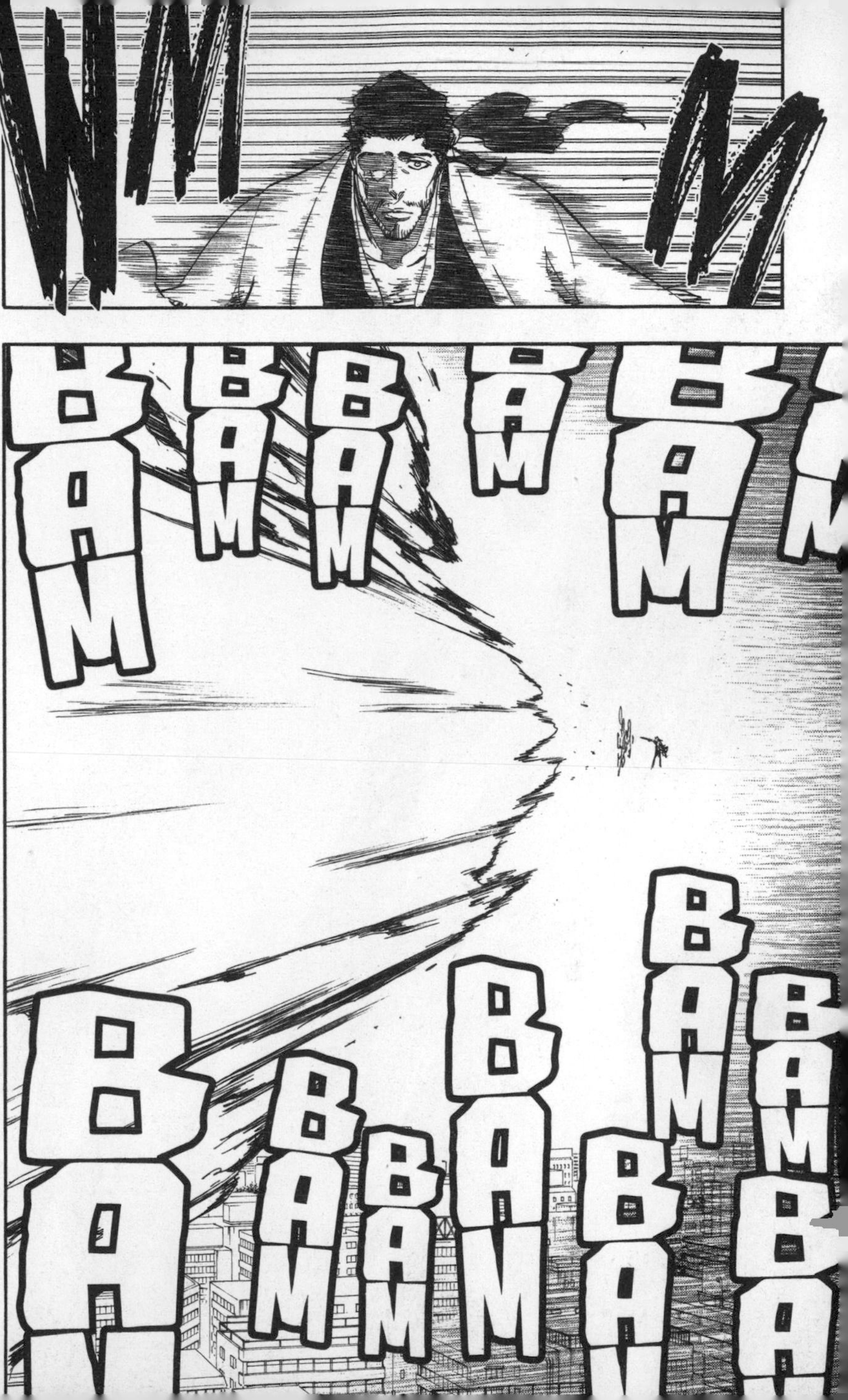
BAM
BAM
BAM
BAM
BAM
BAM
BAM
BAM
BAM
BAM
BAM
BAM
BAM
BAM

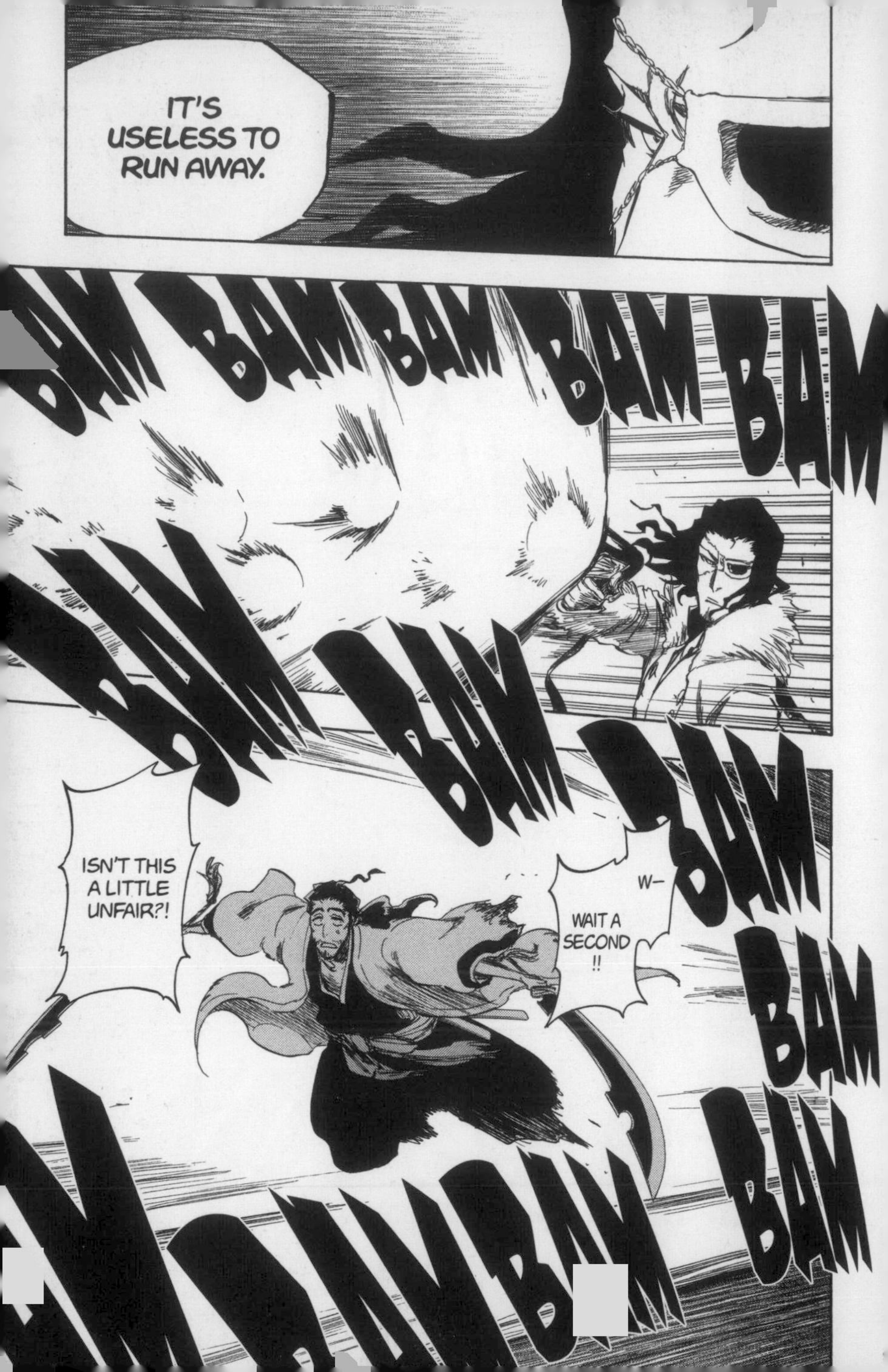
IT'S USELESS TO RUN AWAY.
BAM BAM BAM BAM BAM BAM
BAM BAM BAM BAM BAM BAM BAM
W— WAIT A SECOND!!
ISN'T THIS A LITTLE UNFAIR?!
BAM BAM BAM BAM BAM BAM

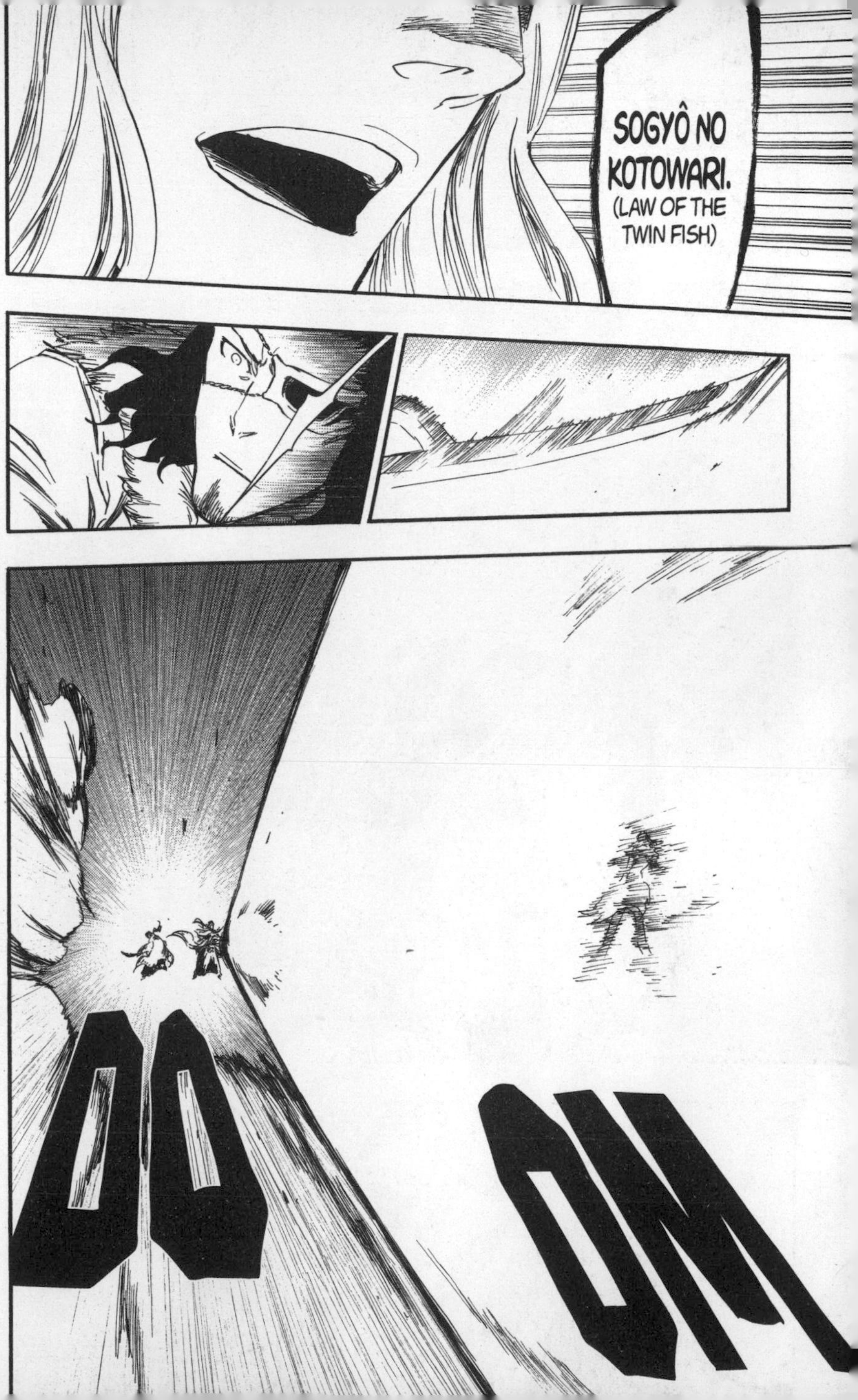
SOGYÔ NO KOTOWARI.
(LAW OF THE TWIN FISH)
DOOM

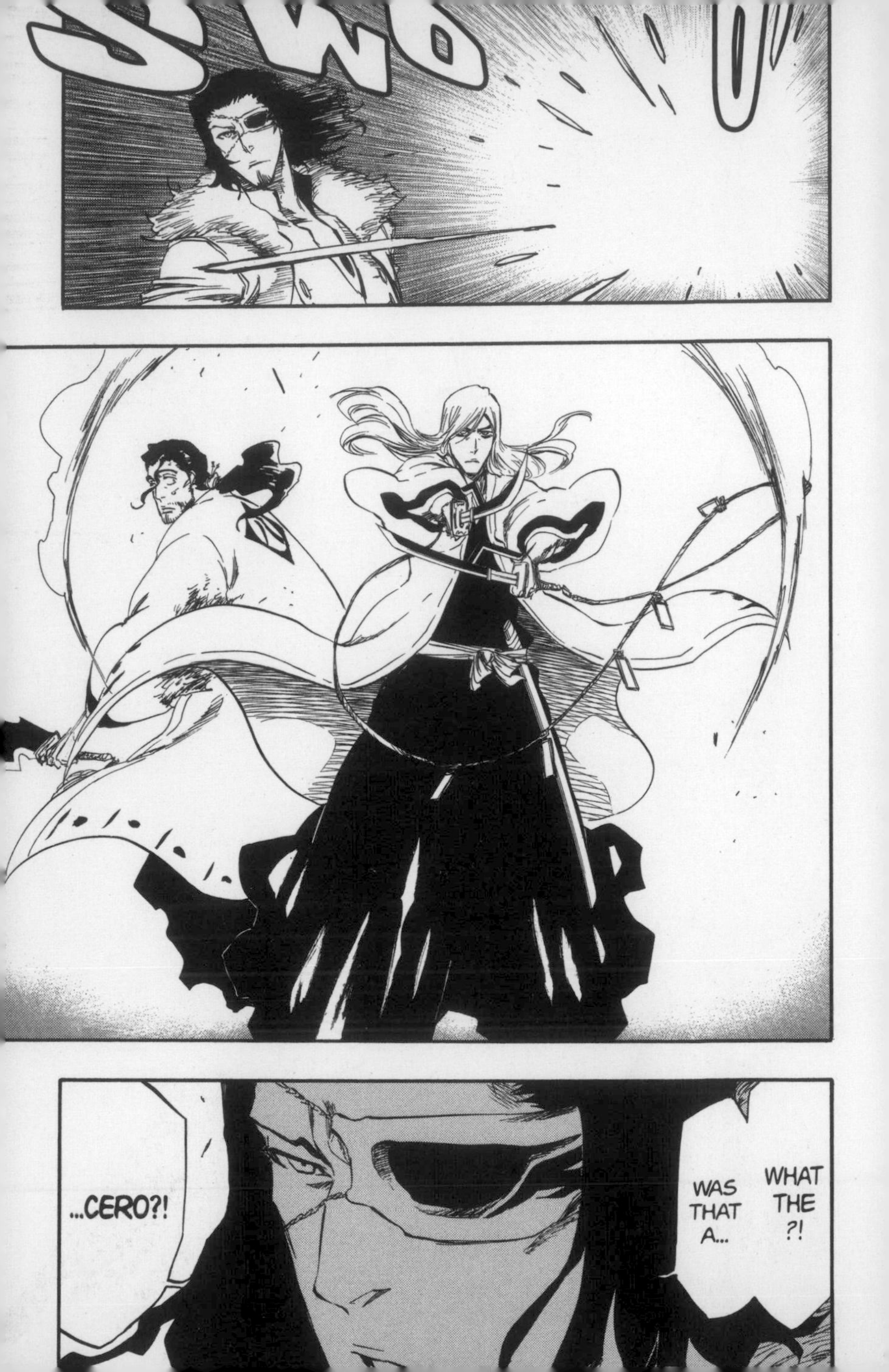
WHAT THE ?!
WAS THAT A...
...CERO?!

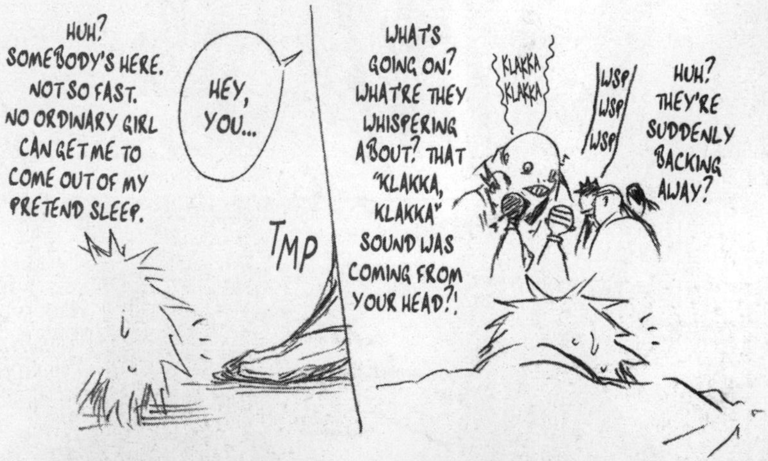
HUH? THEY'RE SUDDENLY BACKING AWAY?
WSP WSP WSP
KLAKKA KLAKKA
WHAT'S GOING ON? WHAT'RE THEY WHISPERING ABOUT? THAT "KLAKKA, KLAKKA" SOUND WAS COMING FROM YOUR HEAD?!
HEY, YOU...
TMP
HUH? SOMEBODY'S HERE. NOT SO FAST. NO ORDINARY GIRL CAN GET ME TO COME OUT OF MY PRETEND SLEEP.

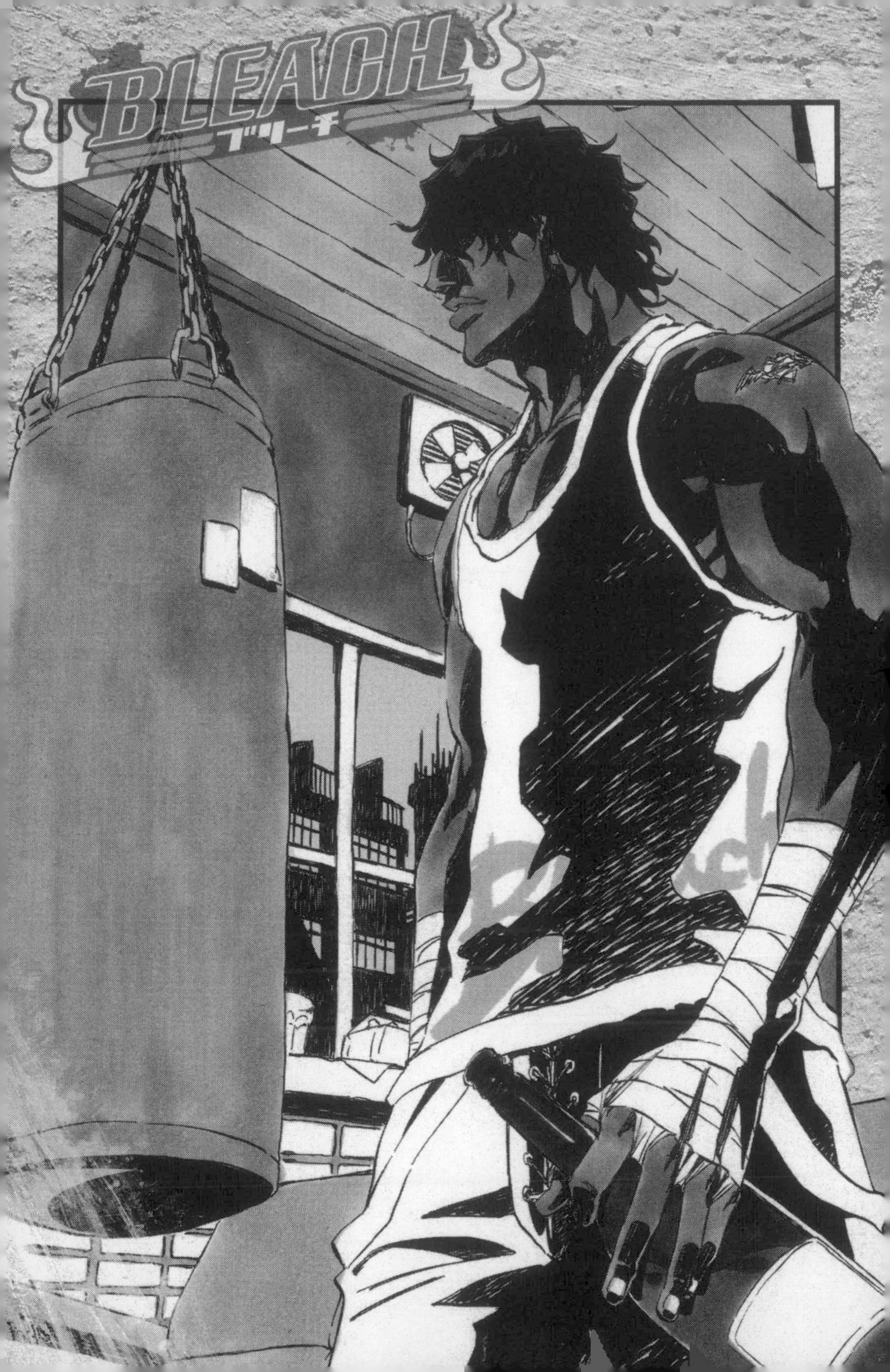
BLEACH
ブリーチ

BLEACH
ブリーチ

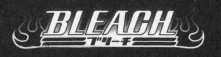

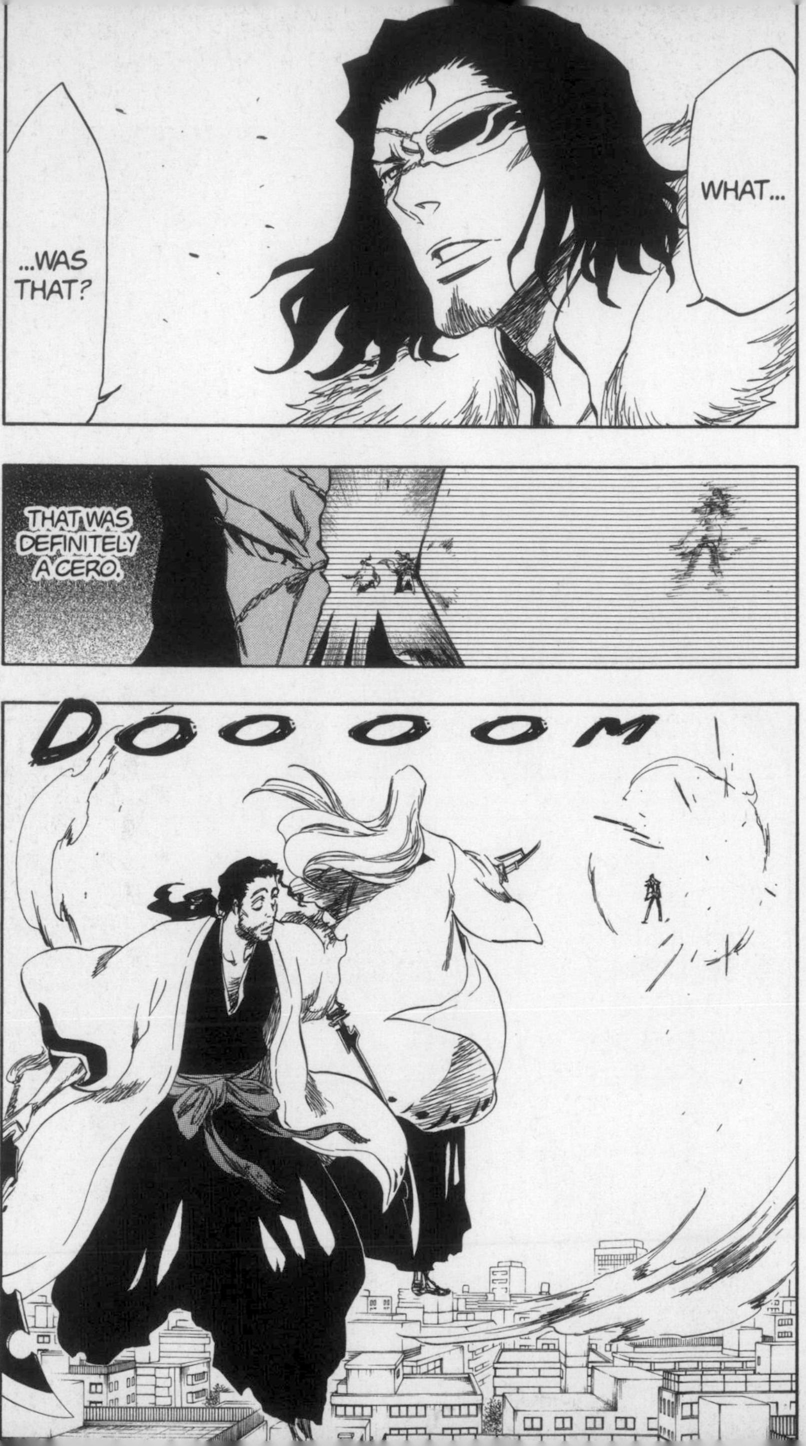
WHAT...
...WAS THAT?
THAT WAS DEFINITELY A CERO.
DOOOOOM

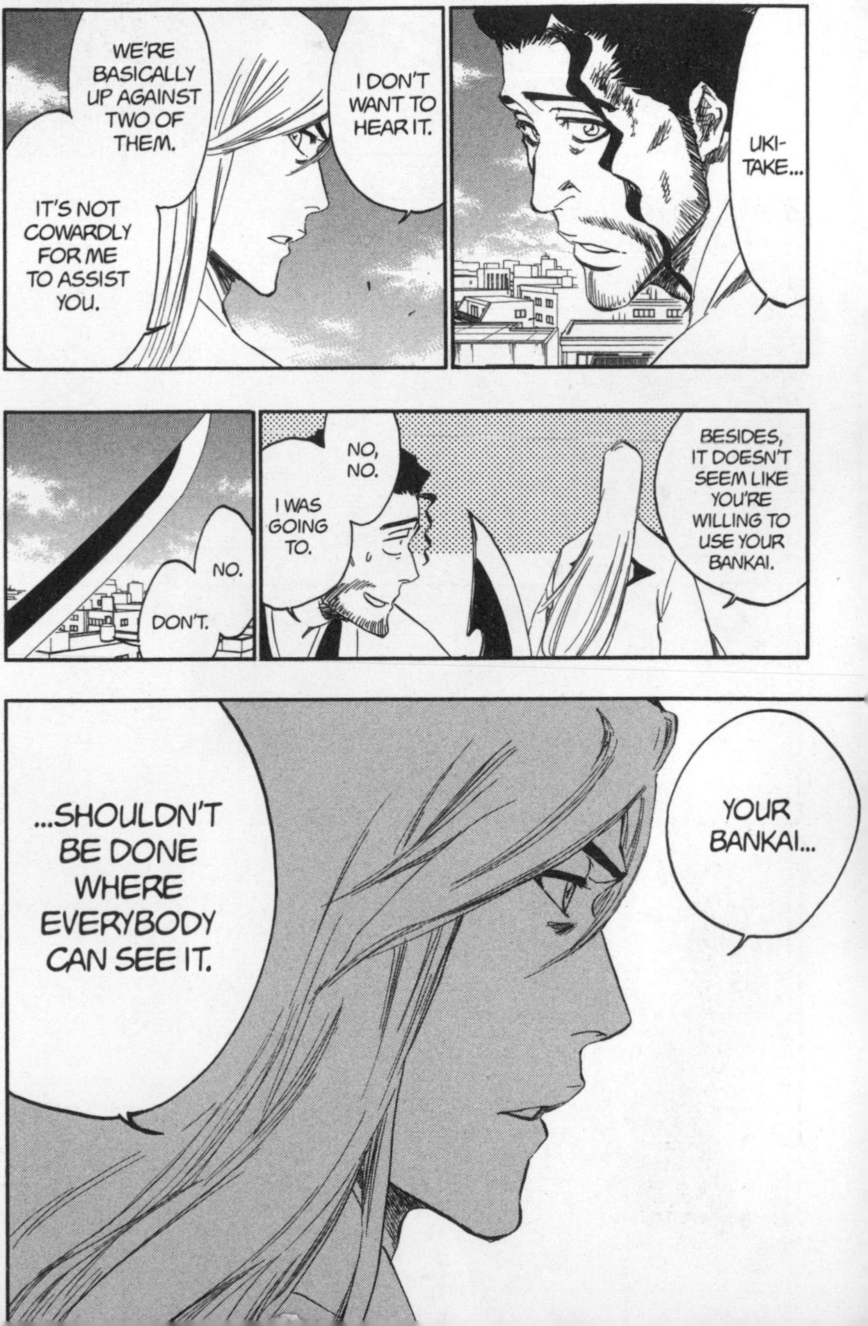
UKI-TAKE...
I DON'T WANT TO HEAR IT.
WE'RE BASICALLY UP AGAINST TWO OF THEM.
IT'S NOT COWARDLY FOR ME TO ASSIST YOU.
BESIDES, IT DOESN'T SEEM LIKE YOU'RE WILLING TO USE YOUR BANKAI.
NO, NO.
I WAS GOING TO.
NO.
DON'T.
YOUR BANKAI...
...SHOULDN'T BE DONE WHERE EVERYBODY CAN SEE IT.

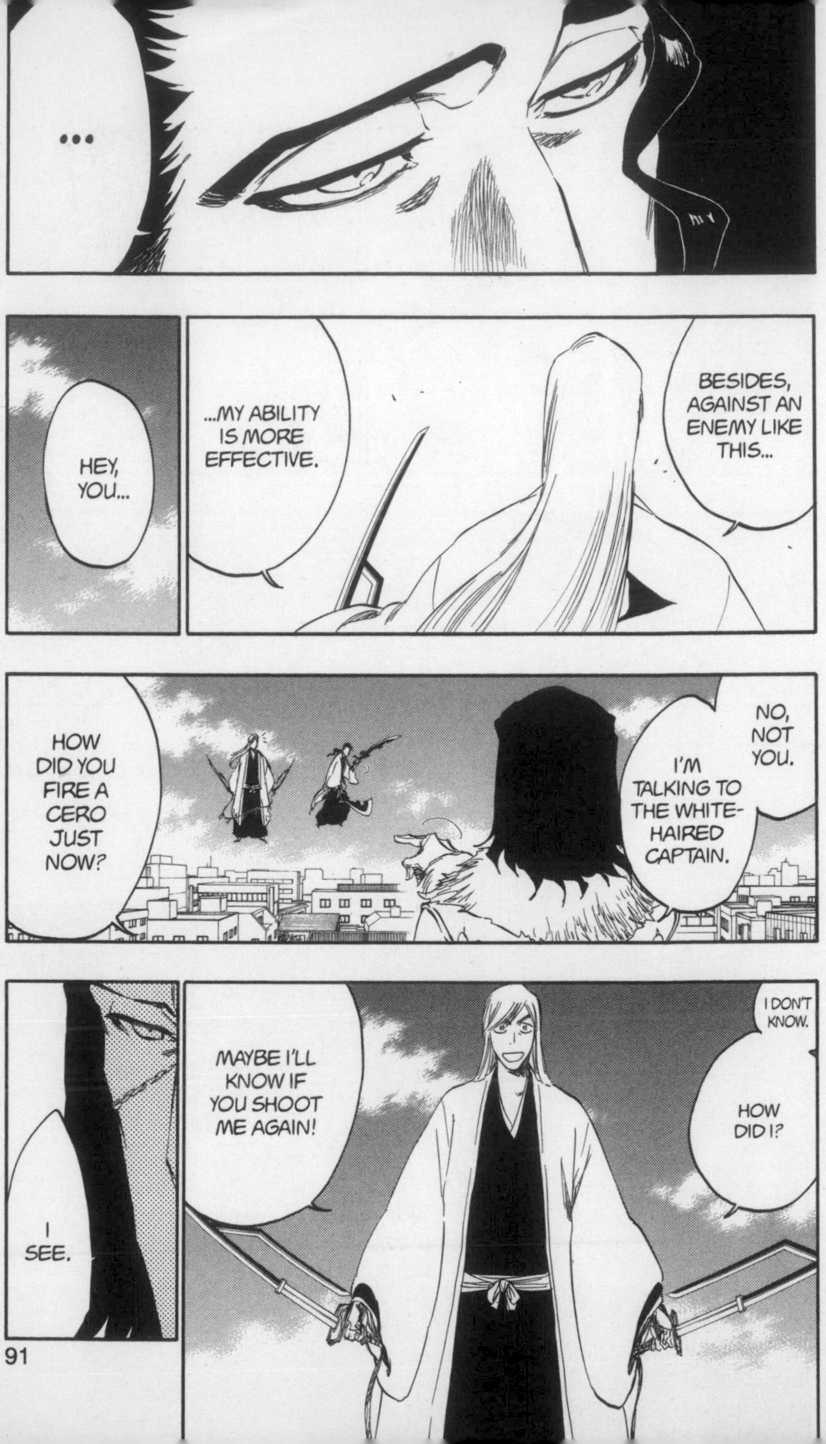
...
BESIDES, AGAINST AN ENEMY LIKE THIS...
...MY ABILITY IS MORE EFFECTIVE.
HEY, YOU...
NO, NOT YOU.
I'M TALKING TO THE WHITE-HAIRED CAPTAIN.
HOW DID YOU FIRE A CERO JUST NOW?
I DON'T KNOW.
HOW DID I?
MAYBE I'LL KNOW IF YOU SHOOT ME AGAIN!
I SEE.

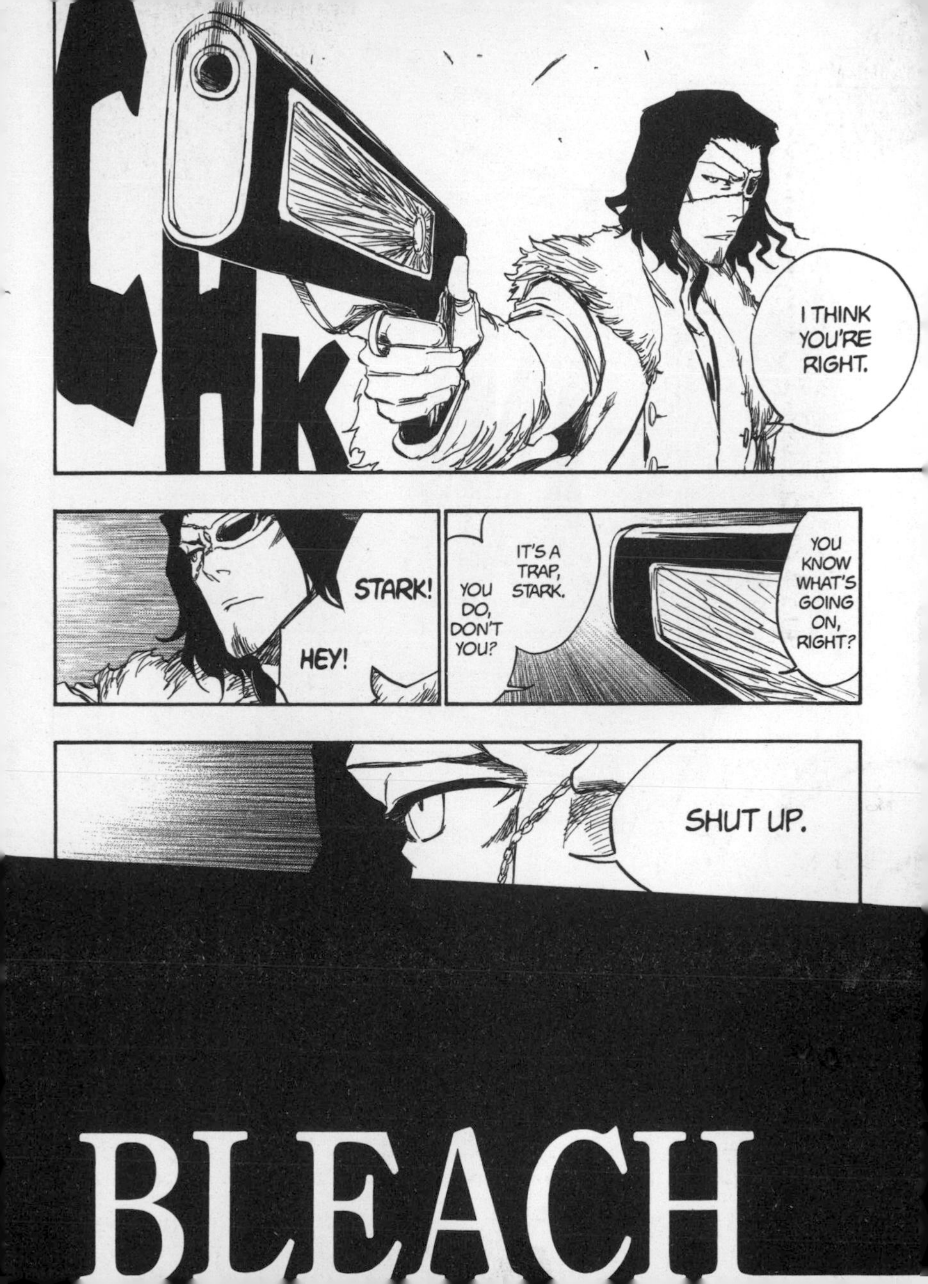
CHK
I THINK YOU'RE RIGHT.
YOU KNOW WHAT'S GOING ON, RIGHT?
IT'S A TRAP, STARK.
YOU DO, DON'T YOU?
STARK!
HEY!
SHUT UP.
BLEACH

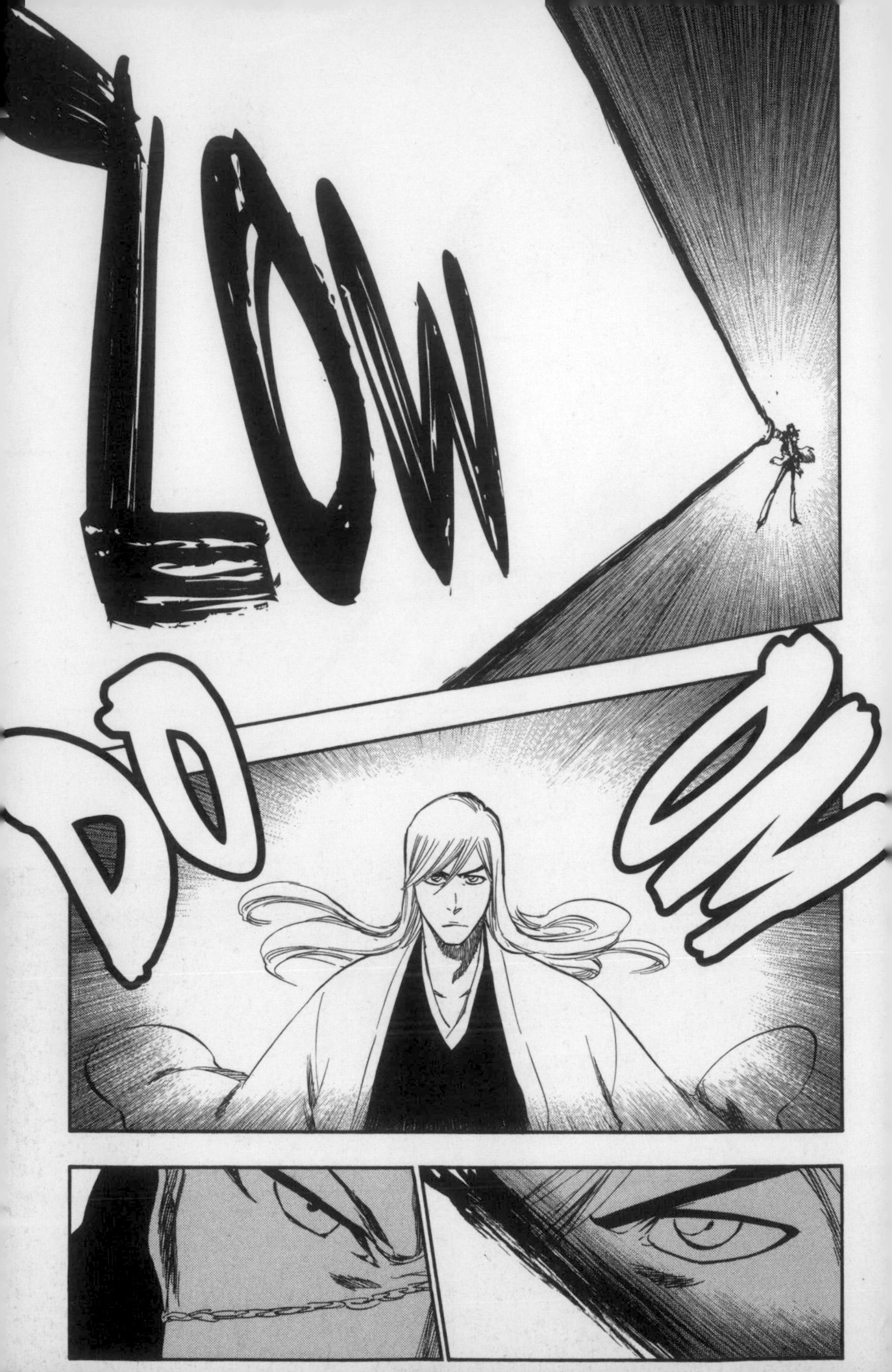
LOW
DOOM

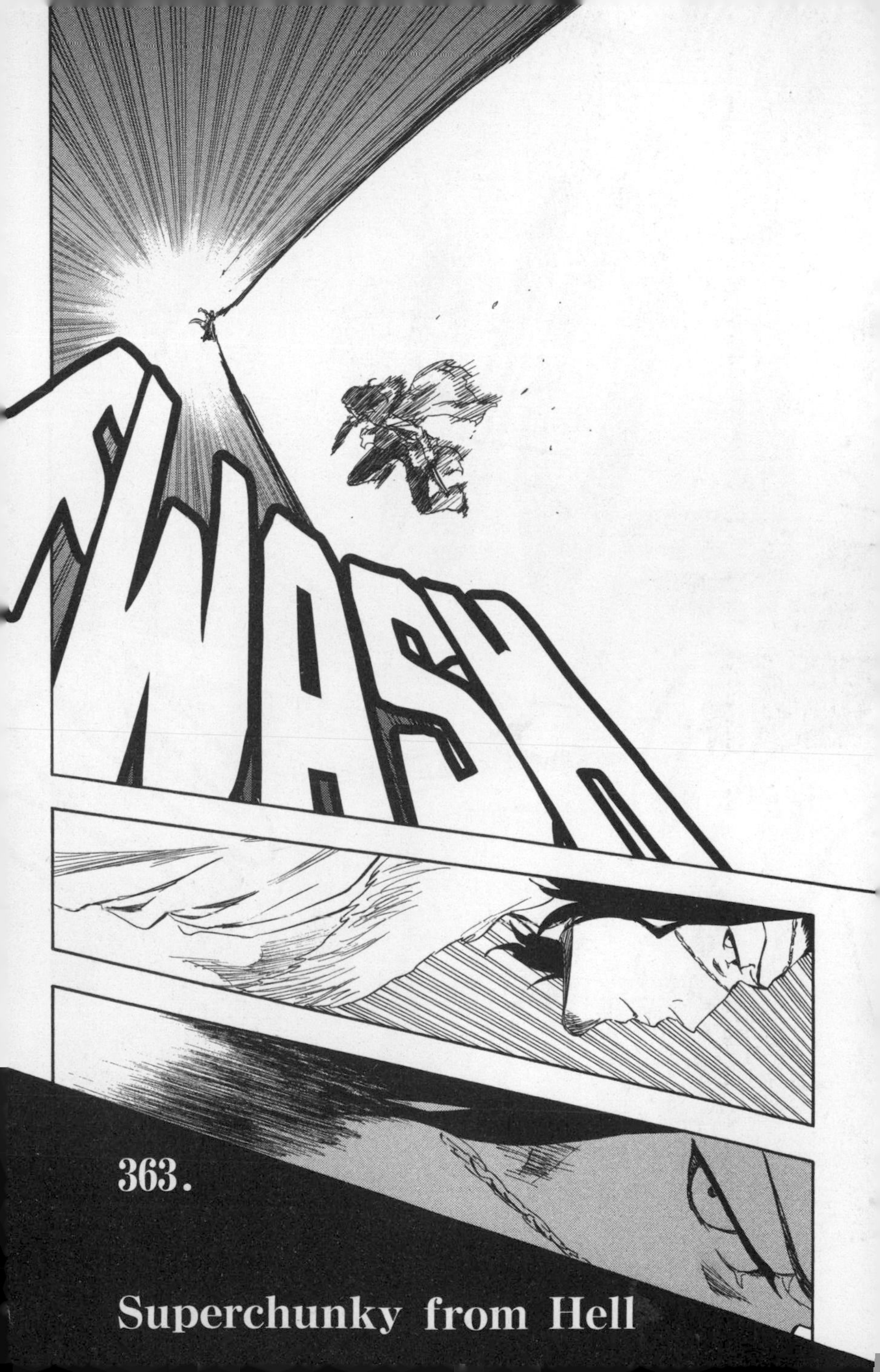
WASH

363.

Superchunky from Hell

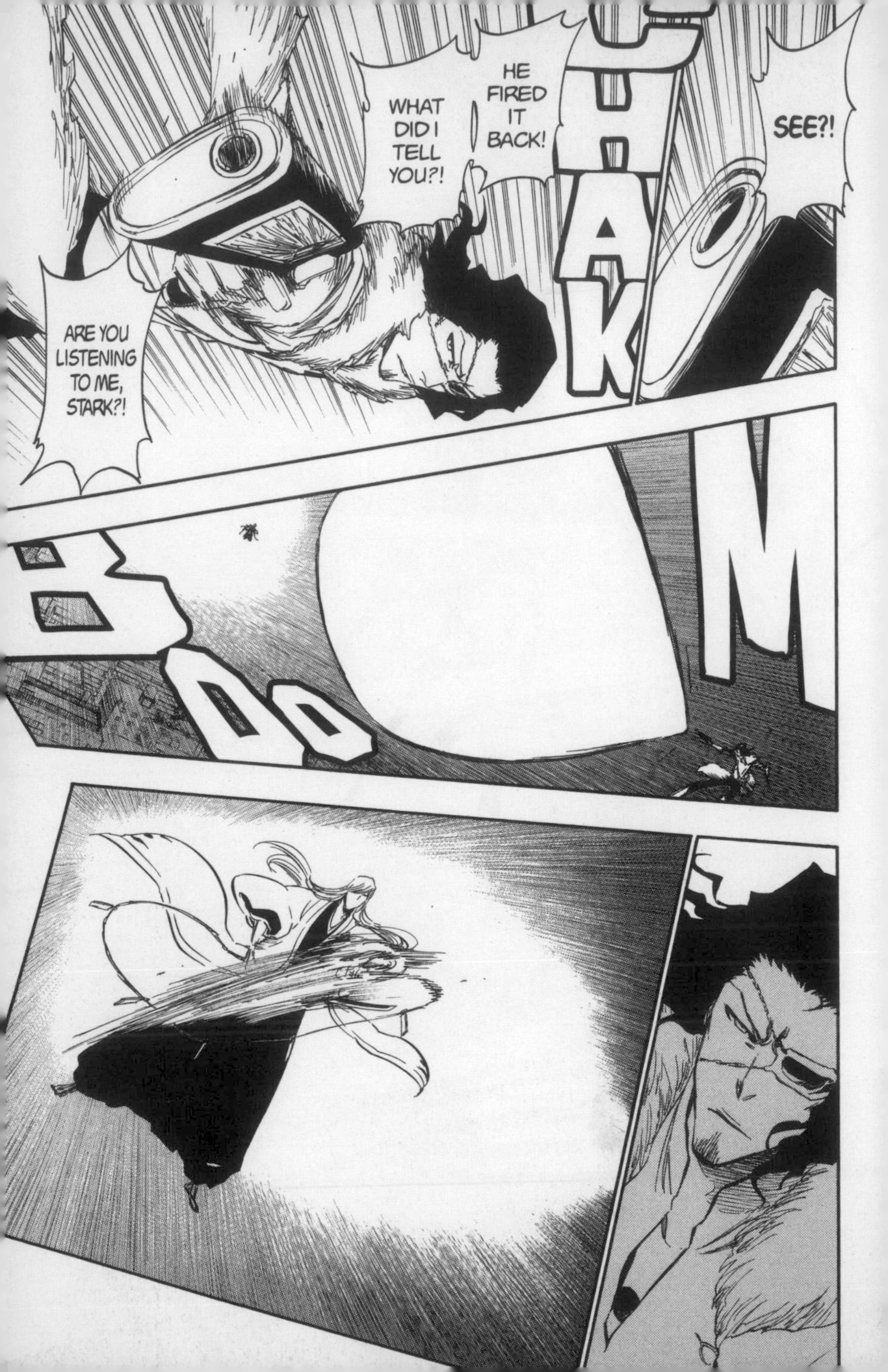
SEE?!
HE FIRED IT BACK!
WHAT DID I TELL YOU?!
ARE YOU LISTENING TO ME, STARK?!
BOOM

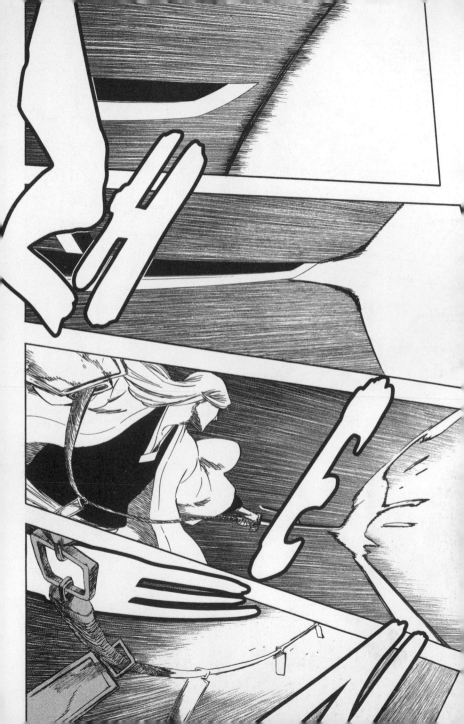

READ THIS WAY

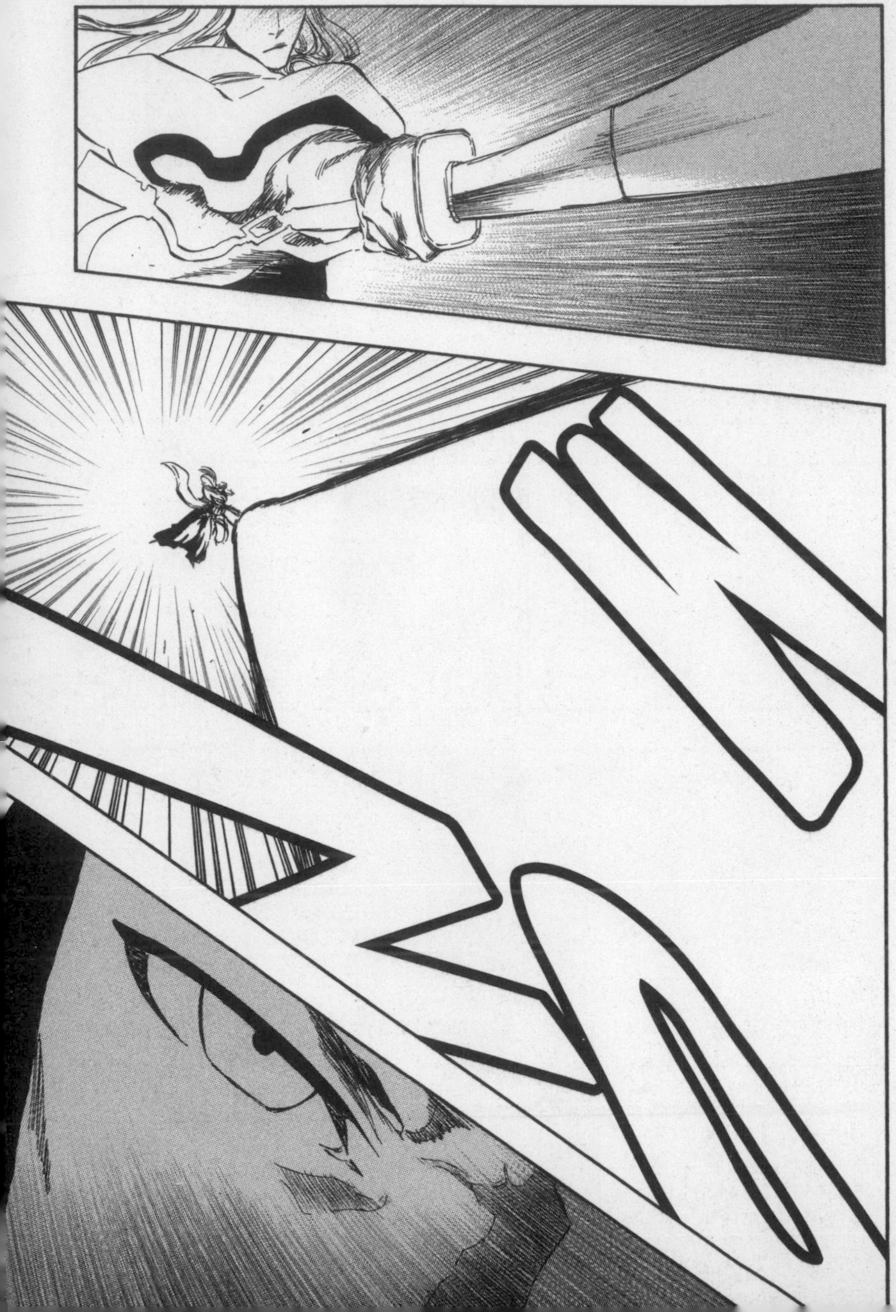

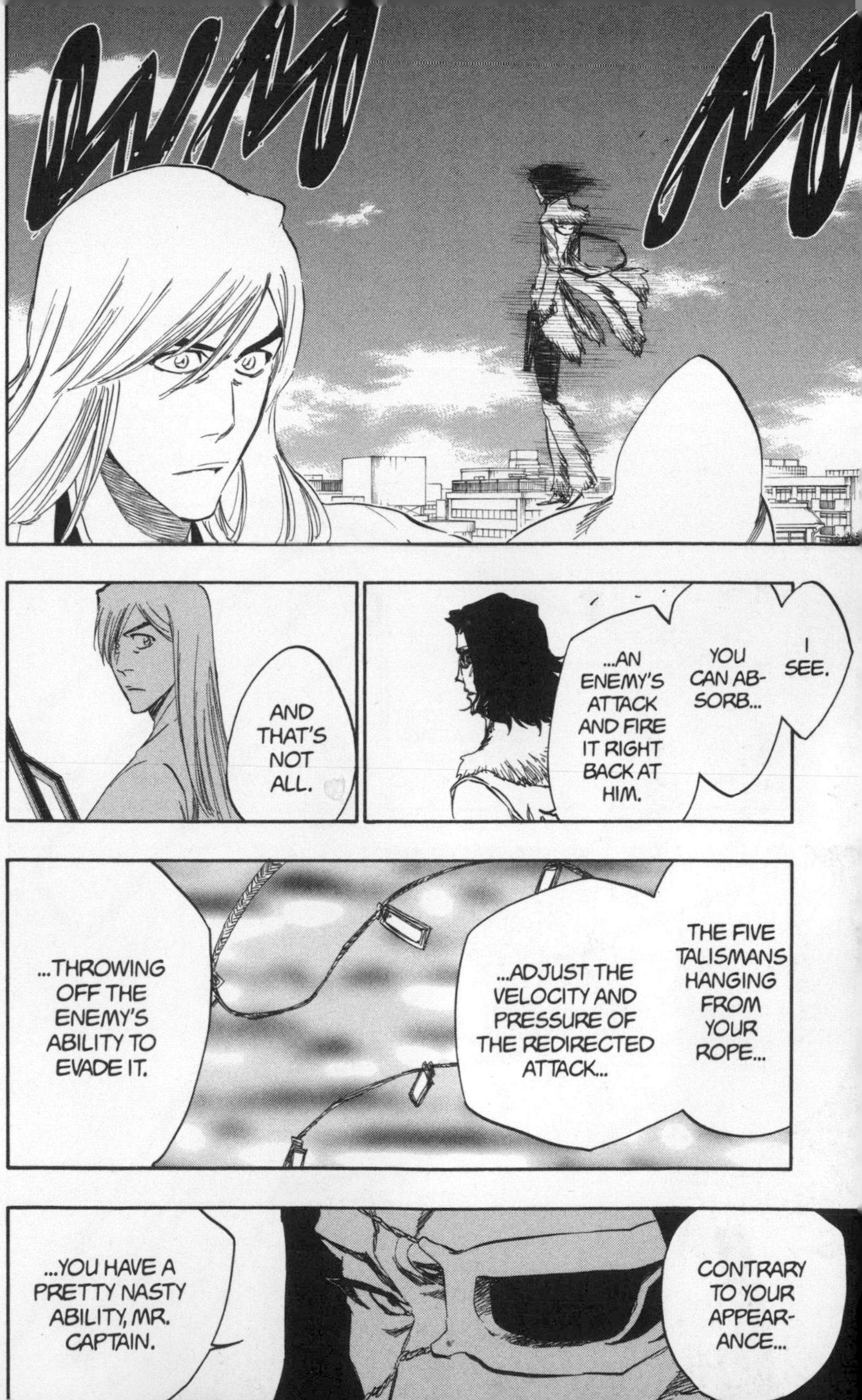
I SEE.
YOU CAN ABSORB...
...AN ENEMY'S ATTACK AND FIRE IT RIGHT BACK AT HIM.
AND THAT'S NOT ALL.
THE FIVE TALISMANS HANGING FROM YOUR ROPE...
...ADJUST THE VELOCITY AND PRESSURE OF THE REDIRECTED ATTACK...
...THROWING OFF THE ENEMY'S ABILITY TO EVADE IT.
CONTRARY TO YOUR APPEARANCE...
...YOU HAVE A PRETTY NASTY ABILITY, MR. CAPTAIN.

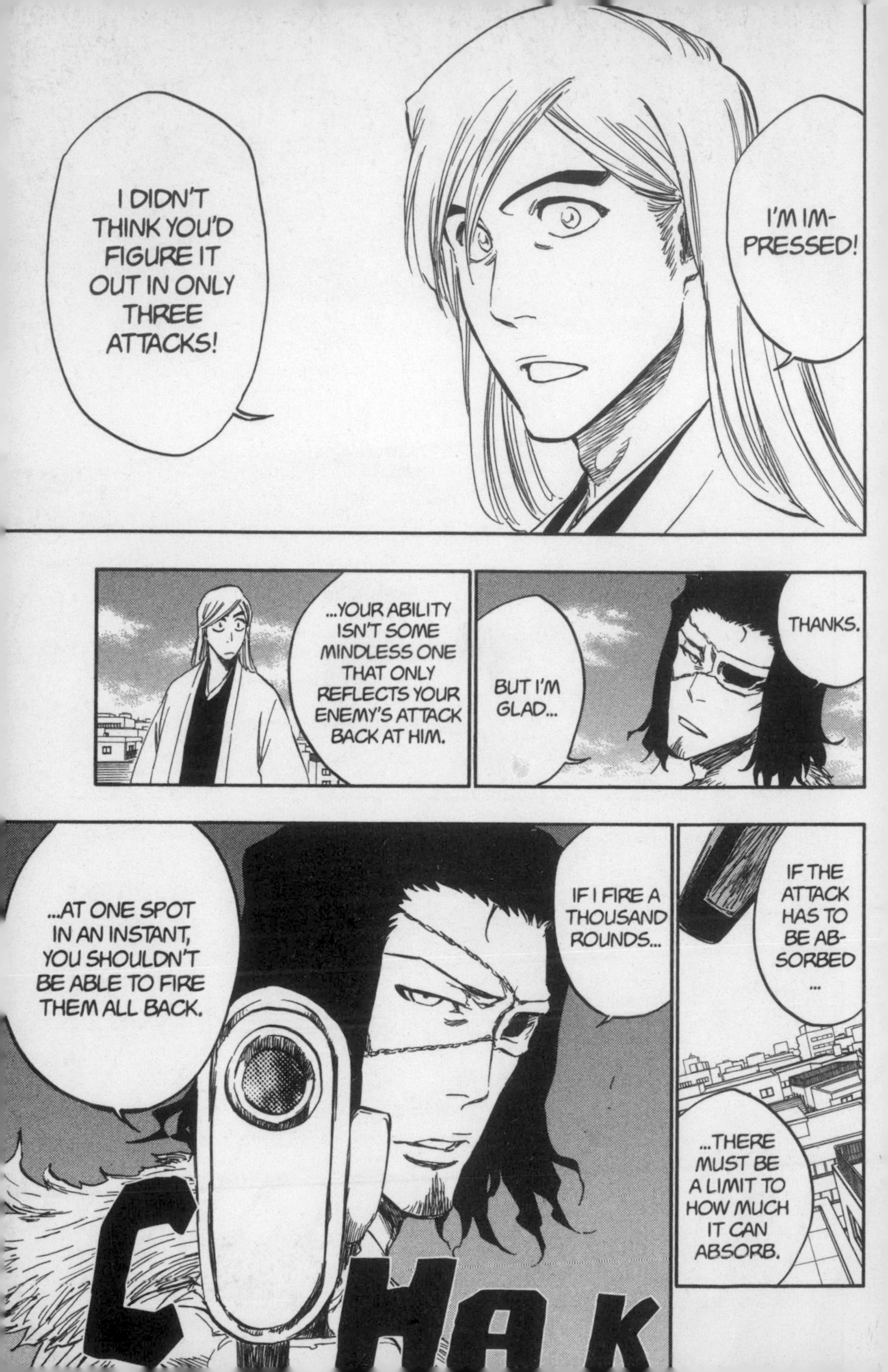
I'M IM-PRESSED!
I DIDN'T THINK YOU'D FIGURE IT OUT IN ONLY THREE ATTACKS!
THANKS.
BUT I'M GLAD...
...YOUR ABILITY ISN'T SOME MINDLESS ONE THAT ONLY REFLECTS YOUR ENEMY'S ATTACK BACK AT HIM.
IF THE ATTACK HAS TO BE ABSORBED...
...THERE MUST BE A LIMIT TO HOW MUCH IT CAN ABSORB.
IF I FIRE A THOUSAND ROUNDS...
...AT ONE SPOT IN AN INSTANT, YOU SHOULDN'T BE ABLE TO FIRE THEM ALL BACK.
CHAK

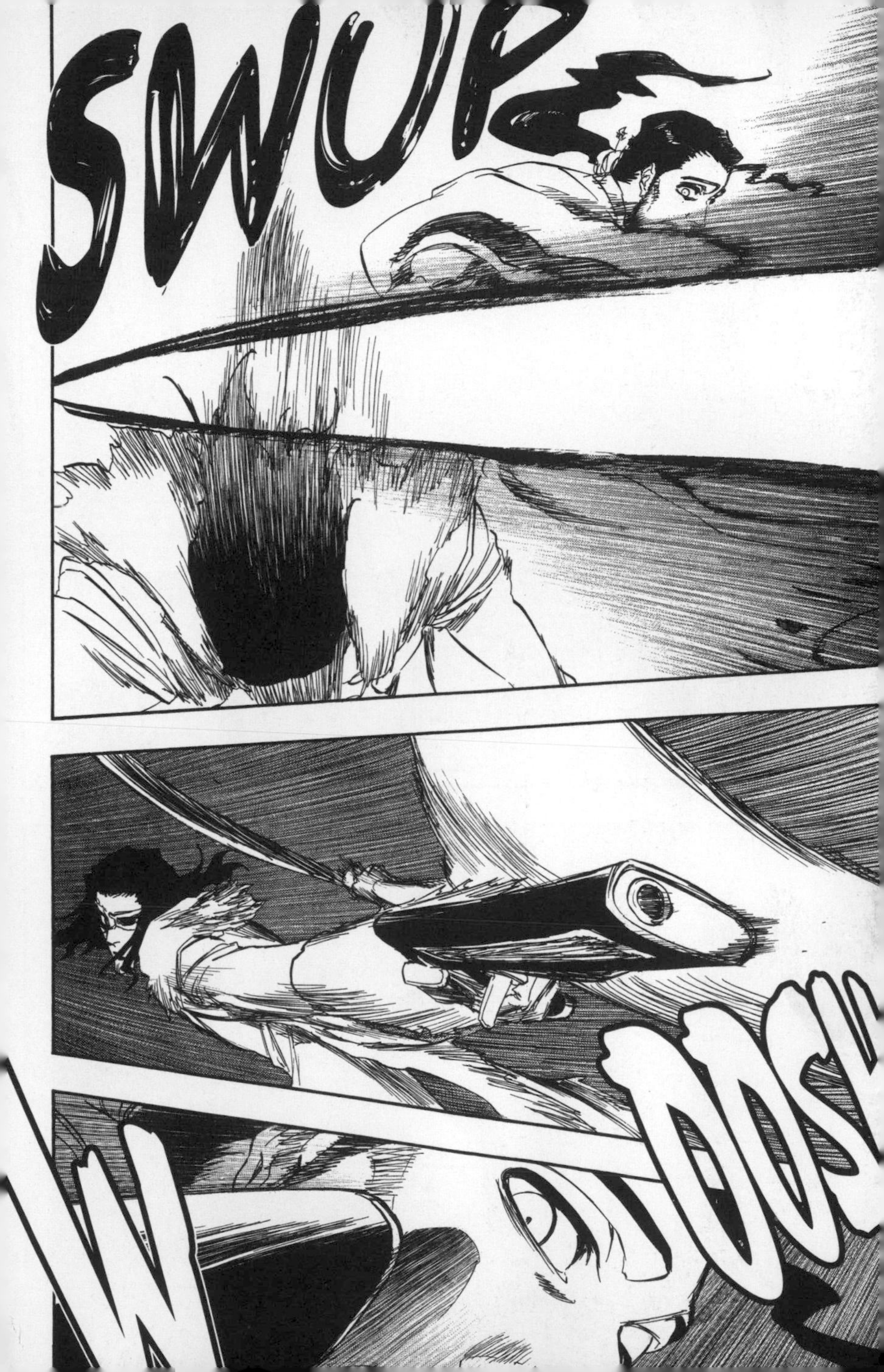
SWUP

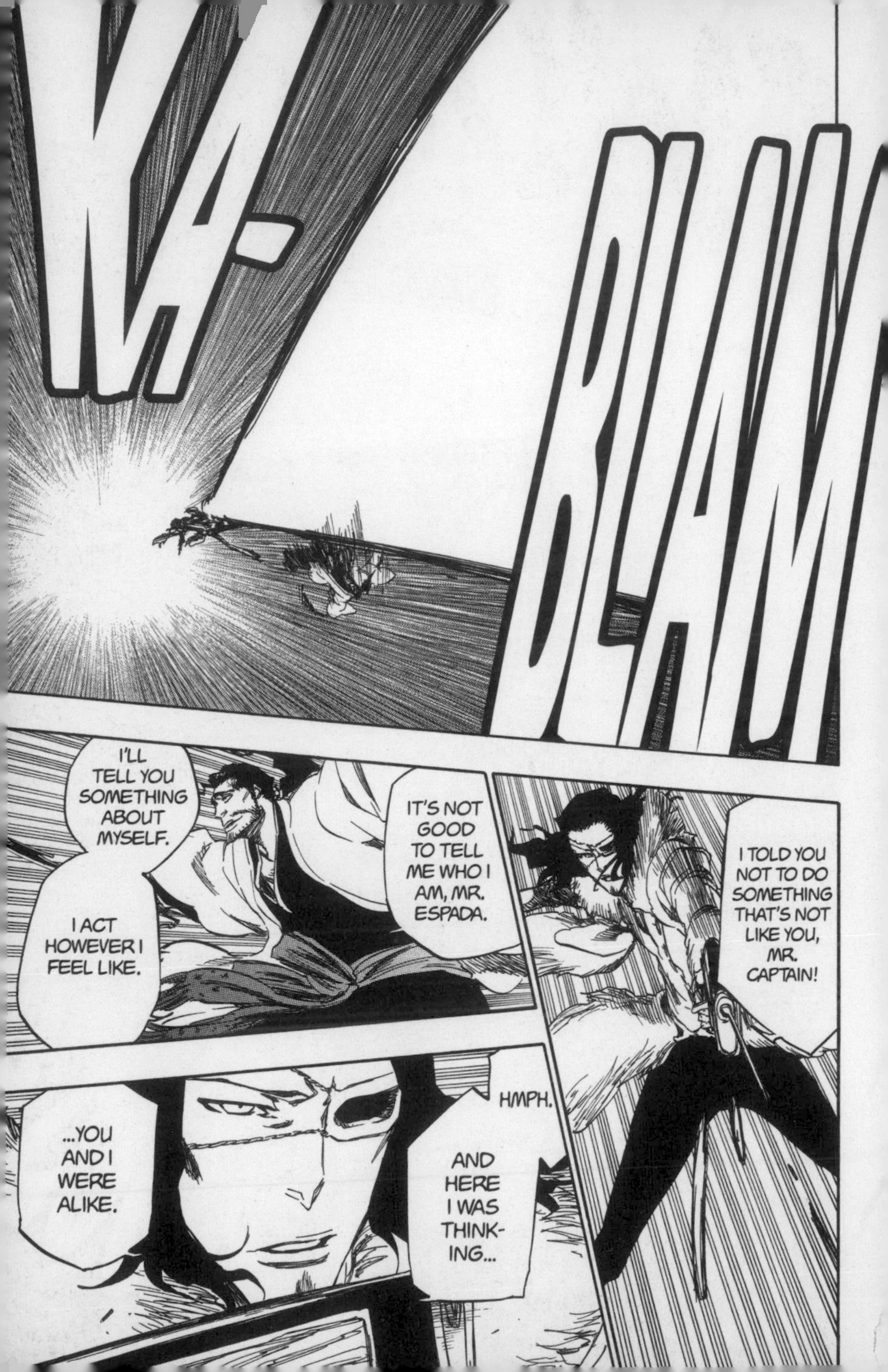
KA-BLAM
I TOLD YOU NOT TO DO SOMETHING THAT'S NOT LIKE YOU, MR. CAPTAIN!
IT'S NOT GOOD TO TELL ME WHO I AM, MR. ESPADA.
I'LL TELL YOU SOMETHING ABOUT MYSELF.
I ACT HOWEVER I FEEL LIKE.
HMPH.
AND HERE I WAS THINKING...
...YOU AND I WERE ALIKE.

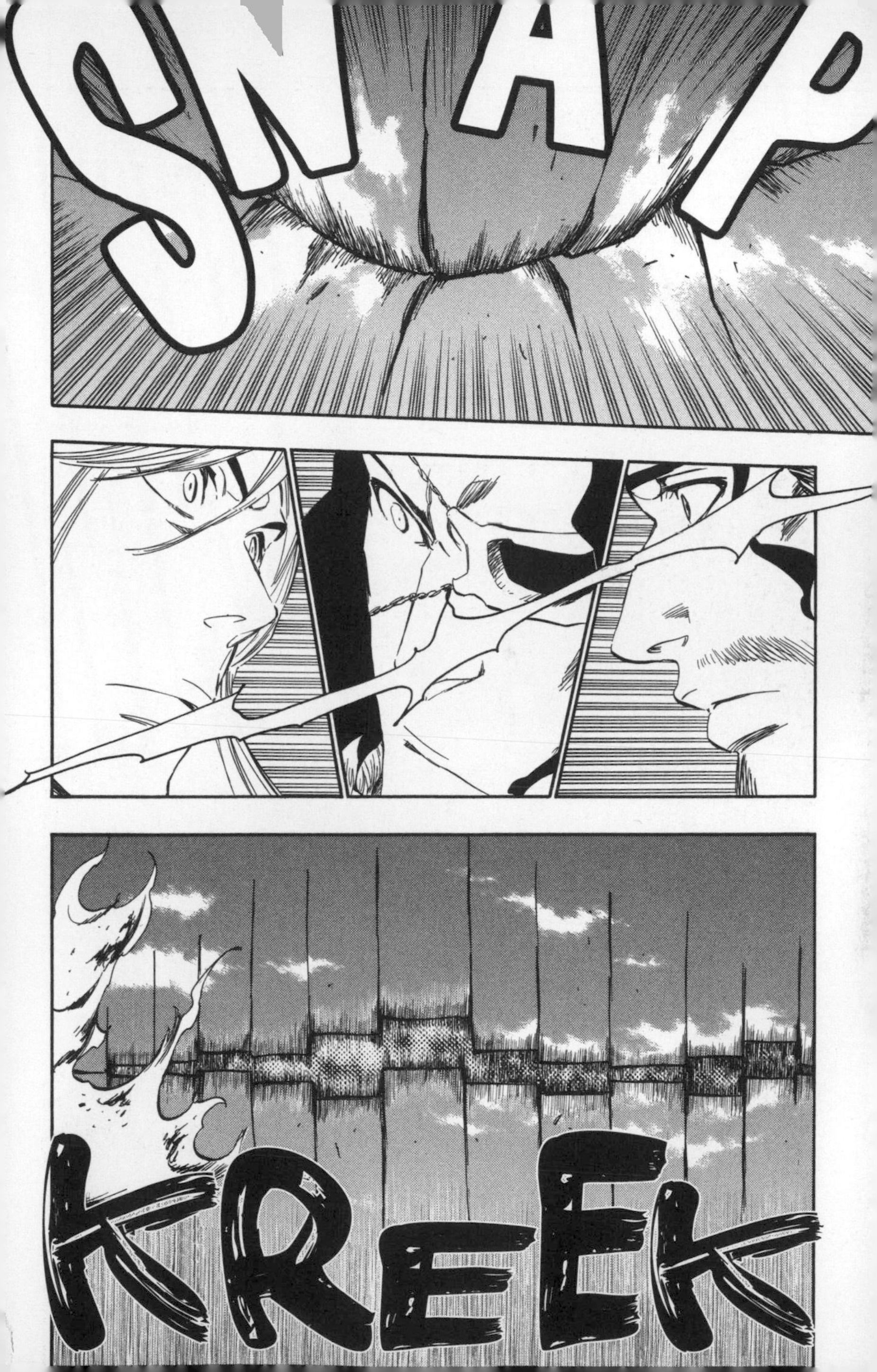
SNAP
KREEK

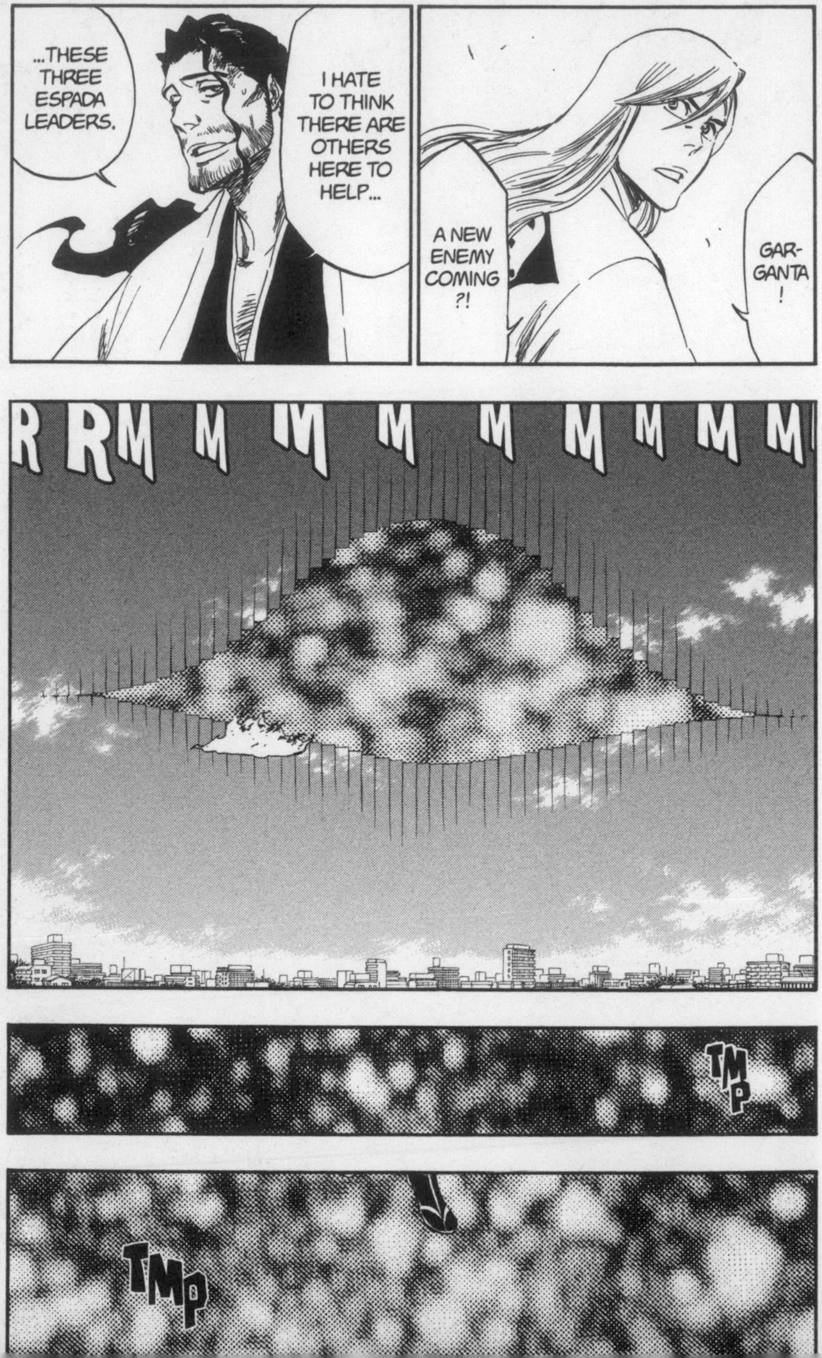
GAR-GANTA!
A NEW ENEMY COMING?!
I HATE TO THINK THERE ARE OTHERS HERE TO HELP...
...THESE THREE ESPADA LEADERS.
RRMMMMMMMMM
TMP
TMP

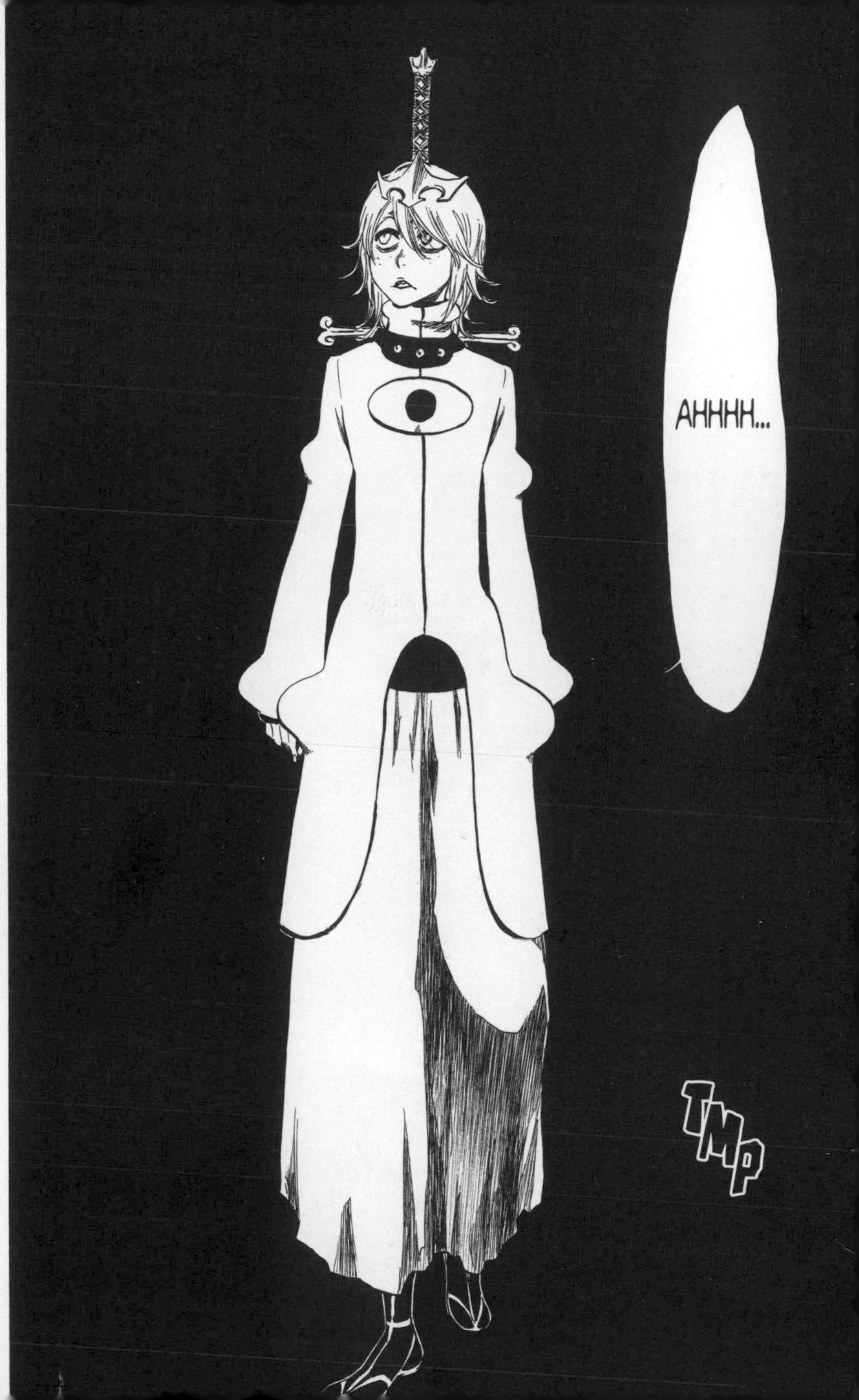
AHHHH...
TMP

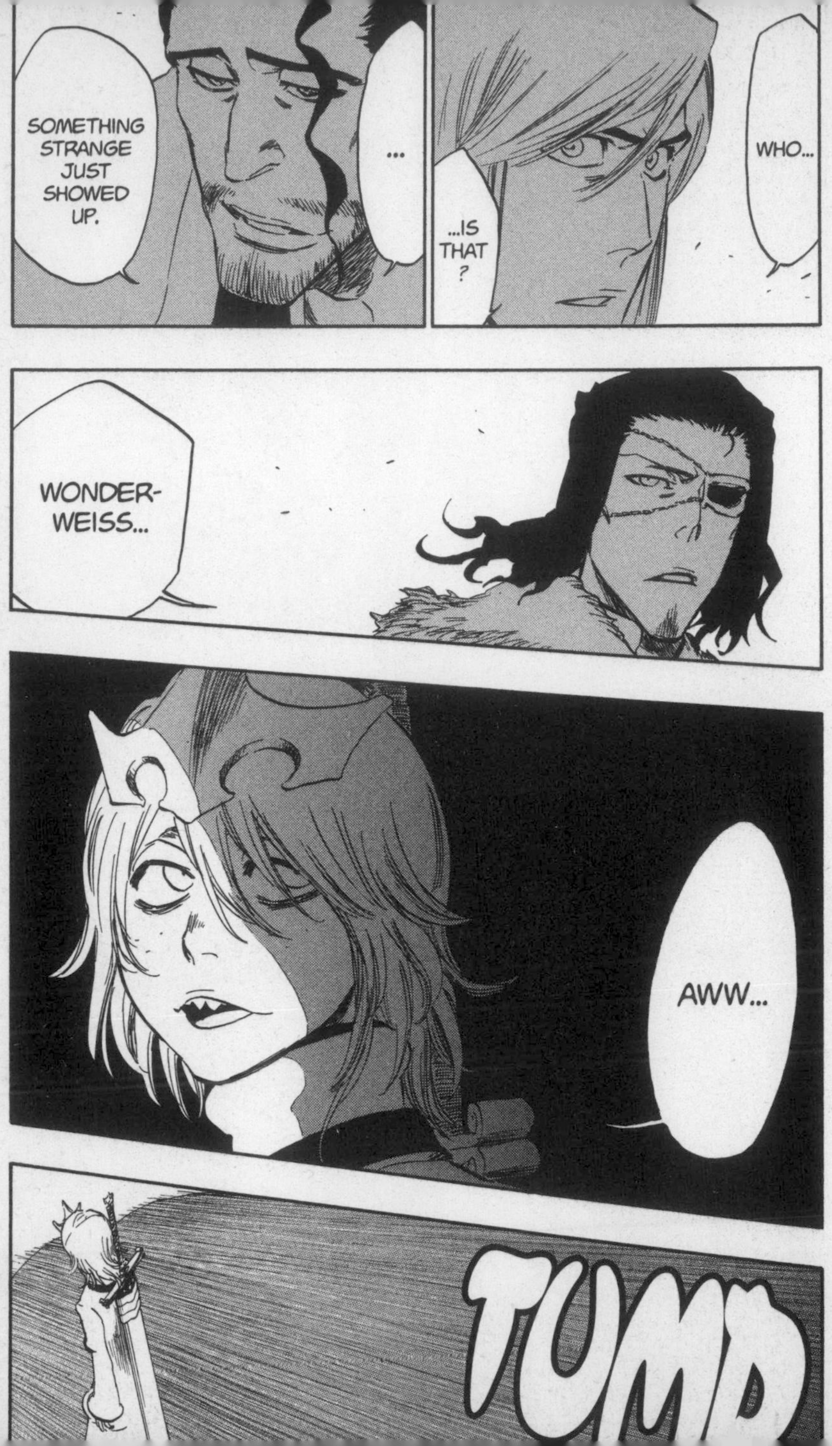
WHO...
...IS THAT ?
...
SOMETHING STRANGE JUST SHOWED UP.
WONDER-WEISS...
AWW...
TUMP

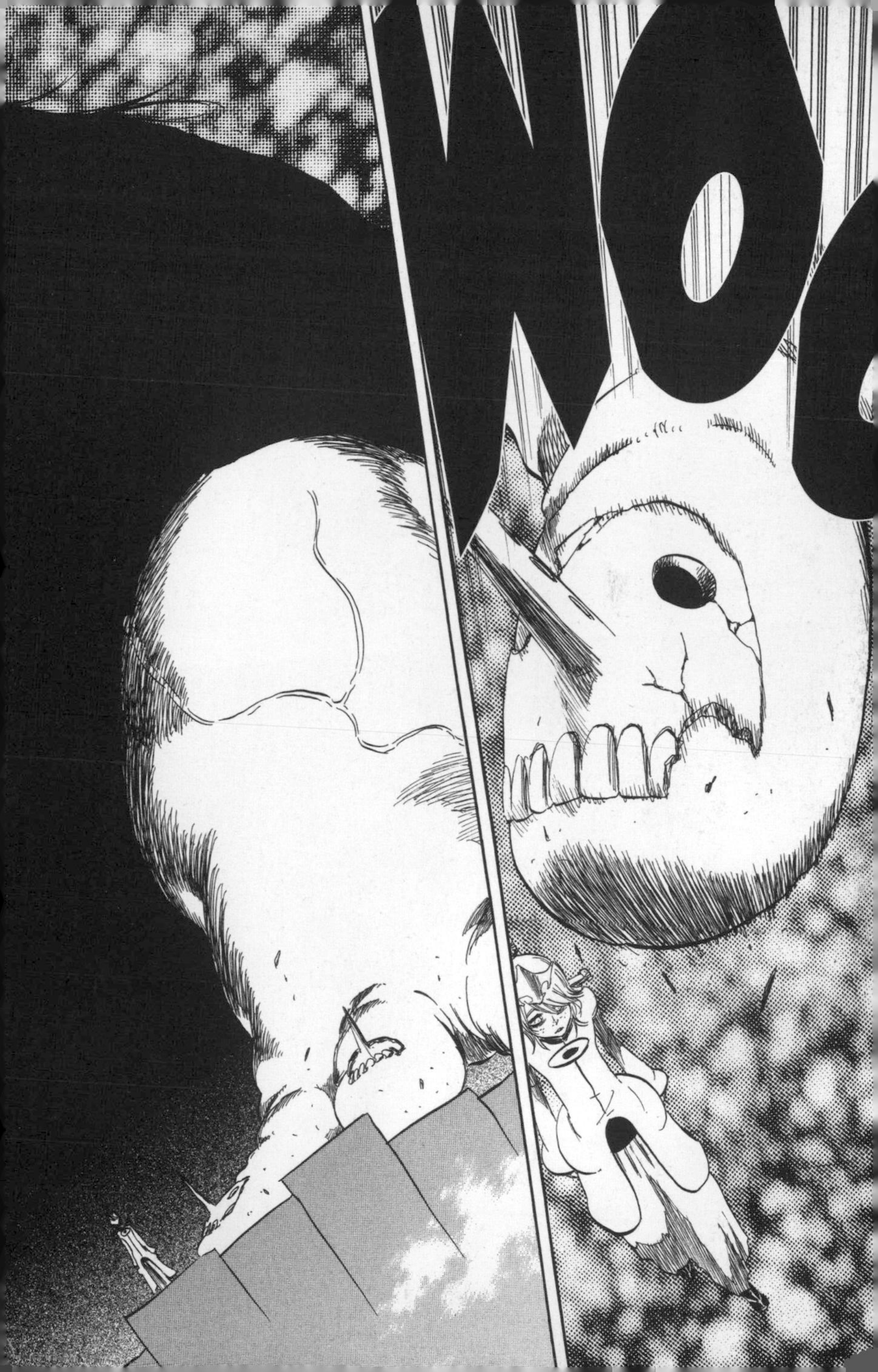
WO

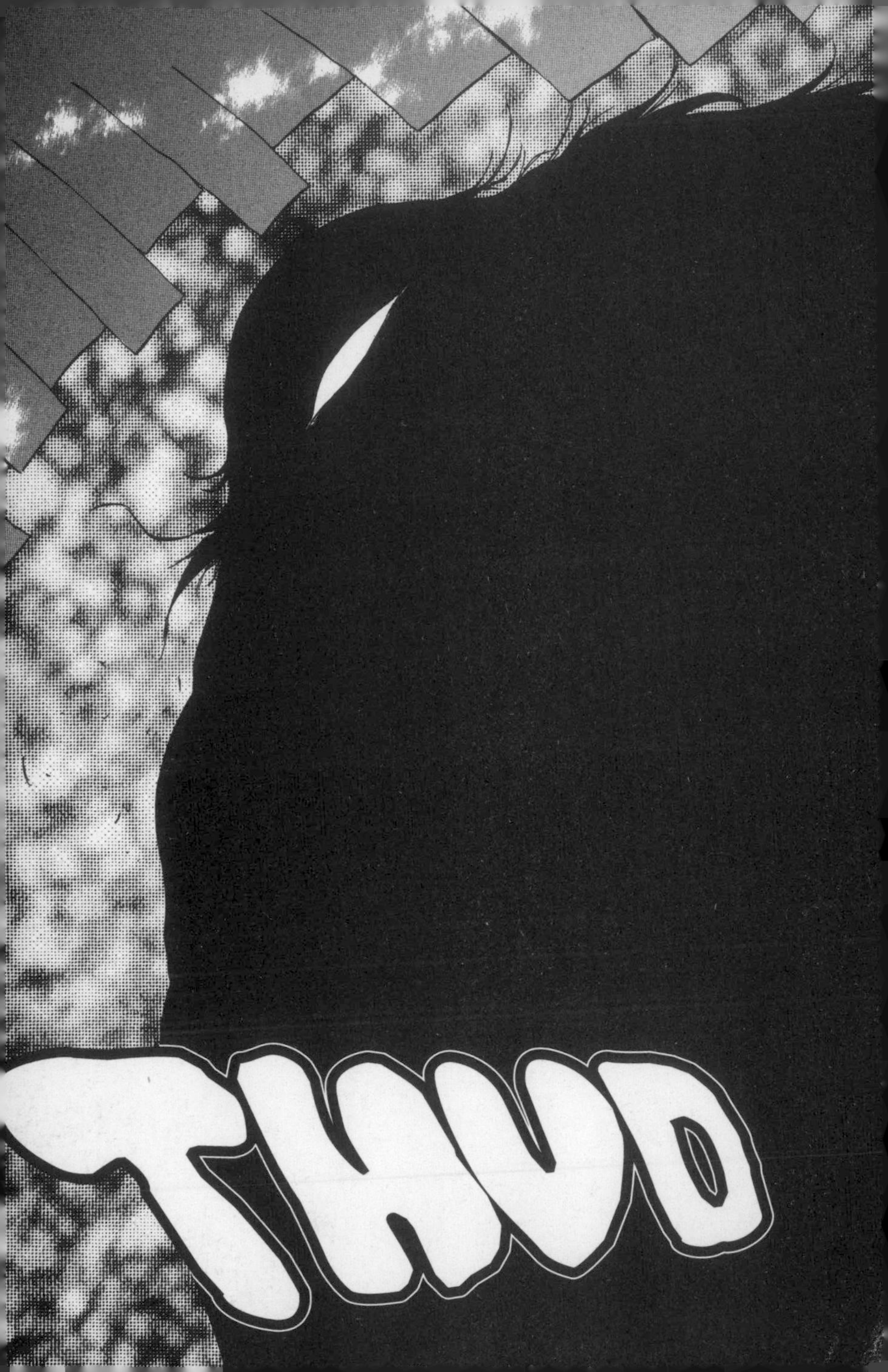
THUD

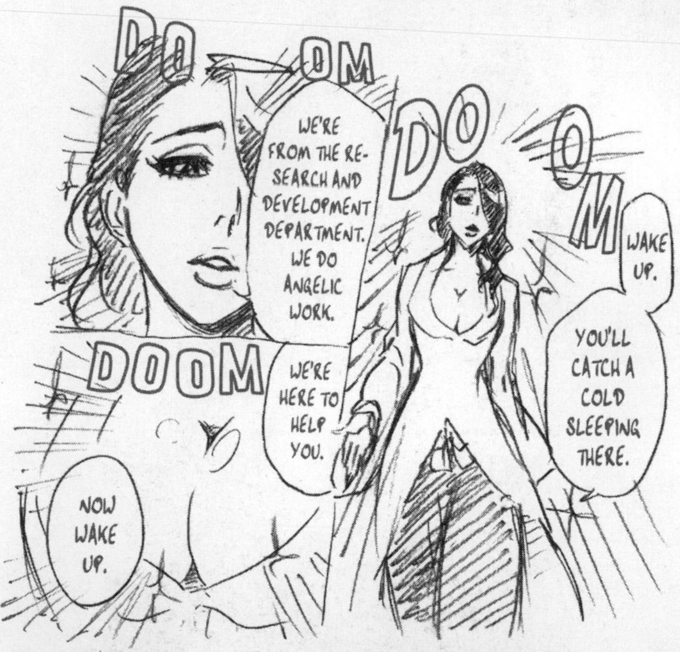
DO O M
WAKE UP.
YOU'LL CATCH A COLD SLEEPING THERE.
DO OM
WE'RE FROM THE RESEARCH AND DEVELOPMENT DEPARTMENT. WE DO ANGELIC WORK.
DOOM
WE'RE HERE TO HELP YOU.
NOW WAKE UP.

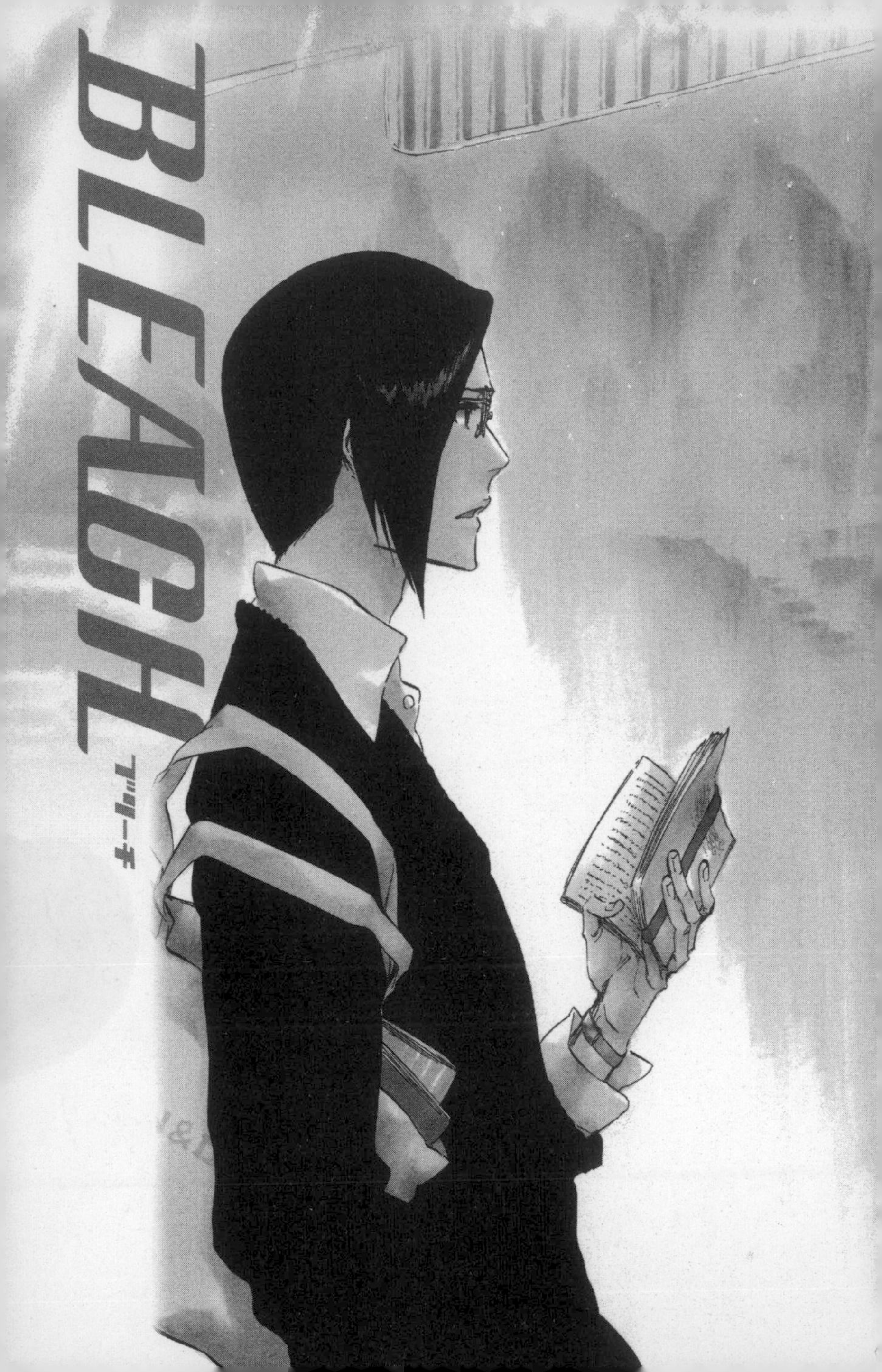
BLEACH
ブリーチ

BLEACH
ブリーチ

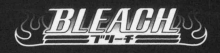

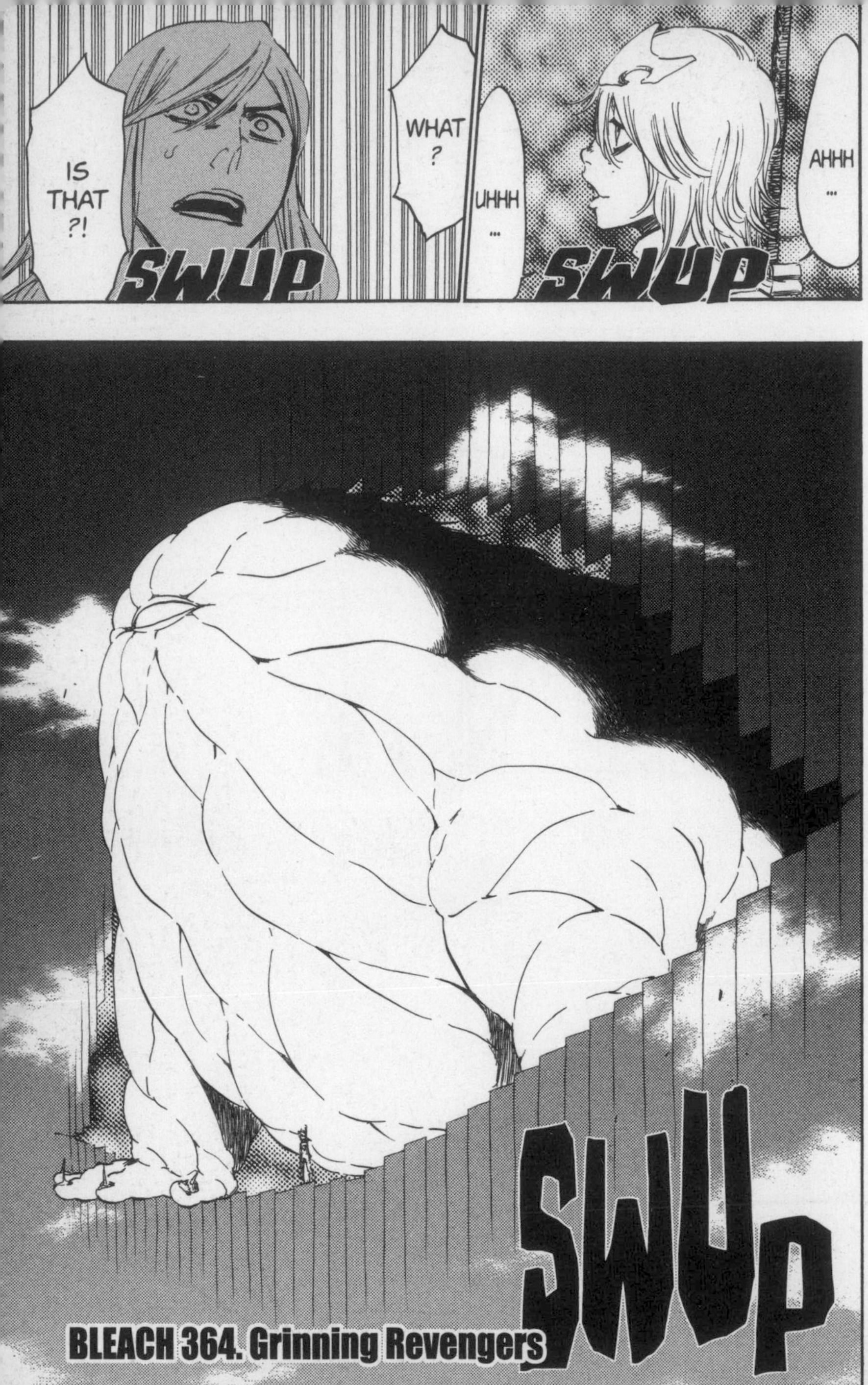
AHHH …
UHHH …
SWUP
WHAT?
IS THAT ?!
SWUP
SWUP
BLEACH 364. Grinning Revengers

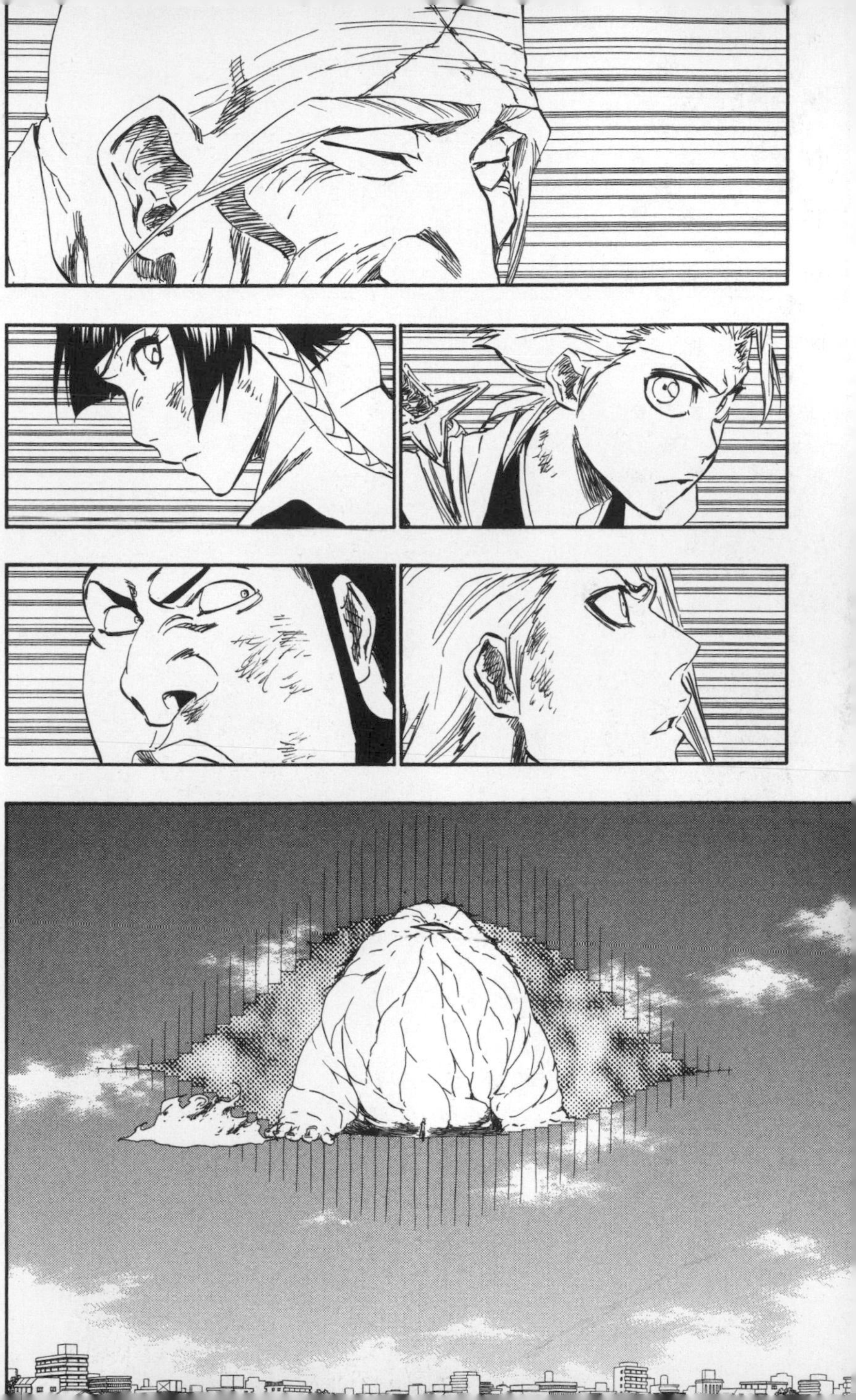

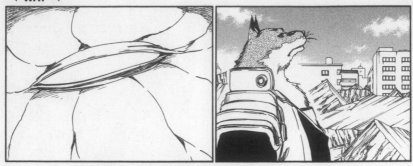

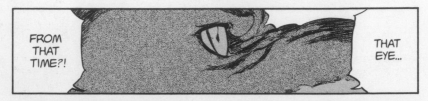

FROM THAT TIME?!

THAT EYE...

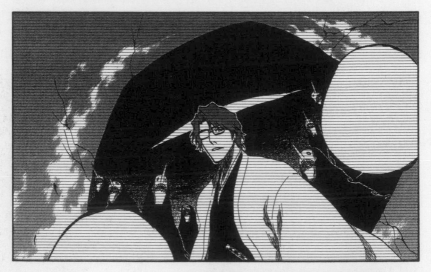

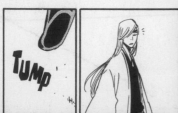

TUMP

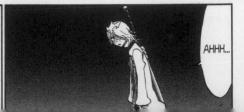

AHHH...

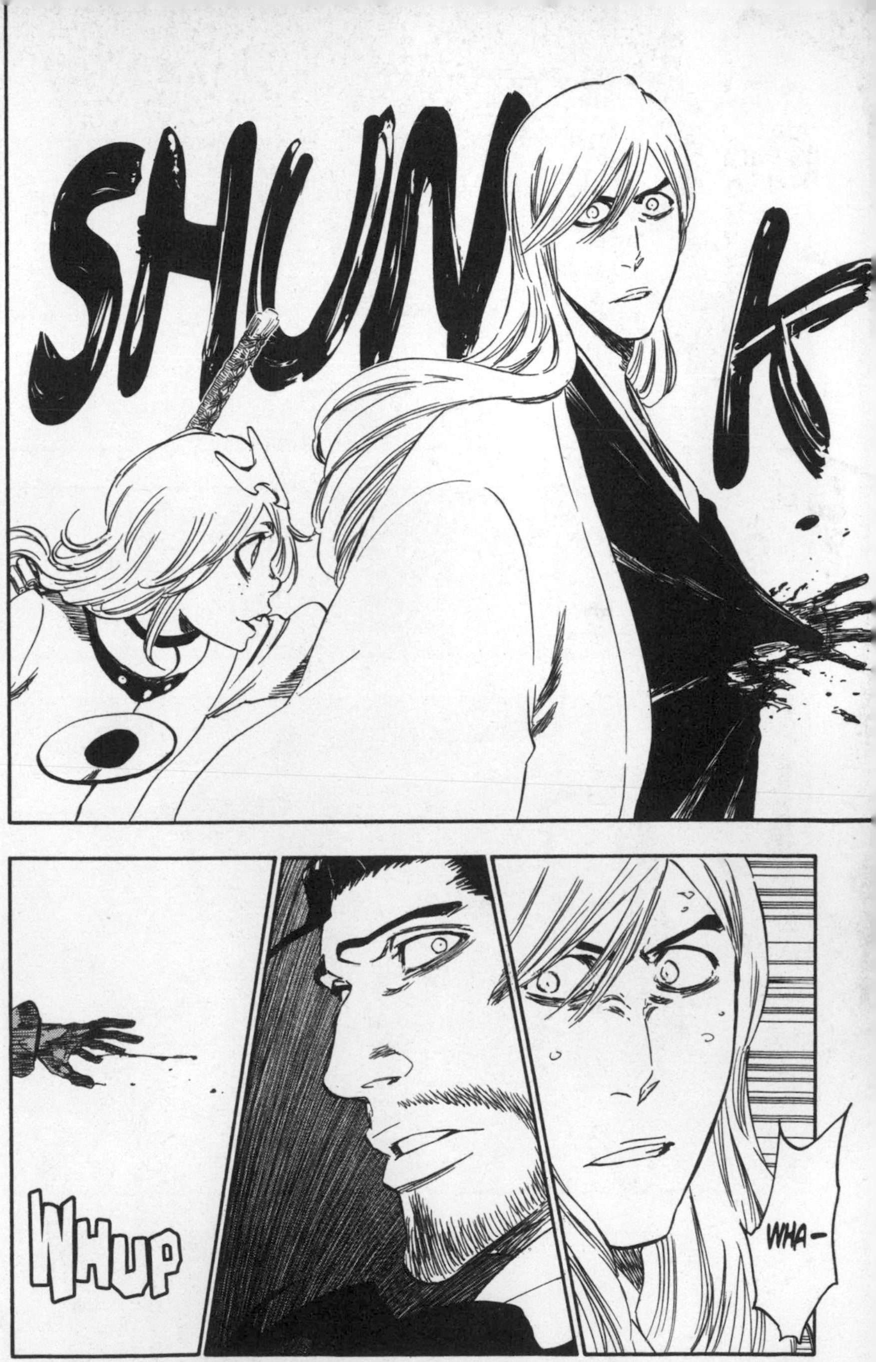
SHUNK
WHA-
WHUP

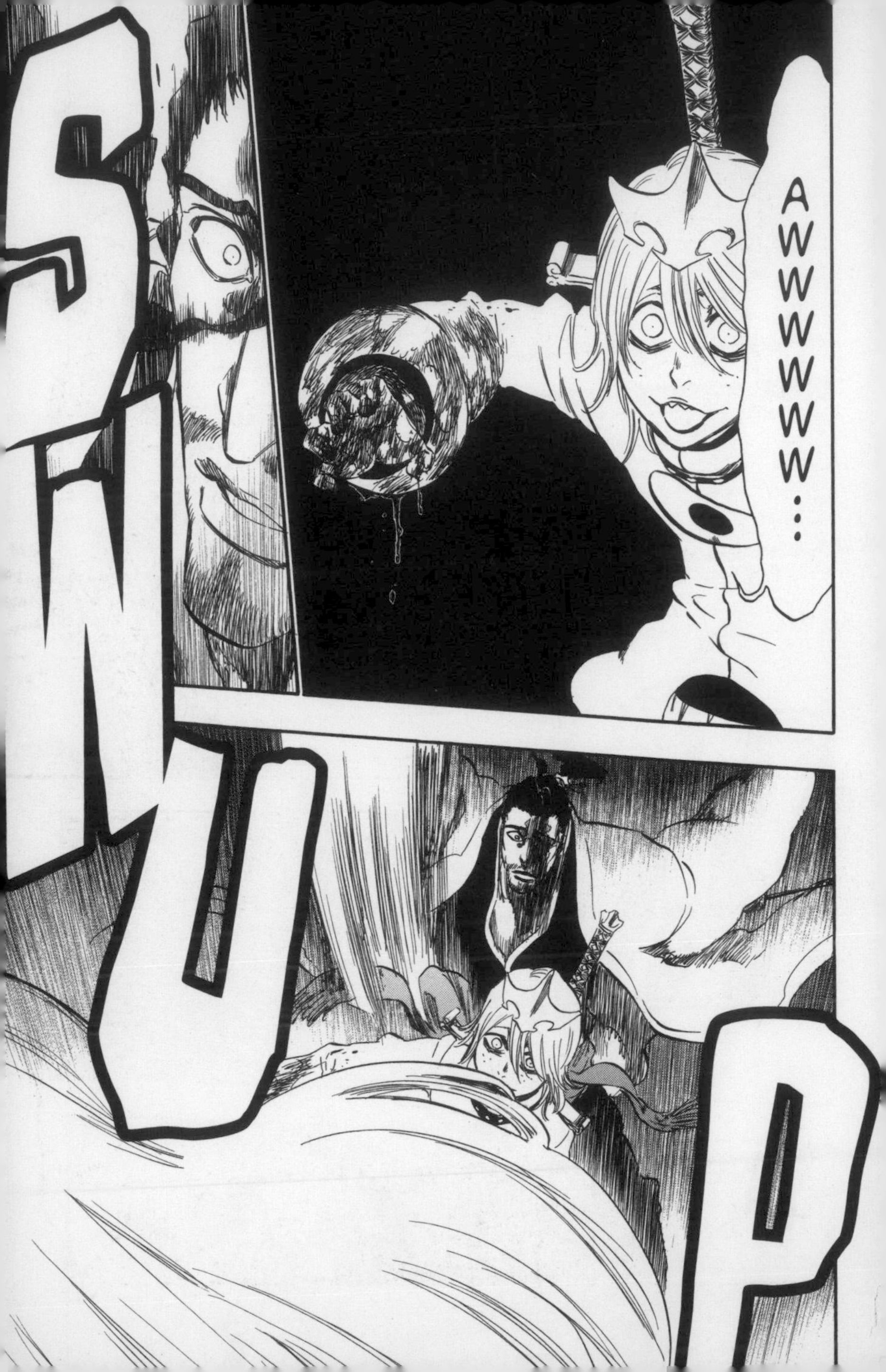
AWWWWWWW...
SWUP

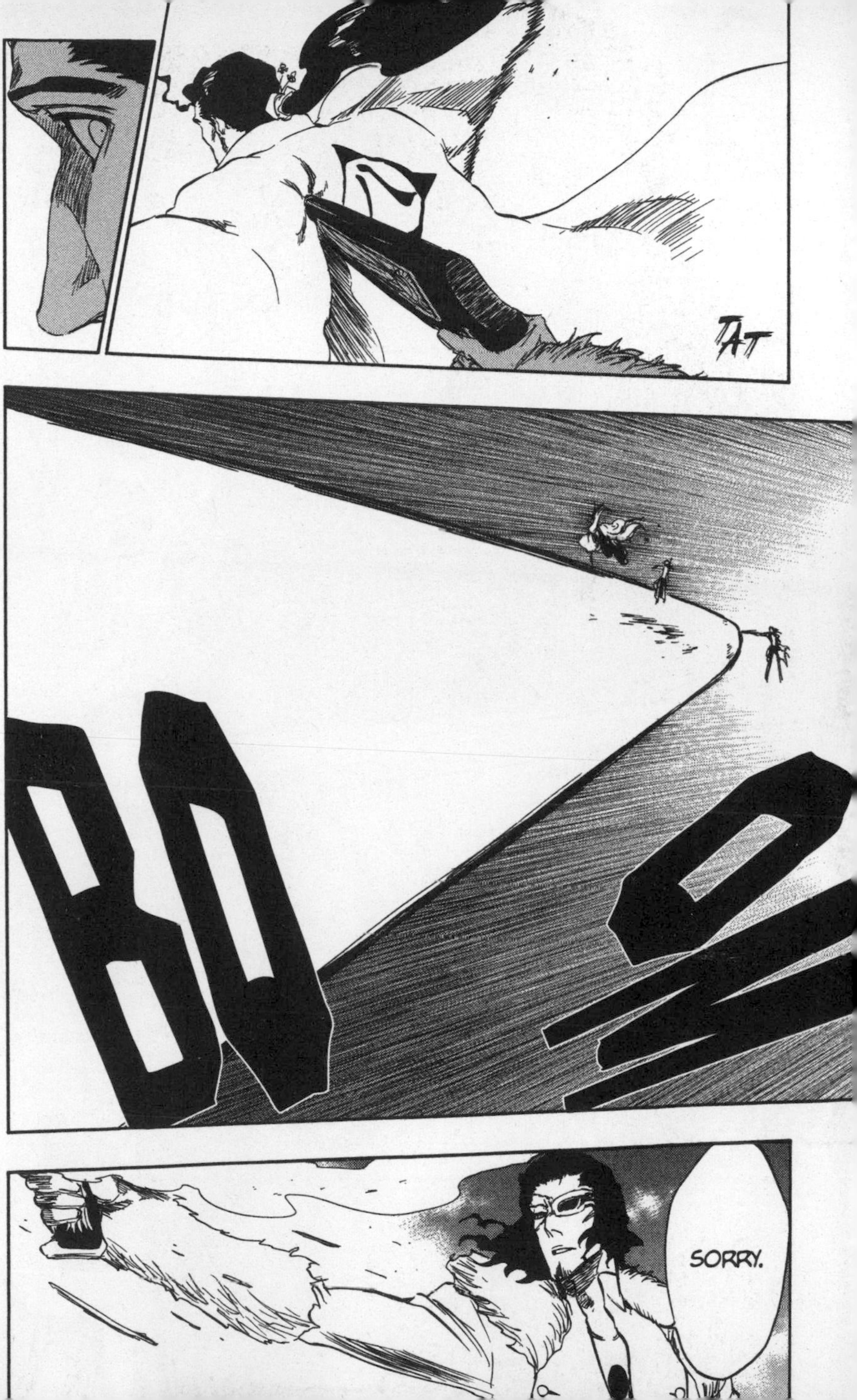
TAT
BOOM
SORRY.

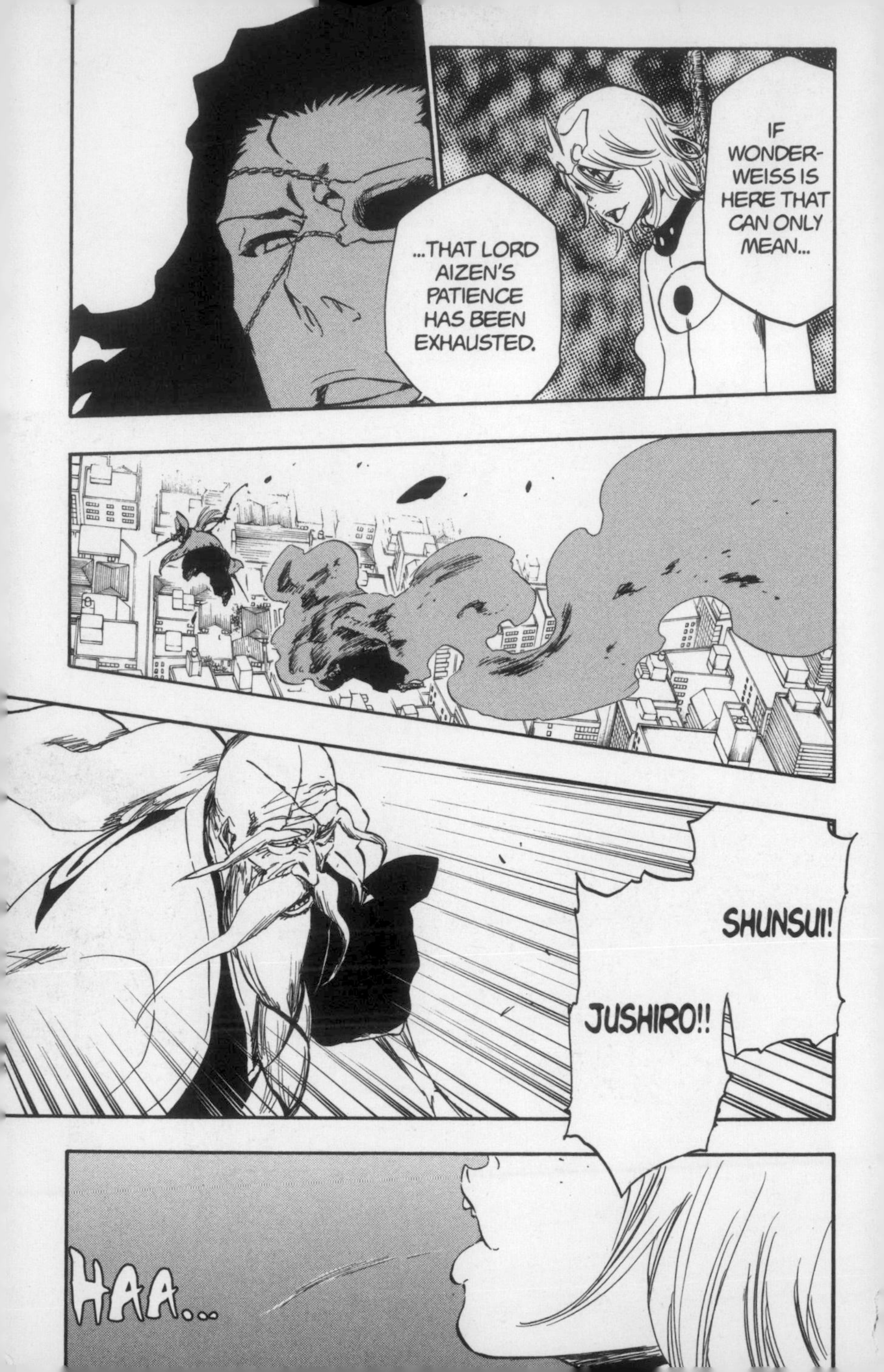
IF WONDER-WEISS IS HERE THAT CAN ONLY MEAN...
...THAT LORD AIZEN'S PATIENCE HAS BEEN EXHAUSTED.
SHUNSUI!
JUSHIRO!!
HAA...

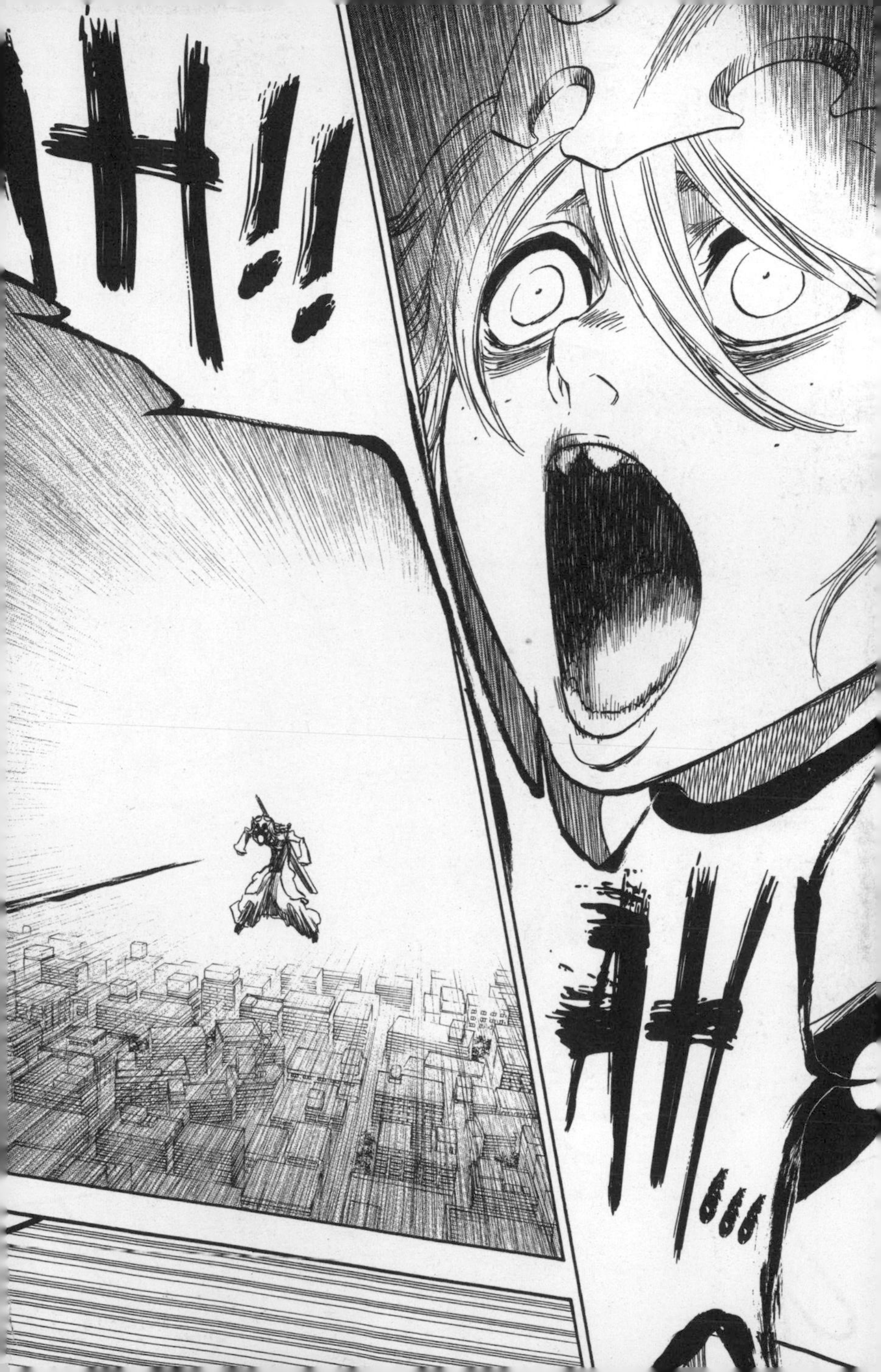
AH...
AH!!

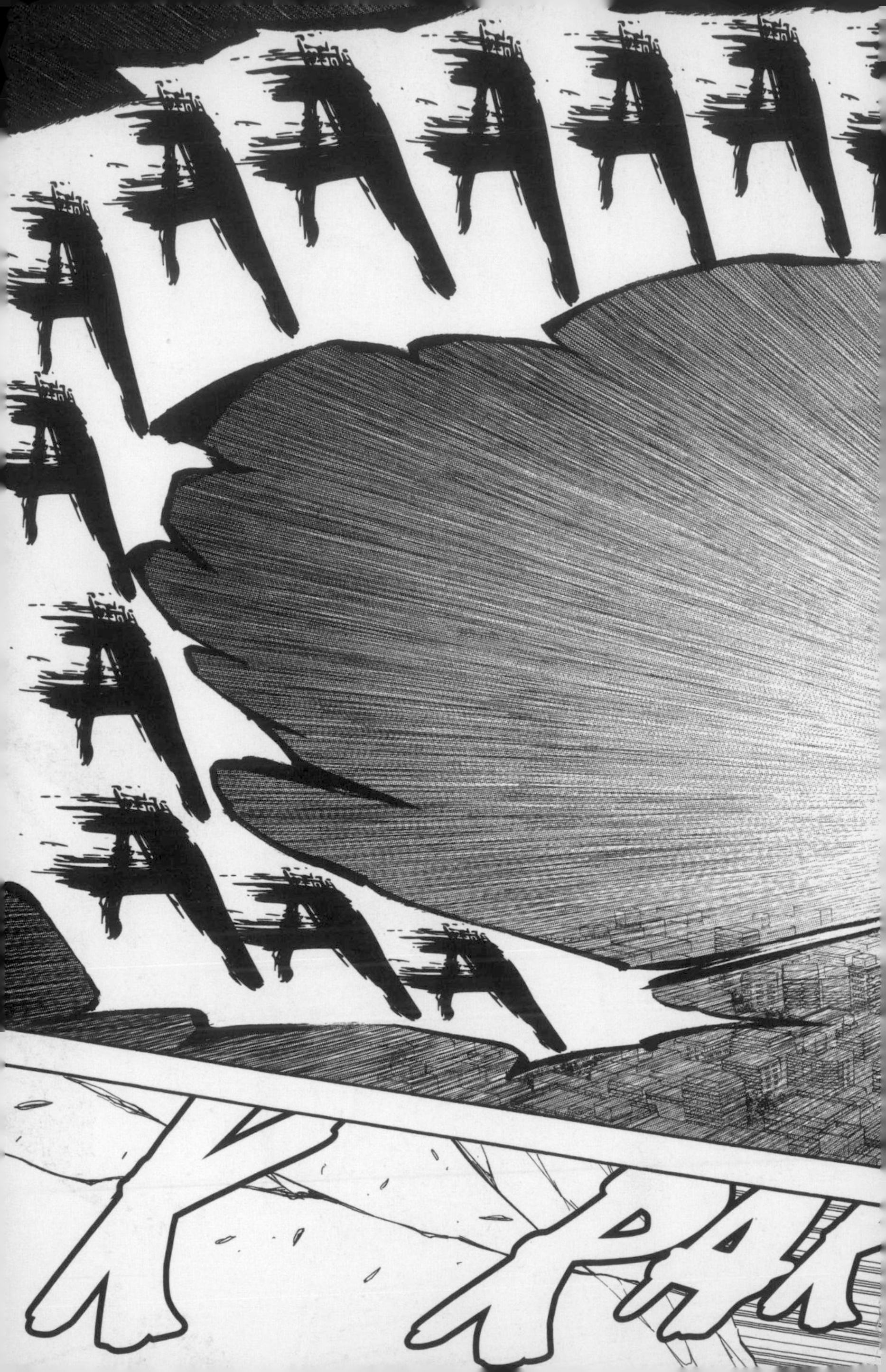
AAAAAAAAAAAA
KPA

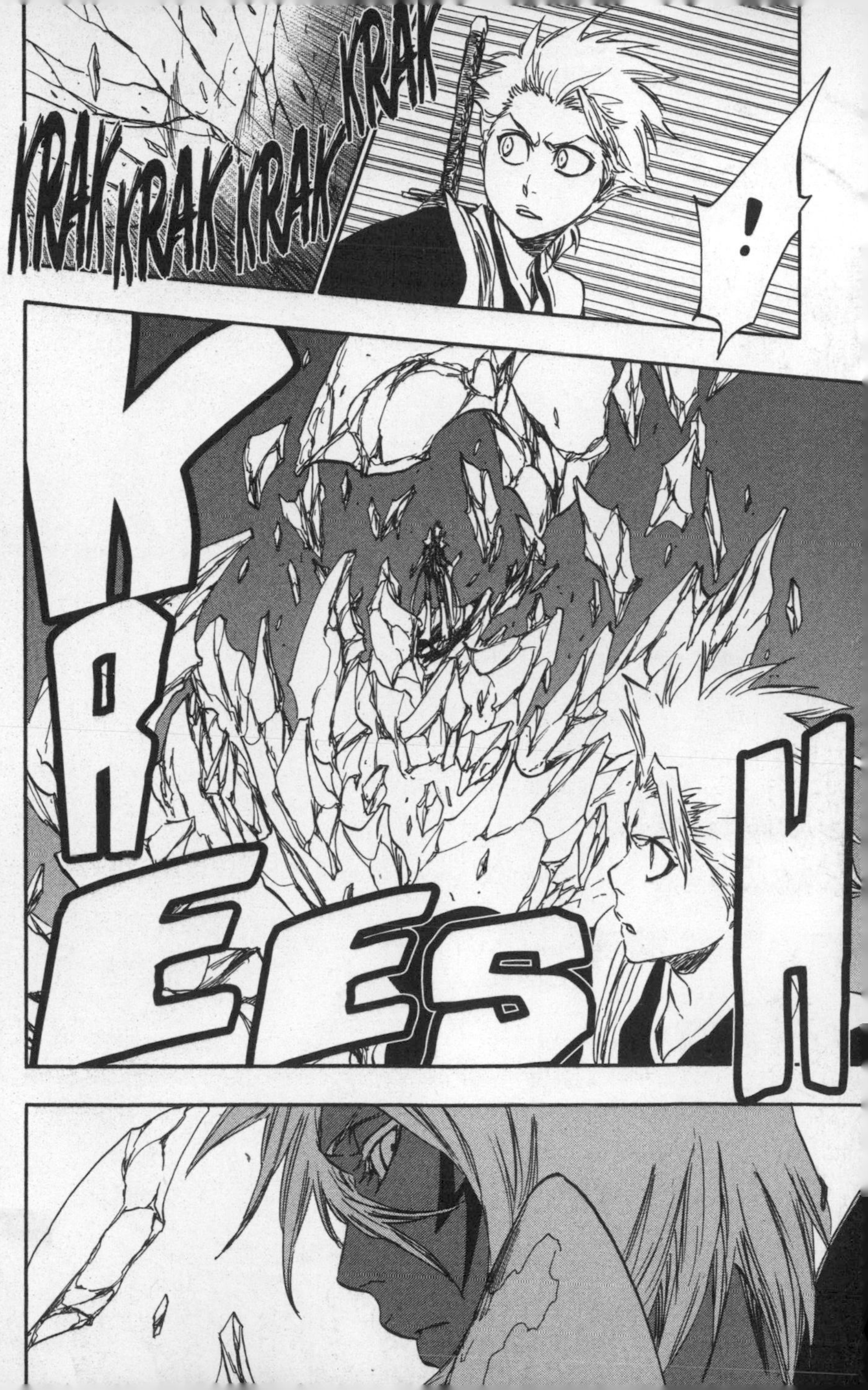

!
KRAK KRAK KRAK KRAK
KRAESH

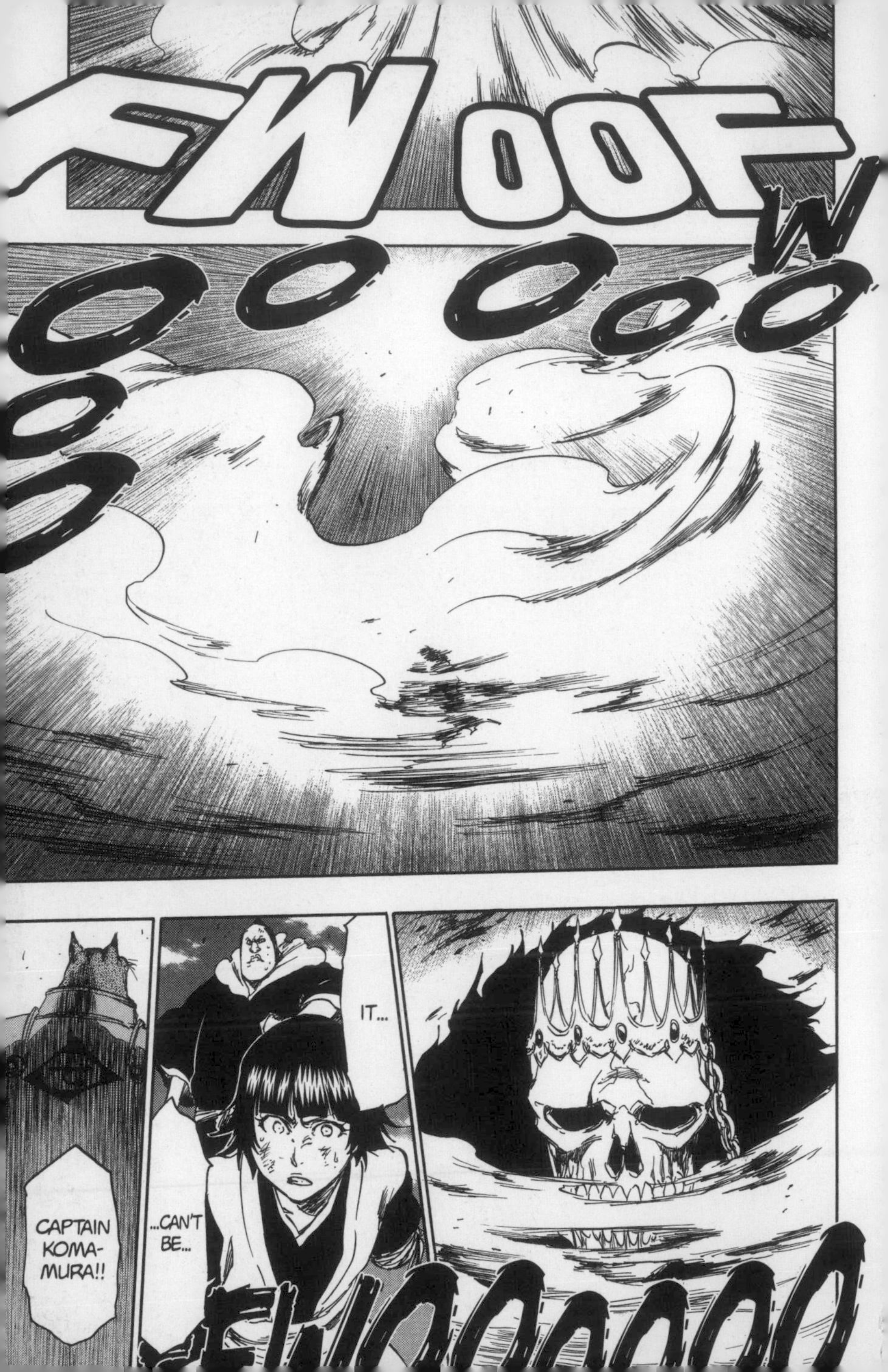
IT...
...CAN'T BE...
CAPTAIN KOMA-MURA!!

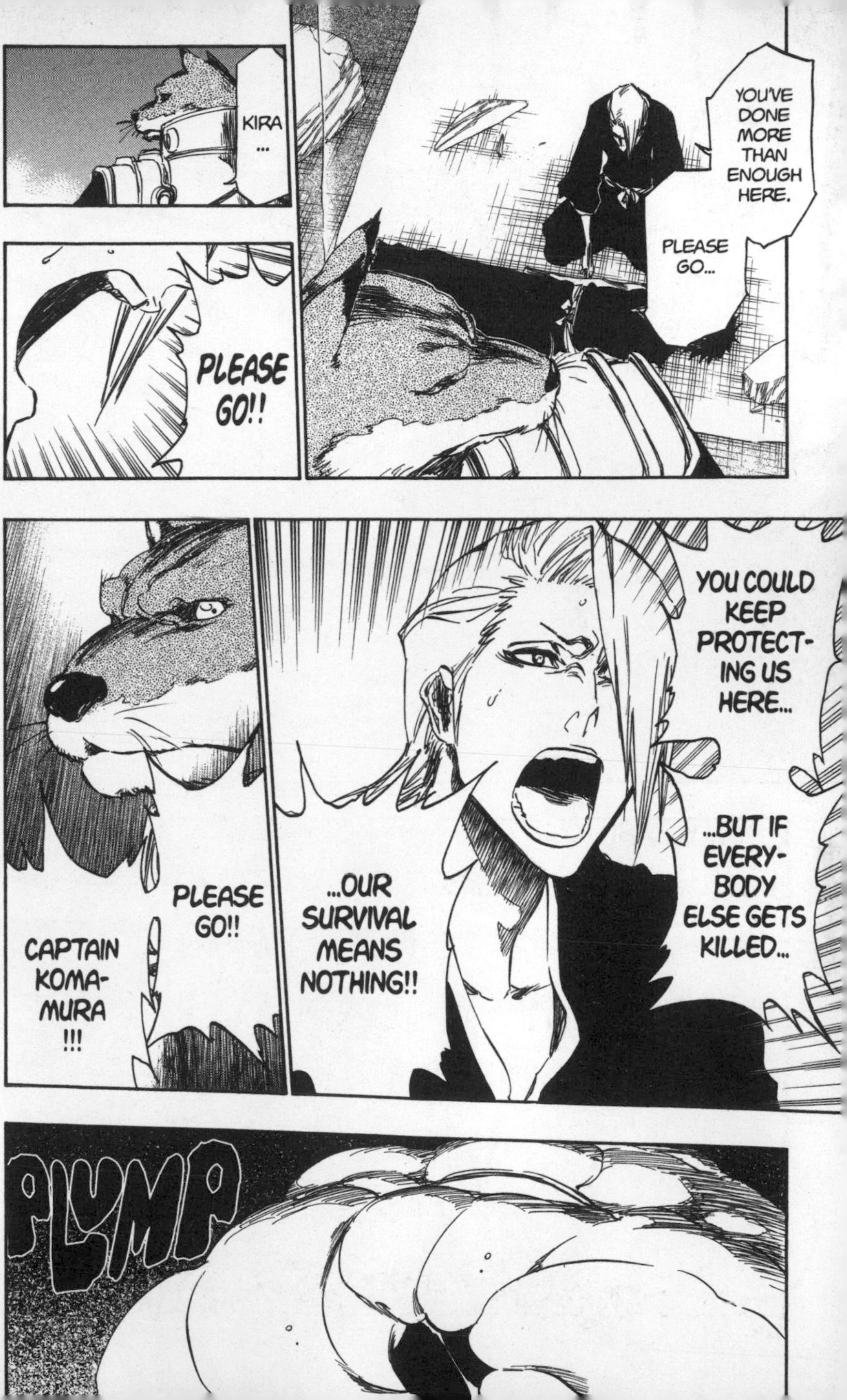
YOU'VE DONE MORE THAN ENOUGH HERE.
PLEASE GO...
KIRA ...
PLEASE GO!!
YOU COULD KEEP PROTECT-ING US HERE...
...BUT IF EVERY-BODY ELSE GETS KILLED...
...OUR SURVIVAL MEANS NOTHING!!
PLEASE GO!!
CAPTAIN KOMA-MURA !!!
PLUMP

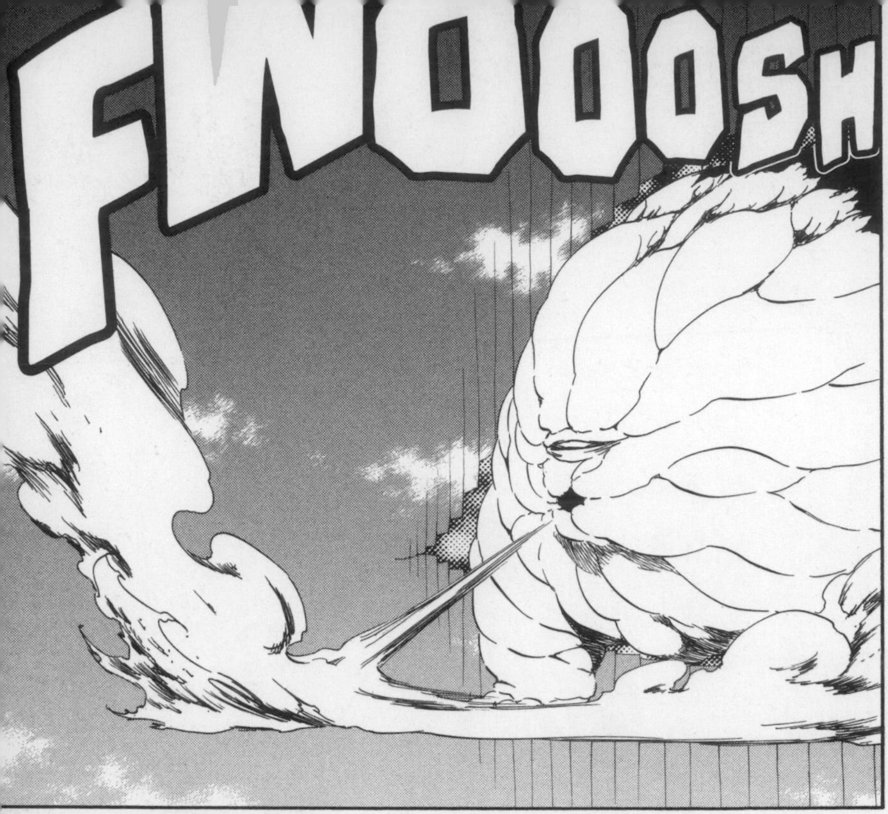
FWOOSH

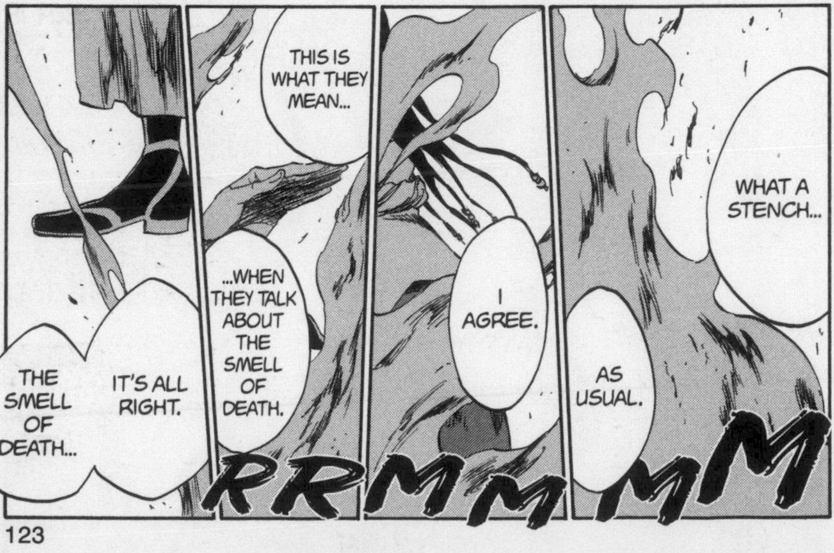
WHAT A STENCH...
AS USUAL.
I AGREE.
THIS IS WHAT THEY MEAN...
...WHEN THEY TALK ABOUT THE SMELL OF DEATH.
IT'S ALL RIGHT.
THE SMELL OF DEATH...
RRMMMMM

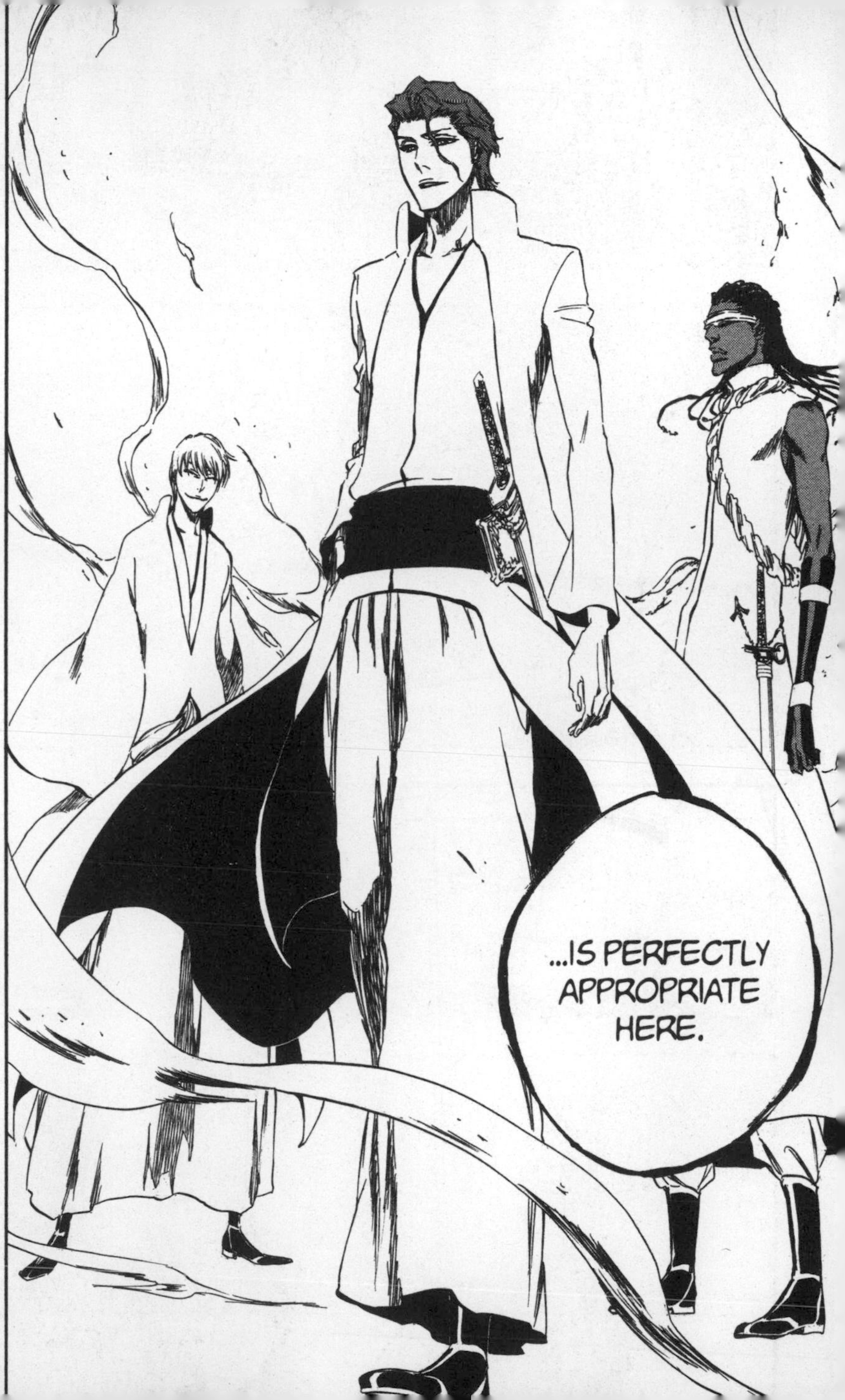
...IS PERFECTLY APPROPRIATE HERE.

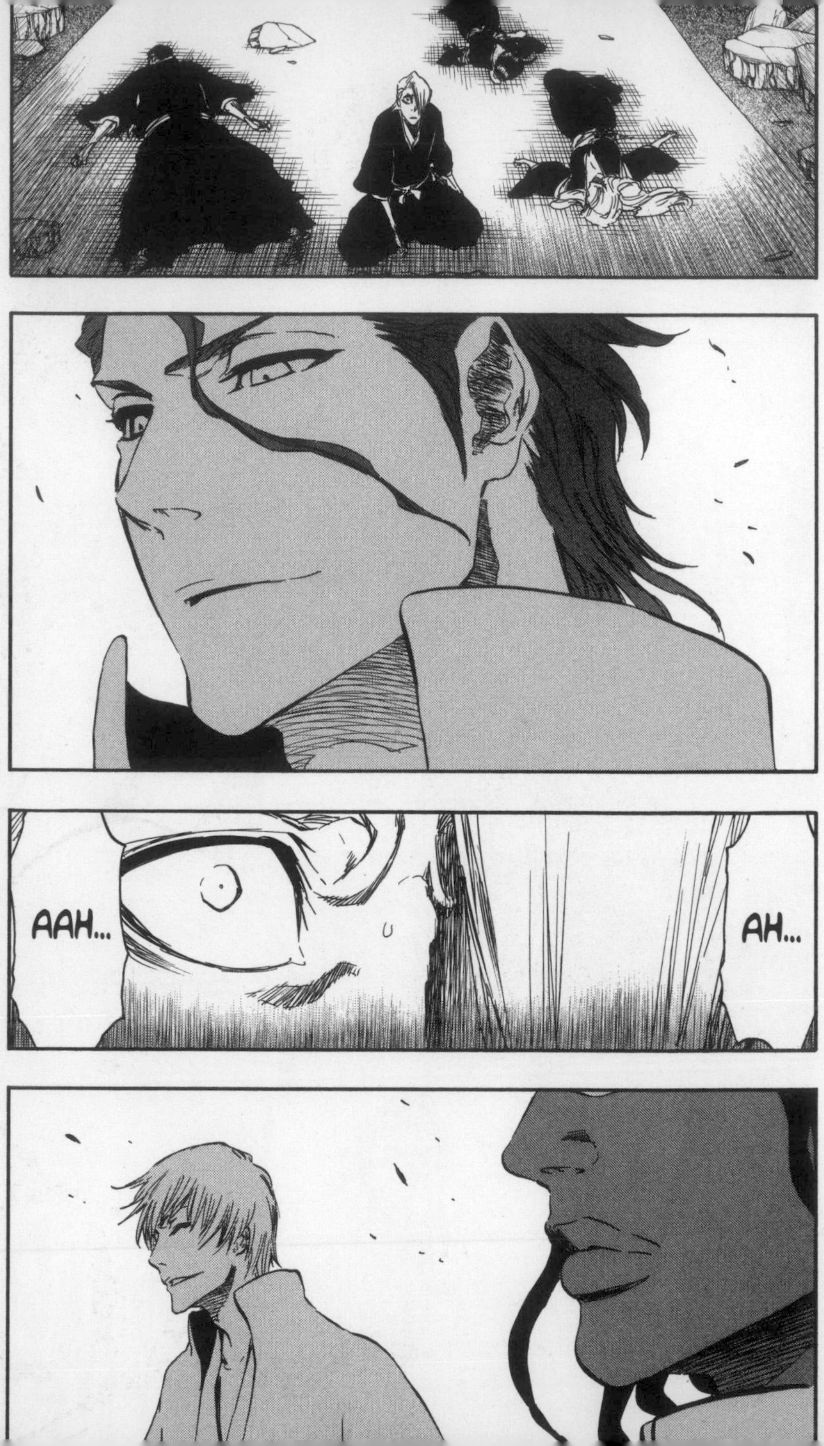
AH...
AAH...

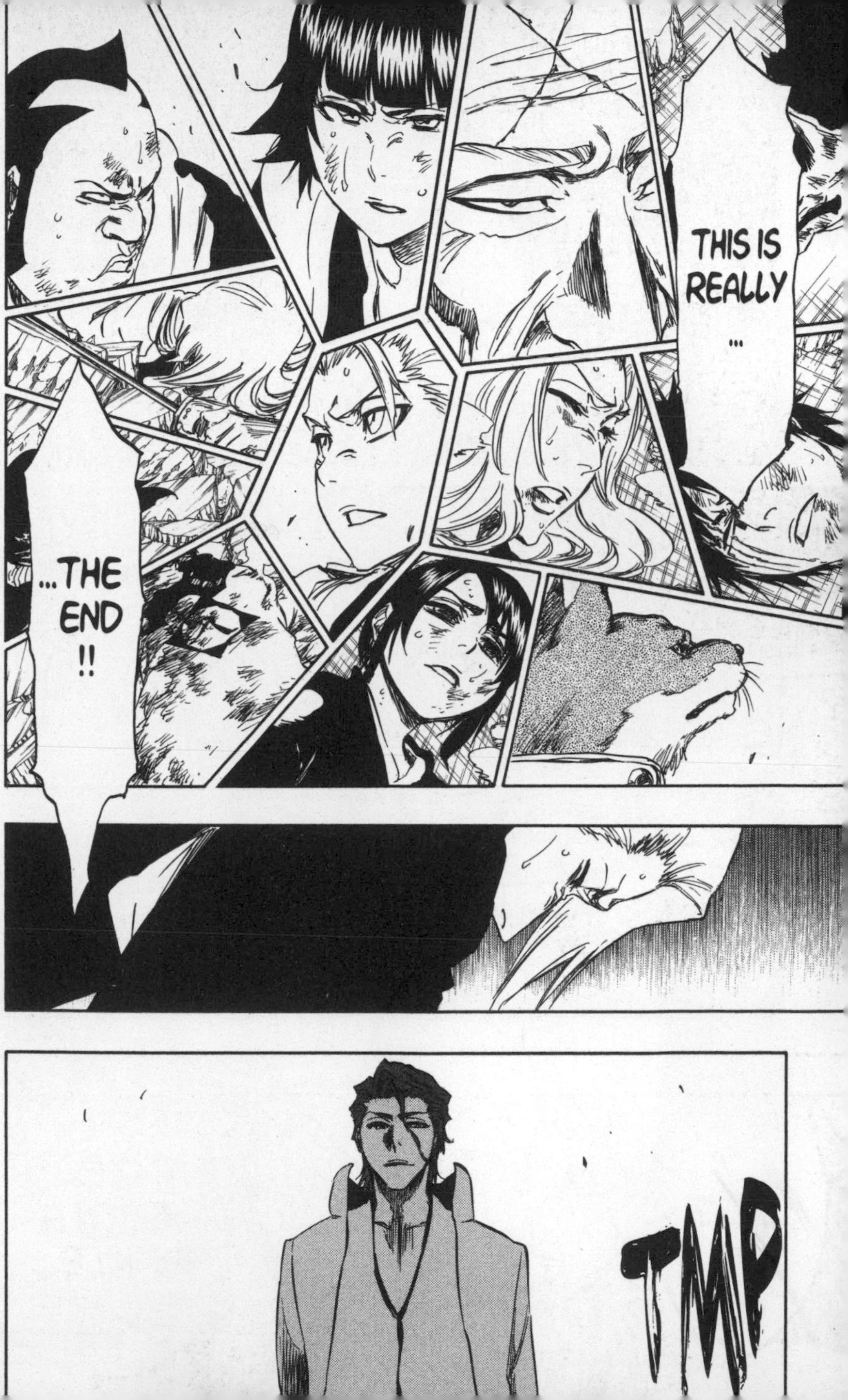
THIS IS REALLY
...
...THE END !!
TMP

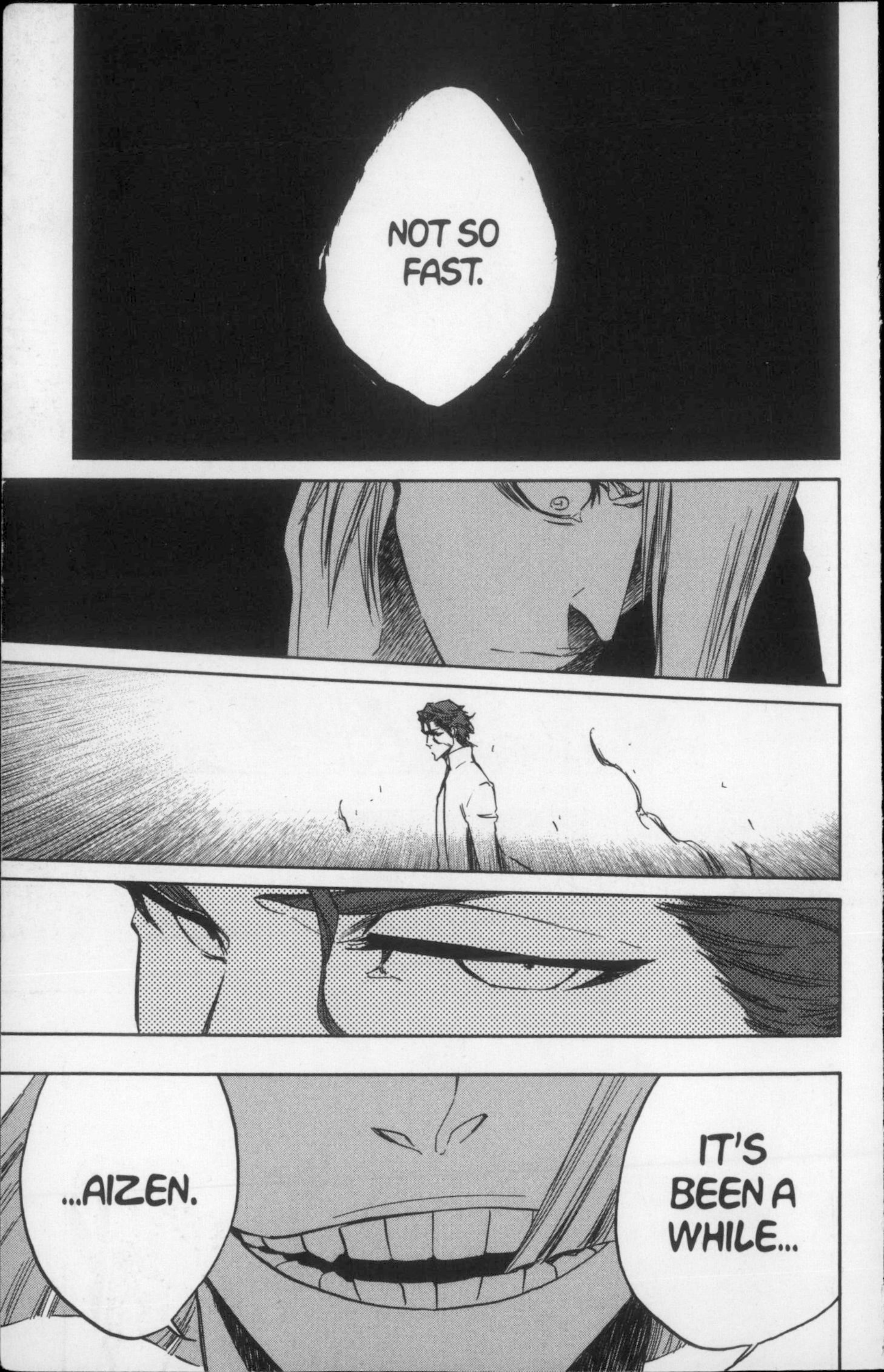
NOT SO FAST.
IT'S BEEN A WHILE...
...AIZEN.

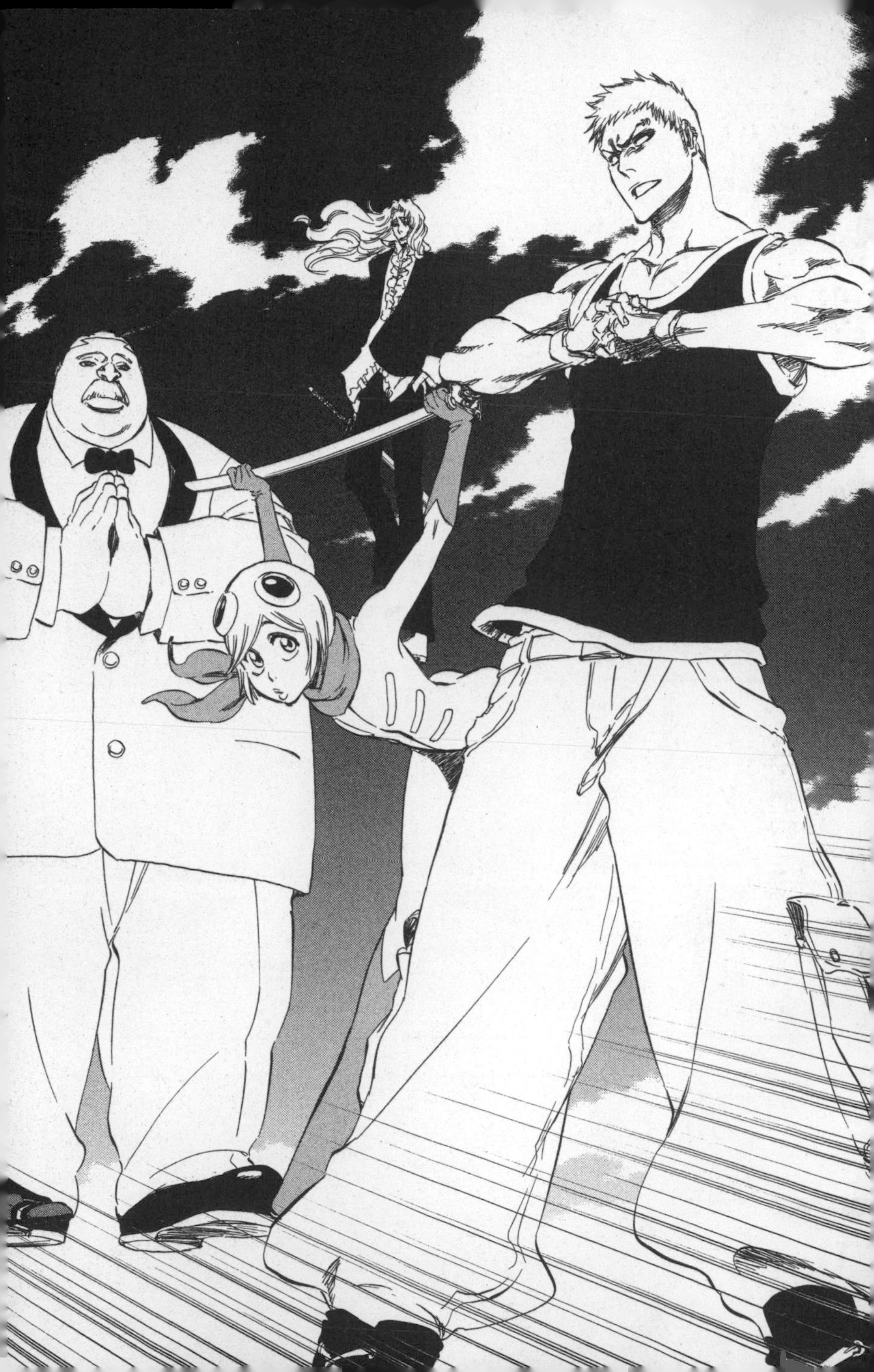

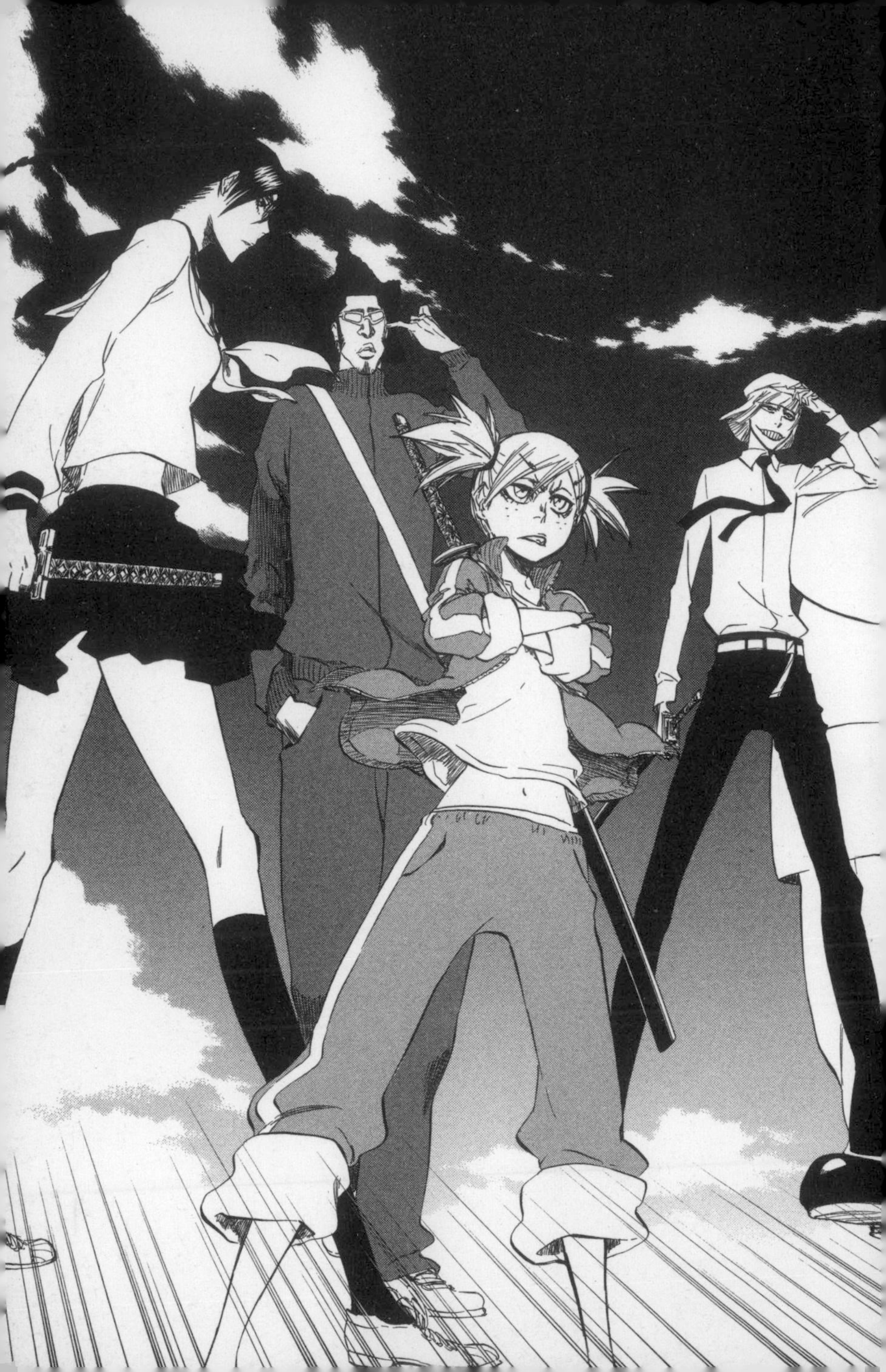

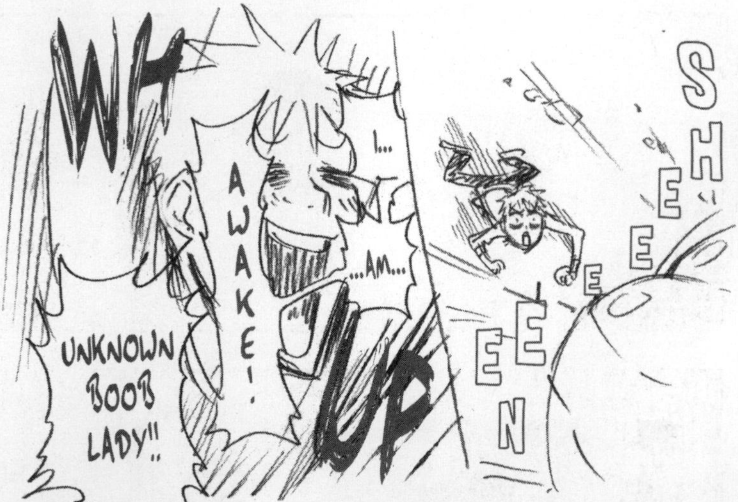
SHEEEEEN
I...
...AM...
AWAKE!
WH
UP
UNKNOWN BOOB LADY!!

365. Whose Side Are We On

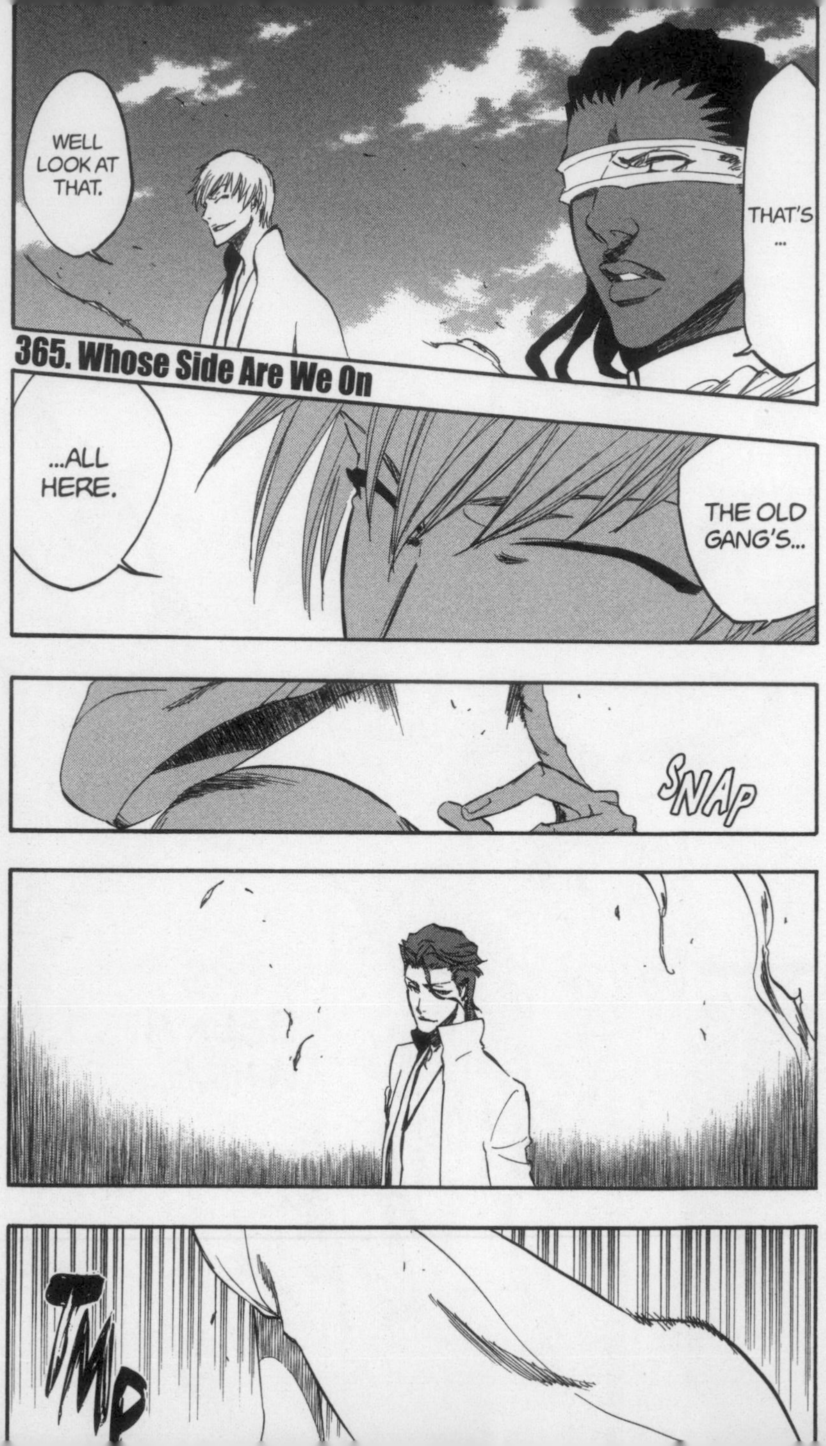
THAT'S...
WELL LOOK AT THAT.
THE OLD GANG'S...
...ALL HERE.
SNAP
TMP

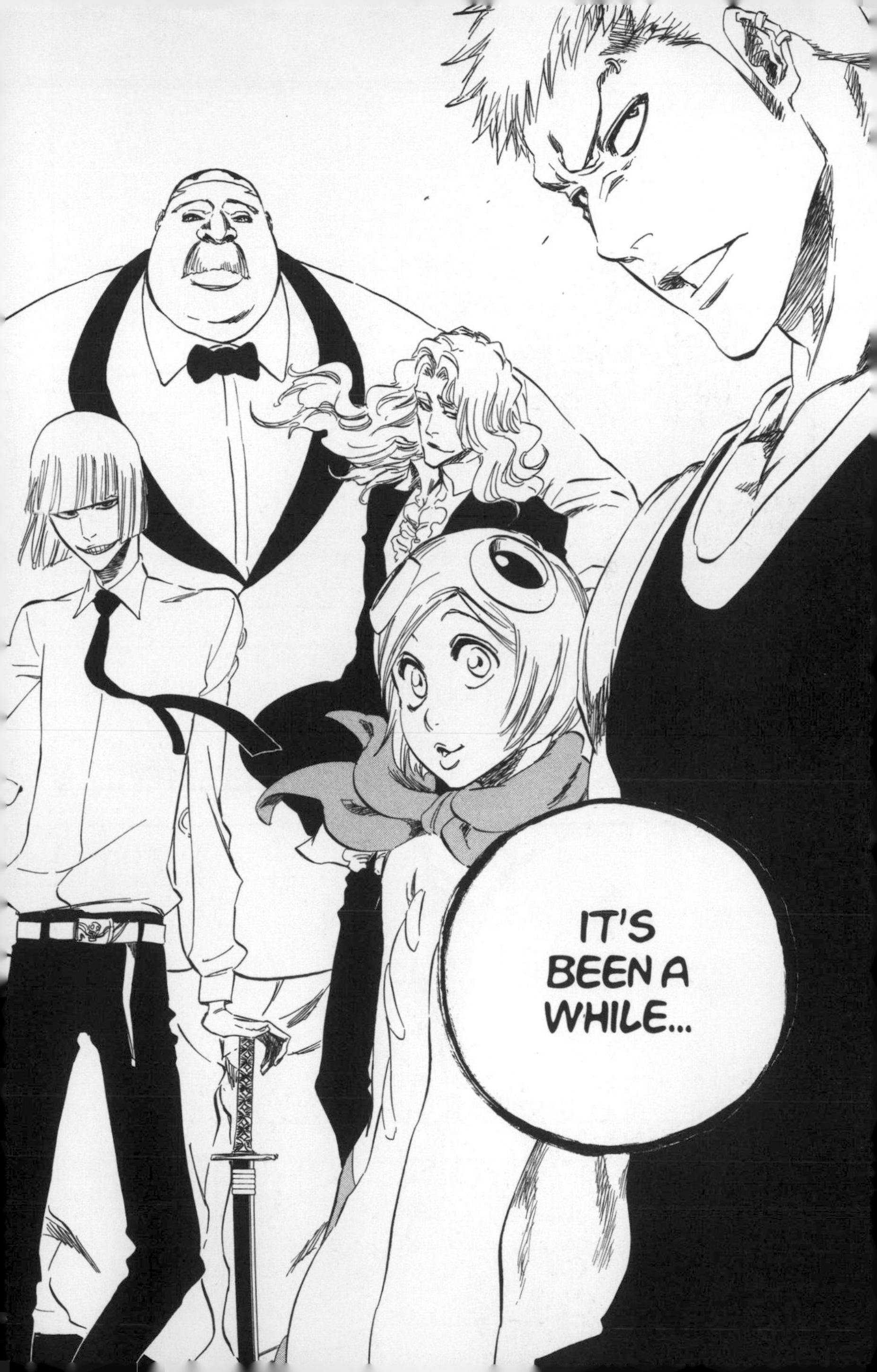
IT'S BEEN A WHILE...

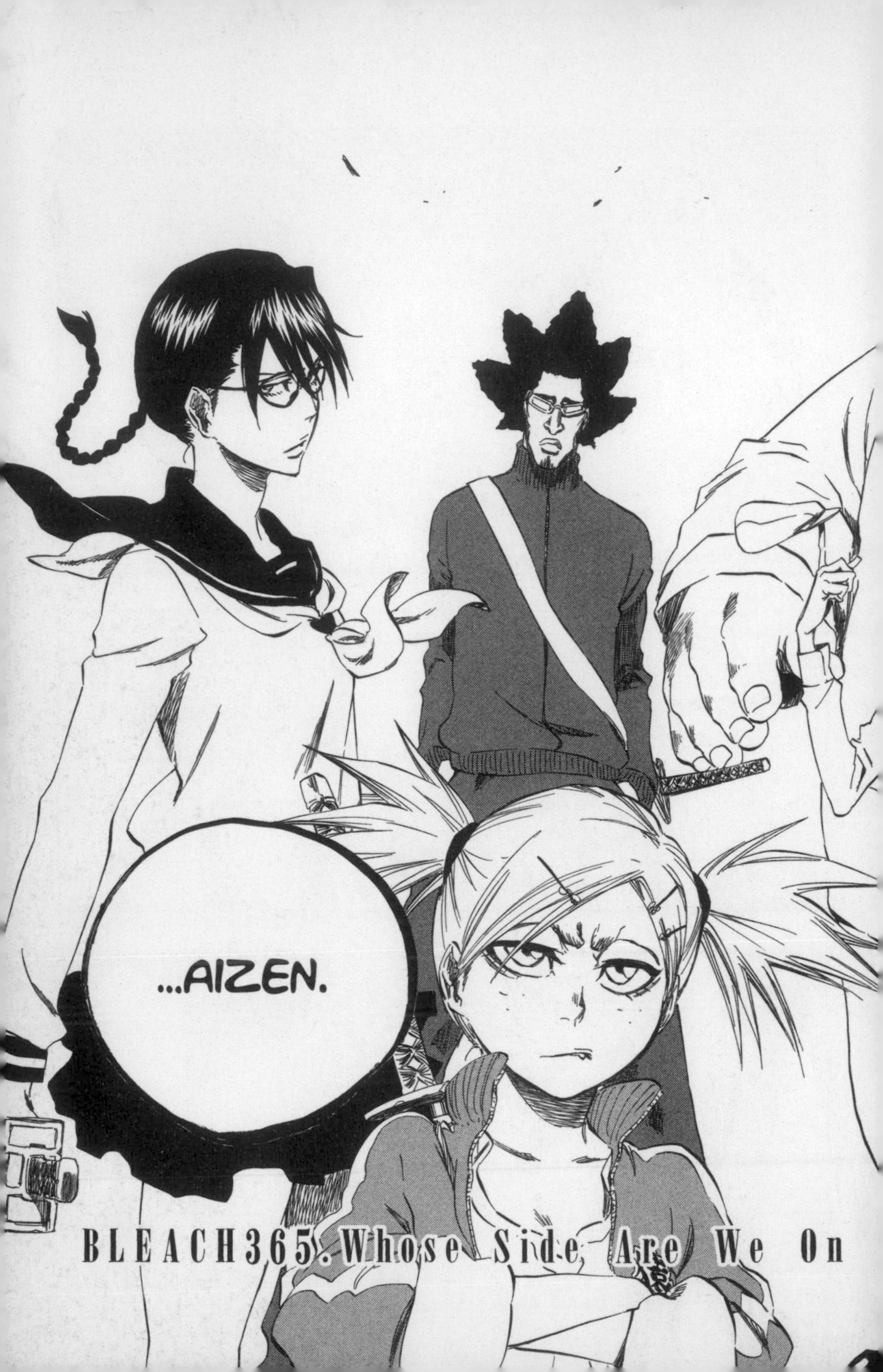
...AIZEN.
BLEACH 365. Whose Side Are We On

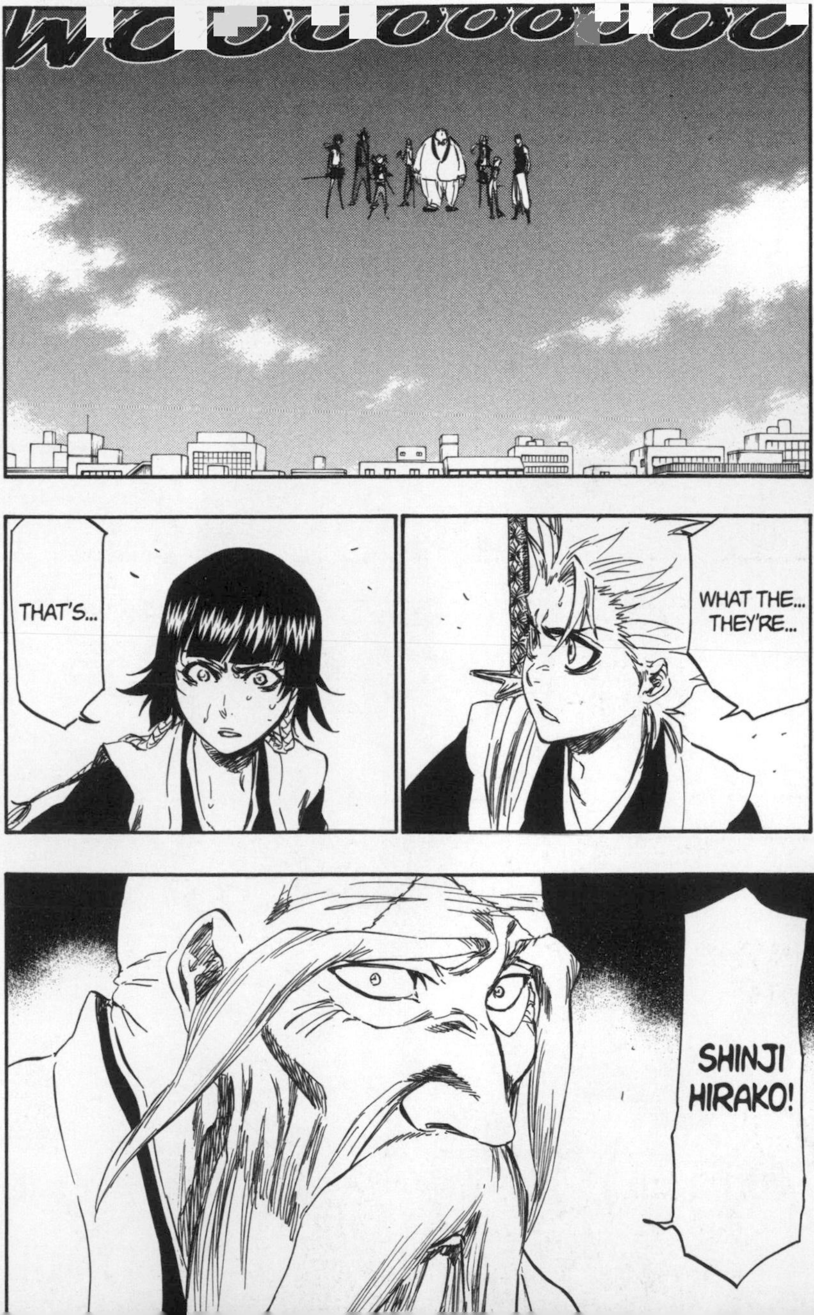
WHAT THE... THEY'RE...
THAT'S...
SHINJI HIRAKO!

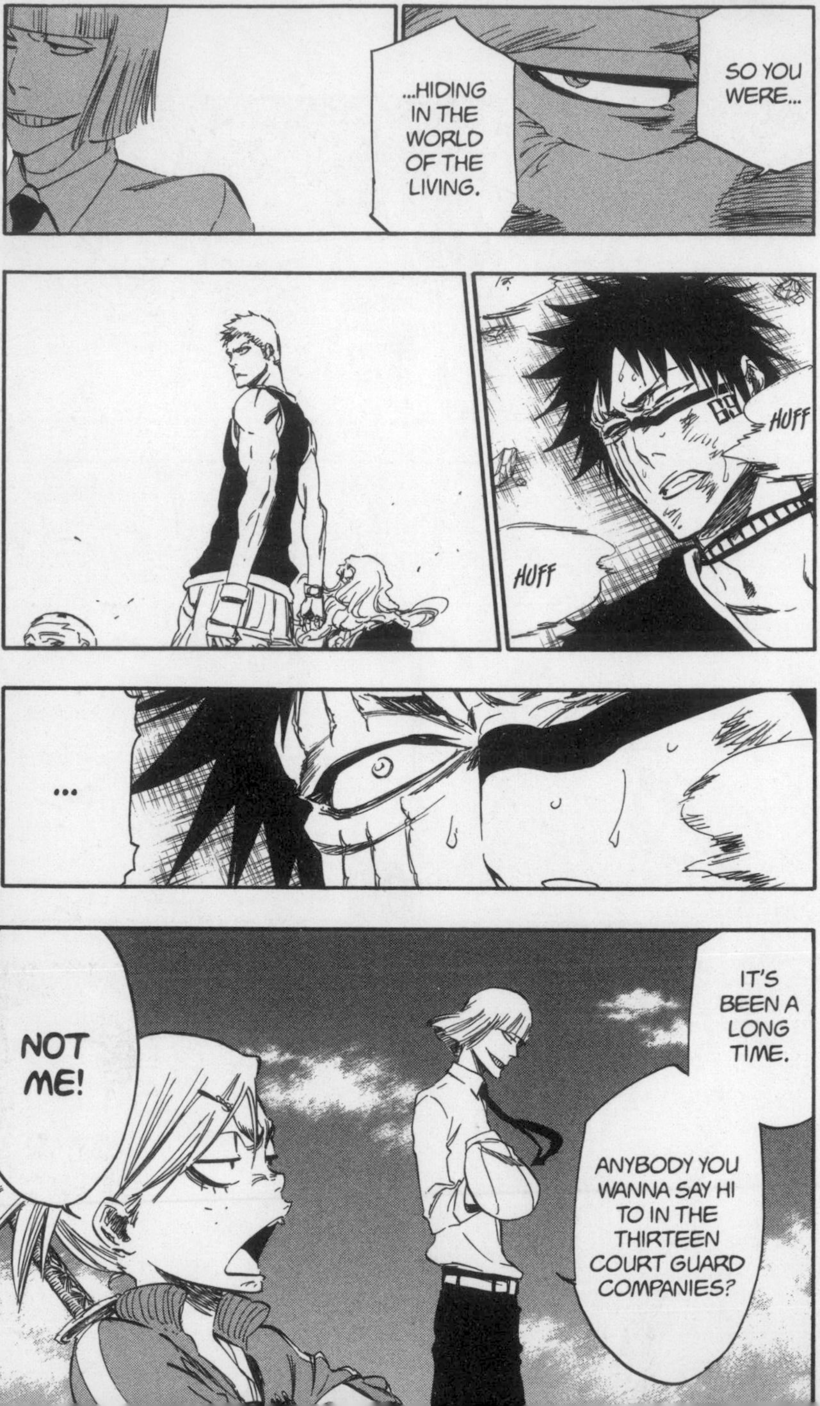
SO YOU WERE...
...HIDING IN THE WORLD OF THE LIVING.
HUFF
HUFF
...
IT'S BEEN A LONG TIME.
ANYBODY YOU WANNA SAY HI TO IN THE THIRTEEN COURT GUARD COMPANIES?
NOT ME!

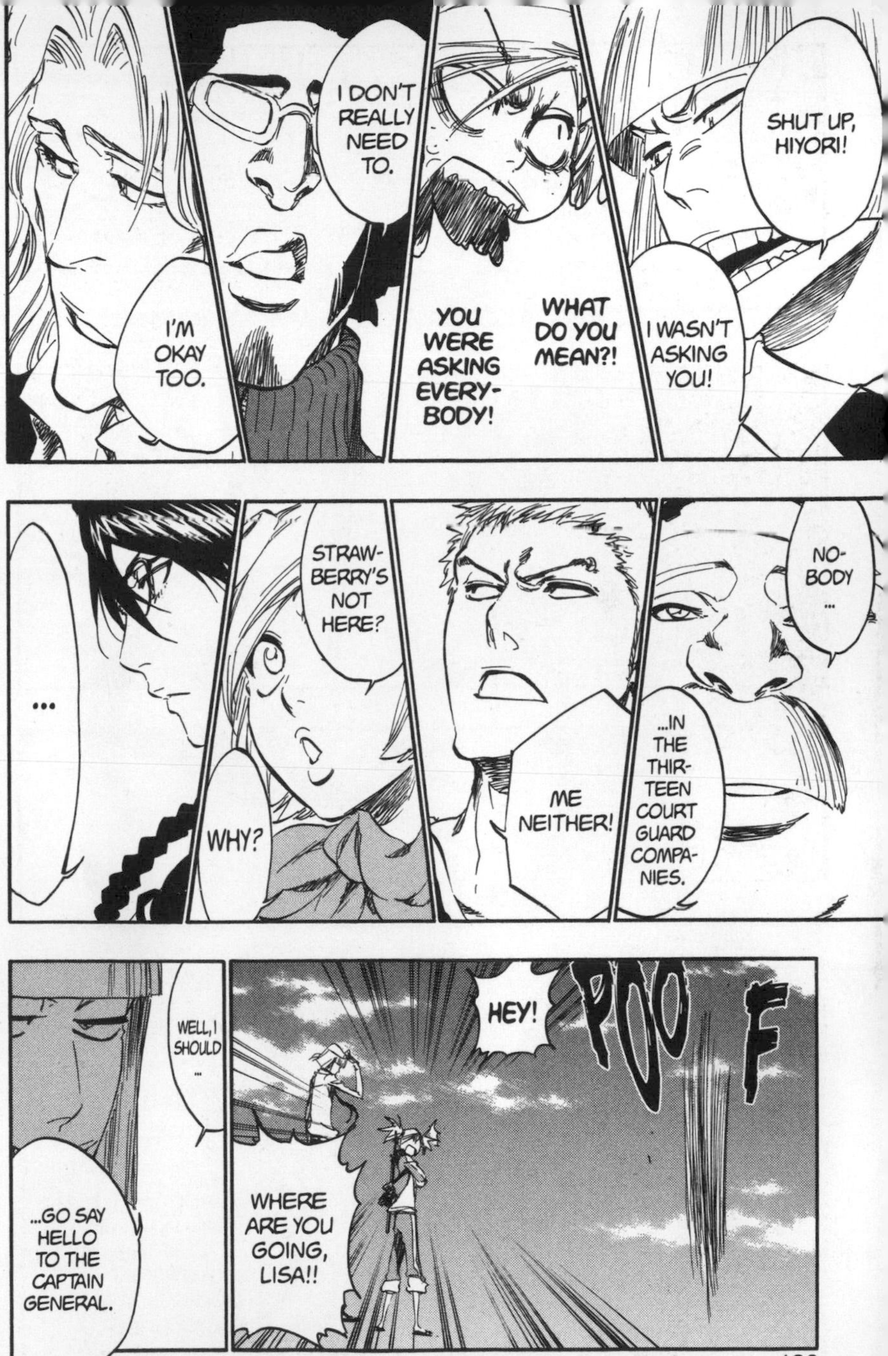
SHUT UP, HIYORI!
I WASN'T ASKING YOU!
WHAT DO YOU MEAN?!
YOU WERE ASKING EVERY-BODY!
I DON'T REALLY NEED TO.
I'M OKAY TOO.
NO-BODY ...
...IN THE THIR-TEEN COURT GUARD COMPA-NIES.
ME NEITHER!
STRAW-BERRY'S NOT HERE?
WHY?
...
HEY!
POOF
WHERE ARE YOU GOING, LISA!!
WELL, I SHOULD ...
...GO SAY HELLO TO THE CAPTAIN GENERAL.

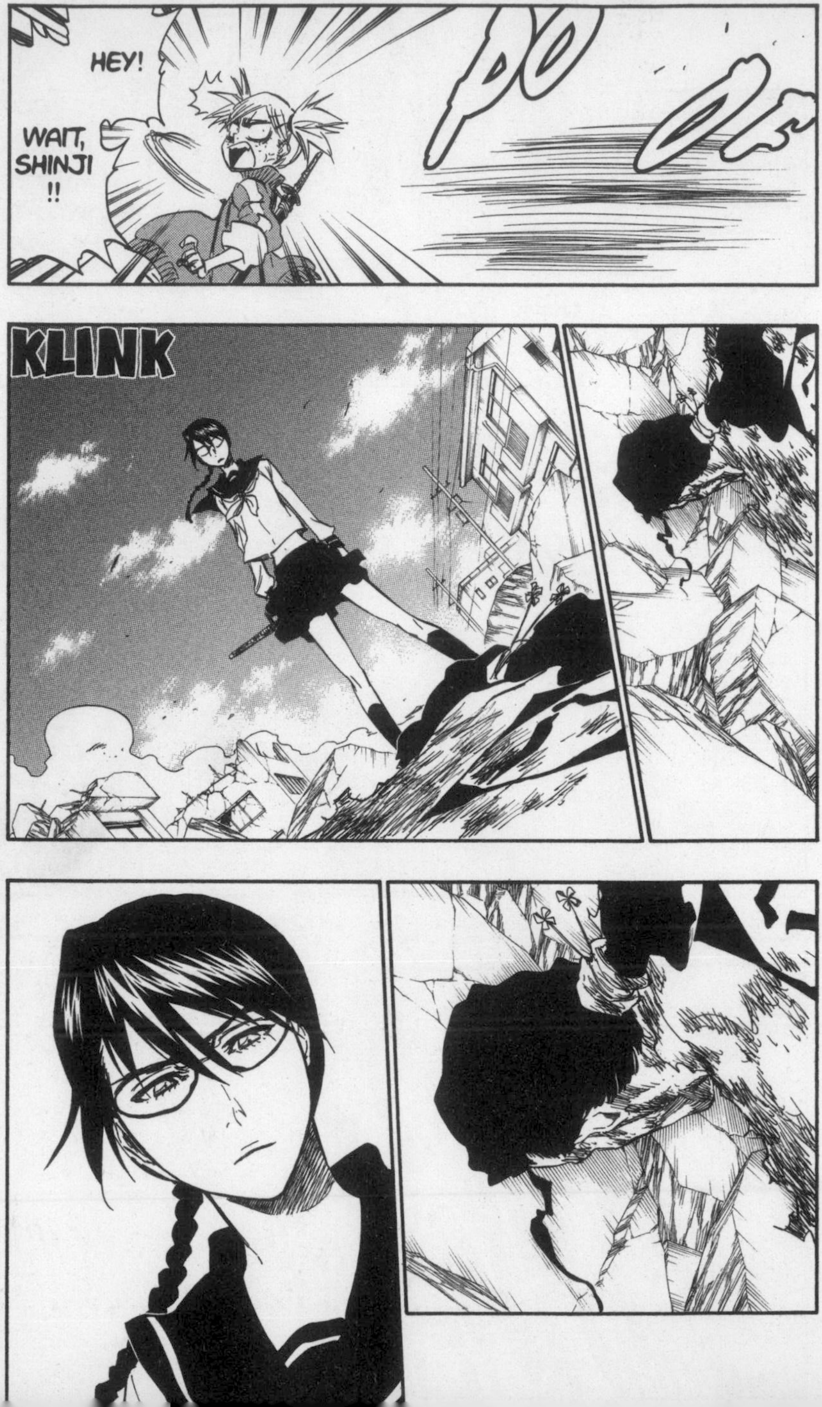
HEY!
WAIT, SHINJI!!
KLINK

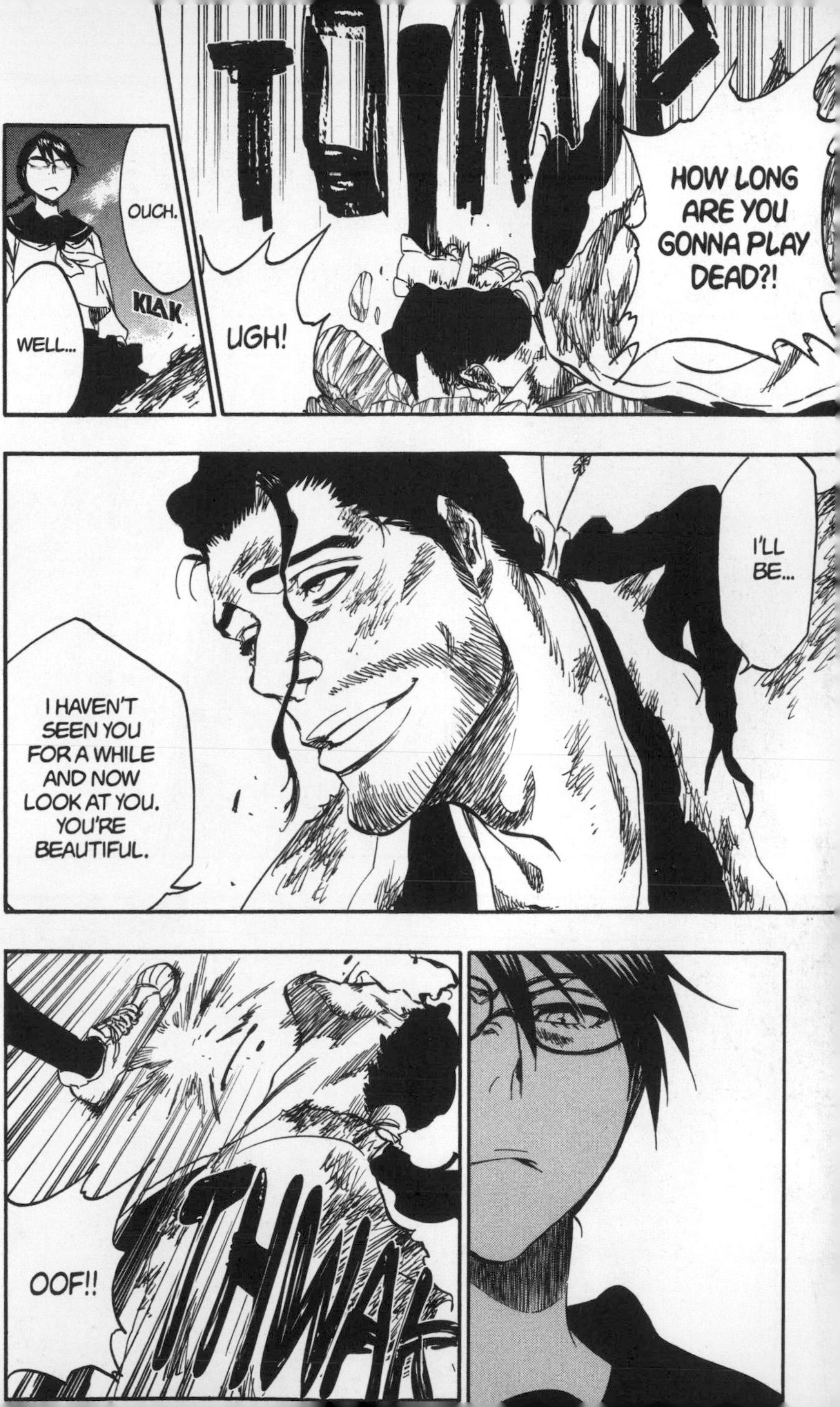
THUMP
HOW LONG ARE YOU GONNA PLAY DEAD?!
UGH!
OUCH.
KLAK
WELL...
I'LL BE...
I HAVEN'T SEEN YOU FOR A WHILE AND NOW LOOK AT YOU. YOU'RE BEAUTIFUL.
THWAK
OOF!!

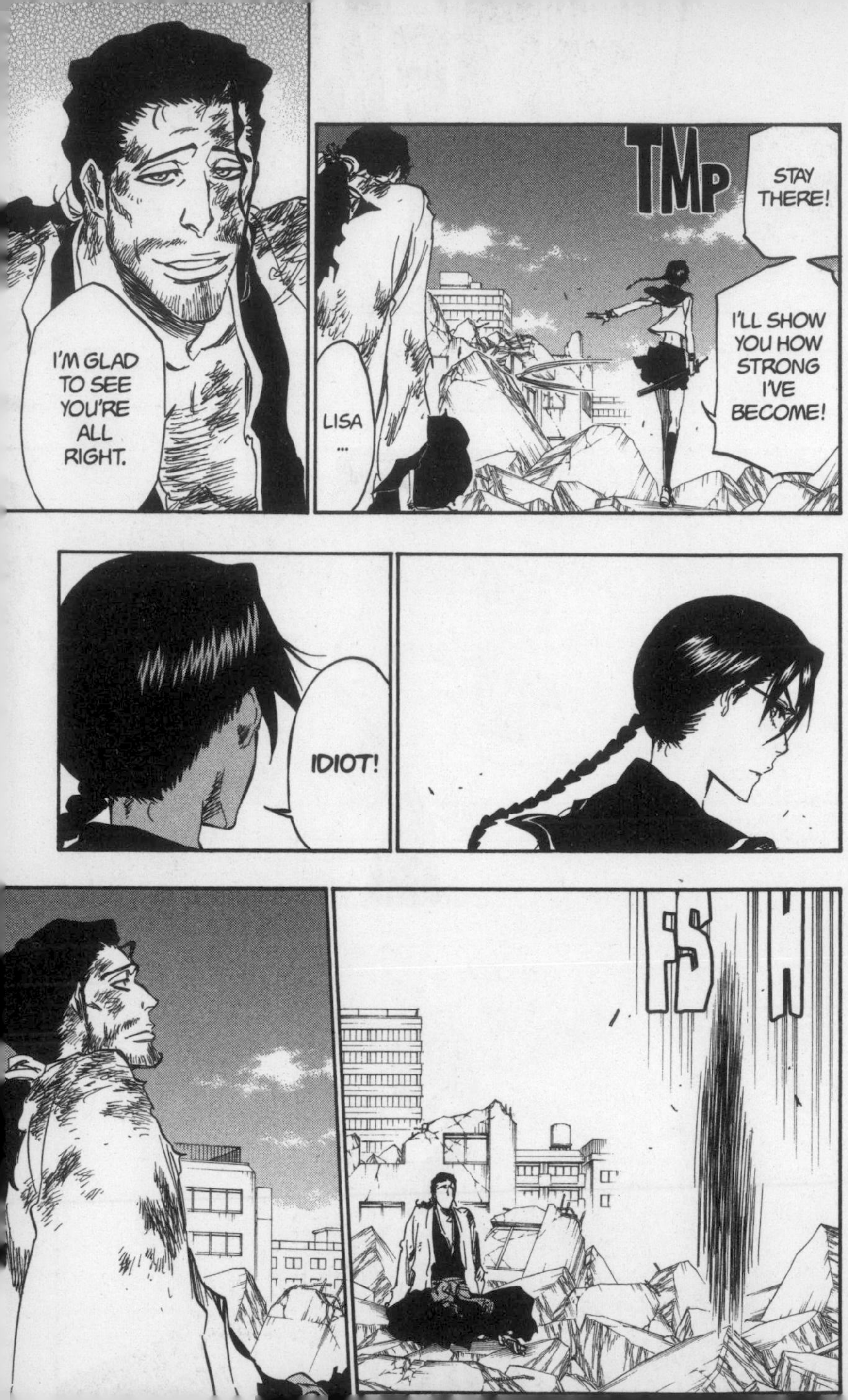
TMP
STAY THERE!
I'LL SHOW YOU HOW STRONG I'VE BECOME!
LISA ...
I'M GLAD TO SEE YOU'RE ALL RIGHT.
IDIOT!
FSH

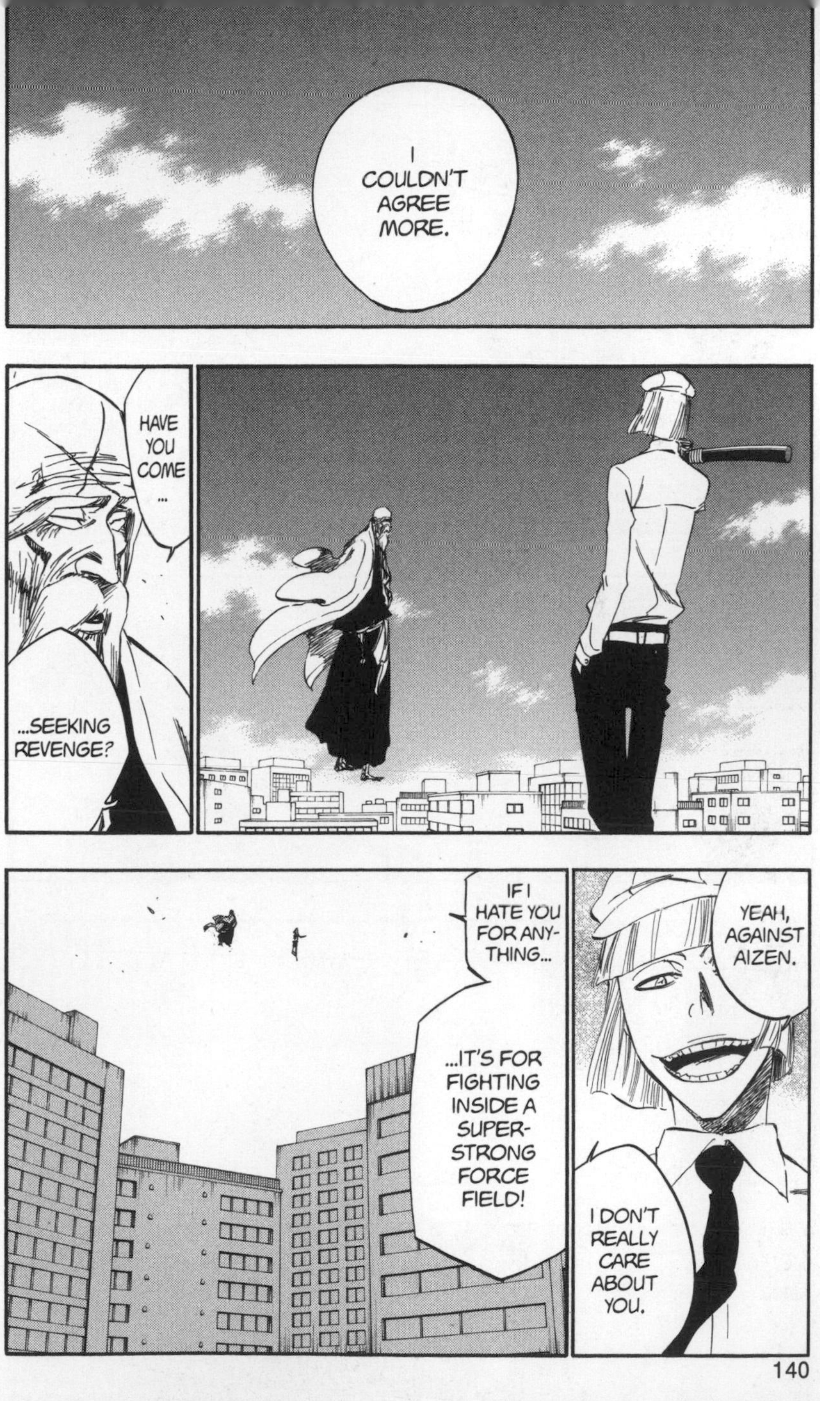
I COULDN'T AGREE MORE.
HAVE YOU COME ...
...SEEKING REVENGE?
YEAH, AGAINST AIZEN.
I DON'T REALLY CARE ABOUT YOU.
IF I HATE YOU FOR ANYTHING...
...IT'S FOR FIGHTING INSIDE A SUPER-STRONG FORCE FIELD!

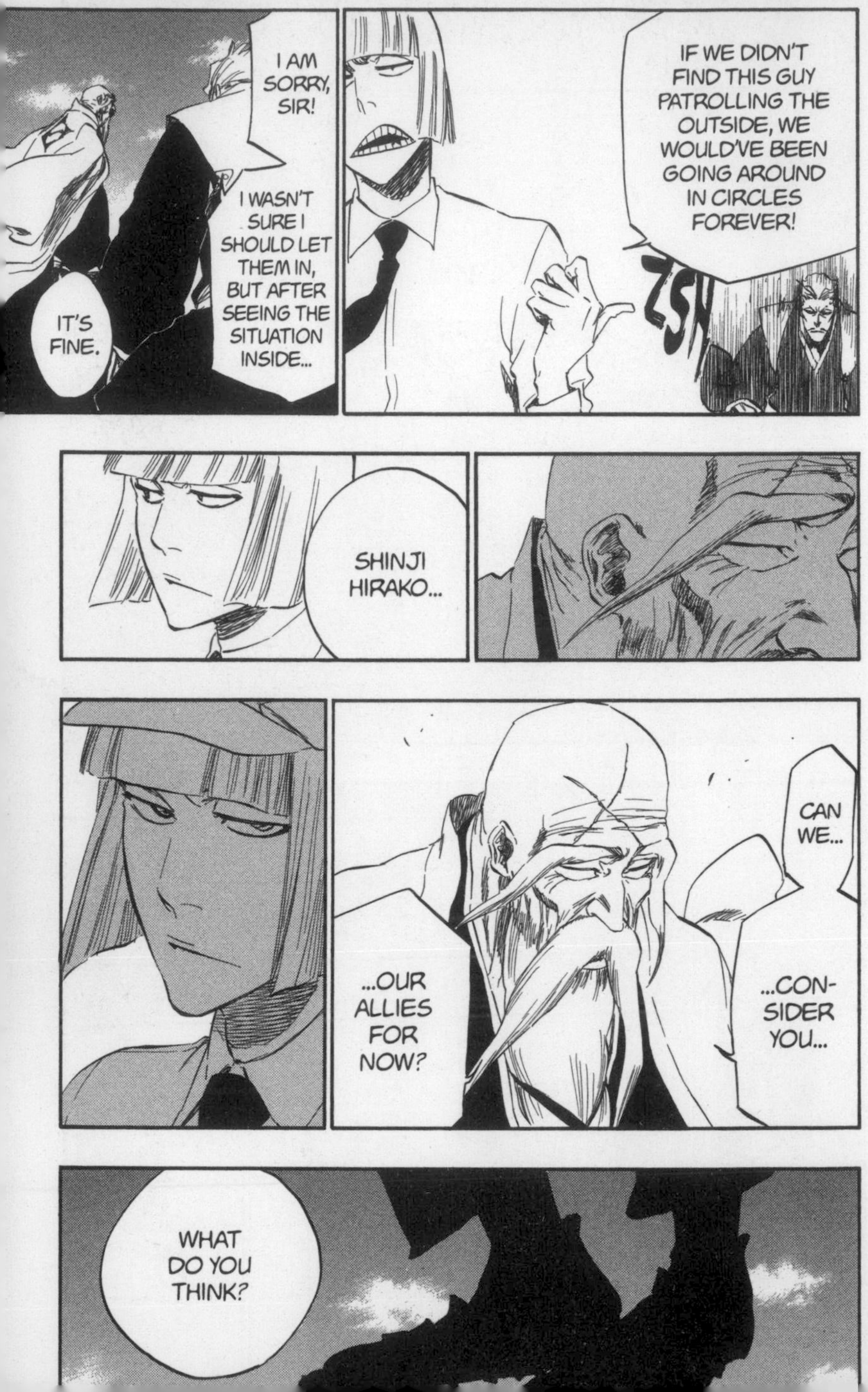
IF WE DIDN'T FIND THIS GUY PATROLLING THE OUTSIDE, WE WOULD'VE BEEN GOING AROUND IN CIRCLES FOREVER!
ZSH
I AM SORRY, SIR!
I WASN'T SURE I SHOULD LET THEM IN, BUT AFTER SEEING THE SITUATION INSIDE...
IT'S FINE.
SHINJI HIRAKO...
CAN WE...
...CON-SIDER YOU...
...OUR ALLIES FOR NOW?
WHAT DO YOU THINK?

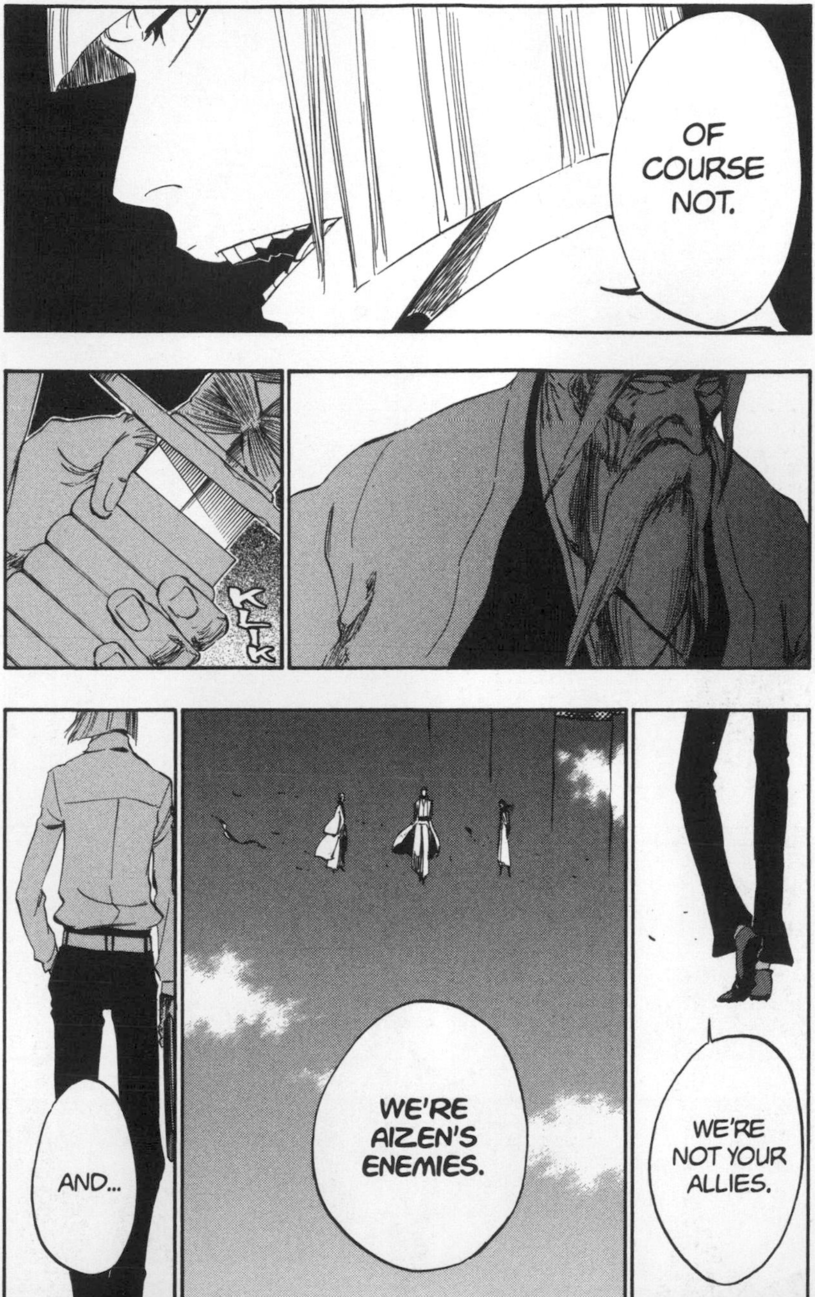
OF COURSE NOT.
KLIK
WE'RE NOT YOUR ALLIES.
WE'RE AIZEN'S ENEMIES.
AND...

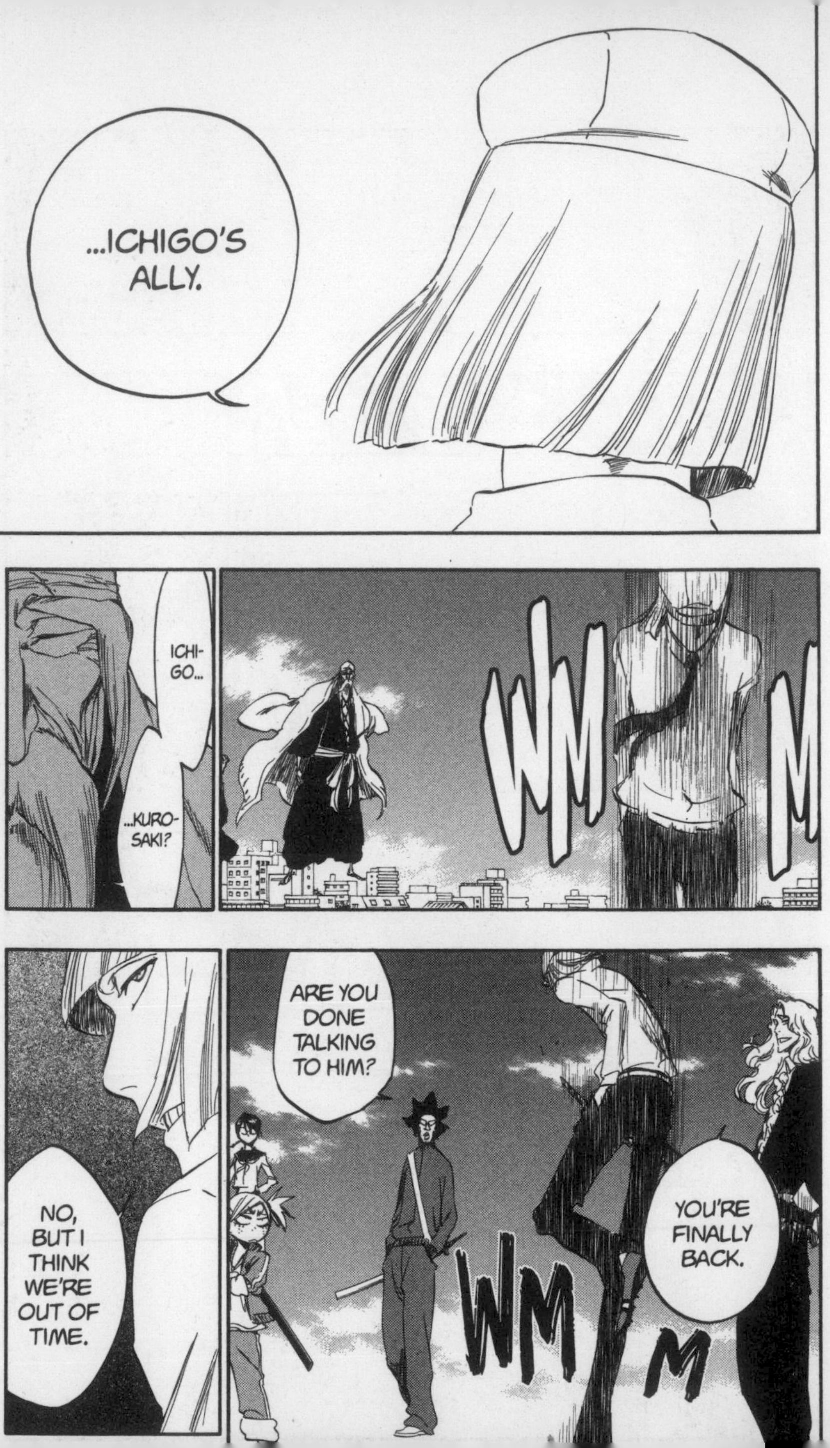
...ICHIGO'S ALLY.
WM
M
ICHI-GO...
...KURO-SAKI?
ARE YOU DONE TALKING TO HIM?
YOU'RE FINALLY BACK.
WM
M
NO, BUT I THINK WE'RE OUT OF TIME.

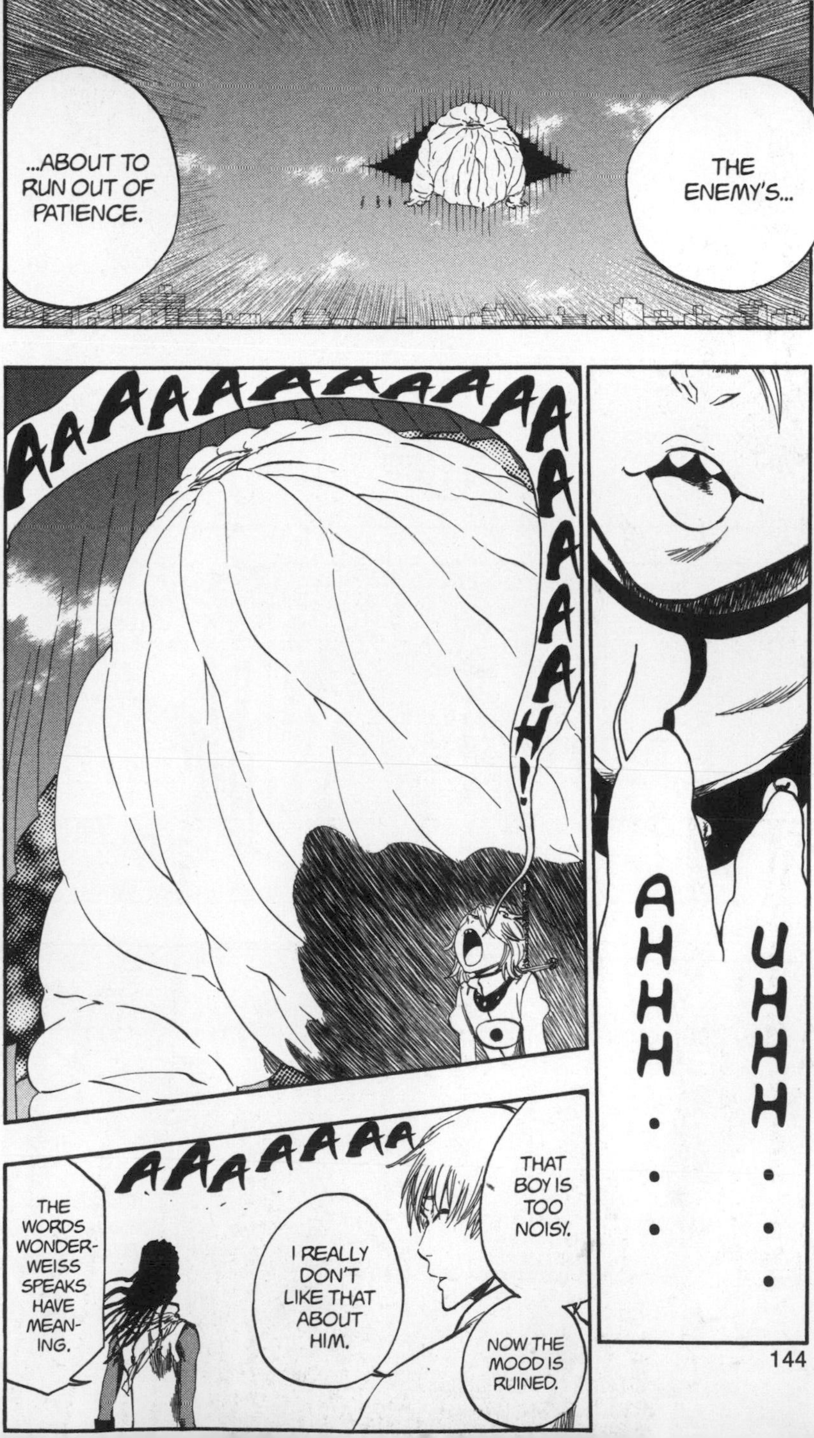
THE ENEMY'S...
...ABOUT TO RUN OUT OF PATIENCE.
UHHH...
AHHH...
AAAAAAAAAAAAAAAAAAAAH!
AAAAAAA
THAT BOY IS TOO NOISY.
NOW THE MOOD IS RUINED.
I REALLY DON'T LIKE THAT ABOUT HIM.
THE WORDS WONDER-WEISS SPEAKS HAVE MEAN-ING.

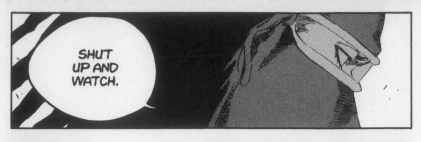

SHUT UP AND WATCH.

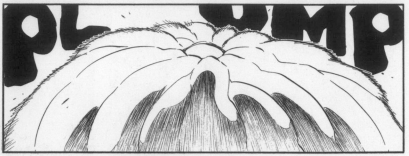

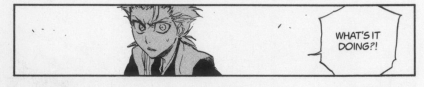

WHAT'S IT DOING?!

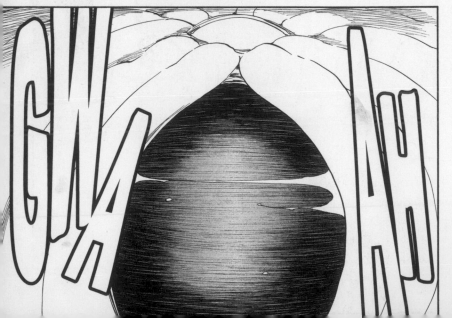

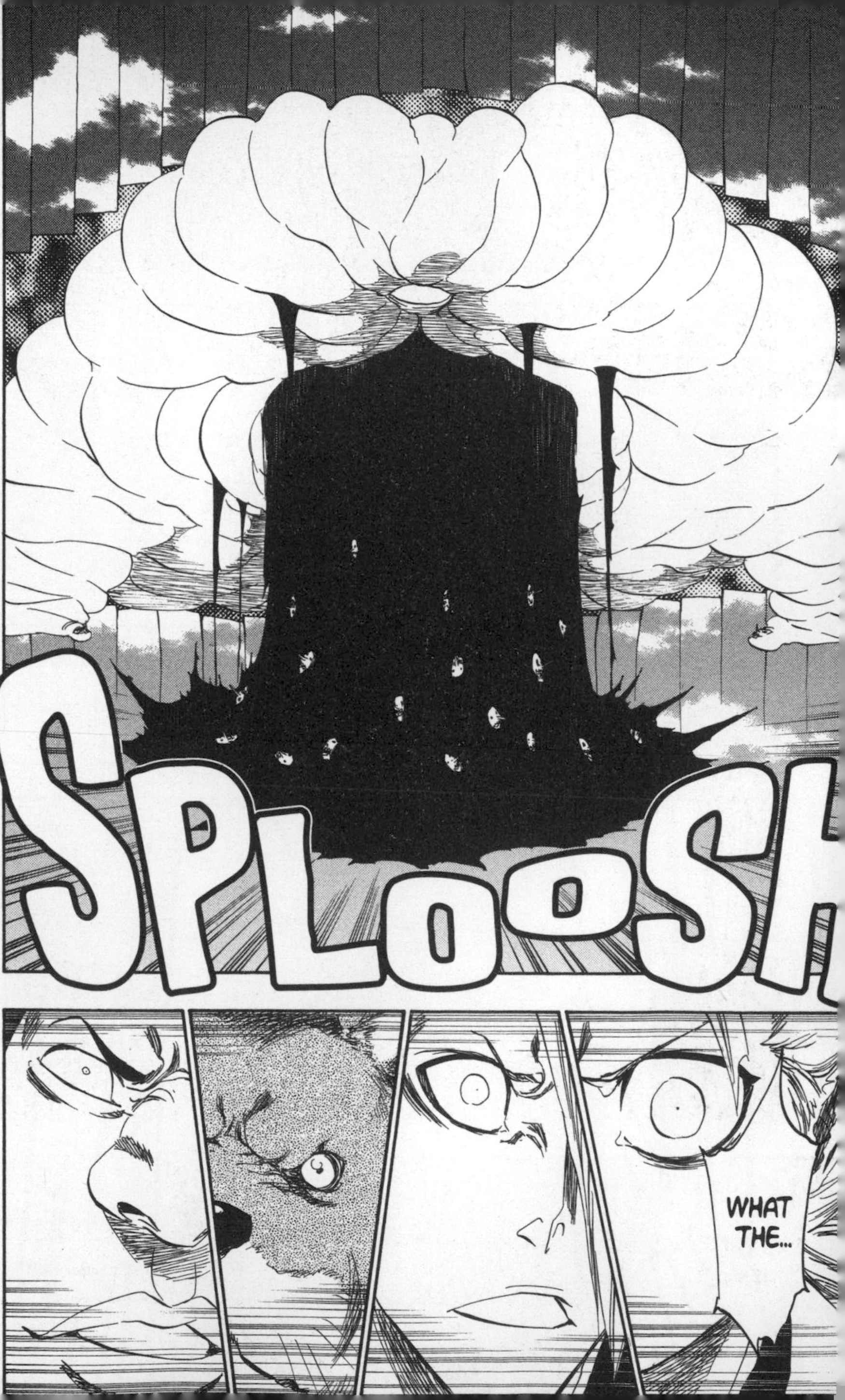
SPLOOSH
WHAT THE...

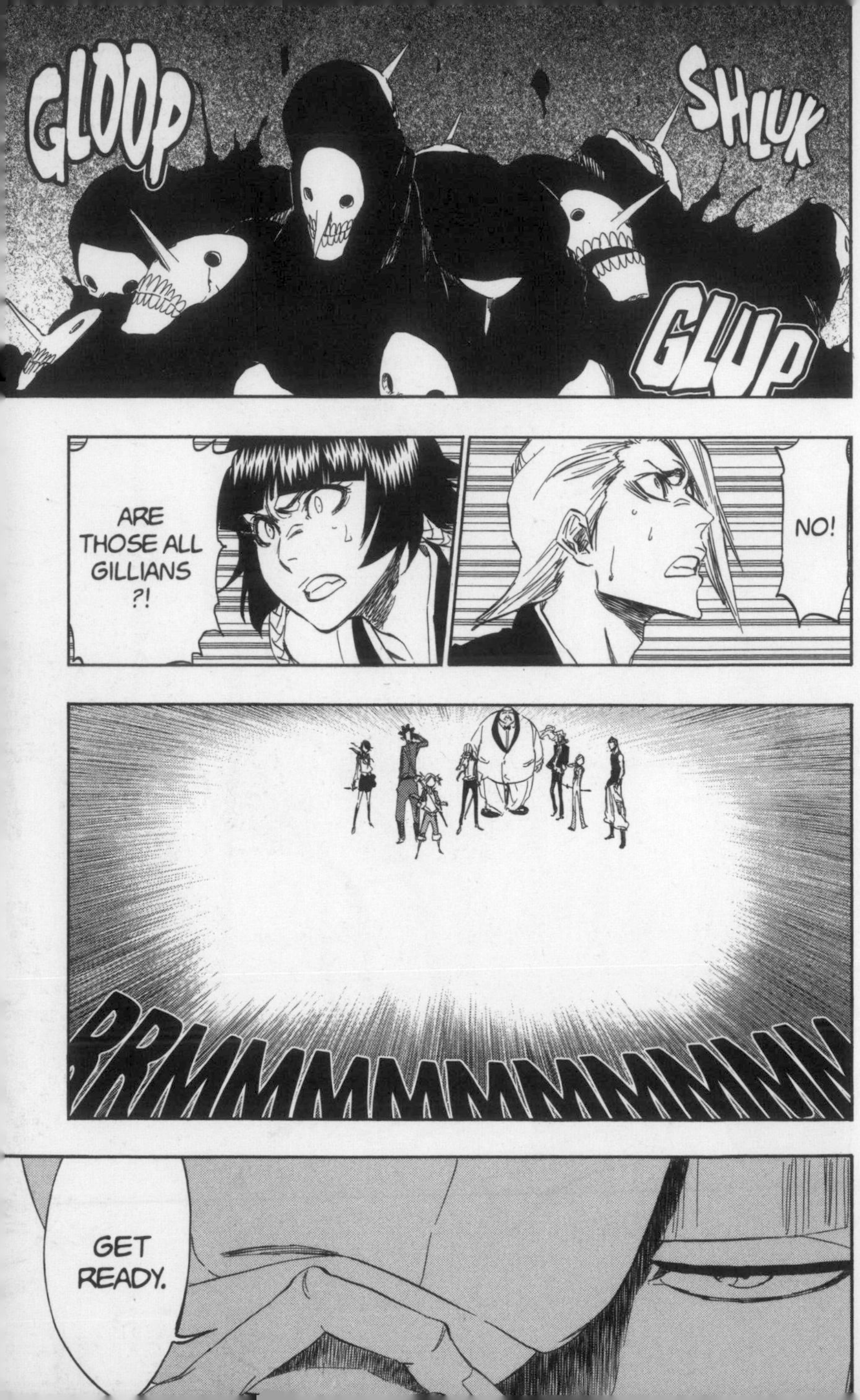
SHLUK
GLOOP
GLUP
NO!
ARE THOSE ALL GILLIANS ?!
BRMMMMMMMMMMMMMN
GET READY.

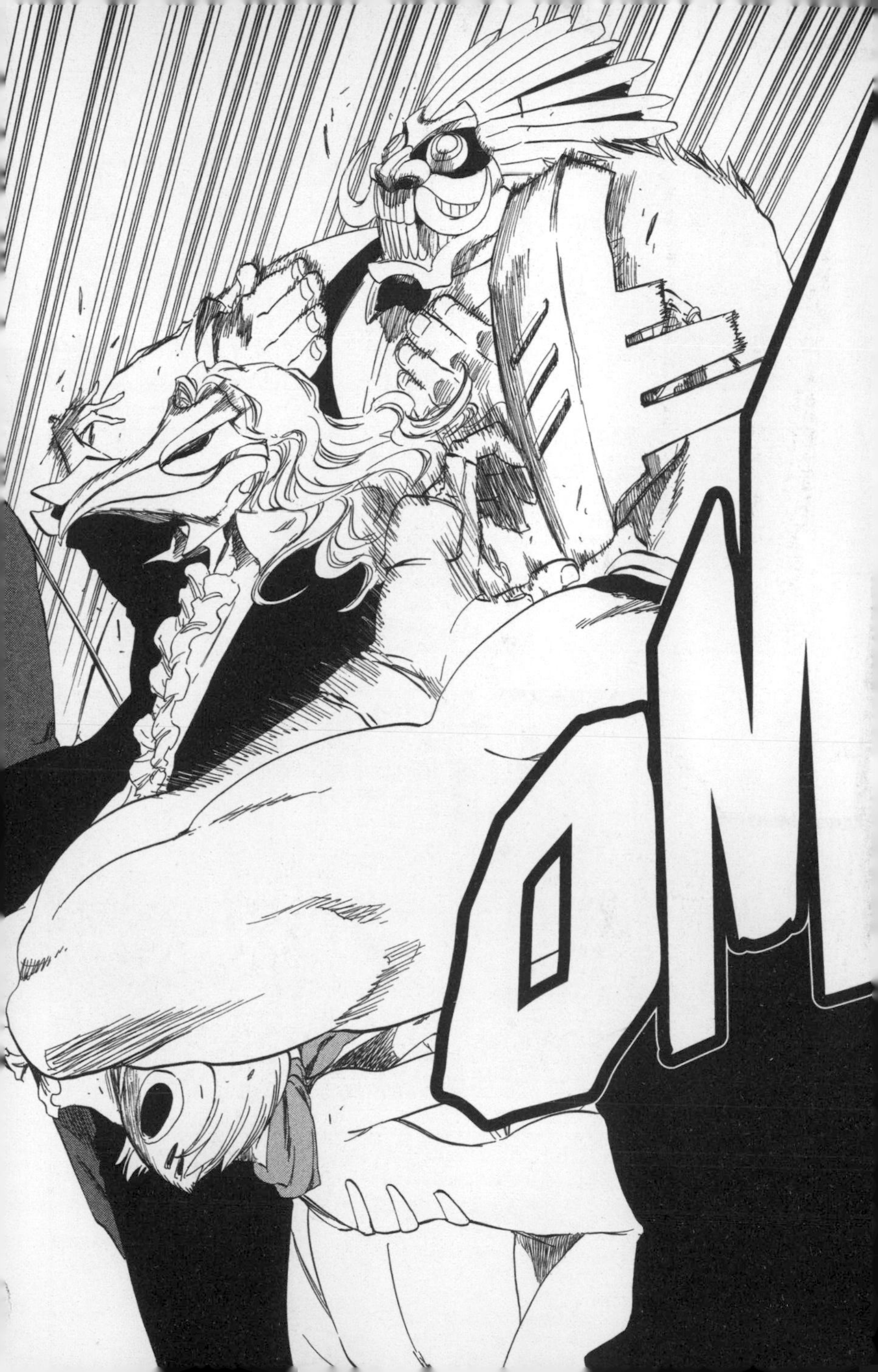
OM

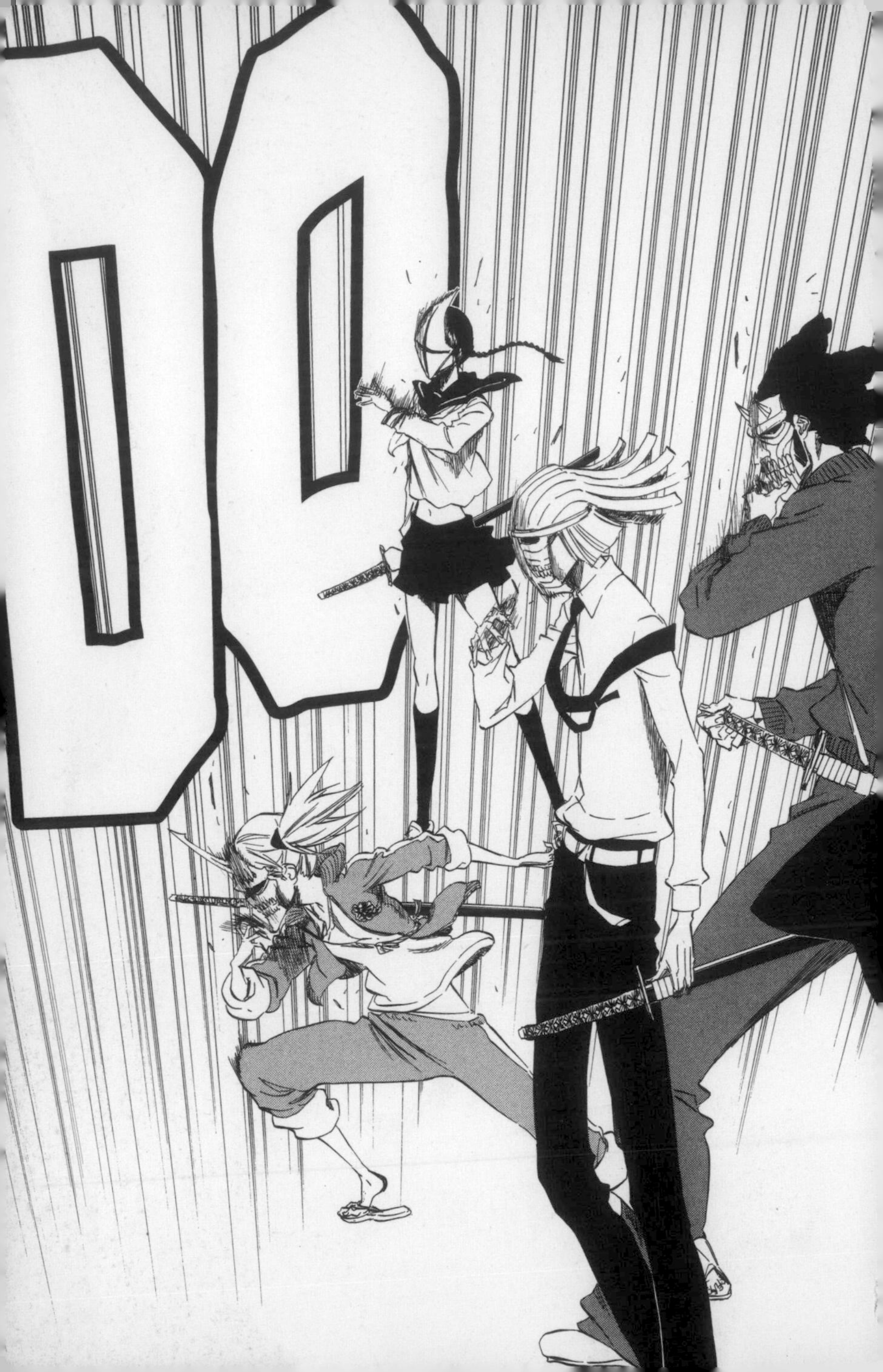
DO

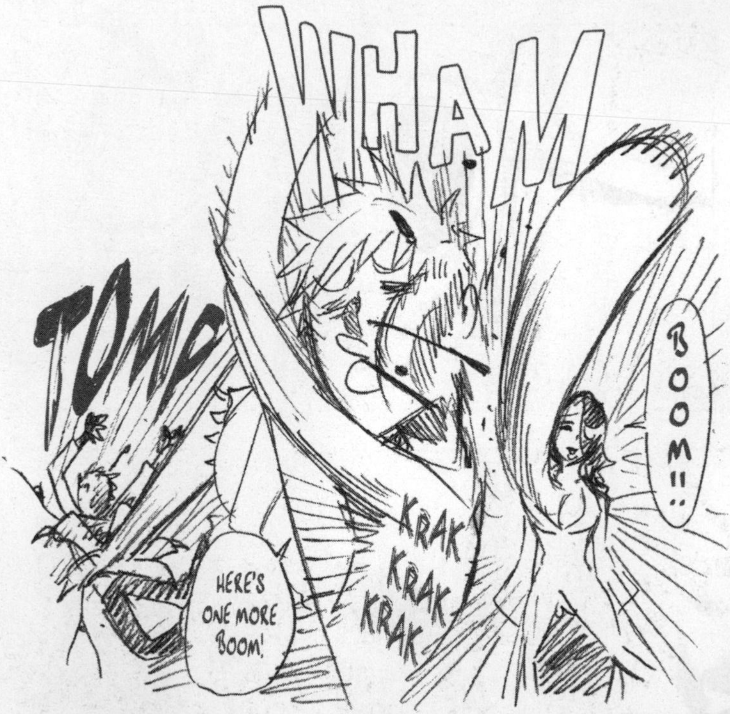
WHAM
BOOM!!
TOMP
KRAK KRAK KRAK
HERE'S ONE MORE BOOM!

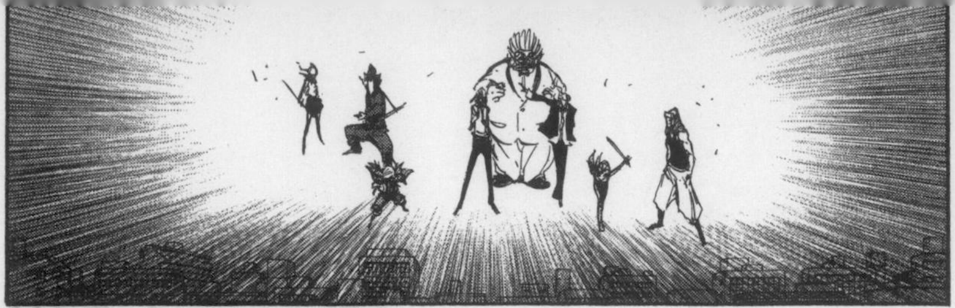

366. The Revenger's High

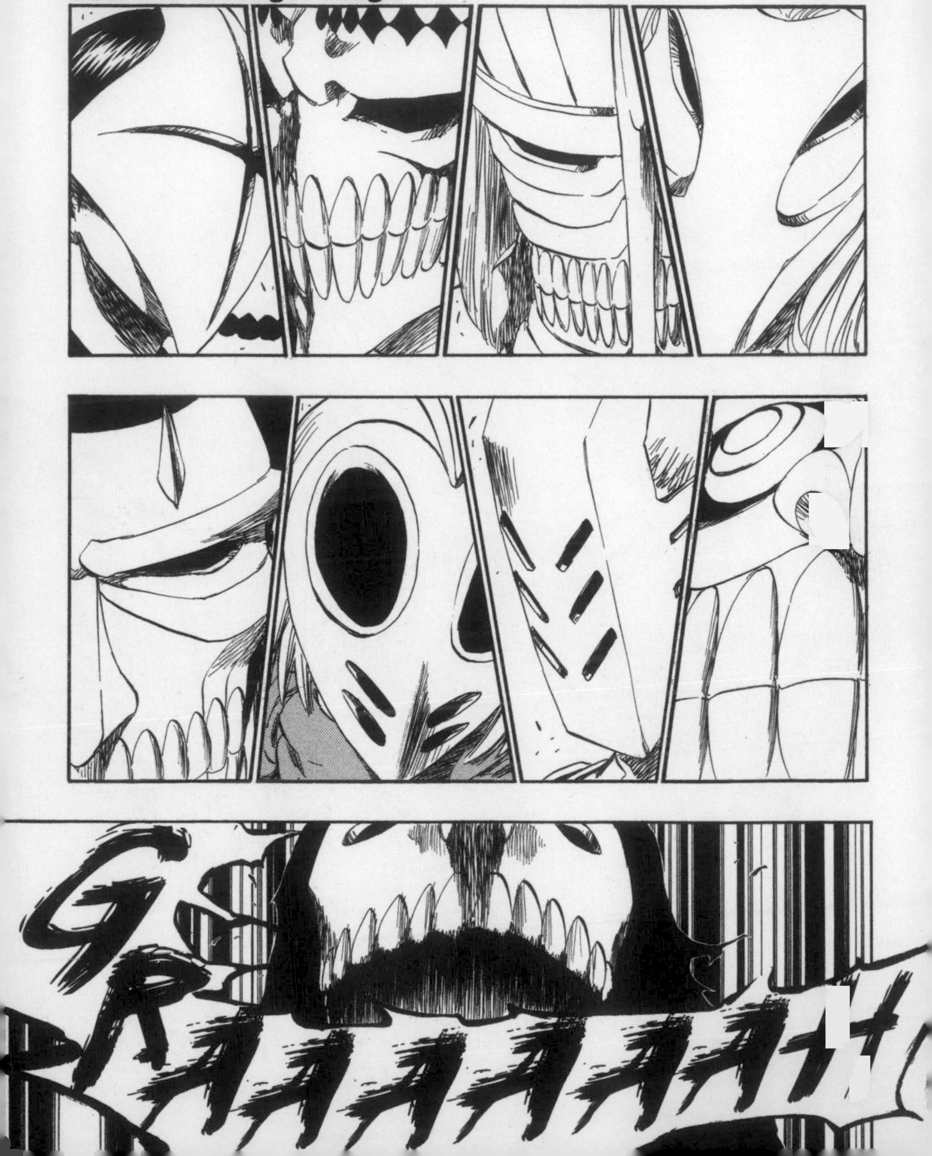
GRAAAAAAH

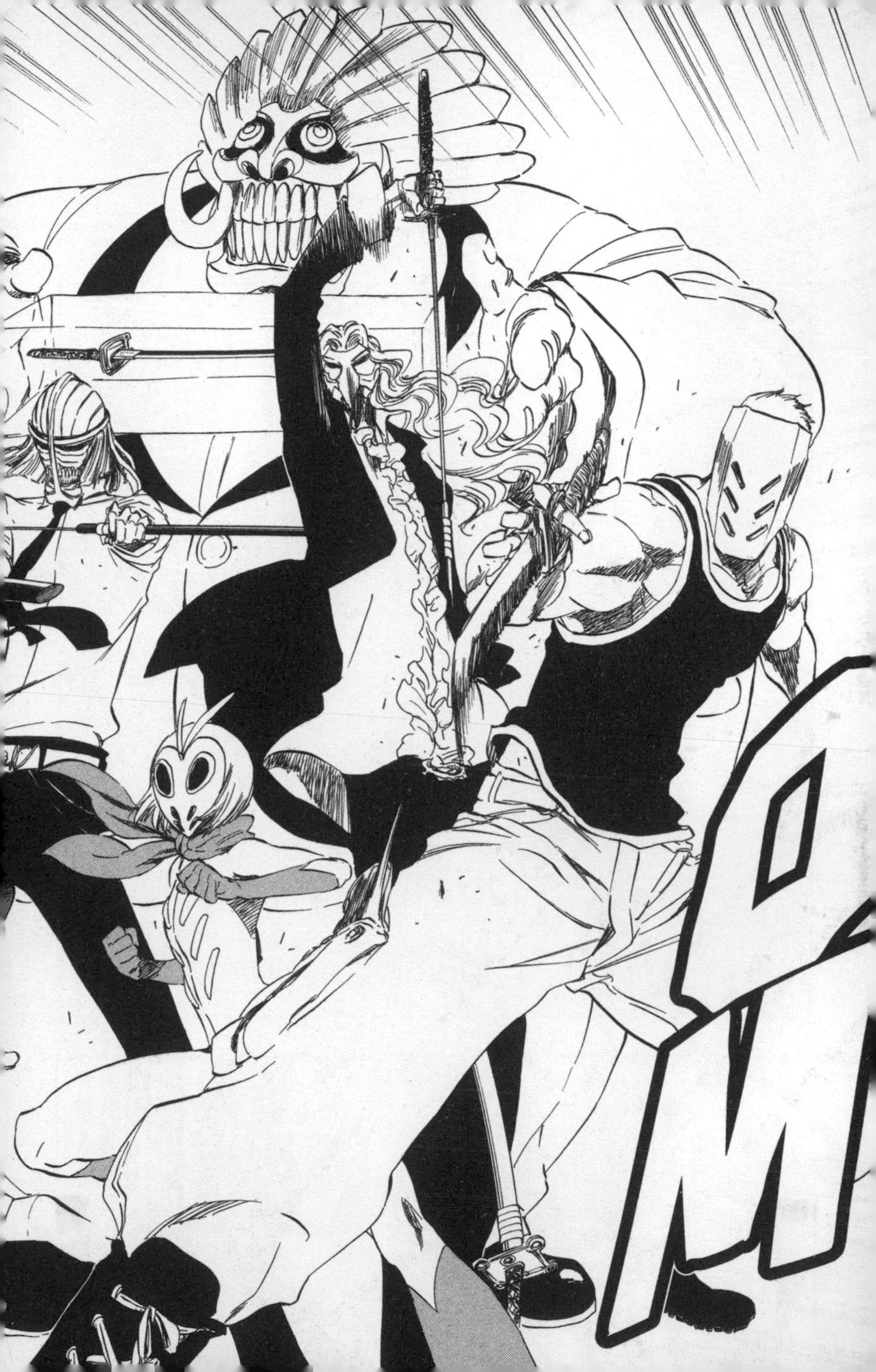

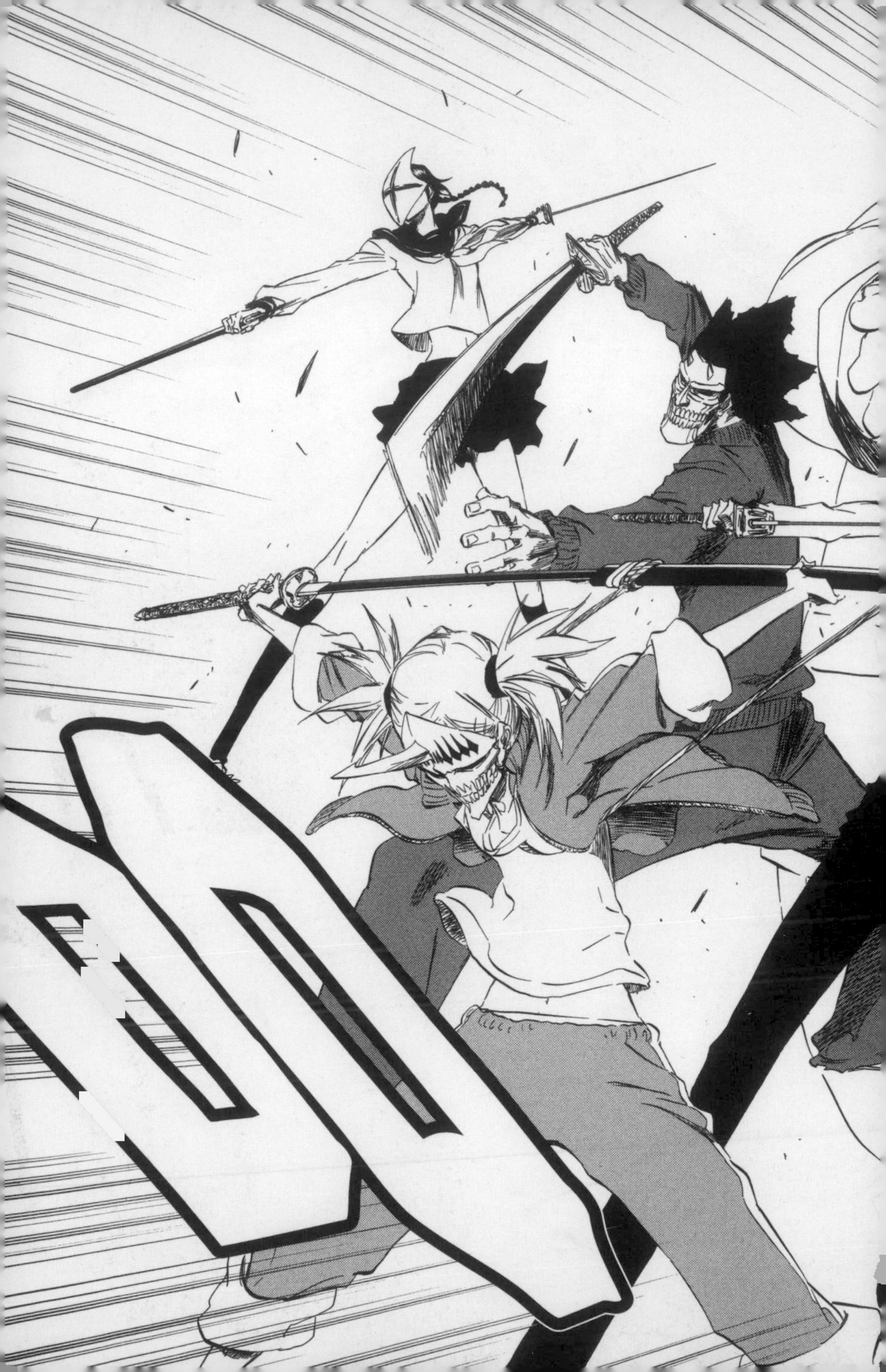

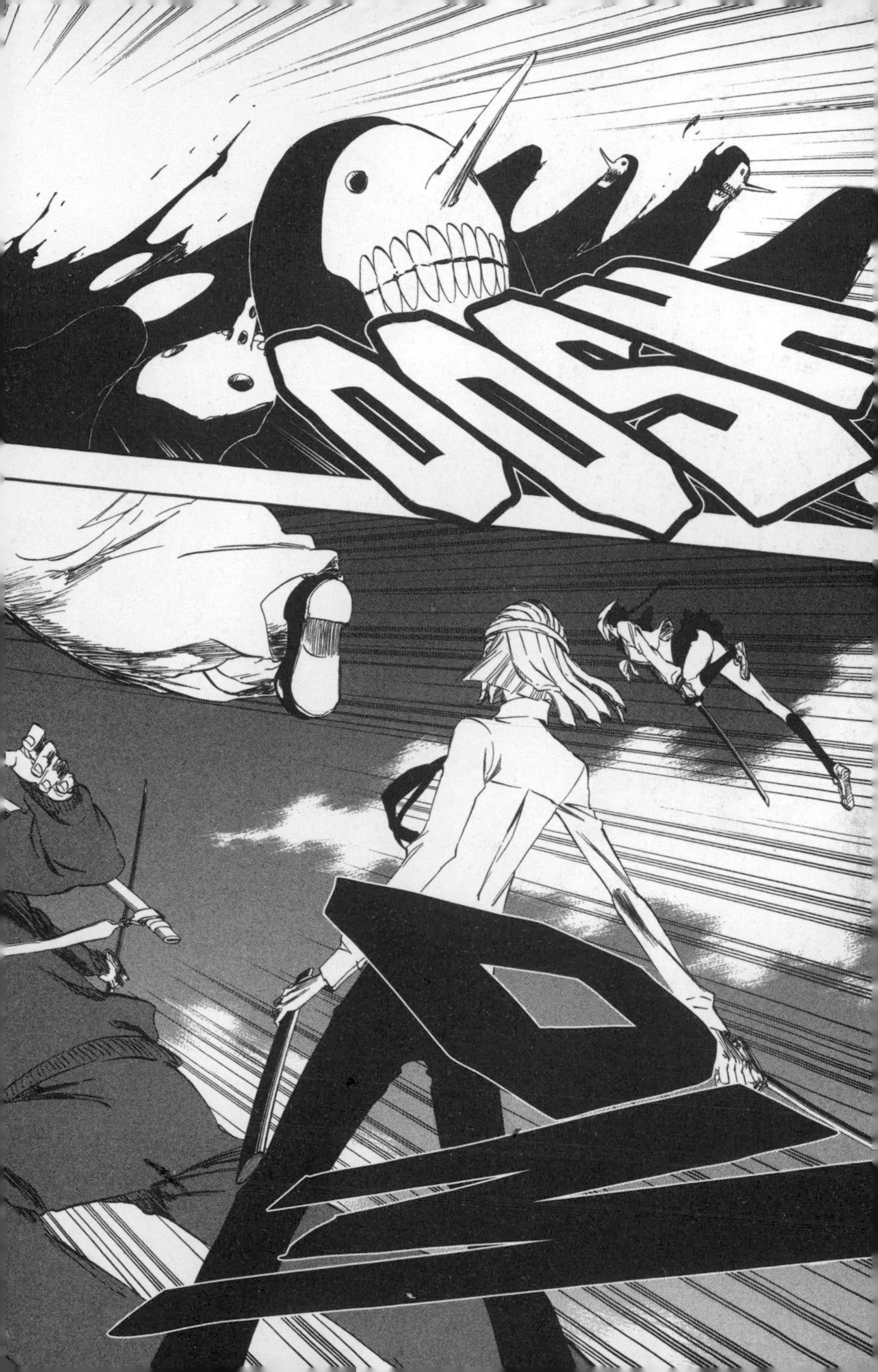

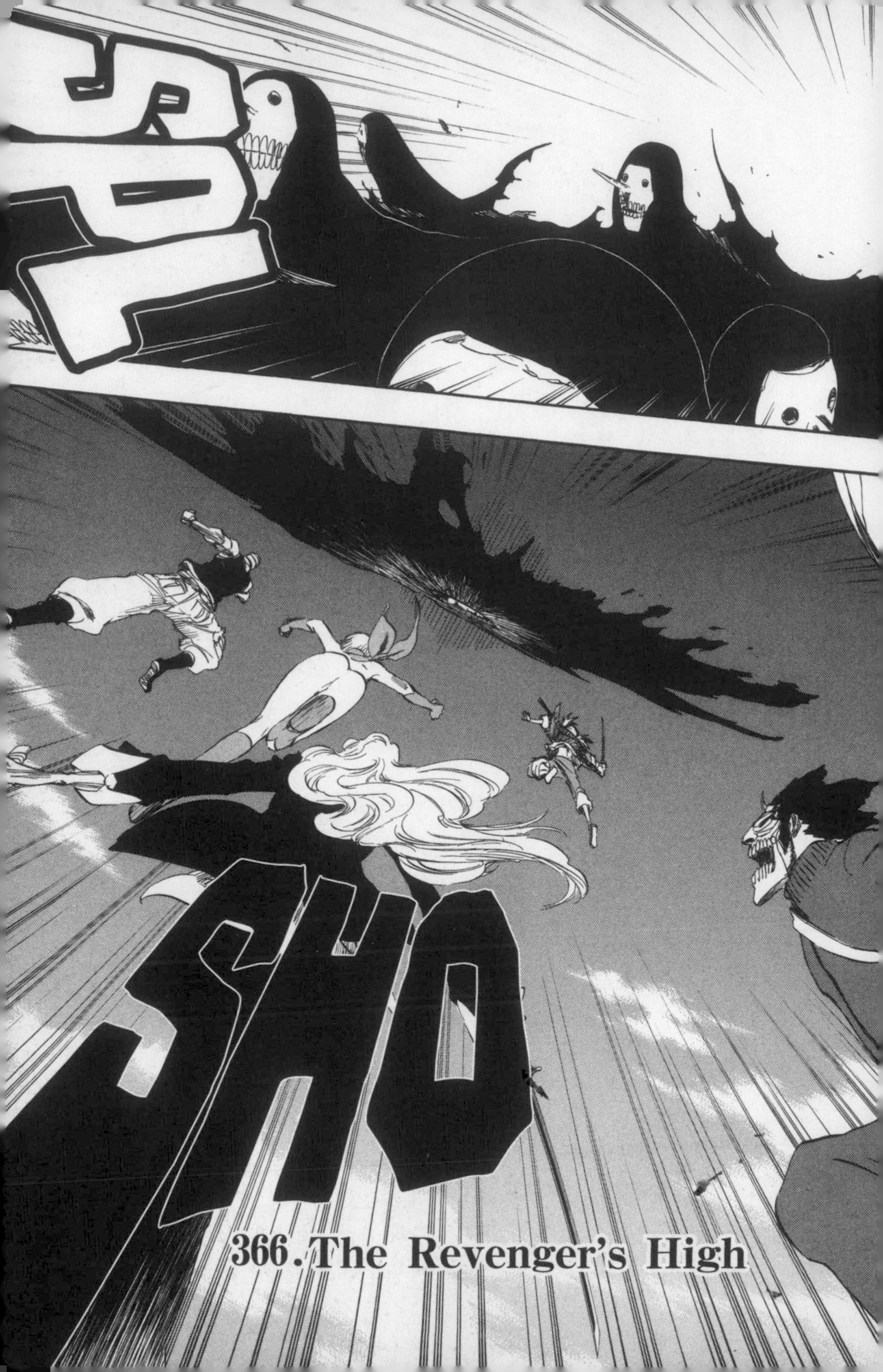
SHO

366. The Revenger's High

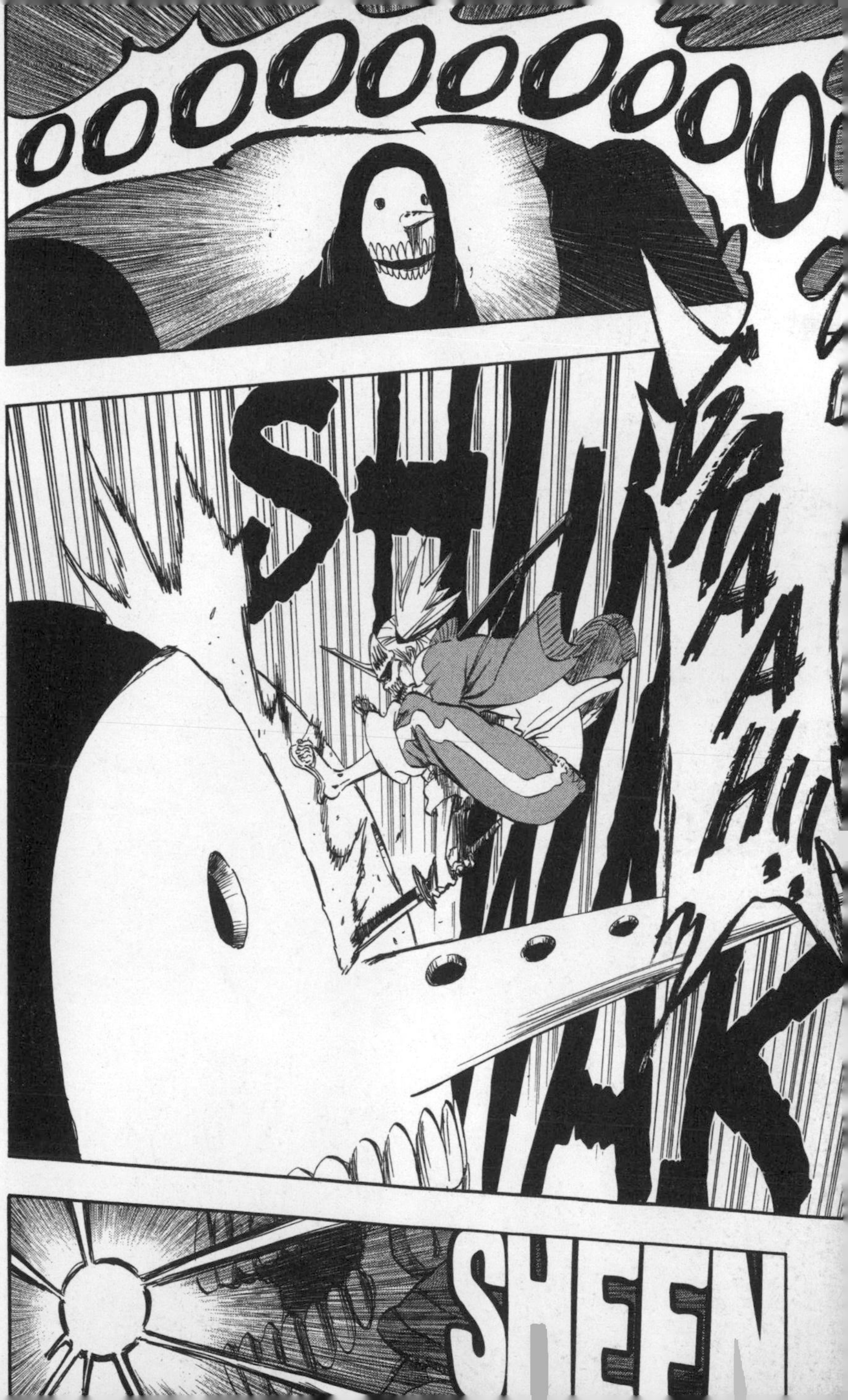
OOOOOOOOOOOO
SHWAK
SHEEN

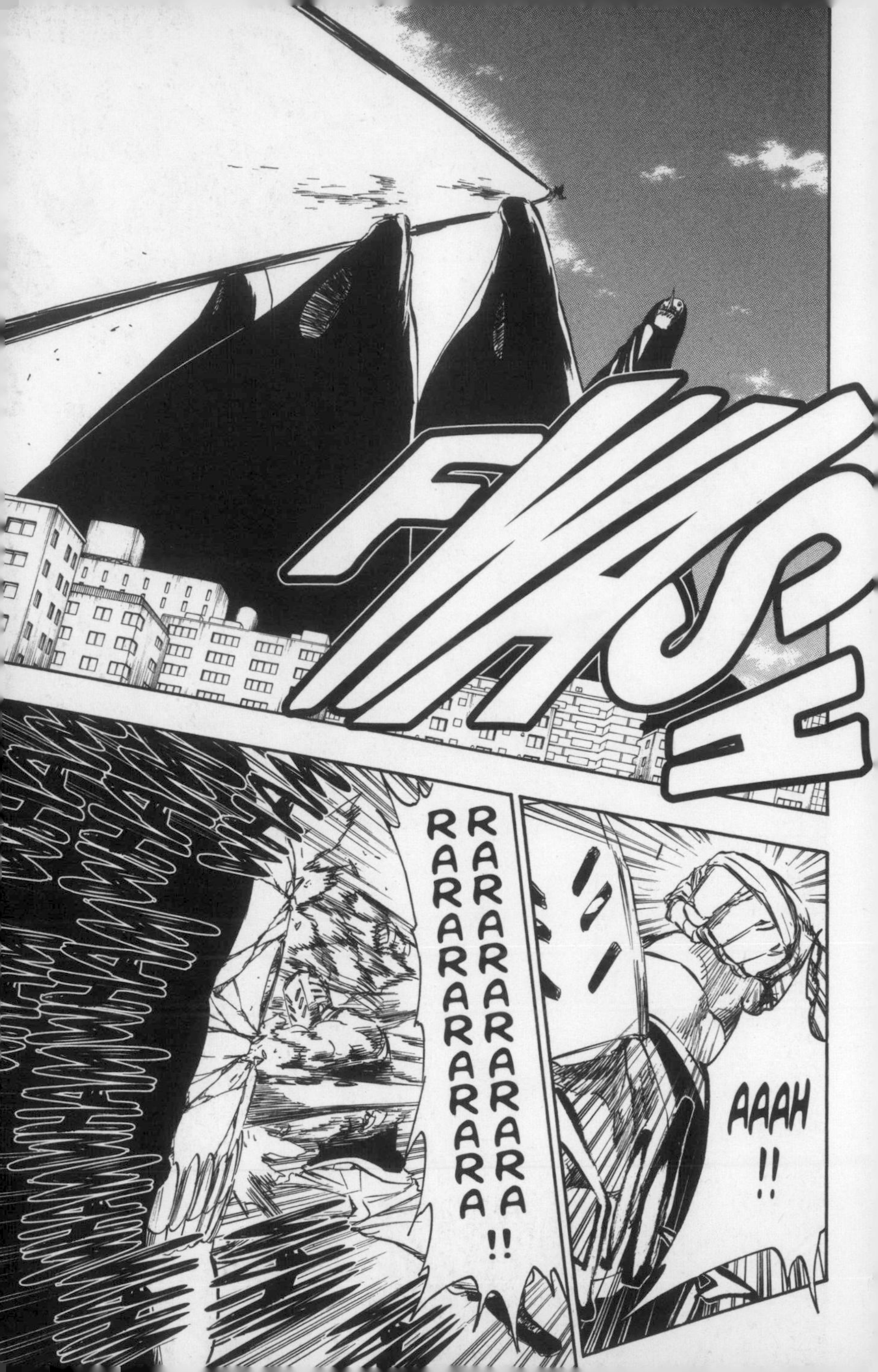
AAAH!!
RARARARARARARA!!
RARARARARARARA

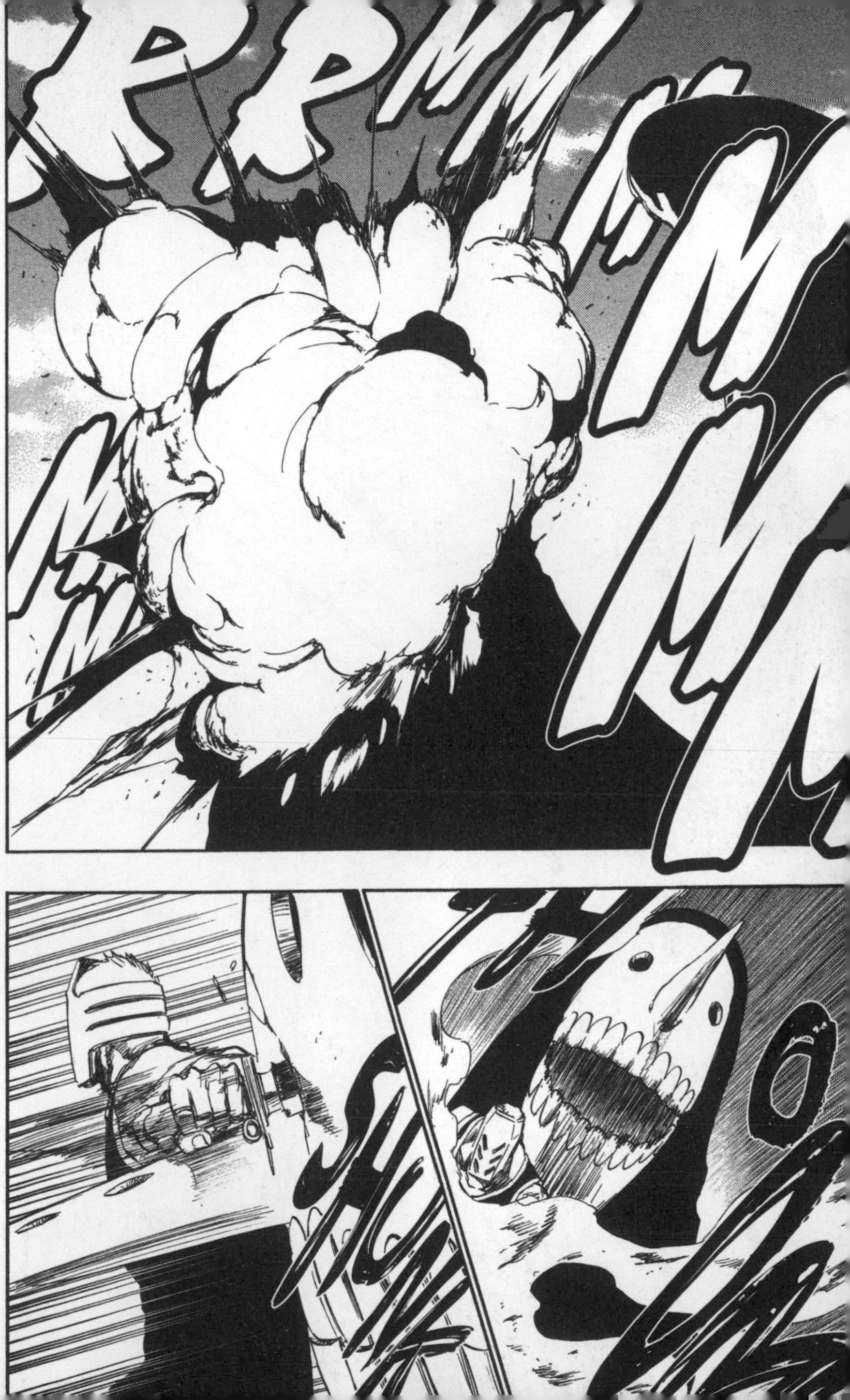

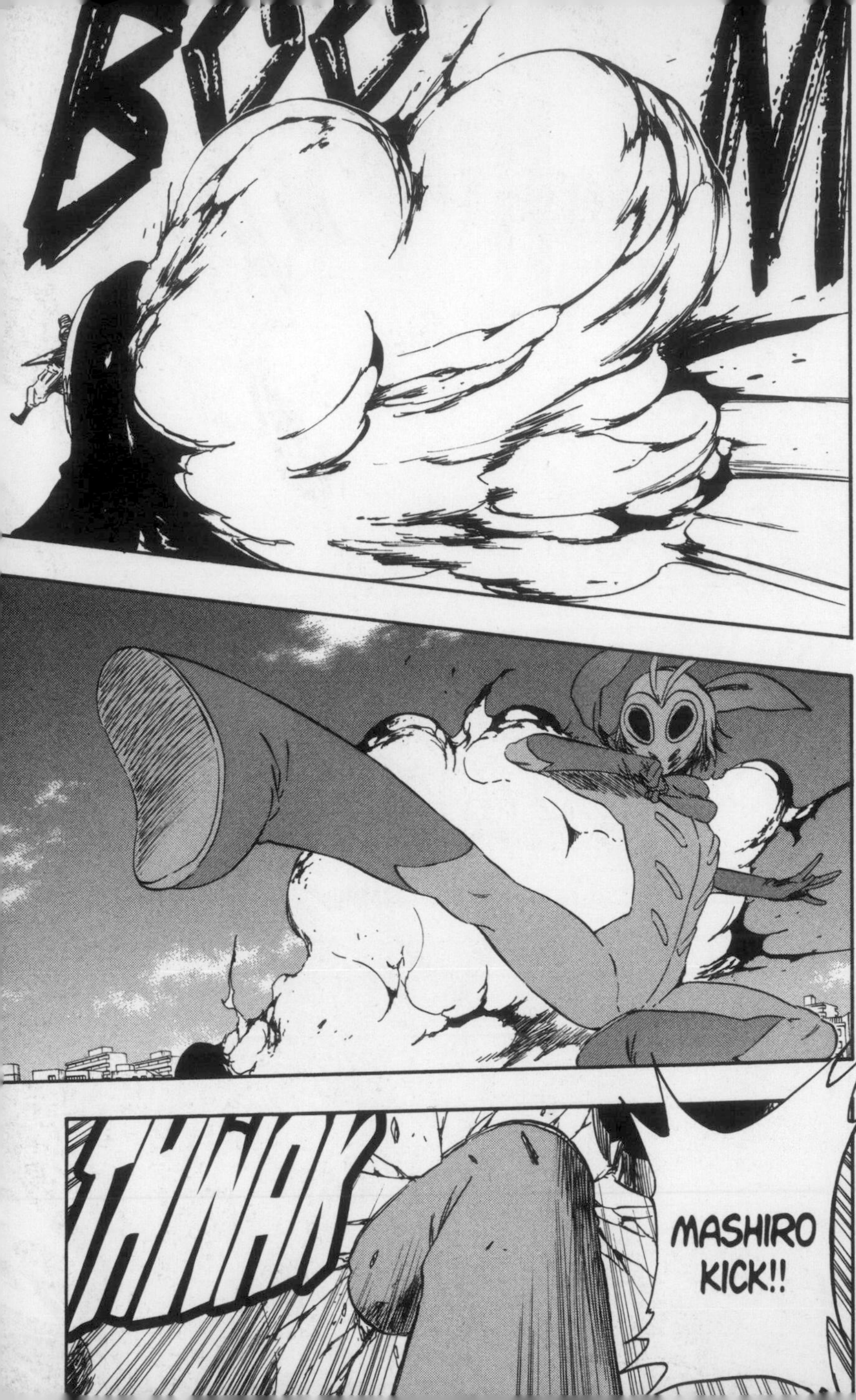
BOOM
THWAK
MASHIRO KICK!!

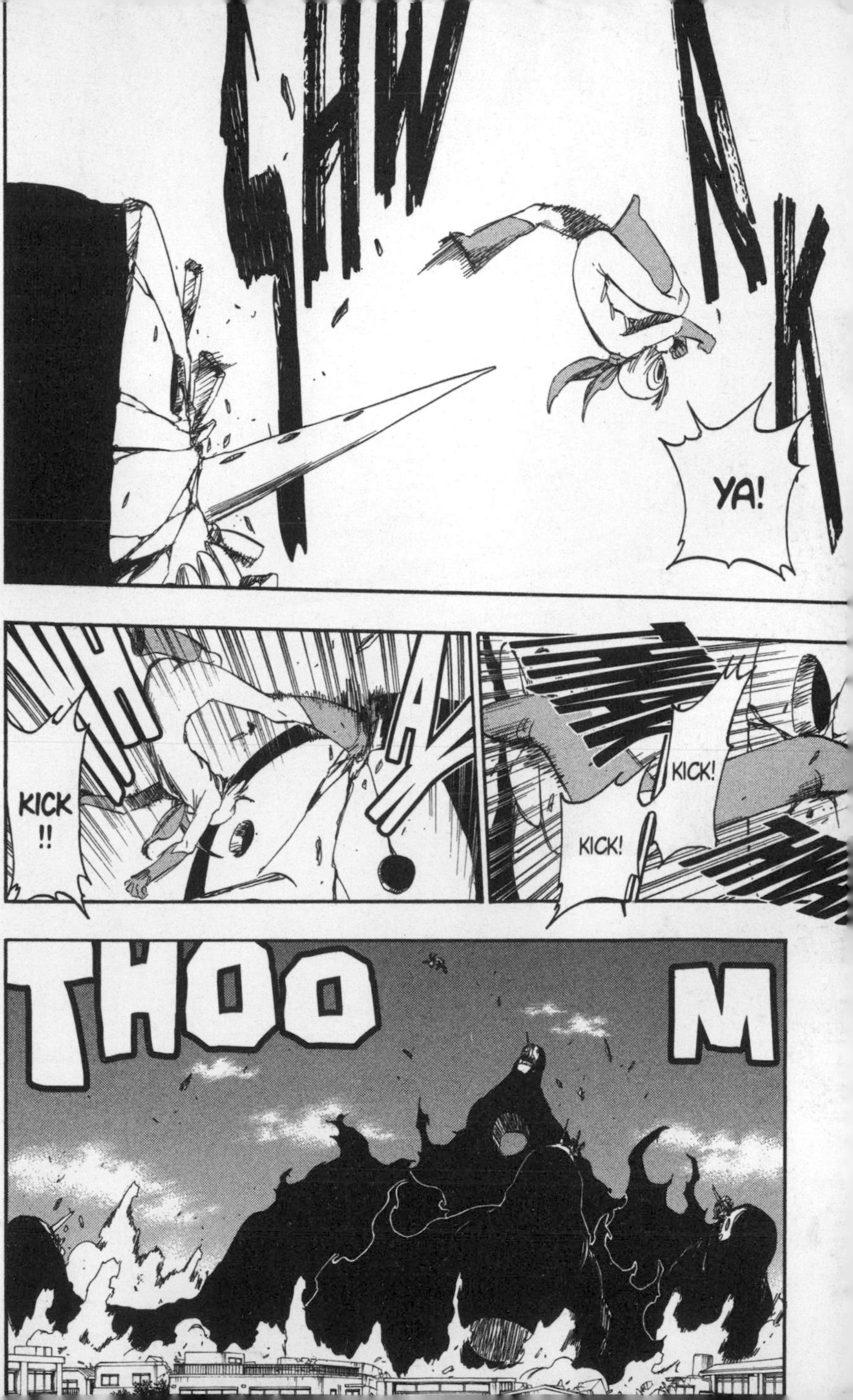
YA!
KICK!
KICK!
KICK !!
THOOM

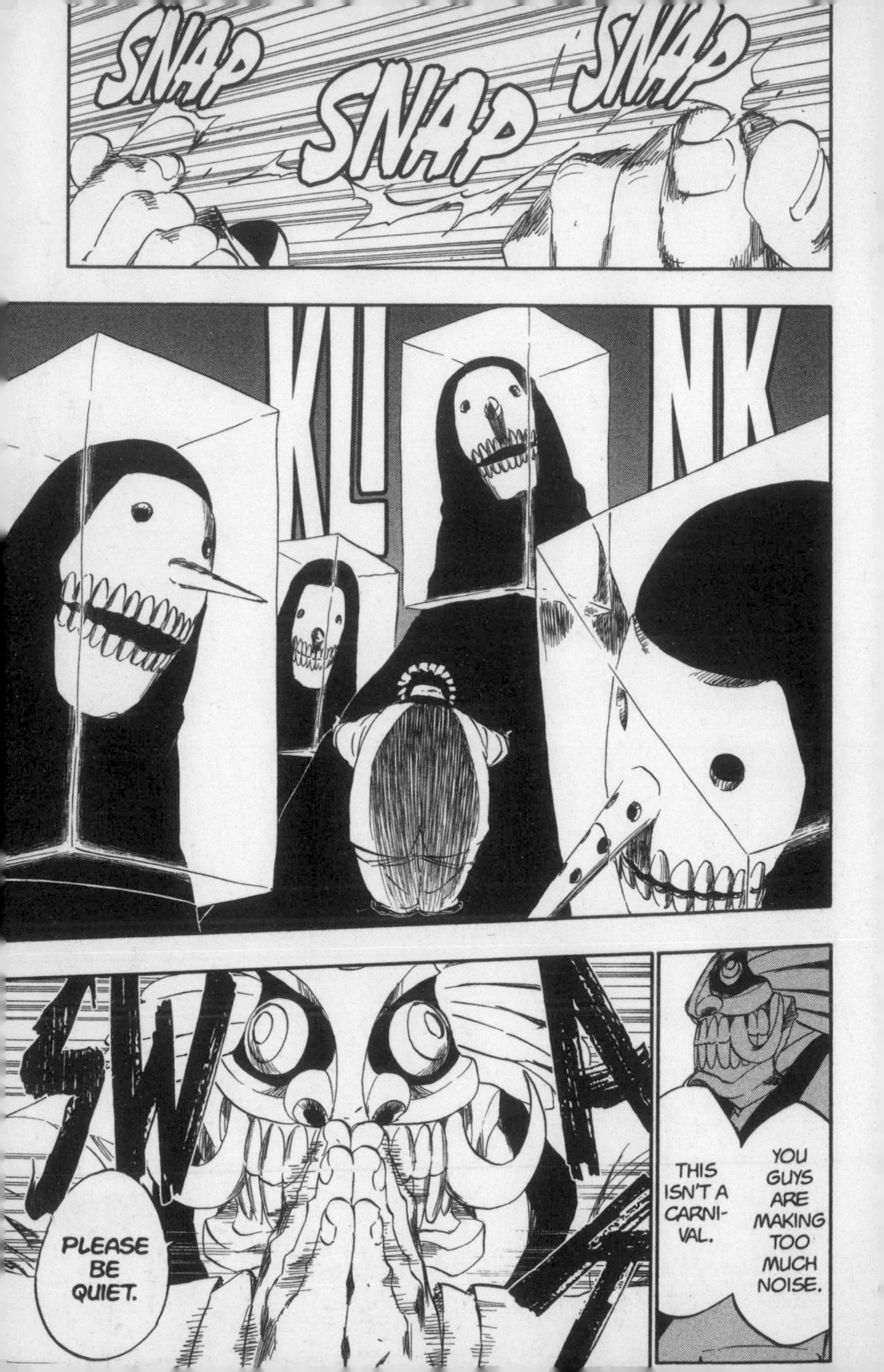
SNAP
SNAP
SNAP
YOU GUYS ARE MAKING TOO MUCH NOISE.
THIS ISN'T A CARNIVAL.
PLEASE BE QUIET.

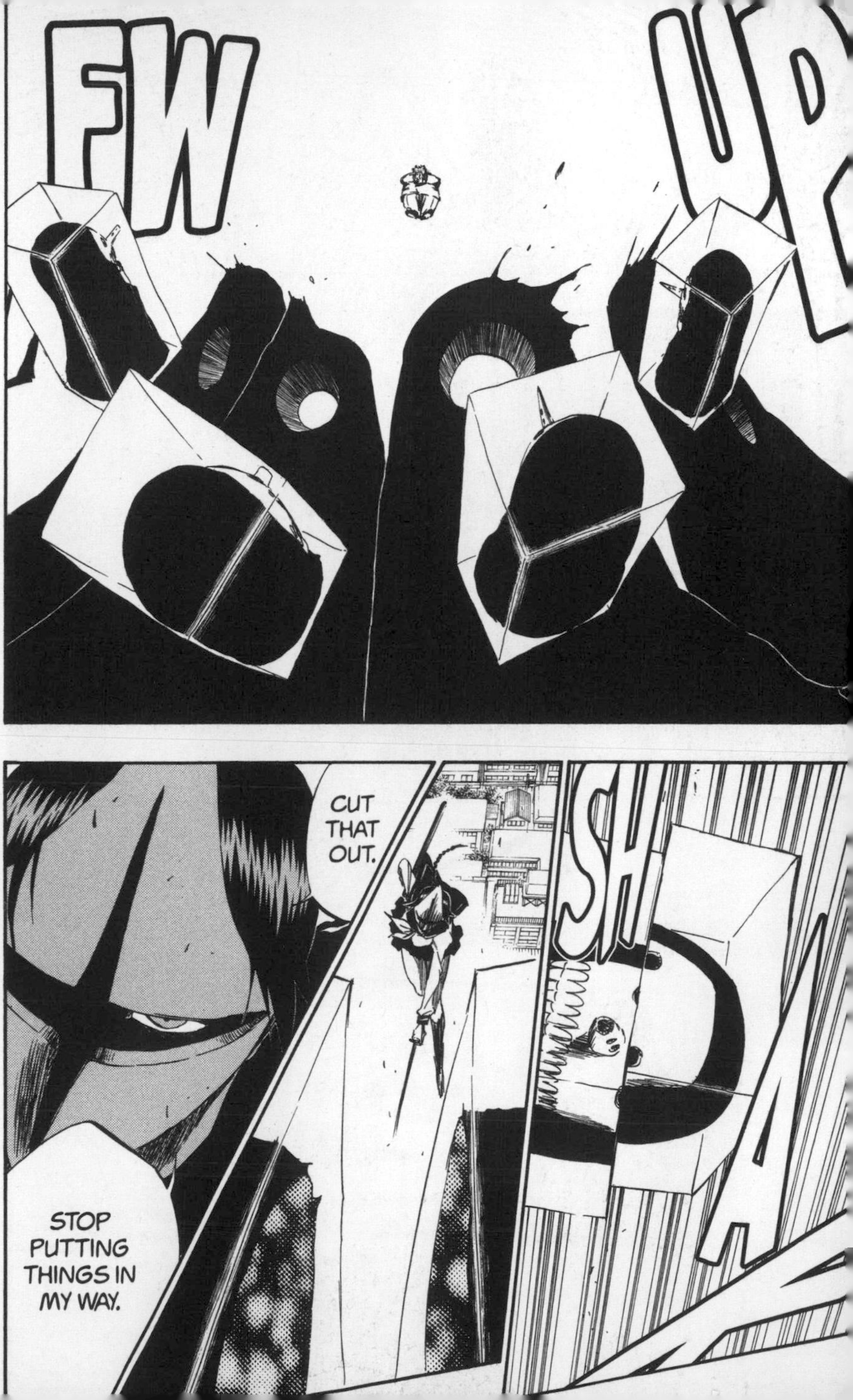
FWUP
SHA
CUT THAT OUT.
STOP PUTTING THINGS IN MY WAY.

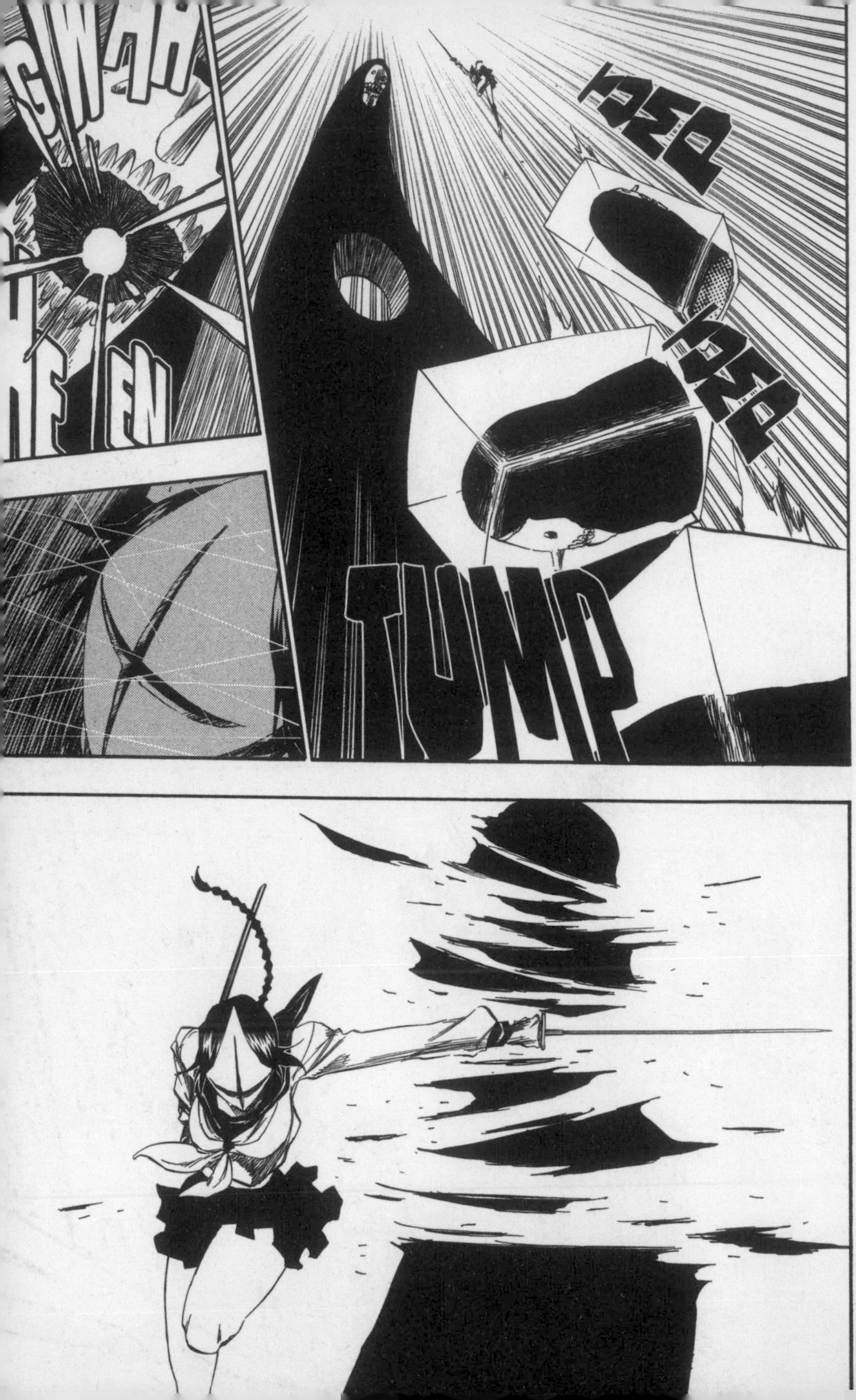
DZSH
DZSH
TUMP
GWAH

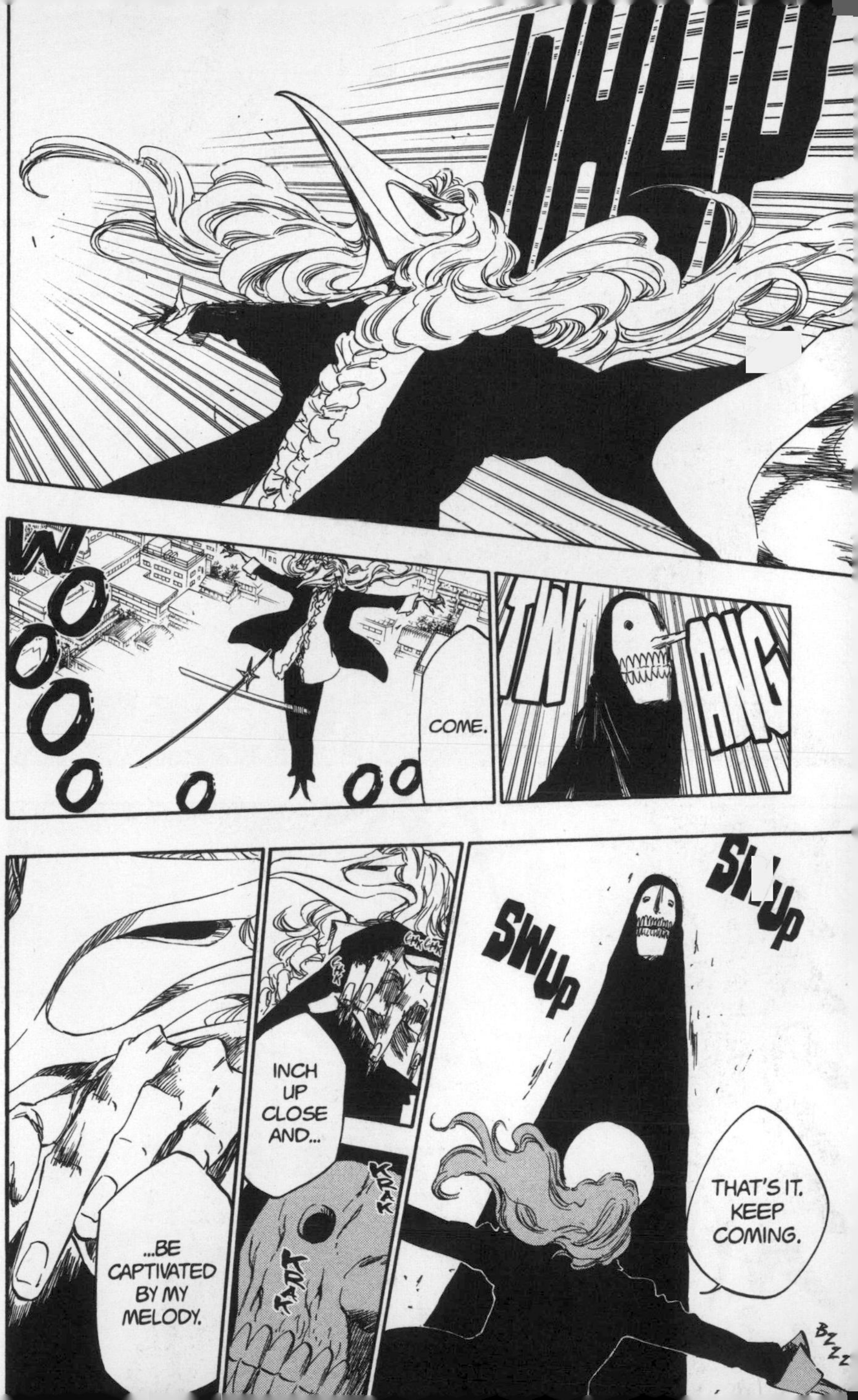
WHIP
TWANG
WOOOOOOOOOO
COME.
SWUP
SWUP
THAT'S IT. KEEP COMING.
BZZZ
INCH UP CLOSE AND...
KRAK
KRAK
...BE CAPTIVATED BY MY MELODY.

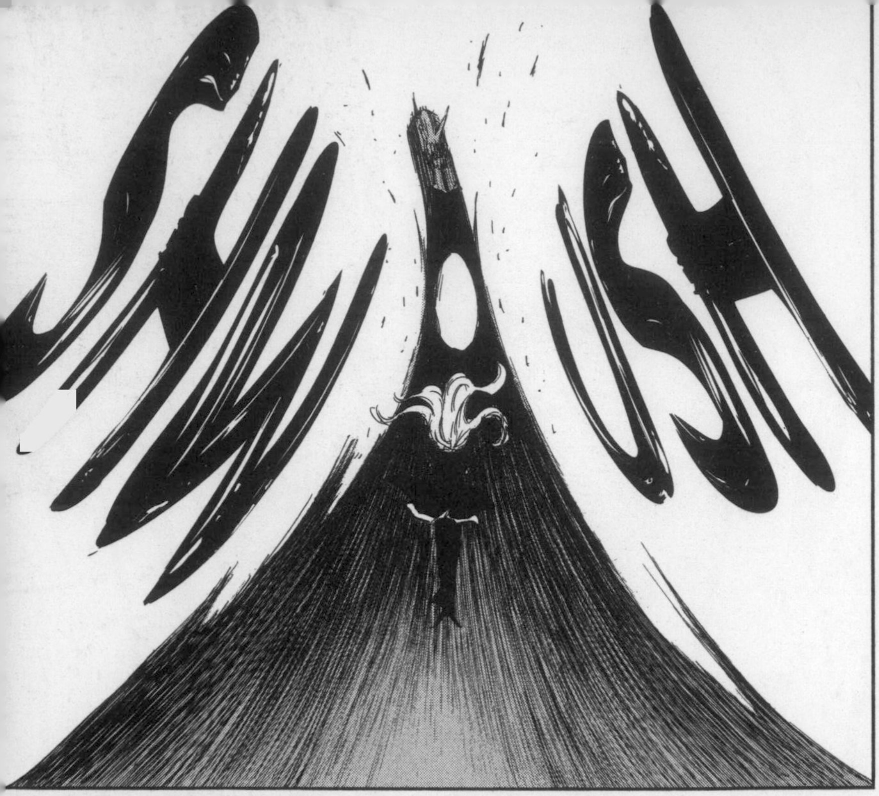
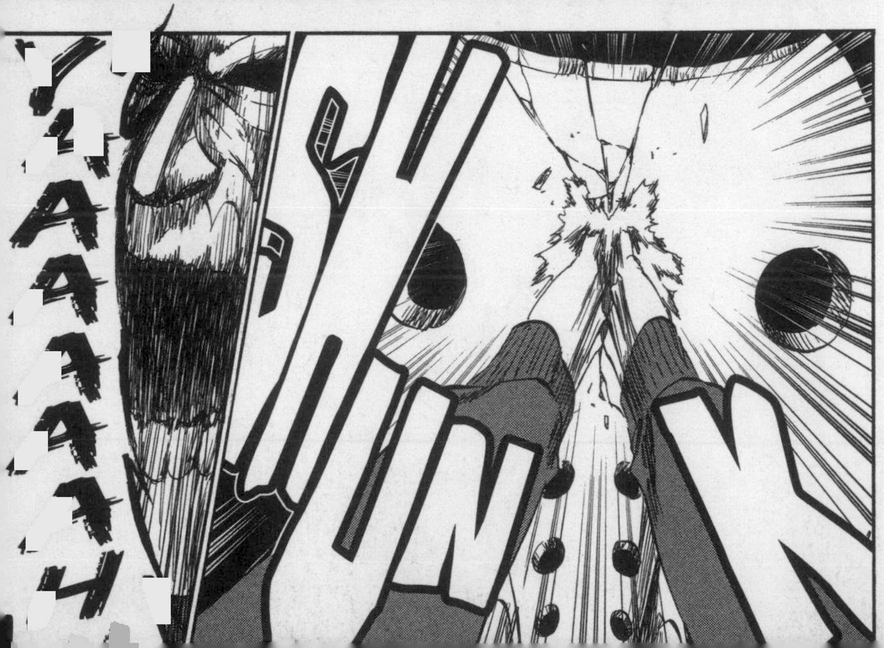

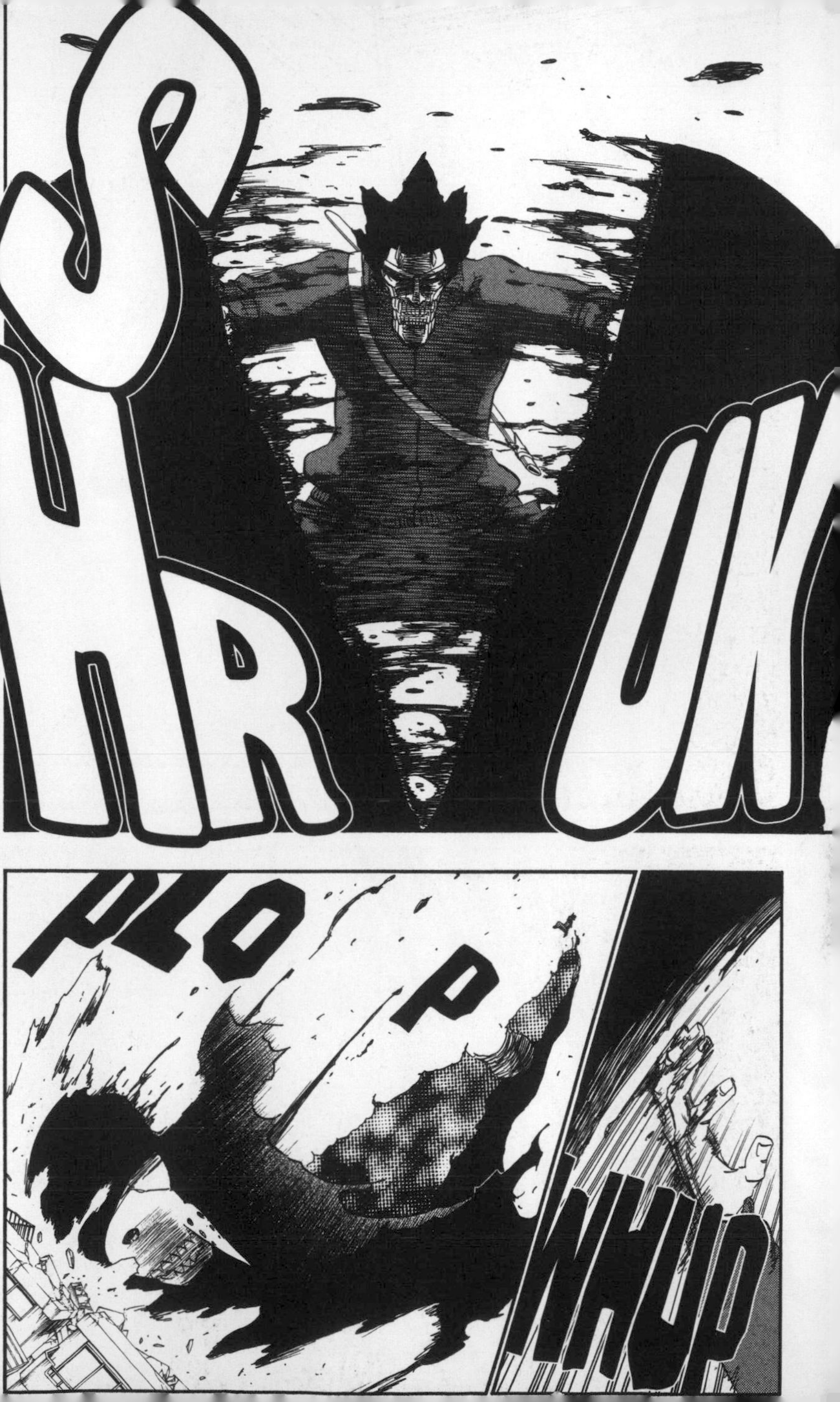
SHRUNK
WHUP
PLOP

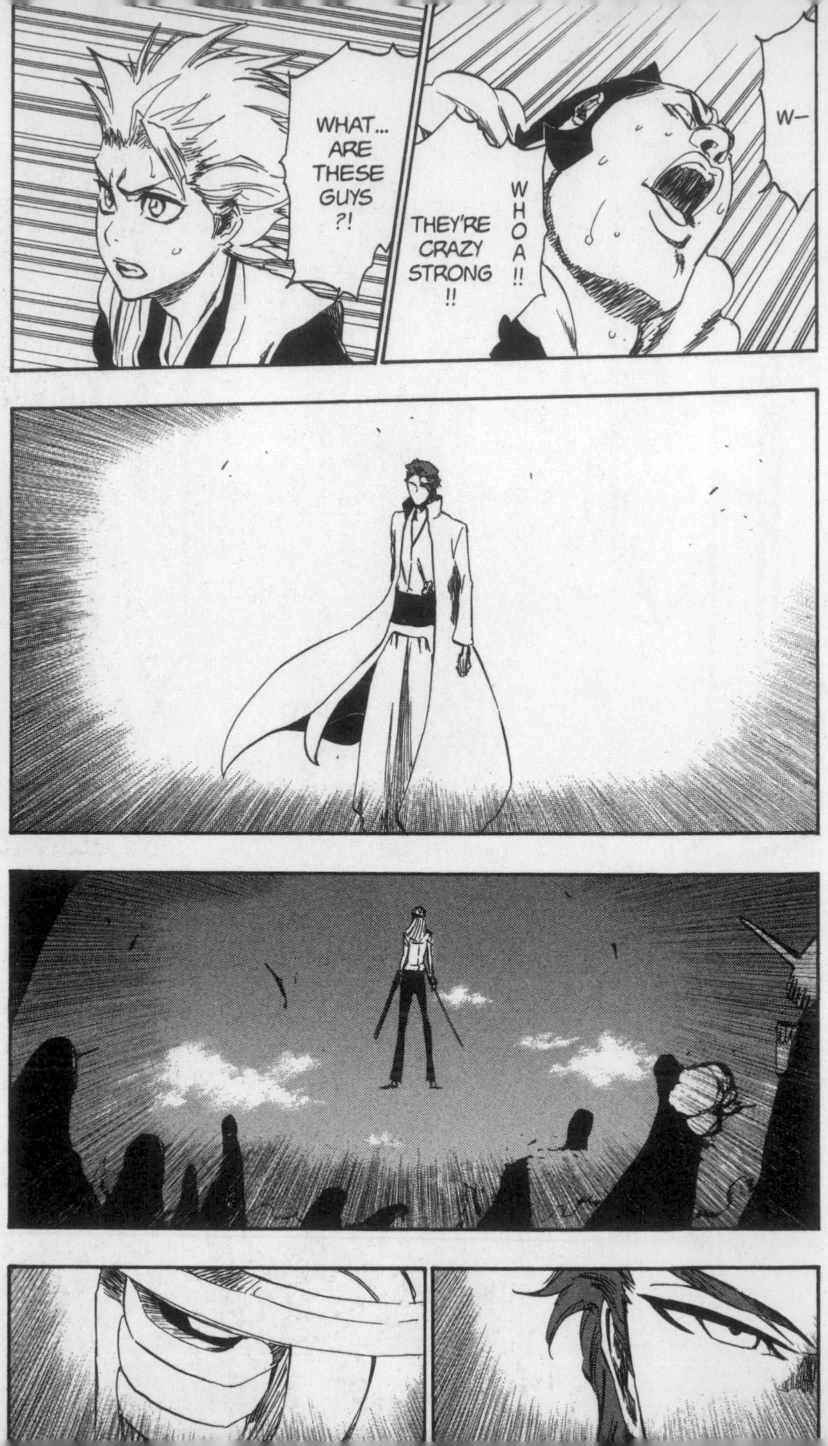
W—
WHOA!!
THEY'RE CRAZY STRONG!!
WHAT... ARE THESE GUYS?!

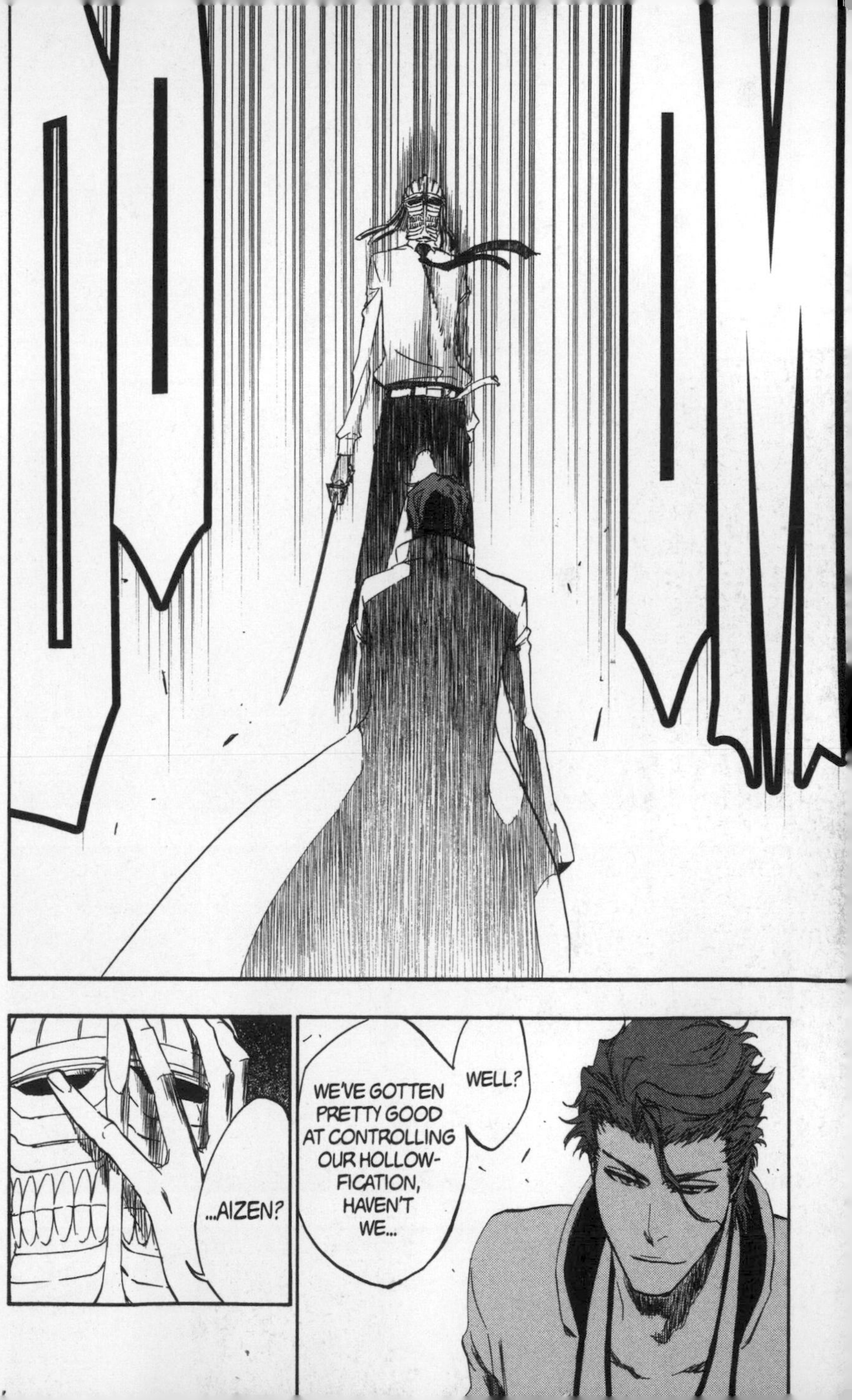
WELL?
WE'VE GOTTEN PRETTY GOOD AT CONTROLLING OUR HOLLOW-FICATION, HAVEN'T WE...
...AIZEN?

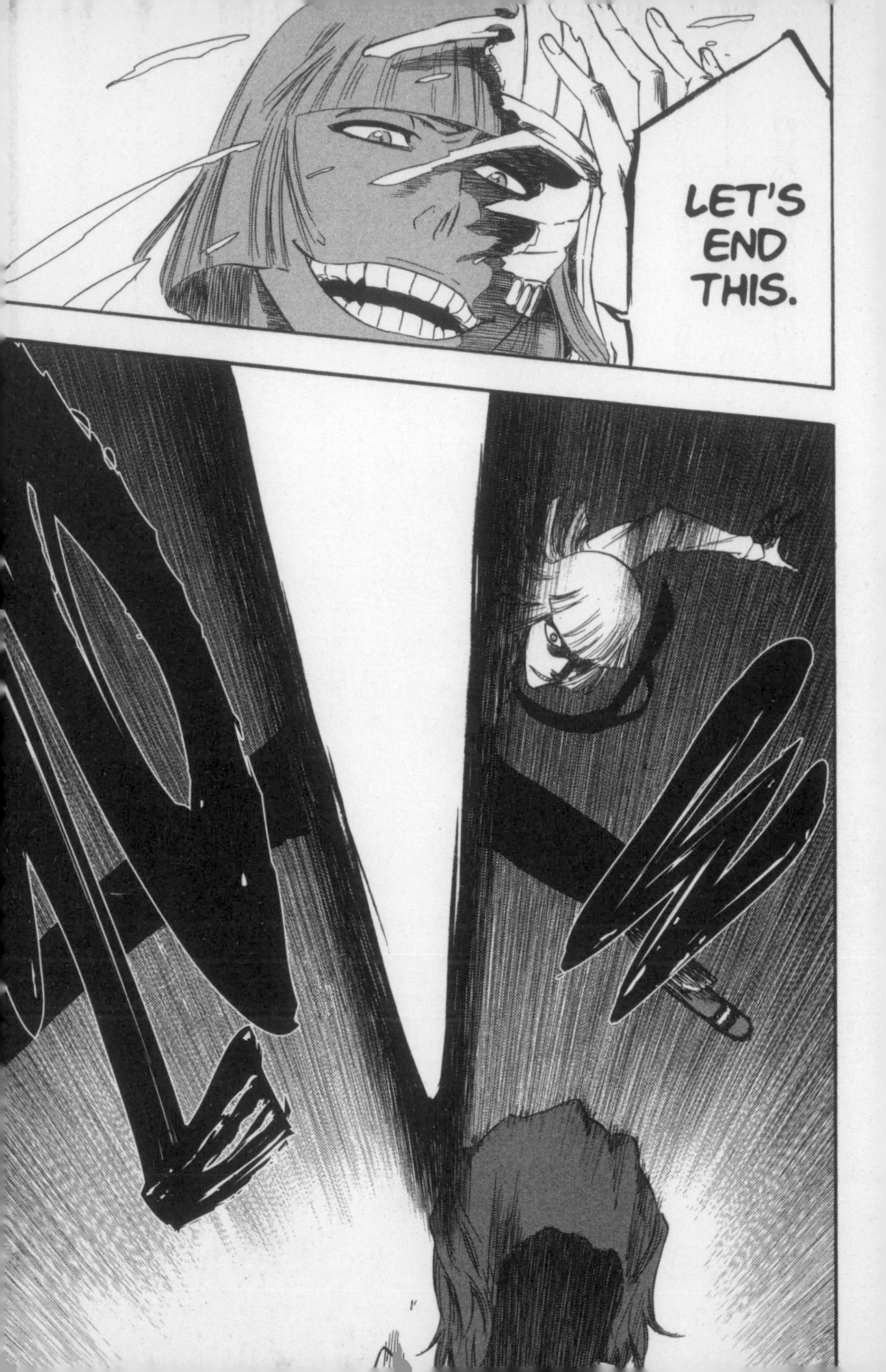
LET'S END THIS.

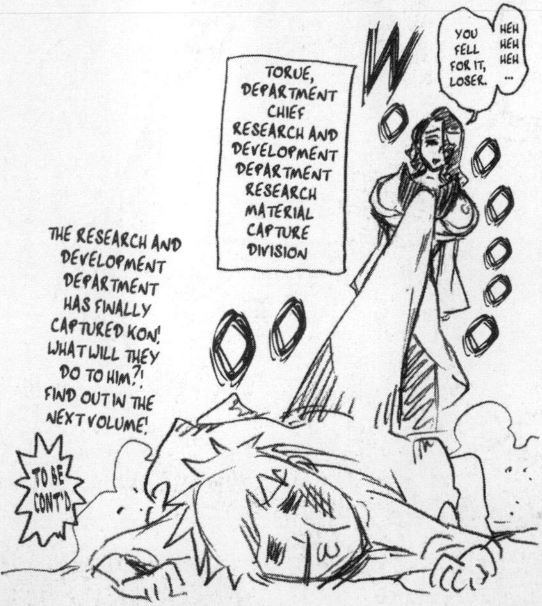
HEH HEH HEH ...
YOU FELL FOR IT, LOSER.
TORUE, DEPARTMENT CHIEF RESEARCH AND DEVELOPMENT DEPARTMENT RESEARCH MATERIAL CAPTURE DIVISION
THE RESEARCH AND DEVELOPMENT DEPARTMENT HAS FINALLY CAPTURED KON! WHAT WILL THEY DO TO HIM?! FIND OUT IN THE NEXT VOLUME!
TO BE CONT'D

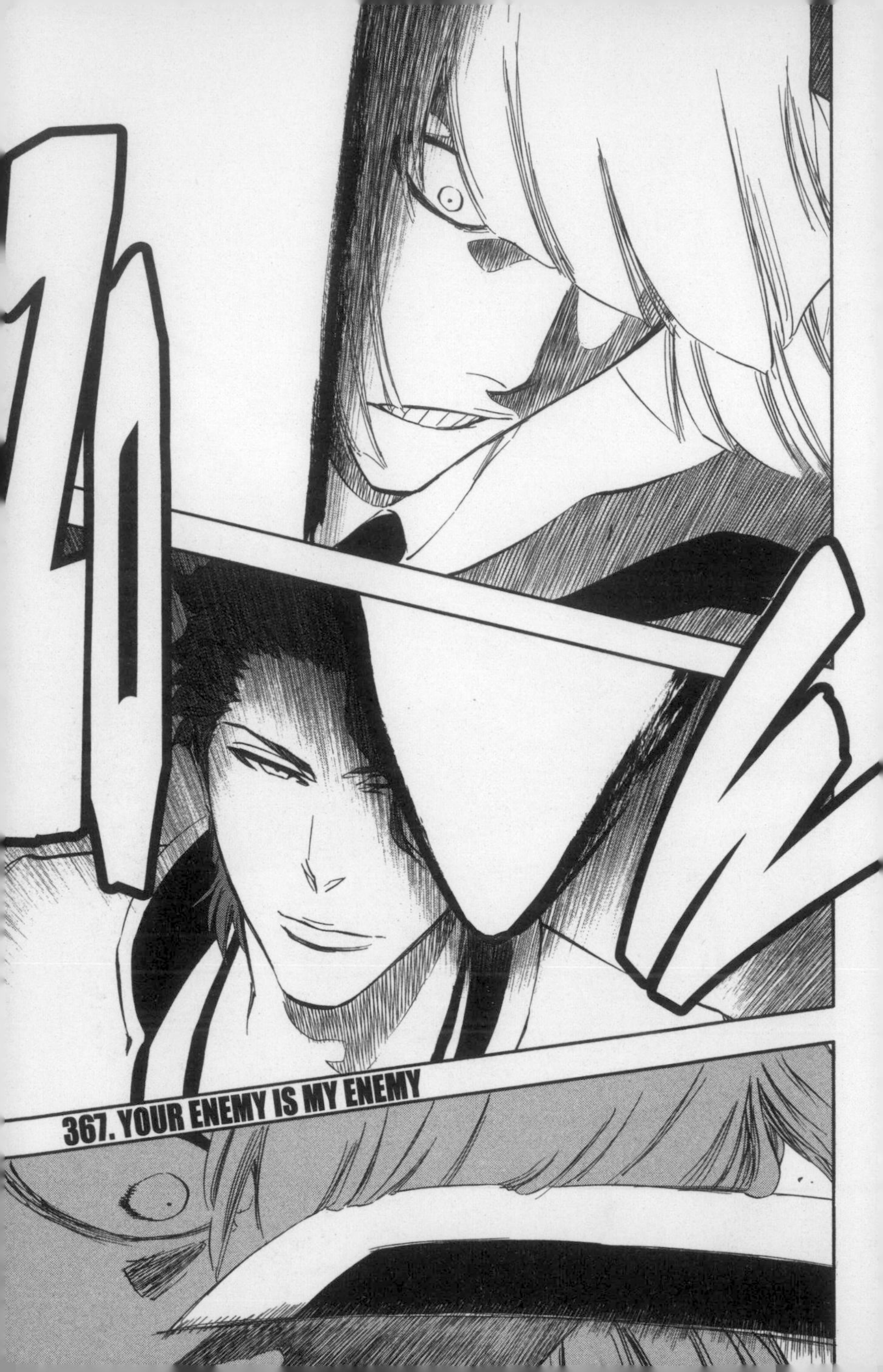
367. YOUR ENEMY IS MY ENEMY

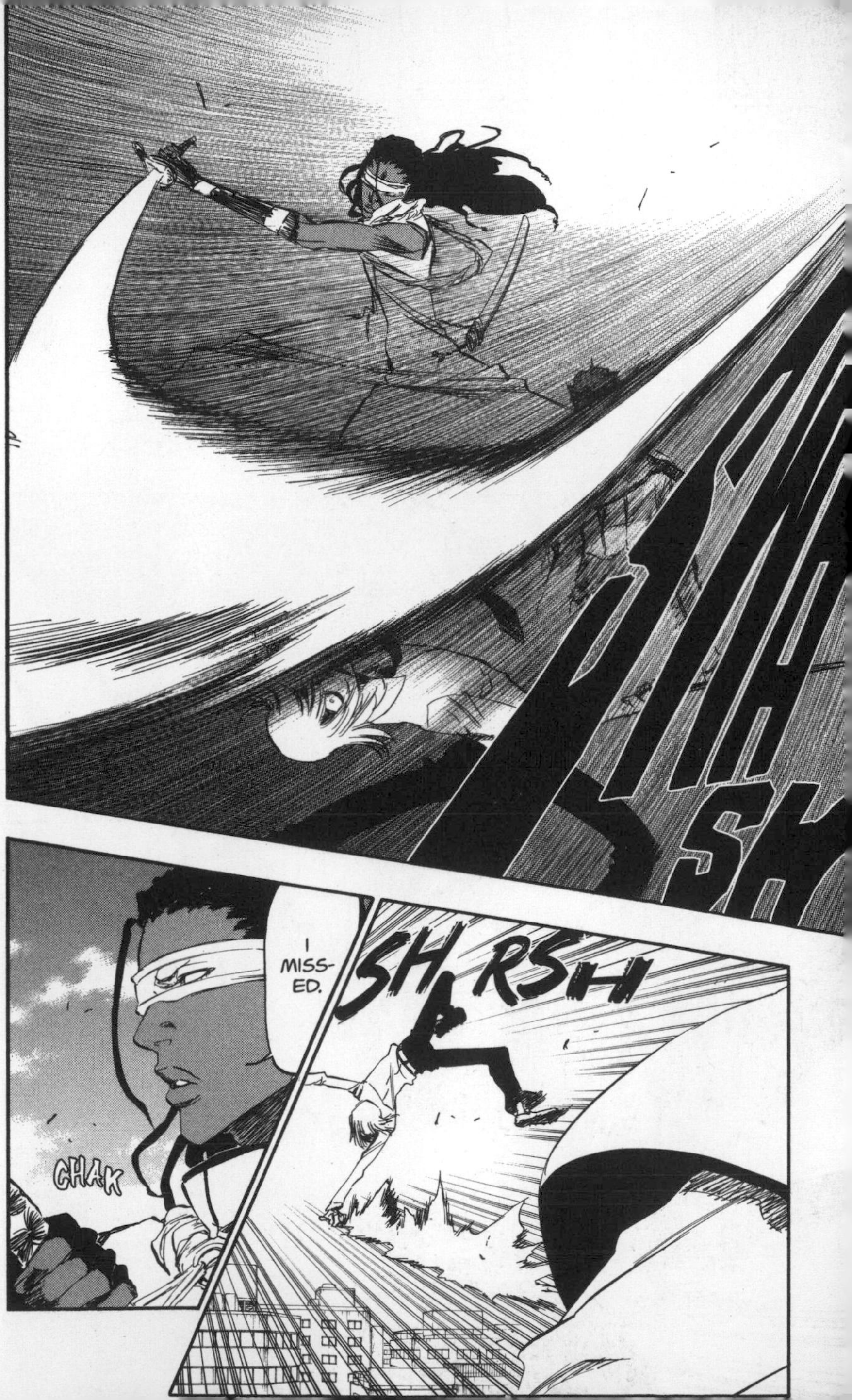
SHRSH
I MISS-ED.
CHAK

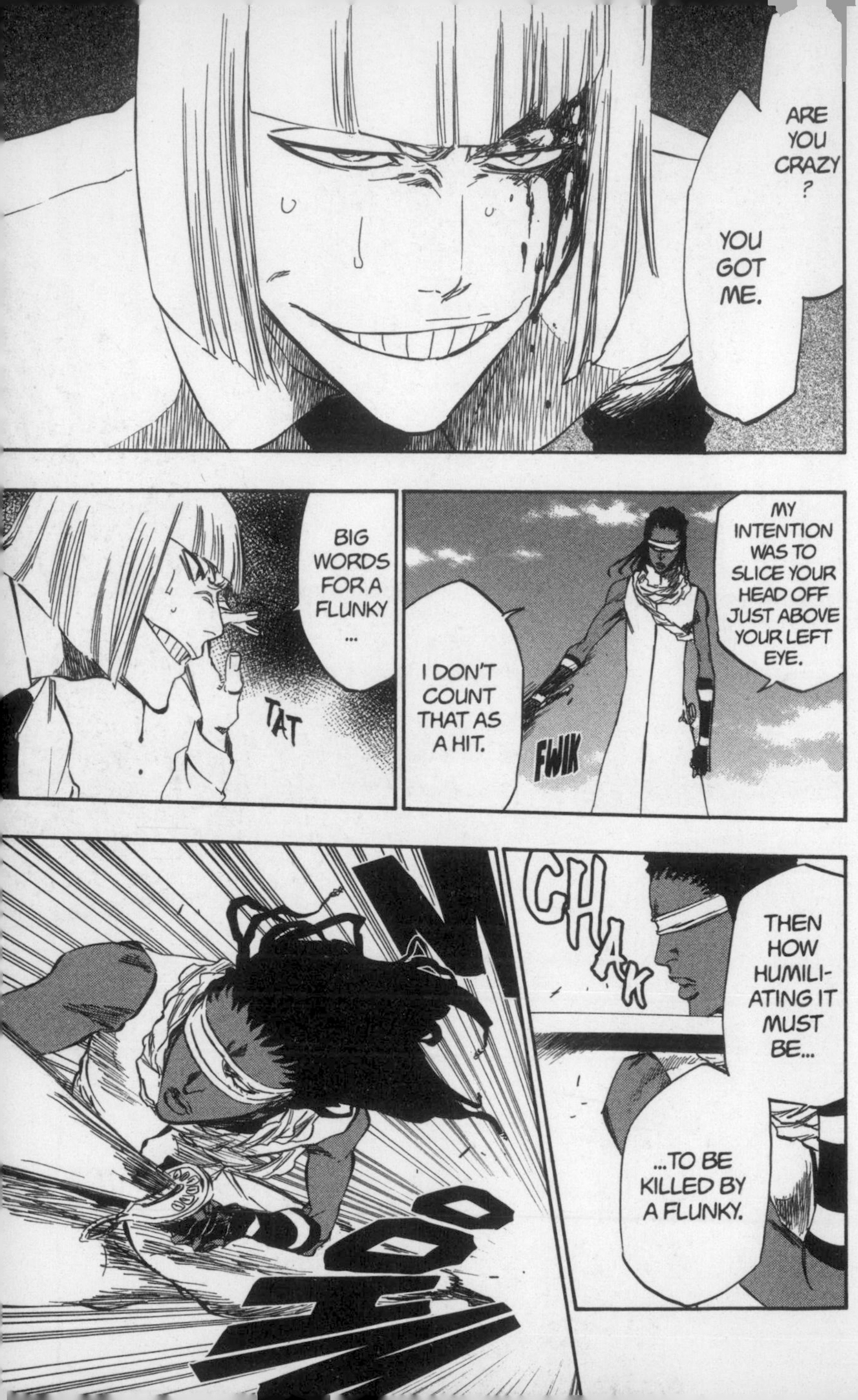
ARE YOU CRAZY?
YOU GOT ME.
MY INTENTION WAS TO SLICE YOUR HEAD OFF JUST ABOVE YOUR LEFT EYE.
I DON'T COUNT THAT AS A HIT.
FWIK
BIG WORDS FOR A FLUNKY...
TAT
CHAK
THEN HOW HUMILIATING IT MUST BE...
...TO BE KILLED BY A FLUNKY.

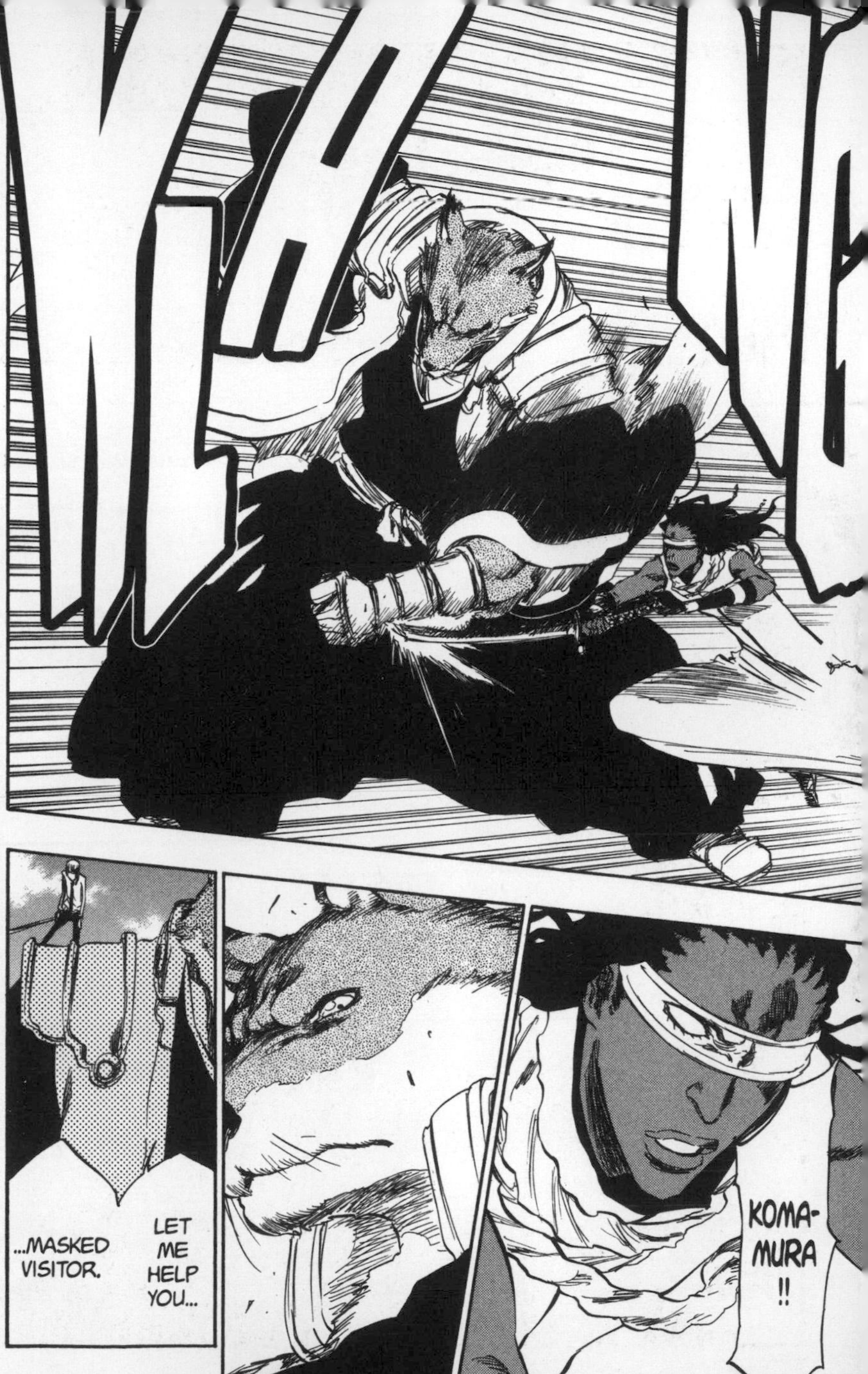
KOMA-MURA!!
LET ME HELP YOU...
...MASKED VISITOR.

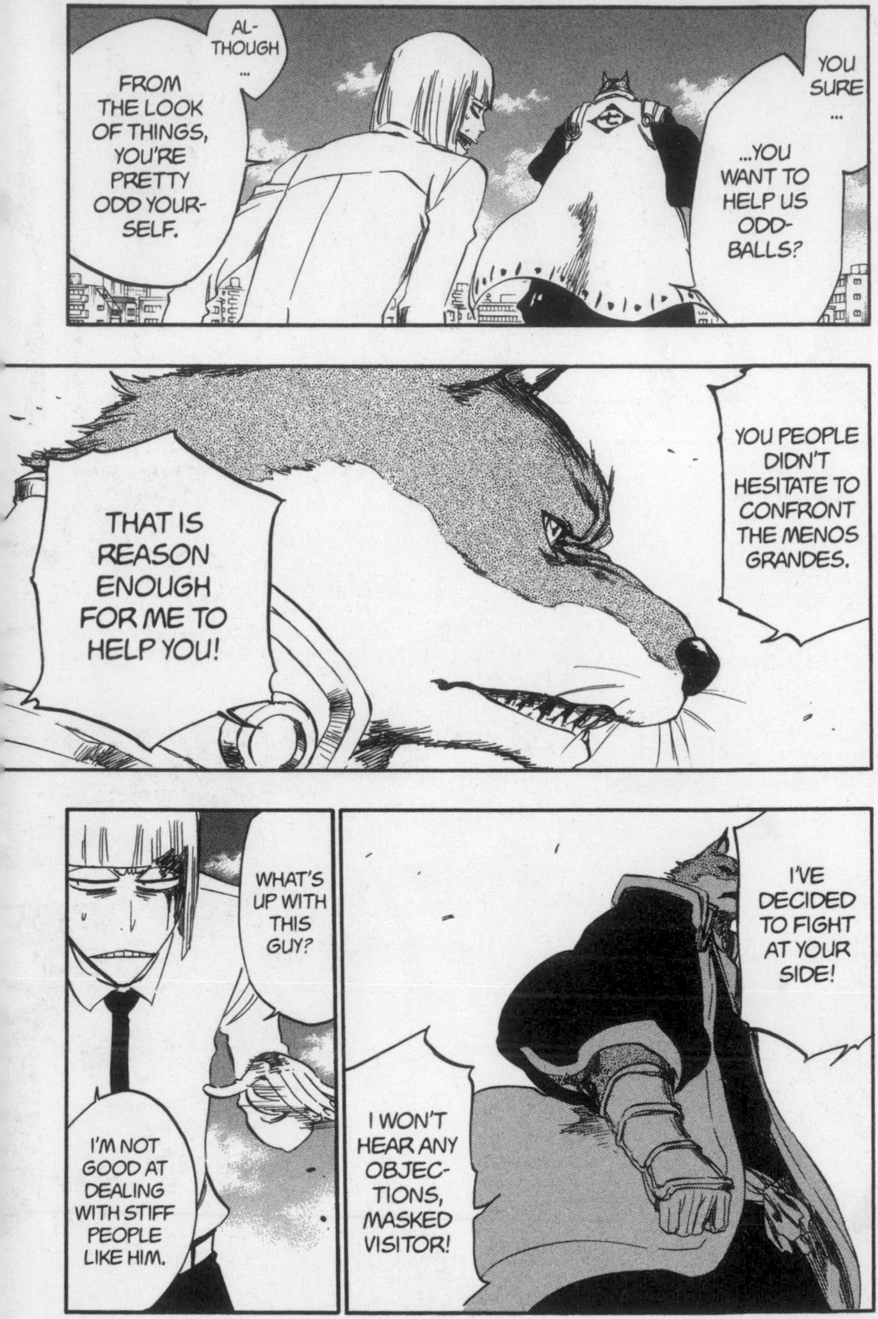
YOU SURE ...
...YOU WANT TO HELP US ODD-BALLS?
AL-THOUGH ...
FROM THE LOOK OF THINGS, YOU'RE PRETTY ODD YOUR-SELF.
YOU PEOPLE DIDN'T HESITATE TO CONFRONT THE MENOS GRANDES.
THAT IS REASON ENOUGH FOR ME TO HELP YOU!
I'VE DECIDED TO FIGHT AT YOUR SIDE!
I WON'T HEAR ANY OBJEC-TIONS, MASKED VISITOR!
WHAT'S UP WITH THIS GUY?
I'M NOT GOOD AT DEALING WITH STIFF PEOPLE LIKE HIM.

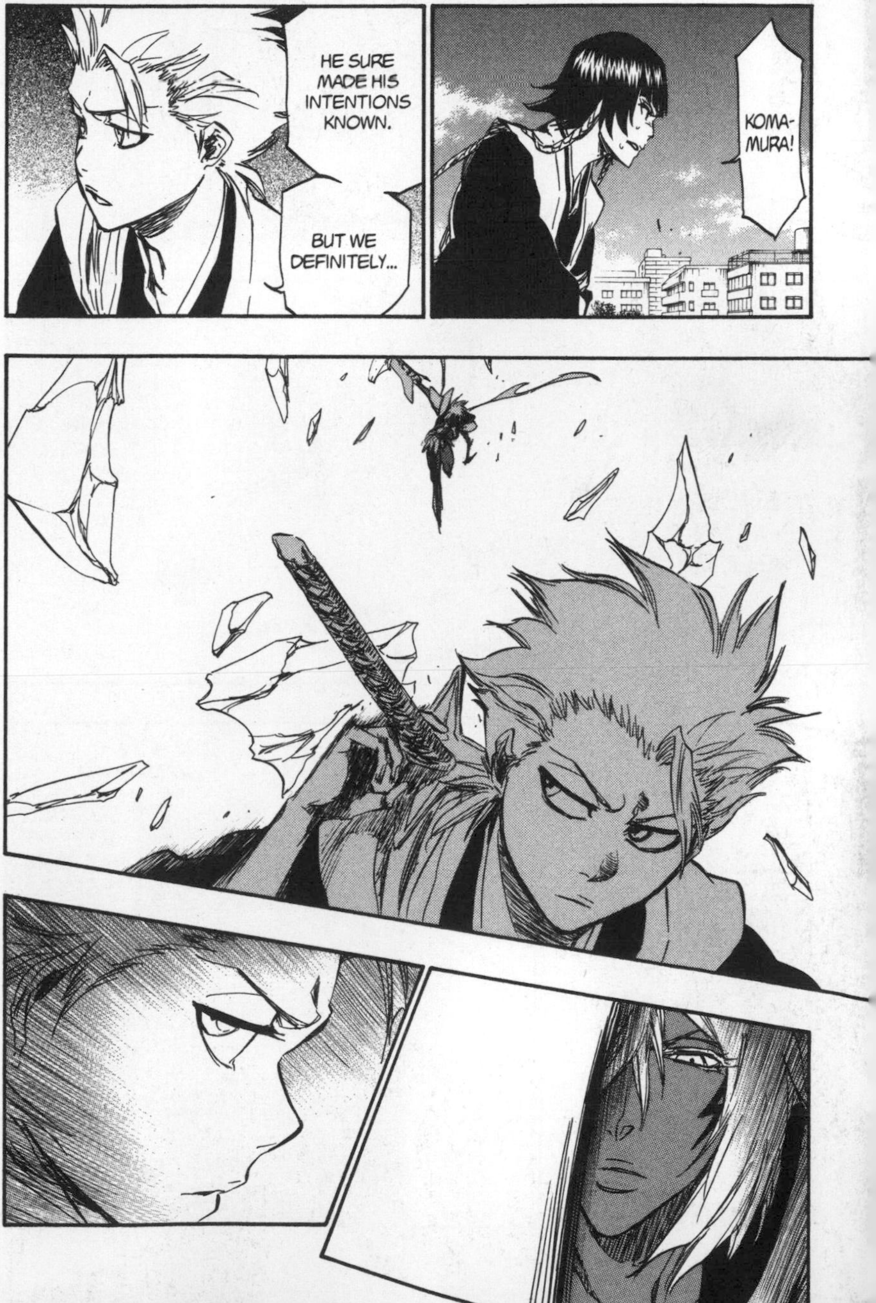
KOMA-MURA!
HE SURE MADE HIS INTENTIONS KNOWN.
BUT WE DEFINITELY...

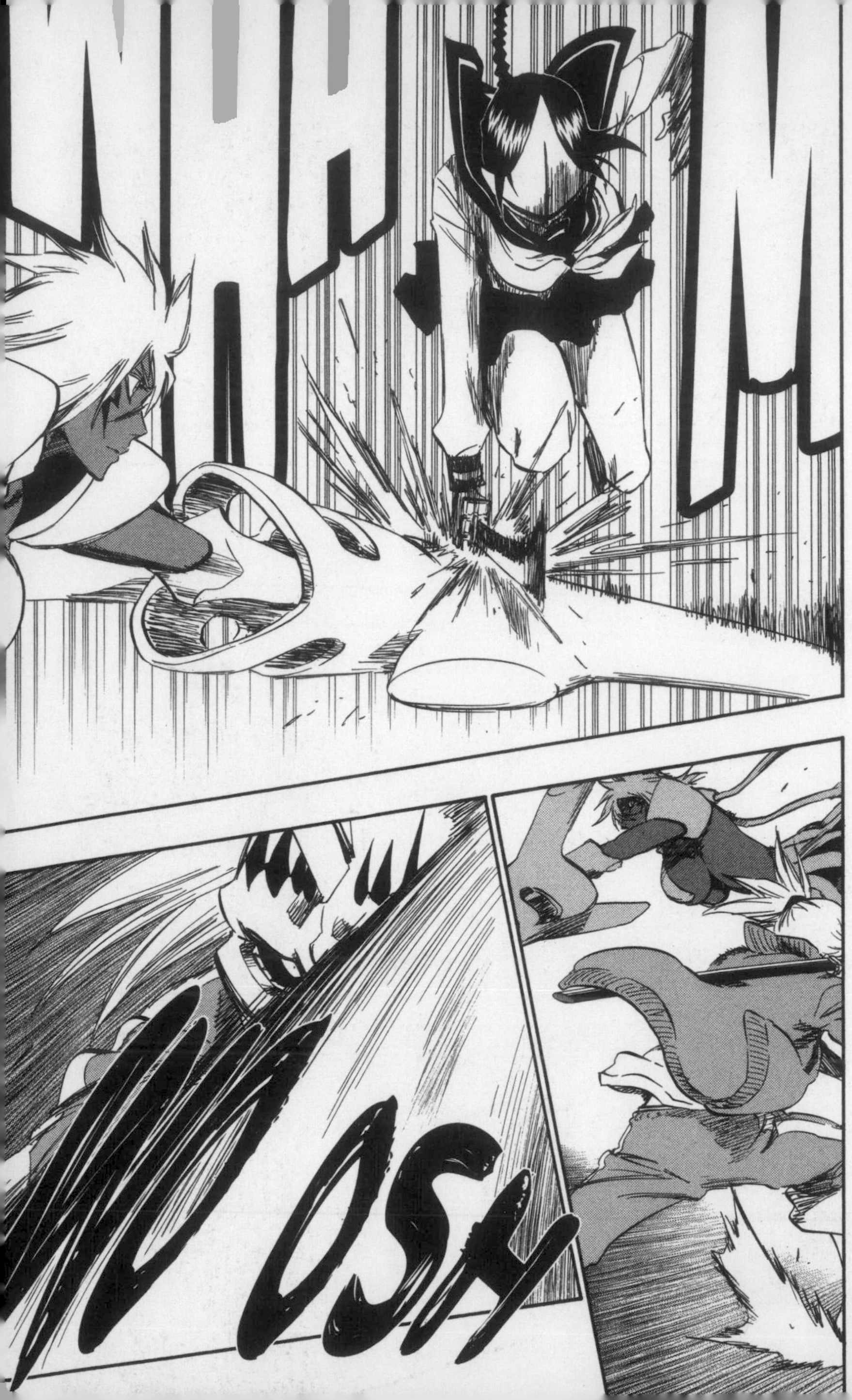
WOOSH

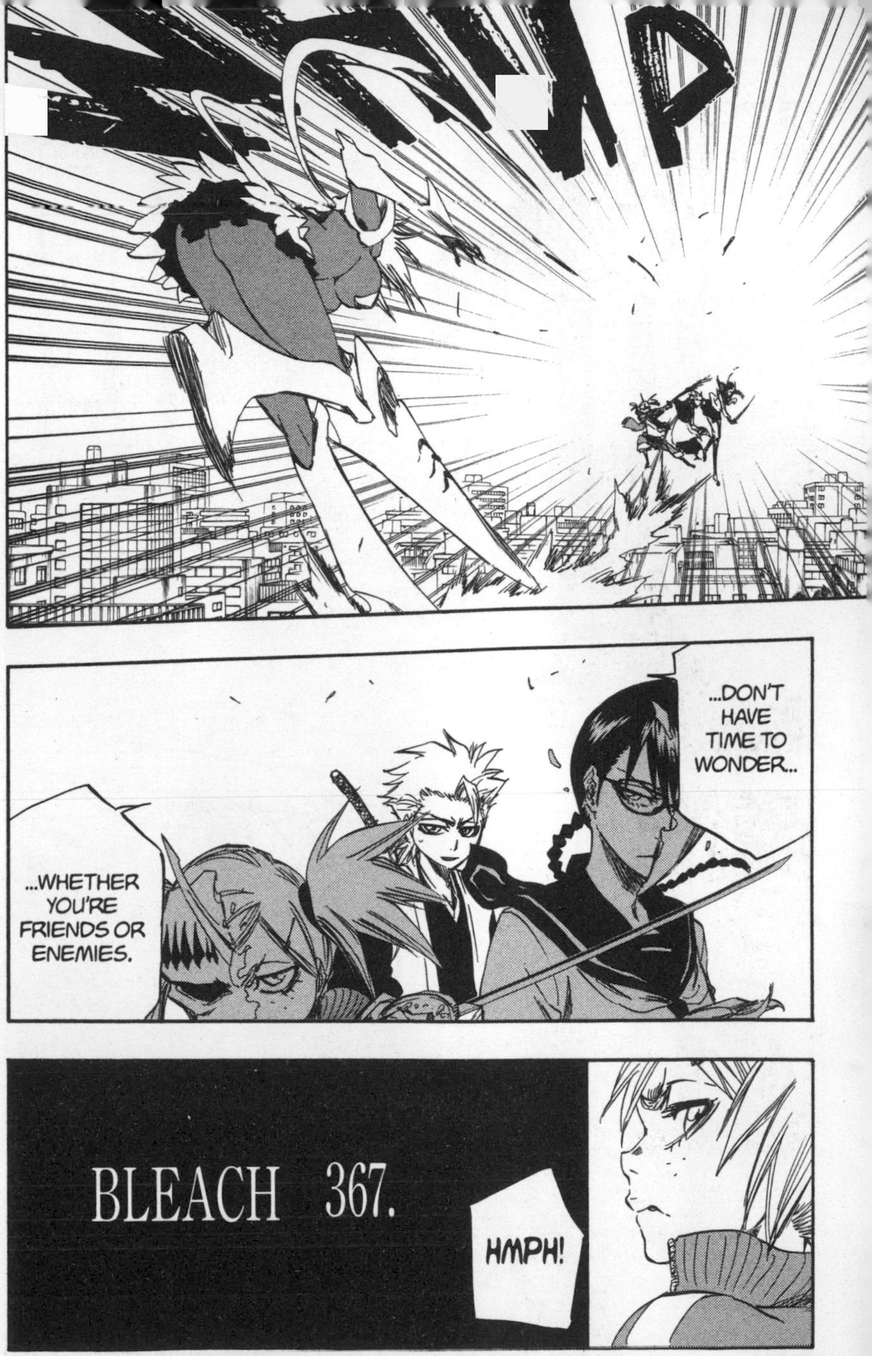
...DON'T HAVE TIME TO WONDER...
...WHETHER YOU'RE FRIENDS OR ENEMIES.
HMPH!
BLEACH 367.

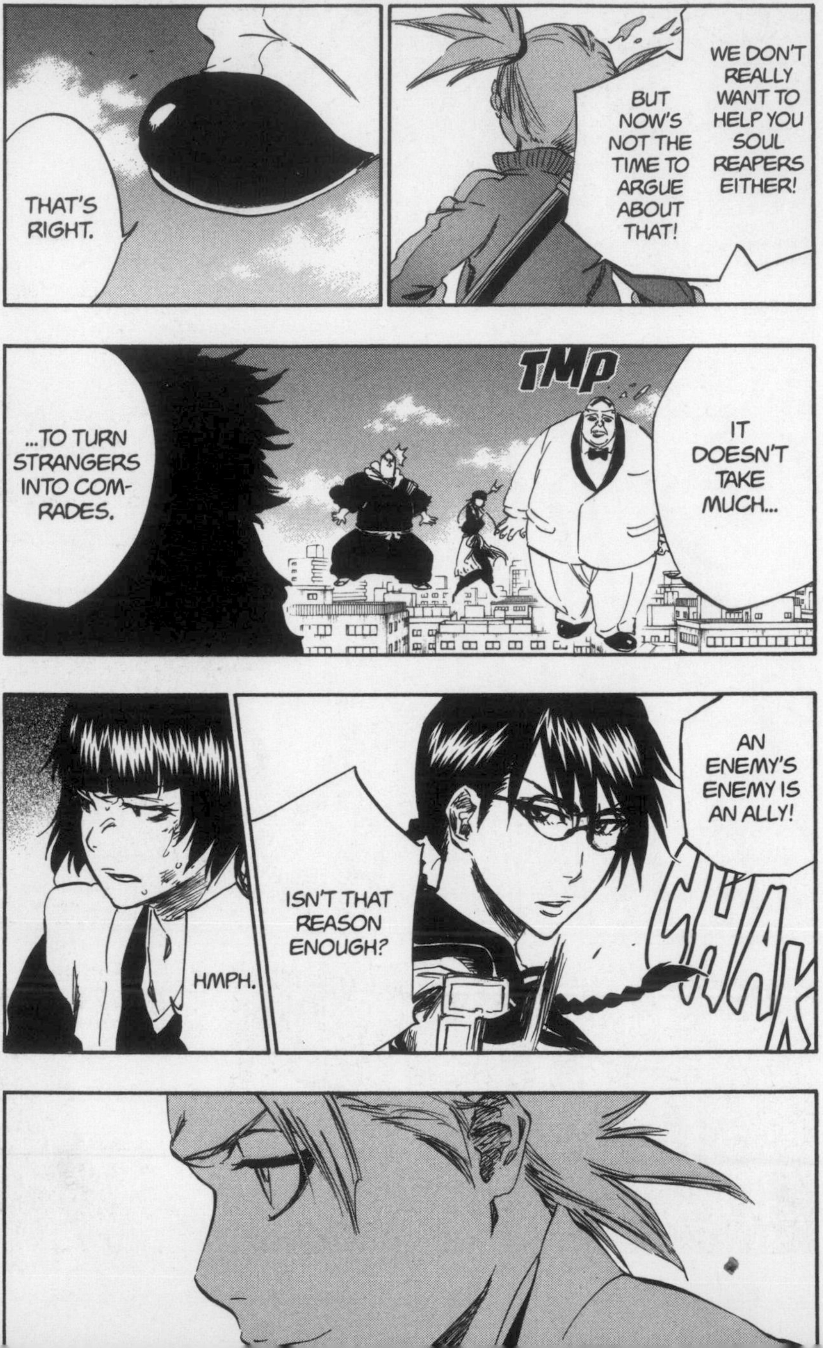
WE DON'T REALLY WANT TO HELP YOU SOUL REAPERS EITHER!
BUT NOW'S NOT THE TIME TO ARGUE ABOUT THAT!
THAT'S RIGHT.
TMP
IT DOESN'T TAKE MUCH...
...TO TURN STRANGERS INTO COM-RADES.
AN ENEMY'S ENEMY IS AN ALLY!
CHAK
ISN'T THAT REASON ENOUGH?
HMPH.

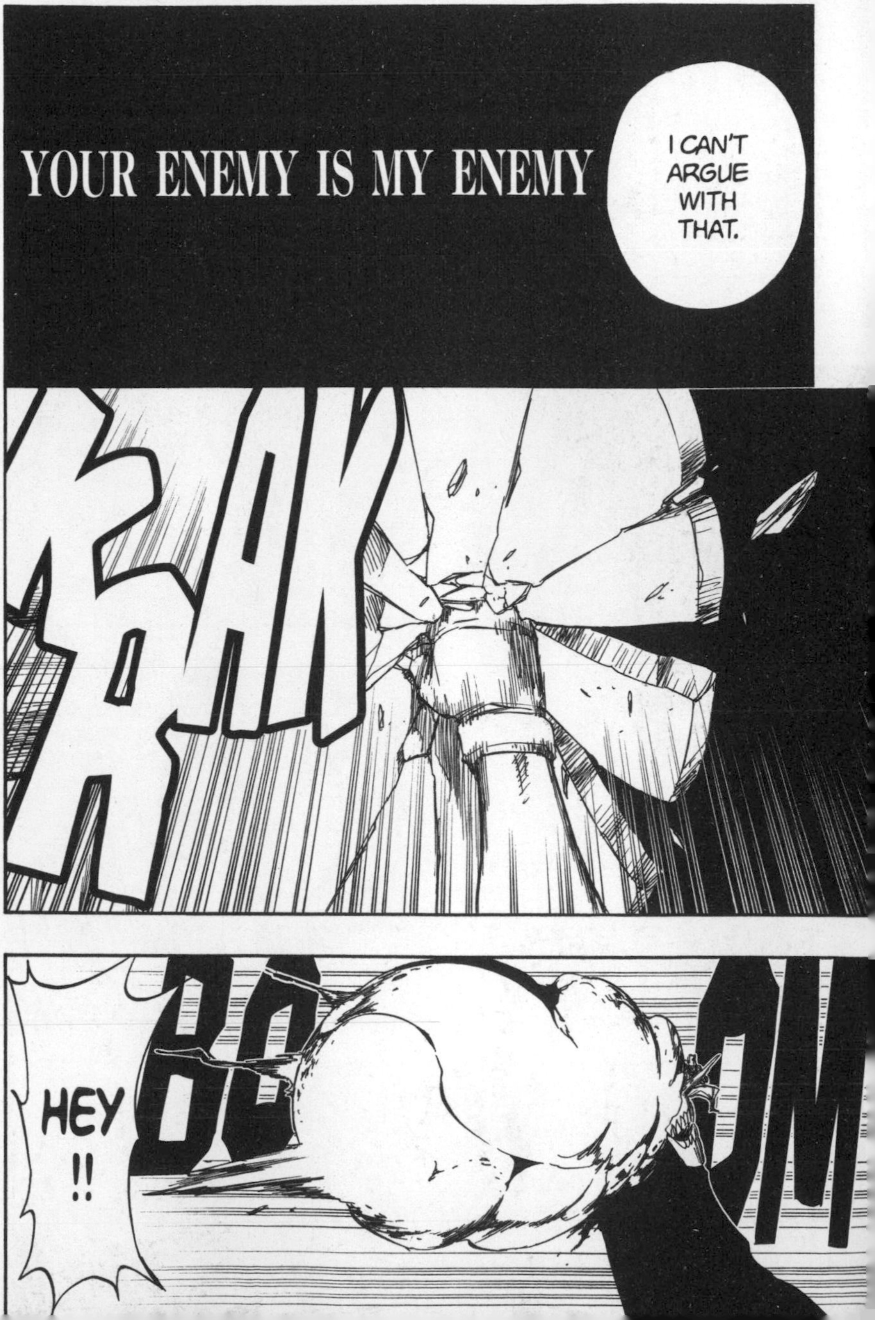
I CAN'T ARGUE WITH THAT.
YOUR ENEMY IS MY ENEMY
HEY !!

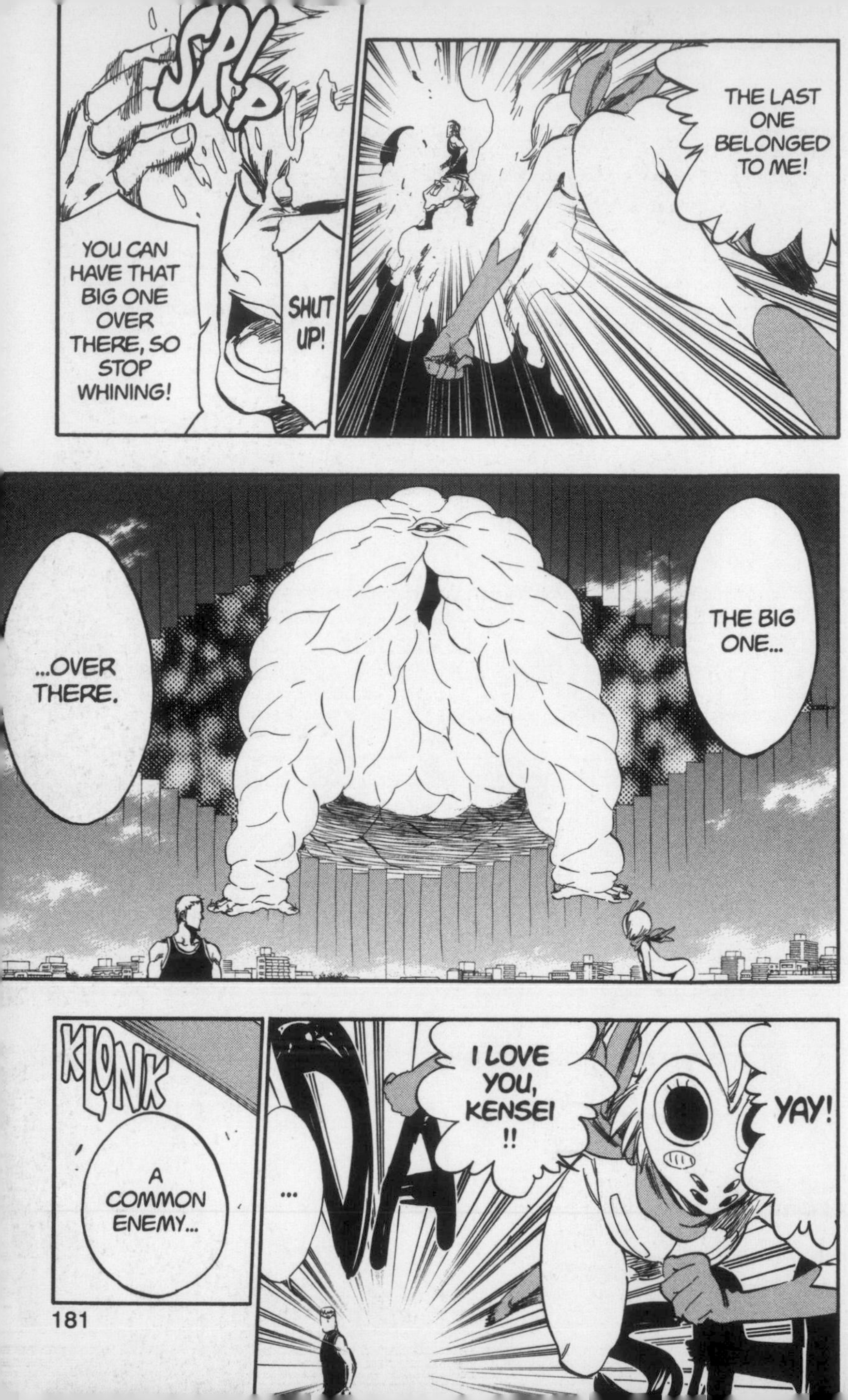
THE LAST ONE BELONGED TO ME!
SPLP
SHUT UP!
YOU CAN HAVE THAT BIG ONE OVER THERE, SO STOP WHINING!
THE BIG ONE...
...OVER THERE.
YAY!
I LOVE YOU, KENSEI !!
...
DASH
KLONK
A COMMON ENEMY...

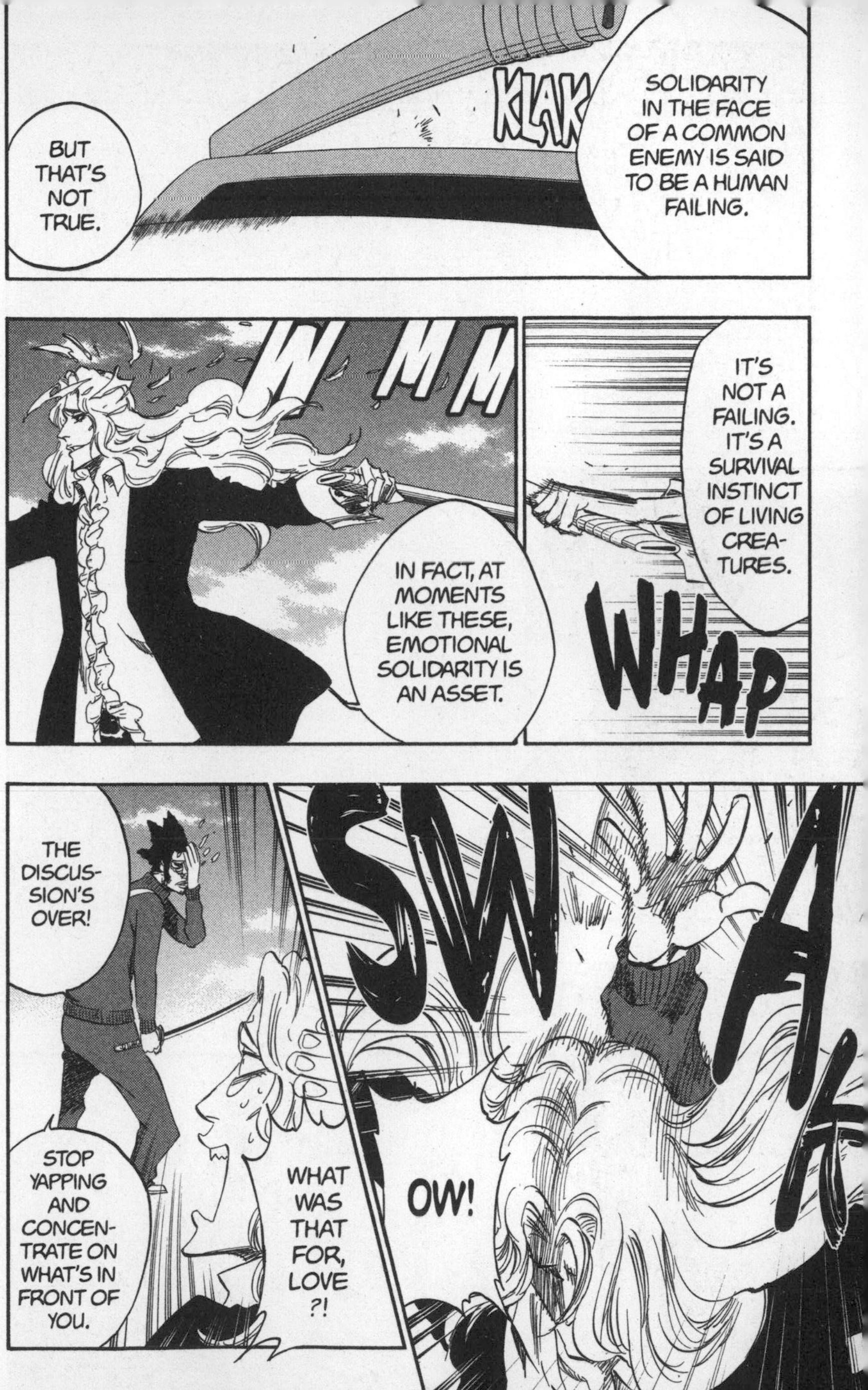
SOLIDARITY IN THE FACE OF A COMMON ENEMY IS SAID TO BE A HUMAN FAILING.
KLAK
BUT THAT'S NOT TRUE.
IT'S NOT A FAILING. IT'S A SURVIVAL INSTINCT OF LIVING CREA-TURES.
WHAP
WMM
IN FACT, AT MOMENTS LIKE THESE, EMOTIONAL SOLIDARITY IS AN ASSET.
OW!
WHAT WAS THAT FOR, LOVE?!
THE DISCUS-SION'S OVER!
STOP YAPPING AND CONCEN-TRATE ON WHAT'S IN FRONT OF YOU.

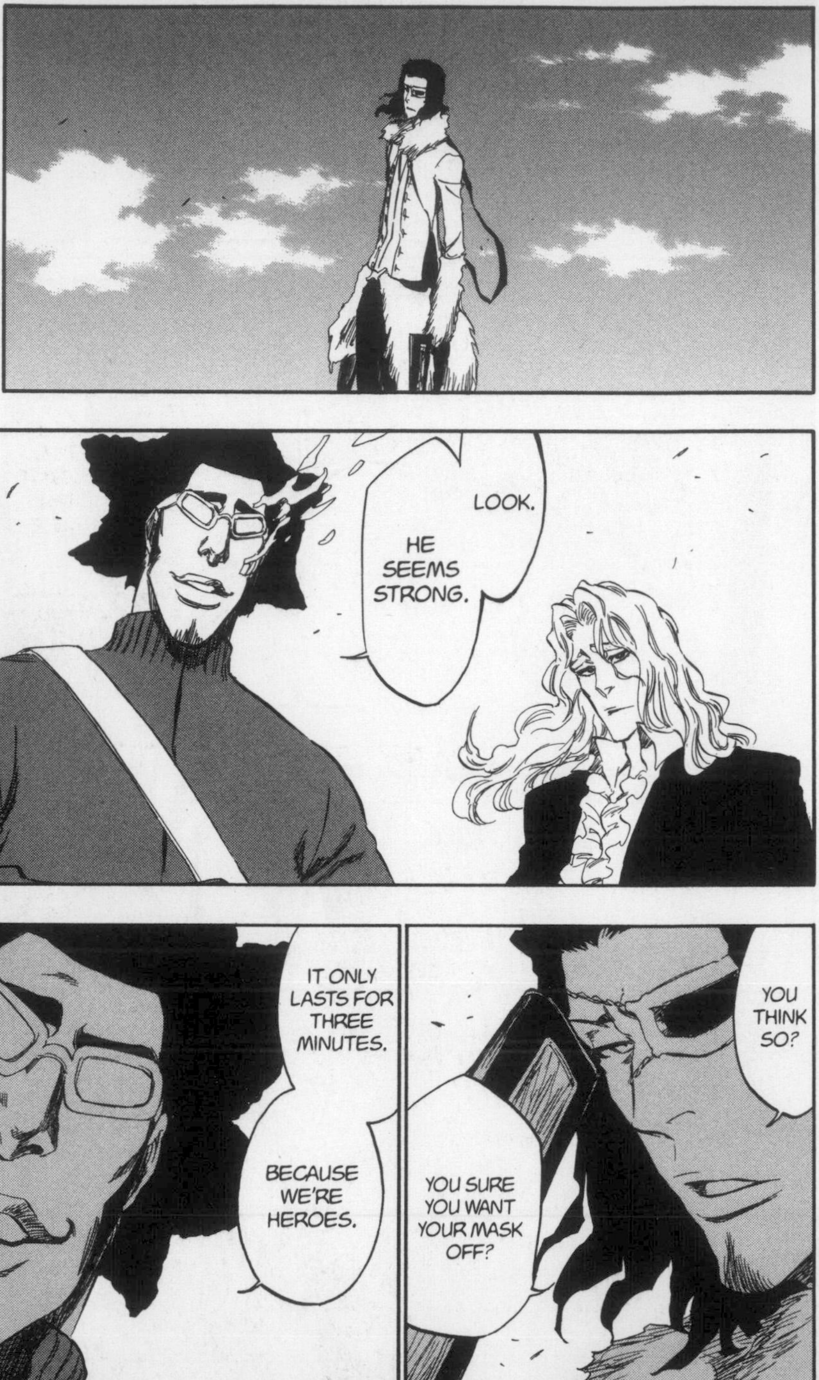
LOOK.
HE SEEMS STRONG.
YOU THINK SO?
YOU SURE YOU WANT YOUR MASK OFF?
IT ONLY LASTS FOR THREE MINUTES.
BECAUSE WE'RE HEROES.

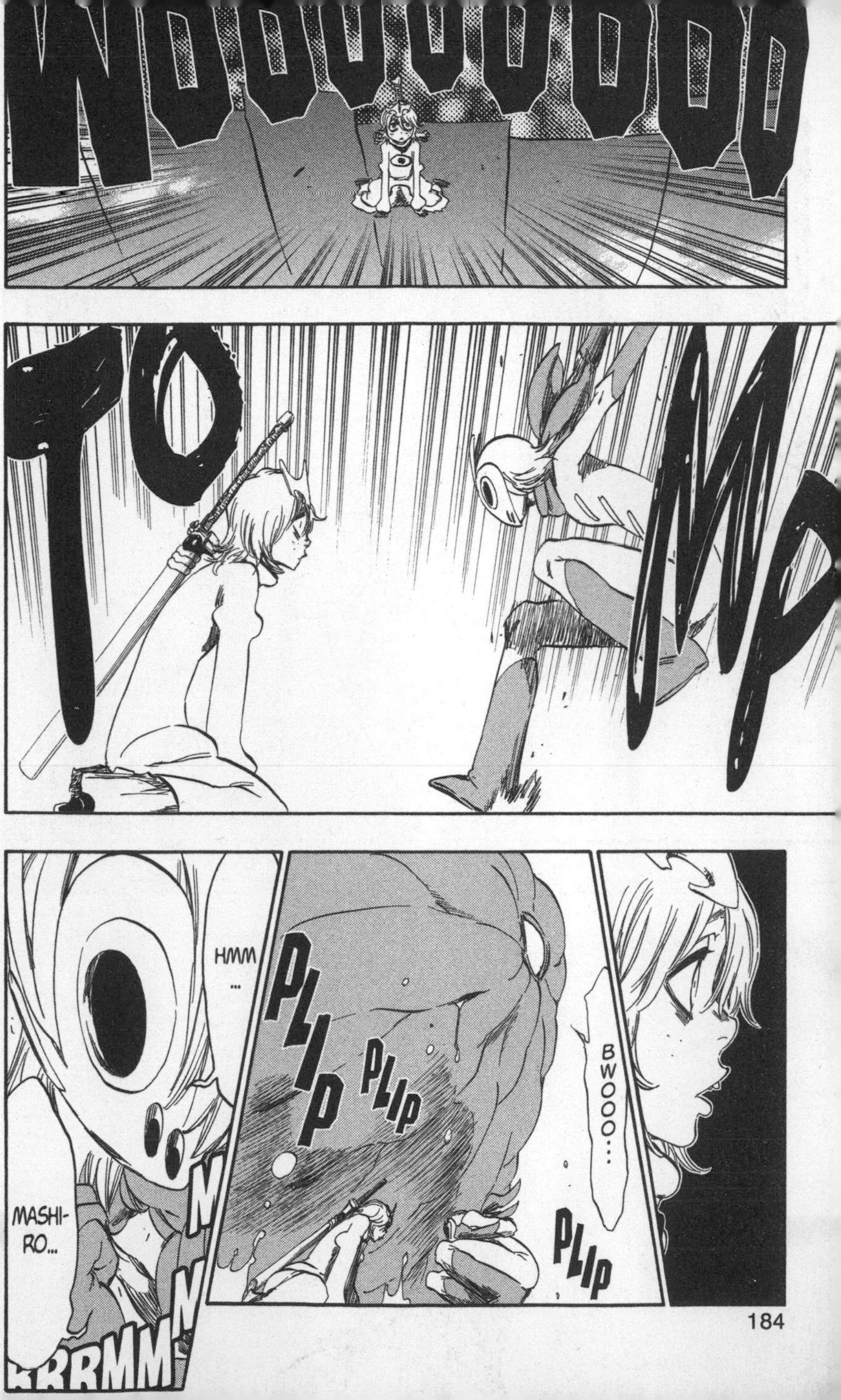
TOMP
BWOOO...
PLIP
PLIP
PLIP
HMM...
MASHIRO...
KRRMM

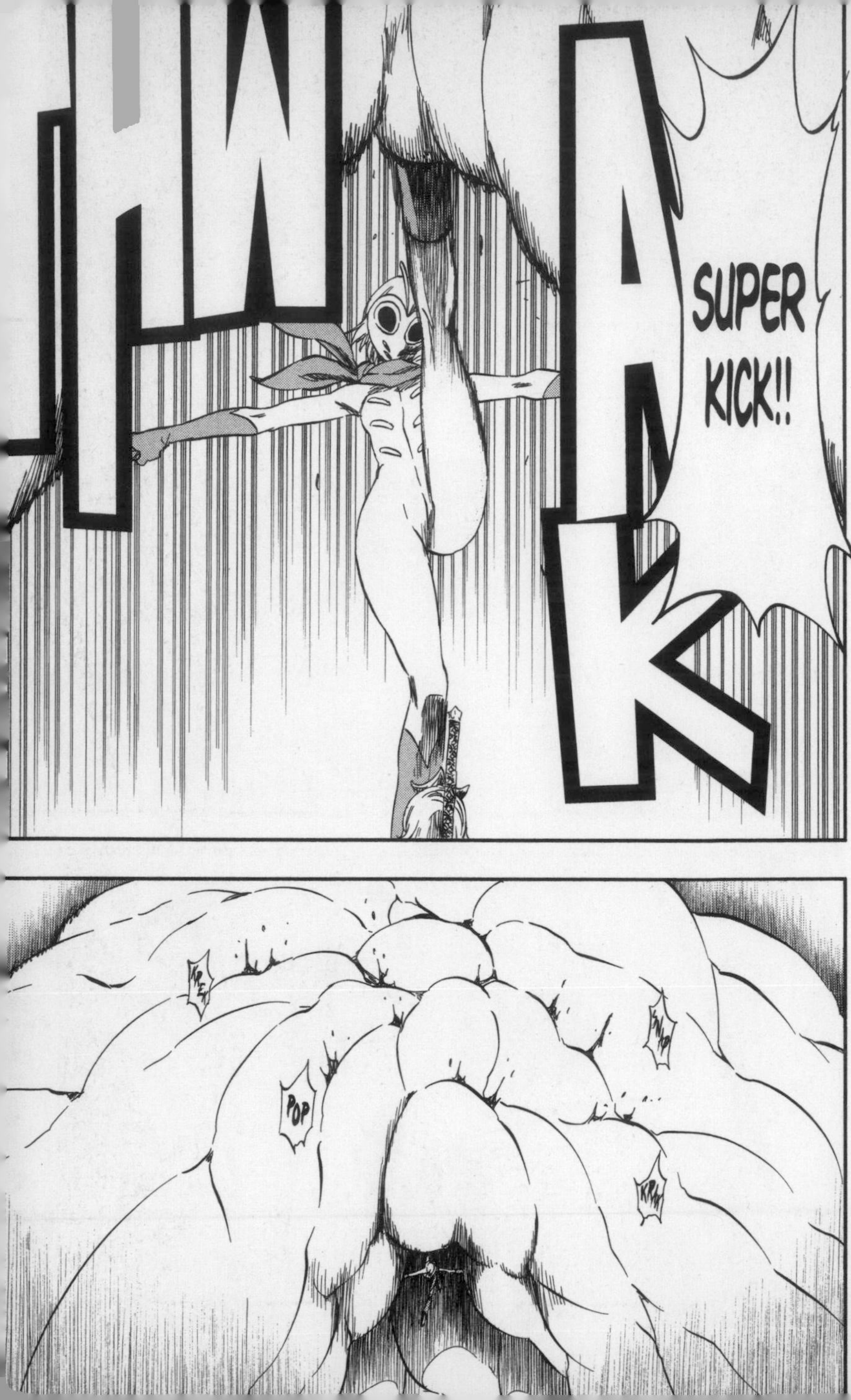
SUPER KICK!!
SNAP
KREK
POP
KRAK

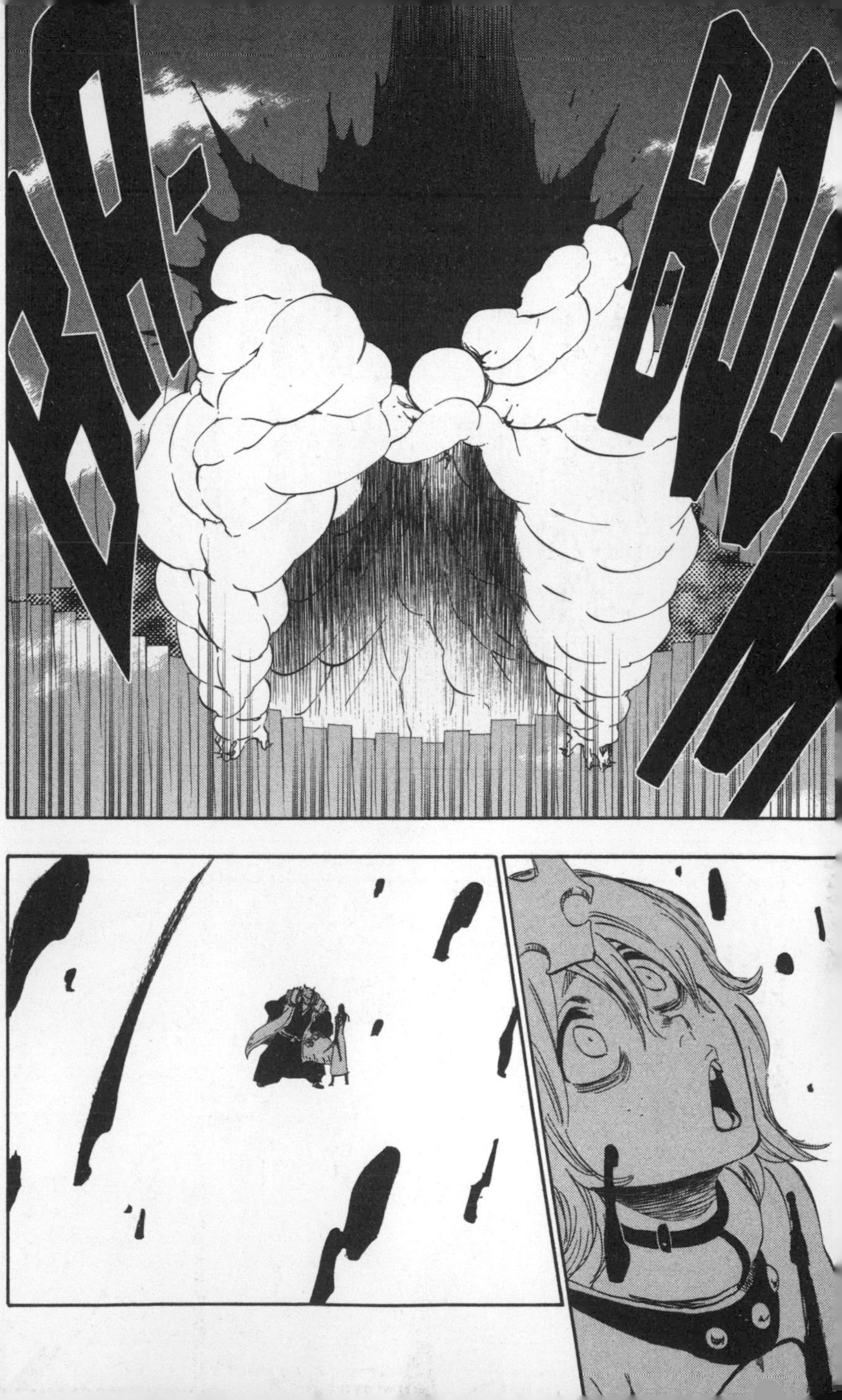

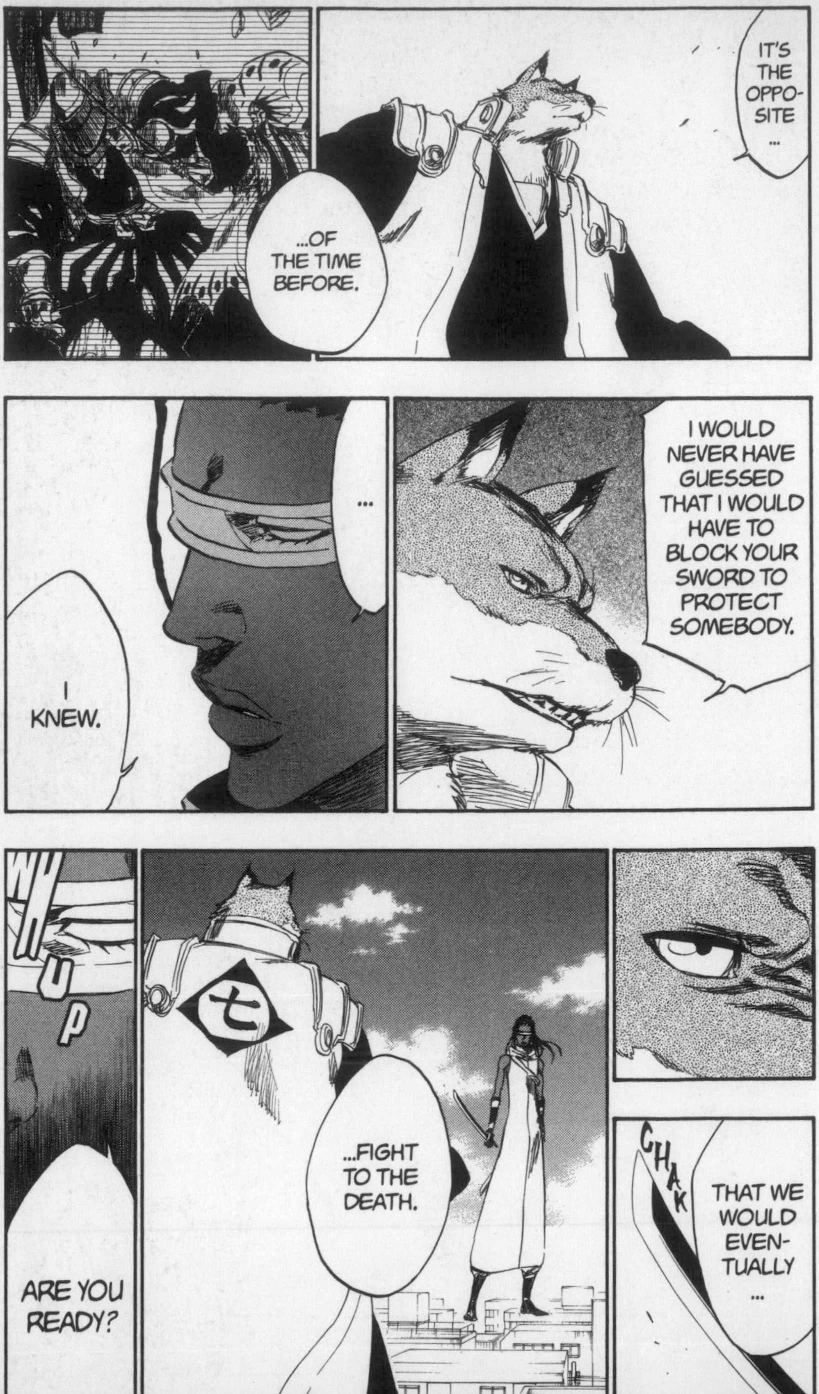
IT'S THE OPPO-SITE ...
...OF THE TIME BEFORE.
I WOULD NEVER HAVE GUESSED THAT I WOULD HAVE TO BLOCK YOUR SWORD TO PROTECT SOMEBODY.
...
I KNEW.
CHAK
THAT WE WOULD EVEN-TUALLY ...
...FIGHT TO THE DEATH.
WHUP
ARE YOU READY?

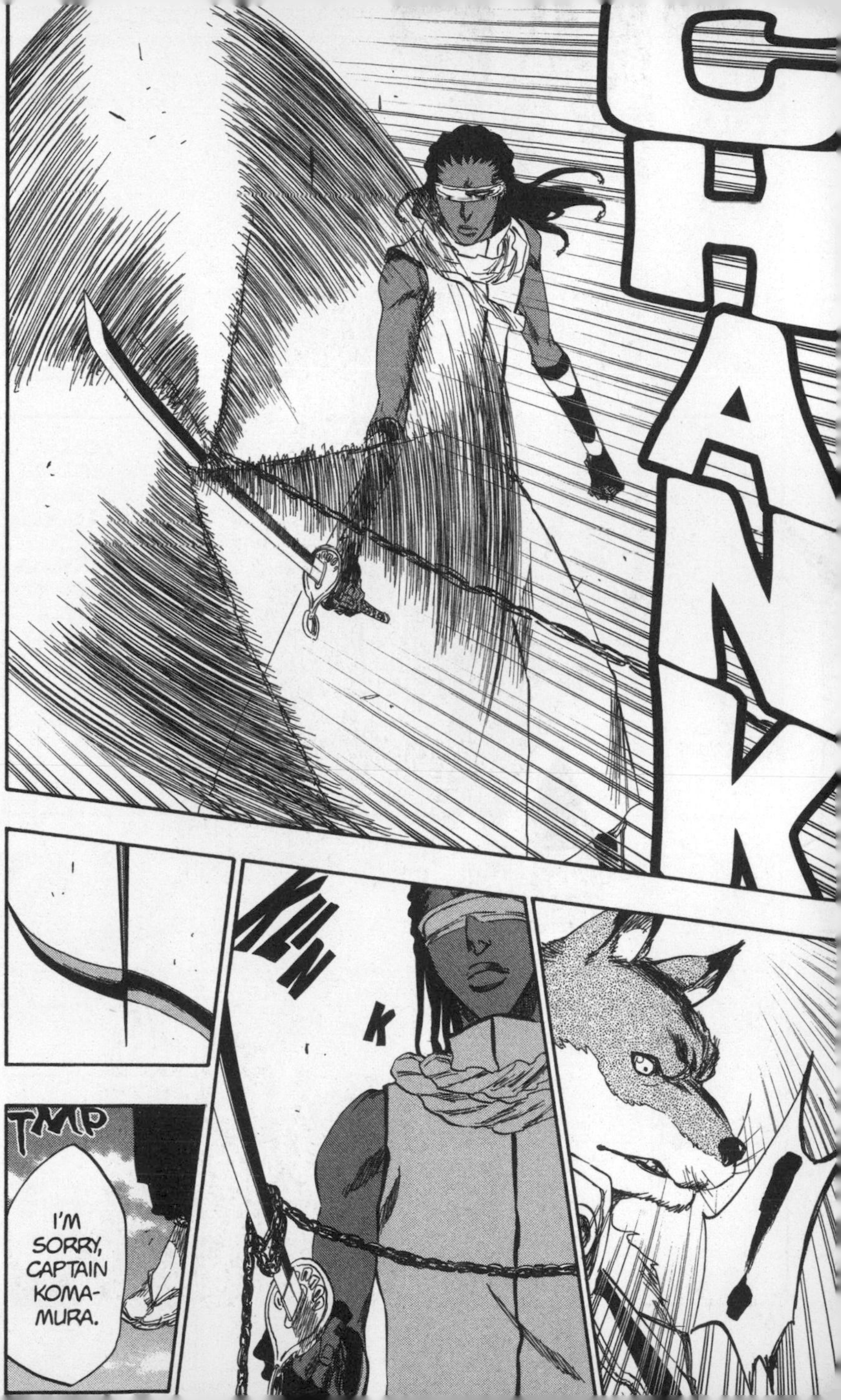
CHANK
!
KLINK
TMP
I'M SORRY, CAPTAIN KOMAMURA.

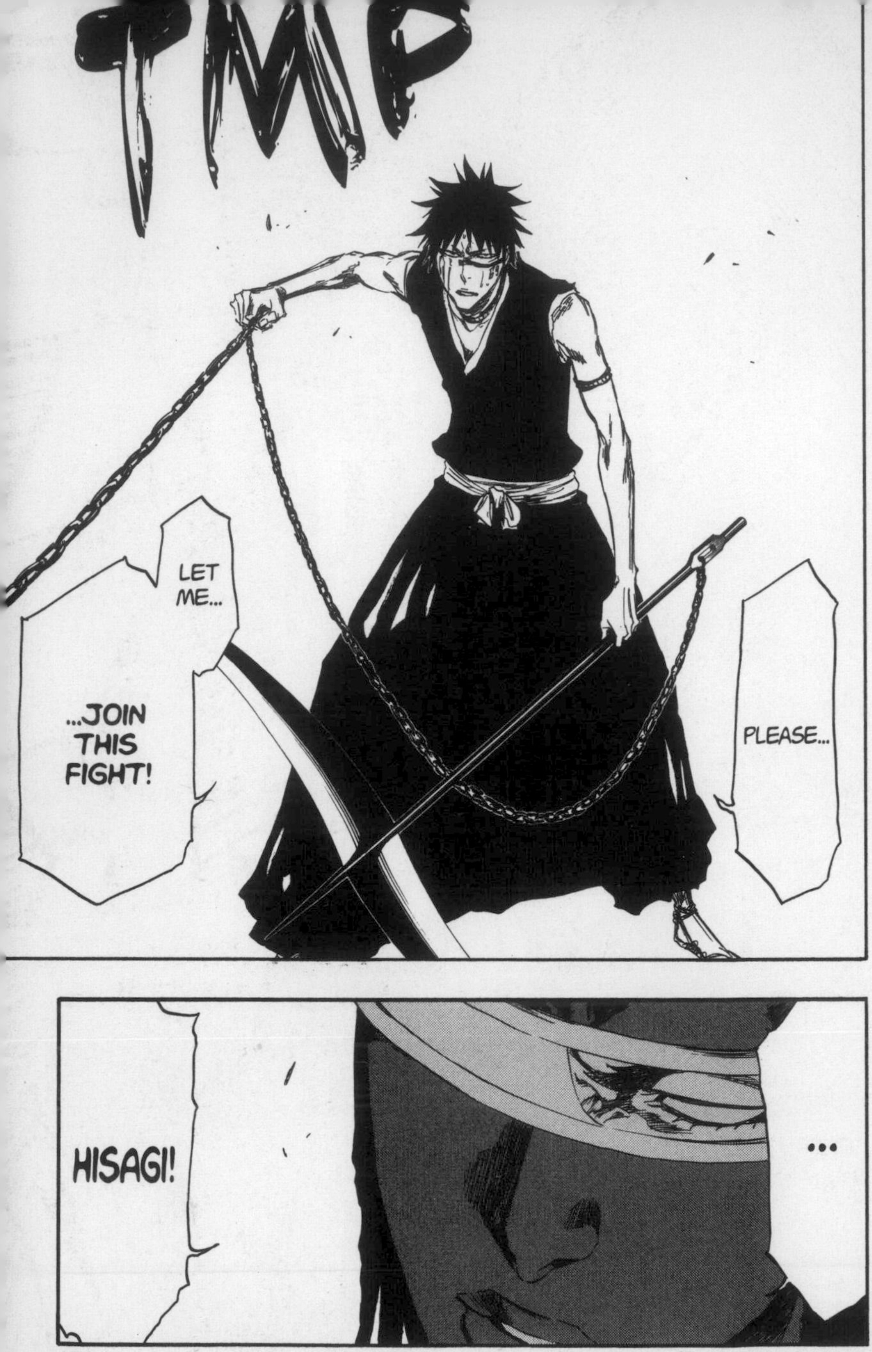
TMP
PLEASE...
LET ME...
...JOIN THIS FIGHT!
...
HISAGI!

CONTI
NUED
IN
BLEACH
43

Next Volume Preview

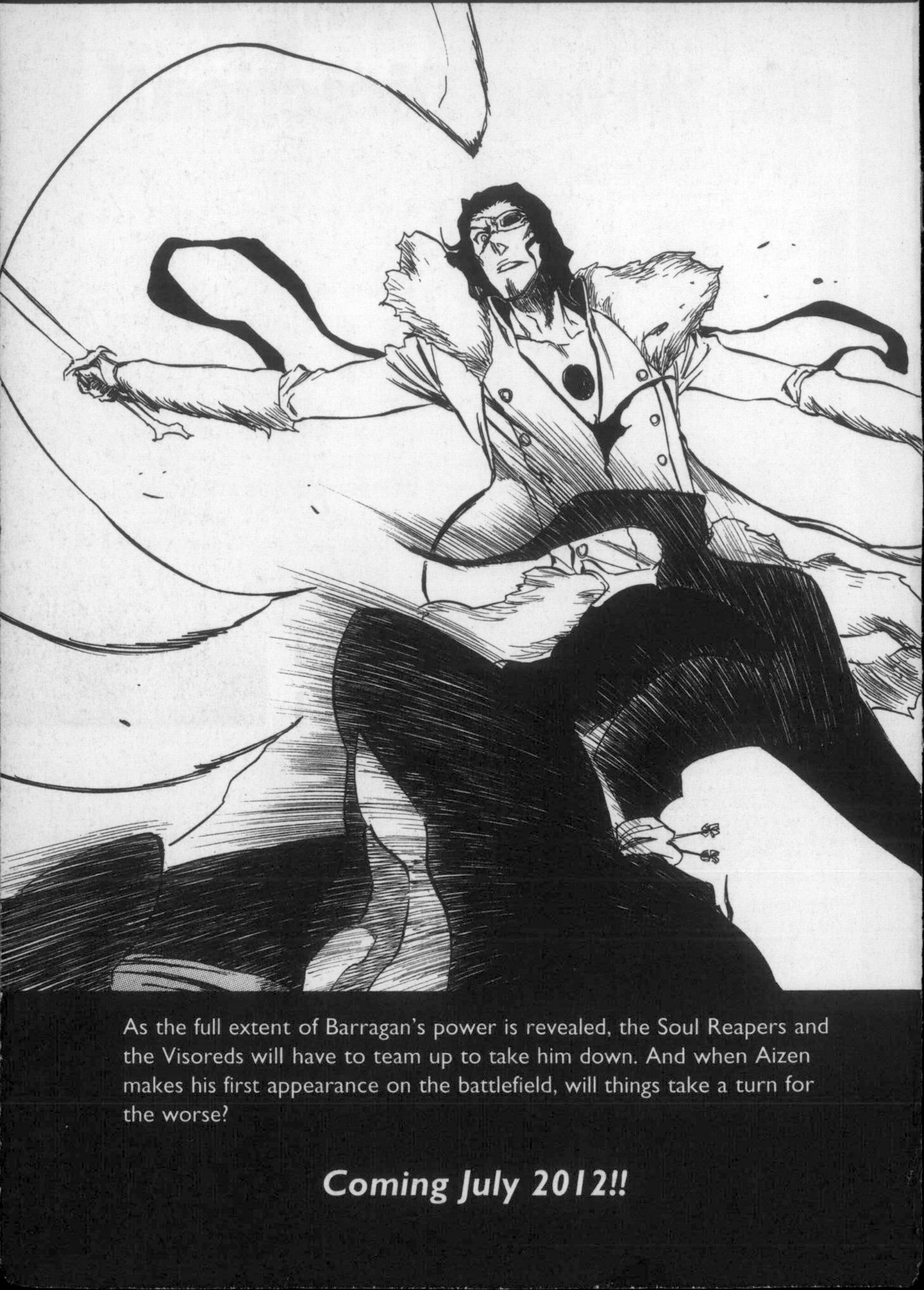

As the full extent of Barragan's power is revealed, the Soul Reapers and the Visoreds will have to team up to take him down. And when Aizen makes his first appearance on the battlefield, will things take a turn for the worse?

Coming July 2012!!

You're Rea~~ding~~
the Wrong Direc~~tion~~!!

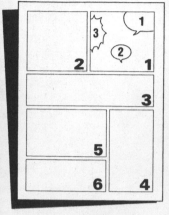

Whoops! Guess what? You're starting at the wrong end of the comic!

…It's true! In keeping with the original Japanese format, **Bleach** is meant to be read from right to left, starting in the upper-right corner.

Unlike English, which is read from left to right, Japanese is read from right to left, meaning that action, sound effects and word-balloon order are completely reversed… something which can make readers unfamiliar with Japanese feel pretty backwards themselves. For this reason, manga or Japanese comics published in the U.S. in English have sometimes been published "flopped"—that is, printed in exact reverse order, as though seen from the other side of a mirror.

By flopping pages, U.S. publishers can avoid confusing readers, but the compromise is not without its downside. For one thing, a character in a flopped manga series who once wore in the original Japanese version a T-shirt emblazoned with "M A Y" (as in "the merry month of") now wears one which reads "Y A M"! Additionally, many manga creators in Japan are themselves unhappy with the process, as some feel the mirror-imaging of their art skews their original intentions.

We are proud to bring you Tite Kubo's **Bleach** in the original unflopped format. For now, though, turn to the other side of the book and let the adventure begin…!

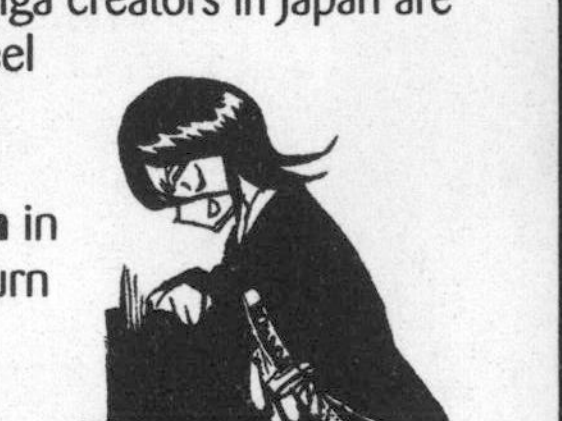

—Editor